Reform and Regulation of Economic Institutions in Afghanistan

Taliban's return to power in August of 2021 caused everyone to ask why the two decades of institution building in Afghanistan failed. This book investigates the root causes of failed reforms in an important area of reform: trade and credit institutions. It explains why the efforts to reform and regulate the economic institutions in Afghanistan failed and what we can learn from their failure. It draws on more than 80 interviews with Afghan merchants, business leaders, money dealers, and government officials in five major provinces of Afghanistan to identify the barriers to access to credit and to understand the performance of formal institutions (banks) and their informal counterparts. This book finds that Afghan merchants were often unable to benefit from the offerings of formal institutions for three reasons: a highly volatile business climate, uncertain contract enforcement, and an unsupportive property rights system. Several informal institutions have emerged that alleviate some of the credit constraints on Afghan merchants. These informal institutions include risk-sharing trade credit operations, money dealers' short-term working capital loans, *Gerawee*, and *Sar qufli*. Although these informal institutions have helped Afghan merchants survive, they are unable to support economic growth. This book argues that countries like Afghanistan should solve their institutional dilemma by adopting an approach which the author calls Grounded Institutional Reform. Using this approach, a country would formalize existing informal institutions, a development that would vastly increase their effectiveness. While this book focuses on credit and trade in Afghanistan, the analysis of "formalizing the informal" can easily be extended to solve other types of economic problems in similarly situated countries. This book should be of great interest to scholars, policy makers, and development workers in the field of law, finance, and development.

Haroun Rahimi has obtained his BA in Law from Herat University, his LLM in Global Business Law from the University of Washington School of Law, and his PhD from the University of Washington. Rahimi is Assistant Professor of Law at the American University of Afghanistan. Rahimi's research focuses on economic laws, institutional reform, Islamic finance, and divergent conceptions of rule of law in the Muslim and modern thoughts. Rahimi's research has appeared in reputable

Routledge Research in International Economic Law

Cost and EU Public Procurement Law
Life-Cycle Costing for Sustainability
Edited by Marta Andhov, Roberto Caranta and Anja Wiesbrock

Promoting and Managing International Investment
Towards an Integrated Policy Approach
Edited by J Anthony VanDuzer and Patrick Leblond

International Investment Law and Gender Equality
Stabilization Clauses and Foreign Investment
Sangwani Patrick Ng'ambi

The Legality of Economic Activities in Occupied Territories
International, EU Law and Business and Human Rights Perspectives
Antoine Duval and Eva Kassoti

International Investment Protection within Europe
The EU's Assertion of Control
Julien Berger

Trade, Migration and Law
Free Movement of Persons in the South African Development Community
Victor Amadi

The Americanization of the World Trade Order
Asif H Qureshi

Reform and Regulation of Economic Institutions in Afghanistan
Haroun Rahimi

For more information about this series, please visit www.routledge.com/Routledge-Research-in-International-Economic-Law/book-series/INTECONLAW

Reform and Regulation of Economic Institutions in Afghanistan

Haroun Rahimi

Routledge
Taylor & Francis Group
LONDON AND NEW YORK

First published 2023
by Routledge
4 Park Square, Milton Park, Abingdon, Oxon OX14 4RN

and by Routledge
605 Third Avenue, New York, NY 10158

Routledge is an imprint of the Taylor & Francis Group, an informa business

British Library Cataloguing-in-Publication Data
A catalogue record for this book is available from the British Library

Library of Congress Cataloging-in-Publication Data
A catalog record for this book has been requested

ISBN: 978-1-032-15735-1 (hbk)
ISBN: 978-1-032-15737-5 (pbk)
ISBN: 978-1-003-24547-6 (ebk)

DOI: 10.4324/9781003245476

Typeset in Times New Roman
by Apex CoVantage, LLC

To my mother and
the memory of my father

I would like to also thank Aysha Marjan Nayer, a bright student of mine, and Siobhan Poole and the rest of the team at the Routledge for helping me finalize this book.

I benefited from the support of several institutions as I worked on this book: Oxford Center for Islamic Studies, the International Institute for the Unification of Private Law (UNIDROIT), Bocconi University School of Law, American University of Afghanistan.

Last but not the least, I would like to thank my family: my mother, to whom I owe everything good; to my older brother, whose support made it possible for me to travel for my education; and to my sister and younger brother, who have given me unconditional love and support throughout writing this book and my life. I would like to also express my deepest gratitude to my beloved wife, Trang Nguyen, who has been my rock. I also pay tribute to the memory of my father, who passed away while I was working on this book. He was my greatest source of strength and my biggest supporter. I owe him everything I ever accomplish.

Preface

As I am writing this introduction, Afghanistan is dubbed the worst humanitarian crisis in the world. On August 15, 2020, Taliban completed a military campaign of dizzying speed which ended with the Taliban in charge of the whole country—Panjsheer province, the only holdout, fell to Taliban a month later. Taliban takeover of the country has given rise to an unprecedented situation where a group sanctioned for terrorism, both by the United Nations and the United States, has become the de facto ruler of a country of near 40 million people. Sanctions meant to weaken Taliban now have devastating consequences on the livelihood of an entire nation—a nation made most dependent on outside assistance through the actions of its leaders and the international community.

In the legal haze that emerged with Taliban in charge, the flow of foreign funds, which made up more than 70% of public expenditure, stopped overnight. The economy contracted by a whopping 30%. Even before sanctions caused economic contraction, the COVID-19 crisis, drought, the bloody tail end of the conflict, and the omnipresence of corruption and poor governance meant that most Afghans already lived in poverty, but now the country is facing universal poverty.

The country's financial system has been hit the hardest. With Taliban in control of Da Afghanistan Bank, the country's central bank, the whole financial system has, in effect, been blacklisted. A liquidity crisis ensued. The economy, which was heavily dollarized—before Taliban takeover, every week millions of USD in crisp 100 dollar bills were flown into the country to finance both the war and service delivery—suddenly has no way to access USD. DAB's foreign reserves held mostly in the American banks are frozen. Even the Afghan currency—which was printed in Europe—may be in short supply.

Most Afghans do not have bank accounts, but the banks nonetheless play a vital role in the economy. Banks mediated the injection of foreign-originated funds into the economy by dispensing government and INGOs payments in forms of salary and vendor payments. Now the faucet is virtually turned off. People line up for hours to withdraw the money they already had in their accounts only to be disappointed by the withdrawal limits Taliban-controlled DAB has enacted to manage the crisis.

The United States and European Union, the main sponsors of the toppled Islamic Republic of Afghanistan, scrambled to respond to the Taliban takeover.

On the one hand, Taliban has defied all the warnings that they would be made a pariah state, and they could not expect to receive foreign assistance if they attempted a military takeover of the country, and that is exactly what they did. On the other hand, Afghanistan is facing a horrible humanitarian crisis.

After a period of unease, and under pressures from allies and the humanitarian aid community, the US has decided to carve out general exemptions from the sanction scheme to allow the flow of humanitarian assistance into the country while keeping the sanctions in place and the foreign reserve funds frozen—now those funds are being claimed by the families of the 9/11 victims in connection to a judgement they had won in absentia against Taliban. The UN and the EU have opted for broader exemptions, often called "humanitarian plus," which includes both humanitarian assistance and funding for basic public services. The United National put forward a Transitional Engagement Framework for the year 2022, which would cost more than 8 billion USD to fund.

Following these mitigating measures, by the time I am writing this introduction, the UNAMA facilitated the shipments of more than 150 million USD into Afghanistan to pay aid, education, and health sector employees and to address food insecurity in the country. Taliban too are estimated to raise around the equivalent of 20 million USD monthly and have taken measures to curb the outflow of USD from the country. These steps have temporarily stabilized the currency crisis and mitigated the liquidity crunch, but the poverty and humanitarian crisis continues unabated.

The formal economic institutions that were erected over two decades collapsed almost overnight. While the informal economic institutions helped mitigate the catastrophe—the money dealer markets, for example, have continued to grease the economic transactions by keeping funds in circulation—they too were severely affected by the scale of the crisis. What happened? How did we get here? What went wrong in the efforts to build working formal economic institutions in Afghanistan? What can explain the shocking lack of resilience in the formal sector in absence of sustained external support? Answering these questions is of utmost importance not only for lessons they can offer for similar efforts going on in other countries but also for the United Nations, which is set to raise billions of dollars—its largest fundraising for a single country yet—to continue the humanitarian and development work in Afghanistan.

This book draws on empirical data to answer the question of why formal economic institutions failed in Afghanistan and what can be done about it. The research used here was conducted before the Taliban takeover, but the dynamics it illustrates have only raised in importance as Afghanistan becomes increasingly dependent on its informal economic institutions, and the United Nations is redefining its development assistance to the country.

Introduction

During the two decades of reform in Afghanistan (2001–2021), as part of efforts to reform the Afghan economy, a number of banks have been established in Afghanistan. Although before the Taliban takeover these banks held large reserves, an increasing number of Afghan merchants were still reporting problems getting the credit they needed to expand their businesses. This book explains why this situation exists and proposes a new approach to designing economic reforms, one that would improve access to finance for Afghan merchants and would generally better policy-making. The book draws on more than 80 interviews with Afghan merchants, business leaders, *Sarrafs*, and government officials in five major provinces of Afghanistan to identify the barriers to access to credit and to understand the performance of formal institutions (banks) and their informal counterparts.

This book shows that Afghan merchants were often unable to benefit from the offerings of formal institutions for three reasons: a highly volatile business climate, uncertain contract enforcement, and an unsupportive property rights system. A number of informal institutions have emerged that alleviate some of the credit constraints on Afghan merchants. These informal institutions include risk-sharing trade credit operations, short-term working capital loans, *Gerawee*, and *Sar qufli*. Although these informal institutions have helped Afghan merchants survive, and now that the formal sector is in a state of ruin, they are even more important, they are unable to support a growing economy. They have only limited capacity to pool savings for investment purposes, and furthermore, their extralegal practices may have negative consequences on long-term economic growth and attraction of foreign investment. In short, the existing formal institutions had sufficient capital, but they could not operate effectively in an environment like Afghanistan. Conversely, the existing informal institutions can operate effectively, but *precisely because they are informal*, they cannot provide a country like Afghanistan the investment capital it requires.

This book argues that Afghanistan should try to address this dilemma using a new approach the author calls Grounded Institutional Reform. Using this approach, Afghanistan would formalize existing informal institutions, a development that would vastly increase their effectiveness. There are, of course, good reasons for Afghanistan to continue in its efforts to save the banks and to encourage Afghans to use them. Nevertheless, as the author explains, this policy is unlikely to be

DOI: 10.4324/9781003245476-1

an immediate success even if we table the politically vexing question of sanctions. Instead, as the banking industry slowly recovers, the formalized "informal" institutions would promote slow but significant economic development. While from an empirical standpoint, this book focuses on credit and trade in Afghanistan before the Taliban takeover, the analysis of how Grounded Institutional Reform and a policy of "formalizing the informal" can easily be extended to solve other types of political and economic problems in Taliban-controlled Afghanistan and, indeed, in many other similarly situated countries.

Broader Theoretical Landscape and the Case of Afghanistan

There is a consensus among economists that the only effective way to alleviate poverty is through sustained economic growth.[1] Economists and legal scholars within the law and development movement generally agree that economic growth is promoted when businesses have access to credit and that improving businesses' access to credit can contribute meaningfully to sustainable economic development and human security.[2] This point is so widely accepted that scholarship no longer focuses on demonstrating the importance of credit transactions to economic growth in developing economies, and it has instead begun to focus on the question of how best to facilitate and encourage credit financing for merchants.

Within the field today, two different theories on institutional development and economic growth compete. One theory, which the author calls Entrepreneurial Institutional Theory,[3] focuses on private entrepreneurs as suppliers of informal institutions and drivers of economic growth. It argues that private entrepreneurs tend to develop the institutions and practices they need to grow their businesses.[4] To the extent that businesses need access to credit, they will develop institutions and practices that will make that credit available. As the private sector grows, the political power of economic entrepreneurs increases, allowing them to demand better formal institutions that are responsive to their needs. A second theory, what the author, following Nee and Opper, calls State-Centered Theory,[5] focuses on the importance of the state's role as the supplier of formal institutions and creator of preconditions for economic growth. This theory proposes that if merchants need access to credit, they are unlikely to independently develop maximally efficient institutions.[6] Development will thus proceed more effectively if states develop formal institutions regulated by courts or state administrative agencies.

Each of these theories has a different normative implication for institution building in the developing world.[7] Government officials today wishing to facilitate economic growth in a developing economy will tend to ally themselves with one of these competing theories. Depending on which of these theories she prefers, she will favor a different set of policies. A champion of Entrepreneurial Institutional Theory will take a reactive approach to institution building, allowing private actors independently to develop institutions, products, and practices. The assumption is that these organically developed institutions will be the best fit to address the needs of private entrepreneurs, and when needed, the private entrepreneurs will advocate for the government to supply the formal institutions that they need. By contrast, a champion of State-Centered Theory will urge the state to adopt institutions that have proven effective in other contexts (best practices) and will encourage the merchants to make use of the new institutions, most often by displacing the organically developed informal institutions.

Afghanistan provides us with a case study that allows us to explore the pros and cons of Entrepreneurial Institutional Theory and of State-Centered Theory in a post-conflict state and to evaluate the advantages and disadvantages of pursuing policies based on each of these theories.[8] It suggests that in a country like Afghanistan, each of the theories is rooted in an important insight. Entrepreneurial Institutional Theory notes correctly that economic actors are well aware of the peculiar challenges that they face and tend to design institutions that address, at least to some level, those particular problems. In support of Entrepreneurial Institutional Theory, the case of Afghanistan suggests that displacing entrepreneurially developed informal institutions is most often unwise and infeasible. On the other hand, in line with the State-Centered Theory, the case of Afghanistan demonstrates that these institutions which develop organically are often insufficient to provide the structure necessary to promote sustainable development because poor infrastructure and limited market expansion opportunities seriously curtail their development. Therefore, save in cases where huge market expansion opportunities and strong infrastructure exist (i.e. the golden case of China), entrepreneurially developed informal institutions, on their own, will not be able to facilitate significant economic growth. The recent history of Afghanistan also suggests, however, that in post-conflict states (and other weak states), the government may have only limited ability to create and enforce new, more effective institutions out of whole cloth. Thus, in a country like Afghanistan, the government should recognize the genius of local institutions, even as it tries to improve upon existing, trusted institutions by formalizing them and supervising them so that these institutions provide the level of predictability that State-Centered Theory says will be required.

After almost 25 years of civil war, Afghanistan was in 2001 invaded by an international force. Thereafter, officials in the new Afghan government and advisors from the international community committed themselves to an ambitious plan of economic and legal reforms all designed to promote sustainable economic growth in Afghanistan.[9] Among the goals of the new reform plan was, naturally, the promotion of more credit transactions. By this time, Afghan merchants had developed institutions and practices that could make a limited amount of credit financing available.[10] Even during the 25-year period of political unrest and civil war that lasted from about 1975 to about 2001, merchants were able to use these institutions and practices to obtain some degree of credit financing for their commercial activities. While post-2001 improvements in infrastructure and new market expansion opportunities aided the improvement of informal institutions, their investment financing capabilities remained limited. These traditional mechanisms did not provide Afghan merchants with the same amount of credit financing that merchants in advanced Western economies can access through Western banking systems, and it did not provide the financing on the same terms. If Afghan merchants were unable to increase the amount of investment financing beyond what the informal institutions made possible, it seemed clear that long-term economic growth would likely be impeded. So how could the foreign-backed Afghan government best increase the amount of credit financing available to Afghan merchants beyond the amount that was being made available through existing institutions?

Instead of formalizing the informal credit institutions that had already emerged organically and, thereby, to increase their efficiency, former Afghan officials and their international advisors decided to displace them. Inspired by the champions of State-Centered development, former Afghan officials and their allies adopted a series of official policies, the Government Strategic Policies, that aimed to replace the existing informal institutions and practices with formal institutions modeled on those that underpin the economies of developed Western economies.[11] Under these new policies, newly formed banks should displace all other sources of credit. Bank credit (mostly bank loans) would become the sole source of credit for merchants in Afghanistan. Banks, it was assumed, would offer loans on terms that Afghan merchants could accept, and merchants would seize the opportunity to borrow money on the terms that banks demanded. Easy access to credit would lead to sustainable economic growth and a measurable increase in Afghans' human security.

As an attempt to facilitate credit financing for Afghan merchants and increase their access to credit, the Government's Strategic Policies were a colossal failure. Since 2014, even before the near-total collapse of the financial system following the Taliban takeover, the number of Afghan businesses reporting problems accessing finance was actually increasing.[12] At the end of 2016, almost half of Afghan businesses surveyed reported they had a problem accessing finance.[13] Even before the COVID-19 crisis, the drop in foreign assistance, and sanctions that brought about the prospect of universal poverty, most Afghans lived below the national poverty line, with a trend toward an increase in poverty.[14] The stickiness of the informal credit institutions could not explain the failure of the formal credit institutions because, as the research presented here shows, the reduction in the use of informal credit institutions in a province did not result in the increased use of bank loans by the merchants in that province.[15] Nor does religious objections to the use of interest explain the unpopularity of bank loans because, as the findings of research conducted for this book demonstrate, the prevalence of pro-interest attitude in a province does not positively correlate with the increased use of bank loans in that province.[16] Additionally, Afghan judges regularly enforced interest-bearing loans under formal rules.[17]

Overview of the Book's Organization and Summary of Its Argument

This book is divided into four chapters. Chapter 1 offers an overview of the state of Afghanistan's economy. A description of the actors involved in Afghanistan's credit economy provides a social and institutional context. Chapter 2 also identifies the fundamental problems that Afghan merchants face when they try to enter into credit transactions. Chapter 2 focuses on informal institutions that have emerged over time in Afghanistan to overcome the problems of credit transactions consequences they pose for allocation of resources and economic growth. Chapter 3 offers an overview of Afghanistan's formal financial institutions before the Taliban takeover and the former Afghan government policies aimed at reforming formal institutions. Chapter 4 defines and develops the approach of Grounded Institutional Reform and explains how it could be applied in Afghanistan to build formal institutions that are based on existing informal institutions. Chapter 4 also explains the problematic theoretical positions that have hindered the adoption of Grounded Institutional Reform as well as the actual problems of implementing Grounded Institutional Reform in Afghanistan. The final section, Conclusions and Recommendations, establishes that Grounded Institutional Reform is the most effective way to create workable institutions that could improve access to investment financing for Afghan merchants.

To understand the failure of the former Afghan government's attempt to create institutions that would give Afghan merchants greater access to credit than they could access through informal institutions and to ascertain how former Afghan officials could have developed more effective institutions, the author carried out more than 80 interviews with Afghan merchants, business leaders, and officials between March and August of 2017 in five major provinces of Afghanistan: Kabul, Herat, Kandahar, Nangarhar, and Balkh. While Afghanistan has 32 provinces, these five provinces collectively represent half of Afghanistan's economy,[18] one-third of Afghanistan's total population,[19] and more than four-fifths of Afghanistan's urban population.[20] The commercial courts that sit in these five provinces were hearing more than 90% of the total commercial court disputes in the country before Taliban overhauled the entire judiciary.[21]

Building on the information gathered in these interviews, this book describes the Afghan economy and the role of merchants within it. It describes the obstacles that Afghan merchants have historically faced when they have sought access to credit on terms that are commercially viable within the Afghan context. Afghan merchants operate in a business environment where credit transactions are inevitably risky. For merchants who want to negotiate a credit transaction, three problems are particularly acute. First, the business climate in Afghanistan is highly volatile. Second, it is difficult to enforce contracts efficiently in the Afghan court system. Third, the property rights system, or rather lack thereof, makes it difficult for merchants to securitize credit transactions.

Having identified the three problems that Afghan merchants find most taxing when trying to enter into a credit transaction, the book describes three informal institutions that merchants have developed, institutions that allowed holders of capitals to make at least some capital available to merchants who needed commercial credit. These three informal institutions are trade credit coupled with *Sarraf*'s working capital loans, *Gerawee*, and *Sar qufli*. These informal institutions have been able to improve access to working capital financing significantly while marginally improving access to investment financing and liquidity in the capital market. These informal institutions have succeeded due to their ability to overcome the problems of credit transactions in Afghanistan. With the complete collapse of the formal economic institutions following Taliban takeover of the country, these informal institutions have become even more important. At the same time, however, the existing informal institutions have not been able to improve access to investment financing significantly and will likely have negative consequences for long-term economic growth and attraction of foreign investment. Informal institutions have not been able to improve access to investment financing because they are neither able to pool disparate savings nor are they capable of diversifying risk. As a result, they cannot be relied on to finance long-term and/or high-risk investments, investments that are instrumental in achieving economic growth. Similarly, while the existing informal institutions are very inclusive with regards to Afghans, they put outsiders at a disadvantage, which impedes foreign investment in Afghanistan.

Having described three informal credit institutions that emerged in Afghanistan, the book analyzes the formal institutions that the former Afghan government and its international partners developed as alternatives to these informal institutions and has determined that Afghan merchants in Afghanistan's commercial centers found that banks and bank loans proved inappropriate for the Afghan context. The terms under which banks offer to lend are unattractive to Afghan merchants. Bank loans entail high-interest rates, inflexible repayment terms, and require real estate with formal deeds as collateral. Afghan merchants cannot pay the high-interest rates or adhere to inflexible repayment terms because they operate in an uncertain business environment with unpredictable cash flows, which keeps the return on investment low and adherence to fixed repayment terms impractical. Furthermore, Afghan merchants have very limited access to formal deeds and thus cannot satisfy the collateral requirements that banks traditionally impose before lending. Informal institutions offer only limited amounts of investment financing, but they do so in the face of a volatile business climate and an unsupportive property right system. Formal banks in Afghanistan, which held as high as 3 billion USD in excessive reserve,[22] theoretically had more money available to borrowers; however, they offered loans on terms that only a few Afghan merchants could meet.

The research presented in this book demonstrates that merchants' failure to take out loans does *not* arise out of a sentimental preference for traditional institutions. Similarly, their resistance to using banks does not primarily arise out of a concern that taking out bank loans violates a religious prohibition on interest, as the demand for Shari'ah-compliant financing (which is offered through Islamic windows of many Afghan banks) and the newly established Islamic Bank of Afghanistan is equally low. Indeed, Afghan merchants, even in provinces with strong anti-interest sentiments, regularly engage in credit transactions that incorporate the time value of money within the *Sarrafi* markets. Nevertheless, in light of the volatility that Afghan businesses face and the difficulties that they face both in enforcing contracts and producing collateral for loans, merchants simply find it impossible to meet the terms that banks (Islamic or conventional) require of their borrowers. Afghan merchants obtain credit from informal institutions that they understand are imperfect, and they obtain less credit than they would ideally like.[23] They do so because these informal institutions are the only ones that are willing to offer credits on terms that Afghan merchants can meet.

Having explained the reasons why Afghan merchants believe that these imperfect informal institutions and practices remain the least bad option available to them, this book explores the implications of these findings. The empirical data in this book is not sufficient by itself to conclusively prove or disprove the claims of Entrepreneurial Institutional Theory or State-Centered Theory. Nevertheless, the data leaves us with provocative evidence suggesting some practical lessons for policy makers who wish to quickly build more effective state-regulated and supervised credit institutions—ones that a weak government can implement and which can provide the lenders and merchants with enough added certainty and predictability that significantly enhances merchants' access to credit. The data collected in the interviews conducted for this book suggests that policies rooted in Entrepreneurial Institutional Theory are not adequate to provide merchants with sufficient access to credit to ensure the economy will support sustainable economic growth. Entrepreneurs have developed institutions and practices that provide some credit but not enough to promote sustainable growth on an ongoing basis because poor infrastructure and limited market expansion opportunities restrain the organic process of institutional development in countries like Afghanistan. In comparison, the proponents of State-Centered Theory have, to date, mostly tried to displace the existing informal institutions by transplanting institutions and practices that are ill-suited to the Afghan context. This book proposes that the policy makers should, going forward, pursue policies that combine a respect for existing informal institutions with an appreciation for the advantages that formalization and state oversight can provide.

This book proposes that governments should develop effective institutions using an approach that this dissertation calls Grounded Institutional Reform. As explained in Chapter 4, the former Afghan government has correctly concluded that existing informal institutions are insufficient to provide the investment financing that its economy will need if it is to develop sustainably. Any new government should reconstitute and promote a series of formal, state-regulated institutions that will provide more access to investment financing than the informal institutions are currently able to provide. These new institutions, however, should be improved versions of existing institutions. The formal institutions should absorb the working informal institutions that are working into the formal system by reshaping and building on them because they provide tried models of workable institutions. Furthermore, Grounded Institutional Reform ensures a smoother transition to a formalized economy because it incorporates the existing institutional knowledge and networks, thus building on them. Grounded Institutional Reform reduces the need to rely on limited coercive power and administrative capacity of the state in the economic realm. By absorbing working informal institutions, Grounded Institutional Reform makes it more likely that weak governments of less-developed countries can overcome the resistance from the invested users of informal institutions. Grounded Institutional Reform accomplishes this task by rendering formalization self-interest compatible. By incorporating informal institutions, Grounded Institutional Reform ensures that invested users will continue to have a role (albeit an altered role) in the formal system. This creates an incentive for the invested users to comply with the formal rules.[24]

A policy based on Grounded Institutional Reform retains the bottom-up and incremental approach to policy-making rooted in Entrepreneurial Institutional Theory. Grounded Institutional Reform leverages the problem-solving abilities of entrepreneurs and ensures user-readiness by absorbing the entrepreneur-developed informal institutions into the formal system. At the same time, however, because the modified institutions are formalized and integrated into the larger state legal apparatus, the institutions will allow lenders to lend (and merchants to borrow) with the added predictability and certainty that State-Centered theorists say, correctly, is necessary for the economy to thrive.

The following examples of reforms that could feasibly be undertaken illustrate what a policy of Grounded Institutional Reform would look like and demonstrate its feasibility.[25]

For example, while Afghanistan's Strategic Economic Policies during the last two decades correctly recognized the need to improve credit for exporters, however, they failed to recognize the potential of leveraging *Sarrafs*' short-term working capital loans for that purpose. Afghanistan's formal policies proposed the creation of an export bank, which would provide credit to exporters at a lower interest rate. The problem with this proposition is that it required resources that the former Afghanistan government and a fortiori the Taliban authorities does not have, as well as institutional knowledge that Afghan merchants and officials do not possess. This is why this proposition has not materialized. A Grounded Institutional Reform approach, on the other hand, would leverage *Sarrafs*' short-term working capital loans, institutions that already help finance import, instead of creating export banks. Leveraging *Sarrafs*' short-term working capital loans would require fewer government resources because it would use the merchants' funds held by *Sarrafs* to provide credit and would build on existing institutional knowledge that Afghan merchants have (they already use short-term working capital loans to finance import).

In addition, while Afghanistan's Government Strategic Policies correctly tried to improve land tenures in the cities to help release the value trapped in the housing market, their strategies failed to capitalize on the potential of *Gerawee* to release the untapped value of the housing market despite imperfect documentation of land tenures. This disregard of *Gerawee* as a financing mechanism deprives Afghan merchants of a valuable source of finance, while the government, both former and possibly the Taliban government, undertakes the incredibly difficult task of reforming Afghanistan's property rights system. *Gerawee* has the added advantage of relying on existing institutional knowledge and networks. Grounded Institutional Reform's policy would seek to improve the efficiency of *Gerawee* by ensuring the protection of creditors' rights, which can be aided by placing *Gerawee* under the jurisdiction of commercial courts. With the caveat that it is not possible yet to say how the Taliban judicial appointees will treat such cases.

And while Afghanistan's Strategic Policies appropriately strived to reform property rights and lower interest rates to expand the provision of bank loans and stimulate economic growth, they failed to recognize the potential of *Sar qufli* in lowering the capital cost of construction projects and improving liquidity in the capital market. Nor did they recognize the role *Sarrafs*' short-term working capital loans play in lowering the capital cost of imports. Policies based on Grounded Institutional Reform would try to leverage *Sar qufli* and *Sarrafs*' short-term working capital loans to improve liquidity in the capital market and improve access to credit for Afghan merchants. Similarly, while Afghanistan's Strategic Policies identified the need to lower the cost of contract enforcement, their solution focused on a formalized Alternative Dispute Resolution Center, disregarding the potential of common and localized business collectives that currently resolve most disputes among merchants. Grounded Institutional Reform's policy would attempt to support localized dispute resolution within local business collectives.

Finally, Afghanistan's Government's Strategic Policies also sought to address the information problems facing banks by proposing the creation of a Credit Bureau to collect and process credit information on businesses. This type of institution would not solve the problem because, given Afghanistan's pervasive informal economy, formal credit information is essentially nonexistent. However, Afghanistan's Strategic Policies disregarded the wealth of information that *Sarrafs*, as the main financial service providers of most businesses in Afghanistan, already possess. If banks could access the information *Sarrafs* hold on their clients, it would greatly improve their ability to assess risk and issue loans. *Sarrafs*, through handling their clients' currency exchange and *hawalas*, have reliable knowledge about their clients' creditworthiness; they use this information to give their clients working capital loans without any collateral or written contract. The Grounded Institutional Reform approach would advocate incentivizing *Sarrafs* to share information with banks, for example, by requiring a *Sarraf* to guarantee a bank loan issued to the *Sarraf*'s client. In this way, *Sarrafs* could provide banks with reliable independently produced data on hard-to-measure metrics of creditworthiness such as cash flow and financial management. Thus, it would allow banks to reduce their reliance on scarce formal collateral to issue loans. Since banks' demanding collateral requirement is an insurmountable barrier for most Afghan merchants, this could greatly increase bank lending in Afghanistan.

This book recommends that Afghanistan adopt the following institutional reforms to improve access to finance and stimulate economic growth:[26] (1) Reform formal property rights to create clear rules to determine legal ownership and to create an integrated system of legal, reliable, and up-to-date titling to reduce transaction costs for property and collateralization; (2) introduce targeted and performance-linked credit guaranty schemes to lower the cost of capital; (3) improve banking regulations to restore people's trust in banks and incentivize savings in banks; (4) improve the process of application for bank loans; support and implement financial literacy programs for Afghan businesses; implement training programs for banks' staff; (5) enact legislation based on the judicial jurisprudence developed in connection with *Sar qufli* to improve the *Sar qufli* market, thereby increasing the incentive for development projects; (6) bring *Gerawee* transactions under the jurisdiction of commercial courts in cases in which the borrower is a merchant, thereby improving the rights of creditors and unleashing the potential trapped in the housing market to finance productive activities; (7) reform commercial courts' procedures and judgment enforcement to improve the comparative competitiveness of formal dispute resolution in relation to informal dispute resolution; (8) promulgate regulations that facilitate the financing role of *Sarrafs*, especially for exporters; and (9) incentivize *Sarrafs* to share information with banks and the Credit Bureau if it is established.

This book accomplishes three undertakings: (1) It identifies the reasons why it is difficult for Afghan merchants to access credit; (2) it describes the main institutional solutions that have emerged organically to improve access to credit for Afghan merchants; and (3) it critically assesses whether, how, and to what extent the emergent institutional solutions improve access to credit for Afghan merchants. Drawing on the case study of Afghanistan, this book concludes by developing a new approach for institutional reform in countries like Afghanistan that are characterized by poor infrastructure, limited market expansion opportunities, and a reformist but weak government—namely Grounded Institutional Reform.

Methodology and Definitions

This book asks how Afghanistan can create better policies to improve its economy, specifically, how Afghanistan can design better policies to improve Afghan merchants' access to credit. To answer this question, this book draws upon qualitative and quantitative data to investigate the following questions: what are the problems of credit transacting in Afghanistan? What are the informal institutions that have organically developed to overcome those problems? Whether, how, and to what extent do these informal institutions work? How well do the formal institutions designed to improve access to credit for Afghan merchants work? If formal institutions have not been able to improve access to credit for Afghan merchants, what can explain their failure? How can Afghanistan create better formal institutions in a way that would work for the Afghan context?

Subscribing to a broad definition of credit in this research, this book uses credit transactions to refer to any non-instantaneous transaction, such as trade credit and bank loans. For the purpose of this study, this book has used the concept of transaction costs to operationalize the effects of different constraints on credit transactions in Afghanistan. Instead of endogenizing institutional transformation to transaction costs, this book posits the fundamental problems of credit transactions in Afghanistan determine the cost of credit transactions and the informal institutions that emerged to overcome those problems. This proposition creates an endogeneity problem: do emergent informal institutions determine the transaction problems, or do the transaction problems determine the informal institutions? To overcome the problem of endogeneity, this dissertation describes the causal pathways that connect the fundamental problems of credit transactions to the emergent informal institutions aimed at resolving those problems. It has also reduced the problem of endogeneity by describing the causes of the fundamental problems of credit transactions; although, it acknowledges that the endogeneity problem is not entirely eliminated.

Grounded Theory

The qualitative research for this book has been designed and conducted using Grounded Theory. Grounded Theory is a qualitative methodology that is specifically suitable for studying an understudied, basic social process with the aim of producing a theory.[27] It entails a dialogical process where the researcher engages in constant comparison between empirical data and explanations of that data to generate a theory that could account for the empirical findings.[28] Grounded Theory prescribes theoretical sampling to ensure theoretical saturation can be achieved.[29] It requires the purposeful selection of a diverse sample so it can produce data on different aspects and variations of the basic social process being studied.

This book uses Grounded Theory to study the problems of and solutions to credit transacting in Afghanistan. It explains how the existing theories of institutional development fail to account for the case of Afghanistan. It generates a new approach for institutional reform based on the case study of Afghanistan for countries with poor infrastructures, limited market expansion opportunists, and reformist but weak governments.

Sampling and Data Collection

To answer this book's research question, the author conducted 83 semi-structured interviews between March and August 2017 in five major provinces of Afghanistan: Herat (24, 29%), Balkh (18, 22%), Nangarhar (16, 19%), Kabul (12, 14%), and Kandahar (17, 20%).[30]

Following Grounded Theory's prescriptions on theoretical sampling,[31] the author chose to focus on these five provinces because they collectively represent half of Afghanistan's economy,[32] one-third of Afghanistan's total population,[33] and more than four-fifth of Afghanistan's urban population.[34] The commercial courts that sit in these five provinces used to hear more than 90% of total commercial disputes in the country. The faith of those courts is unclear with Taliban in power.

The majority of merchants in the sample are sellers/creditors. However, the data collected from these interviews describe the operation of buyers/debtors, as far as credit transaction is concerned, because they are the receiver of trade credit issued by sellers/creditors. The sample also includes *Sarrafs*, judges, Huquq Department Judgment Enforcement Specialists,[35] and leaders of business associations.

The sample of interviews conducted for this book does not include female merchants because the experience of women in business merits independent research.[36] While the number of women-owned businesses in Afghanistan was increasing since 2001, men still dominated commerce and industries in Afghanistan even before Taliban takeover rolled back women's rights significantly.[37] According to

Afghanistan's Investment Support Agency's data, only 4.2% of the businesses registered between 2003 and 2013 are owned by women (i.e. 1,600 out of 37,767 registered companies),[38] most of which are in the handicraft and service industry and are subsidized by international donors.[39] However, this is not to underestimate women's contribution to Afghanistan's economy. Afghan women are active participants in the economy. For example, Afghan women account for 65% of the workforce in agriculture, which constitutes one-third of Afghanistan's GDP. One rough estimate on the contribution of Afghan women to the GDP, *which by definition excludes household work*, suggests that women are responsible for 11–14% of Afghanistan's GDP.[40]

The available data on the women-owned businesses suggest that female merchants had considerably less access to credit than their male counterparts. For example, 81% of 298 Afghan women business owners surveyed in 2013 reported that they were unable to access any credit or financing,[41] whereas in 2014 only 36% of merchants in the Business Climate Report's sample, which consisted of all men-owned businesses, reported having a problem with access to finance. Although the smaller size of women-owned businesses may explain some of the difference,[42] it cannot account for the entire 45% difference. Likewise, the available data on the operation of women-owned businesses suggest that they have more difficulty establishing business relations. For example, the 2013 Afghan Women's Economic Participation Survey found that almost 90% of women-owned businesses do not have partnerships with other businesses or institutions, and nearly 75% do not belong to a business association.[43] While some of the analysis presented in this book (particularly concerning the property rights system and family businesses in Afghanistan) sheds light upon the ways the prevailing institutional arrangements handicap women-owned businesses, the vast differences between the experience of Afghan businesswomen and Afghan businessmen suggest independent studies are needed to illustrate the ways businesswomen interacted with the prevailing formal and informal institutions in Afghanistan even during the period of 2001–2021. The increased restrictions on women's participation in public life following the Taliban takeover of the country in August of 2021 also presents a fundamental change in a context whose consequences for women's economic activities merit special attention.

The author chose this sample through his own networks of relationships and the networks of relationships of his local informants, while purposefully attempting to create as diverse of a sample as possible, with the aim of collecting data on different aspects and variations of credit transactions in Afghanistan. The author has also randomized the sample by (1) walking through the marketplace and randomly choosing merchants to interview and (2) driving around industrial towns and randomly choosing factory owners to interview.

A goal of a minimum of fifteen interviews per province was set; however, the author stopped when he concluded that thematic saturation was reached. Alternatively, the author did more interviews in a province when additional interviews were needed to reach thematic saturation. The sectoral breakdown of the sample is presented in the next section. A majority of merchants who were interviewed are active in more than one sector. The most common combinations are manufacturing/trade, service/trade, and manufacturing/service/trade.[44]

- 28/83: Manufacturers and producers who produce cleaning products, furniture, wheel caps, UPVC, cookies, cooking oil, bricks, plastic bags, flavors, chocolates, nonalcoholic beverages, steel rods, aluminum plates, 3D panels, dairy products, iodized salt, carton boxes, stoves, and marble.
- 34/83: Traders who import, sell, and distribute furniture, oil and gas, rugs and carpets, construction materials, power generators and construction machinery, tea, cooking oil, food items, cell phones, tractors, wheat, flavor, woods, household necessities, cleaning products, fabrics and clothes, medicines, valuable stones, electronics, seeds, blankets, and home appliances.
- 7/83: Merchants in the service industry that provide construction, logistics, transportation, printing, and processing services.
- 13/83: *Sarrafs*.
- 5/83: Specialists at Huquq Department.
- 8/83: Commercial judges.
- 8/83: Leaders of unions of *Sarrafs*, manufacturers, and chambers of commerce and industries.

This book has used macroeconomic and demographic statistics supplied by Afghanistan's government (most often Afghanistan's Central Statistics Organization), Afghanistan Chamber of Commerce, the World Bank, the International Monetary Fund, other international organizations, and some academic sources. When reading these statistics, the reader must exercise caution because all quantitative data on Afghanistan, more or less, suffer from a set of systematic problems that stem from the incredible level of informality of Afghanistan's economy, the prevalence of insecurity that has made a large part of the country inaccessible until very recently when the war ended, the prevalence of a sizable underground economy that operates illegally, and political sensitivity that surround some types of data. As a result, for example, estimates on Afghanistan's population range from 29m provided by the Afghan government, and 31m provided by the World Bank. Similarly, the data on Afghanistan's GDP does not include income generated from opium, corruption, illegal trade, and a sizable war economy.

Statistics and surveys on the access to finance, used here and elsewhere, do not account for *Gerawee*, *Sar qufli*, trade credit, and *Sarraf*'s short-term working capital loans because merchants do not consider them financing devices. This is because the credit provided by these devices are most often short-term and embedded in different transactions, such as credit sales, *hawala*, currency exchanges, or leases. Additionally, in the case of *Sarraf*'s short-term working capital loans and *Gerawee*, the non-financing conceptualization allows actors to obscure the appearance of interest-bearing transactions, thereby avoiding possible religious objections to their use.

Definitions

Here a number of terms used throughout this book are defined:

Institution: for the purpose of this study, institutions are the set of formal and informal rules, norms, and conventions, as well as their enforcement mechanisms, that facilitate, coordinate, and constrain behaviors. This definition has a close affinity with the North's definition of the institutions. However, here this study does not consider beliefs and "mental models" of individuals as constitutive parts of institutions.[45]

Formal and informal institutions: this study uses the concept of formal institutions to refer to the use of legal rules and state-sanctioned mechanisms to facilitate credit transactions. It uses the term *informal institutions* to refer to the use of norms that are not legally enacted and mechanisms that are not state-sanctioned to facilitate credit transactions. This study does not mean to dichotomize formal and informal institutions; rather, in this book, they are meant to represent two ends of a spectrum. When a merchant registers property in a court as collateral to receive a loan from a bank, he is using formal institutions. On the other hand, when a merchant uses his/her relationship with a *Sarraf* to receive a working capital loan so he can transfer money to a foreign supplier, he is using informal institutions. Similarly, when a merchant goes to court to enforce a contract, he is using formal institutions. However, when a merchant goes to a business association to enforce a contract, he is using informal institutions.

Trade credit: trade credit is when a person purchases goods and services but does not immediately pay for them—instead, promising to pay at a later date.

Credit transactions: for the purpose of this study, this study uses credit transactions to refer to any non-instantaneous transaction such as trade credit and bank loans.

Transaction costs: this study focuses on information, enforcement, and the costs of making transactions. Information costs encompass the costs involved in determining with whom one should transact and the economically important descriptions of the thing that is being transacted. Enforcement costs comprise of the costs involved in monitoring and enforcing transactions. The costs of making transactions refer to the costs one has to incur in order to make a transaction, for example the cost of negotiating an agreement.

Property rights: this study adopts a legal definition of property rights, that is, a legally enforceable right with relation to a thing; however, it acknowledges that property rights are not uniformly protected by formal institutions. For example, in Afghanistan *Sar qufli* has managed to gain more formal legal protection compared to *Gerawee* because the former has been more effectively incorporated into formal institutions, while the holder of both types of property rights, arguably, has some legal claims that are theoretically protected by formal rules.

Merchants, Sellers/Creditors, and Buyer/Debtor: this study classifies actors in Afghanistan's credit economy into three main actor-types: buyers/debtors, who are most often retailers and receivers of trade credit; sellers/creditors, who are most often importer and/or manufacturers and suppliers of trade credit; and *Sarrafs*, who are the main financial service providers in Afghanistan.

In Afghanistan, merchants at the top of supply chains are importers, manufacturers, and service providers. They are the main source of trade credit; hence, this study refers to them as sellers/creditors. Importers do not usually receive trade credit because it is difficult to receive credit from a supplier located outside of Afghanistan.

Manufacturers, on the other hand, differ. If a manufacturer can procure the necessary input from domestic sources, he can easily do so on credit; in which case, he would become a buyer/debtor with respect to his domestic suppliers. If a manufacturer cannot procure the necessary input domestically, he will have to import them; in which case, he usually cannot secure trade credit.

Service providers are sellers/creditors because they do sell their services in exchange for a promise to receive regular payment in the future. Service providers are often not debtors/buyers because their main input is labor, which is bought through a completely different process, that is, employment agreements. In some instances, service providers import and sell goods that are connected to the service they provide. In those cases, depending on their position in the supply chain, they may be either a seller/creditor or a buyer/debtor.

Merchants at the lower end of supply chains are retailers who sell imported and domestically produced products directly to the consumers; hence, this study refers to them as buyers/debtors. Within some supply chains, there are wholesale distributors who buy from importers/manufacturers and sell to retailers wholesale. These wholesale distributors fall in the middle. They are debtors/buyers with respect to importers and producers, and sellers/creditors with respect to retailers.

The impermanence of the buyer/debtor and the seller/creditor roles does not pose a significant analytical problem because wherever a seller/creditor-buyer/debtor exists, the analyses presented here apply. When discussing a topic that concerns both functions of sellers/creditors and buyers/debtors, this study uses the term *merchant*.

Notes

1 *See* e.g. Dani Rodrik, *One Economics, Many Recipes: Globalization, Institutions and Economic Growth* (2007) 2 (stating that "Historically nothing has worked better than economic growth in enabling societies to improve the life chances of their members, including those at the very bottom"); Richard H. Adams Jr., The World Bank, Economic Growth, Inequality, and Poverty: Findings from a New Data Set (Policy Research Working Paper 2972, SSRN 2003), http://siteresources.worldbank.org/INTPGI/Resources/14021_WPS_2972_adams.pdf; *see also* Martin Ravallion & Shaohua Chen, *World Bank, What Can New Survey Data Tell Us about Recent Changes in*

Distribution and Poverty, 11(2) The World Bank Economic Review 357, 380 (1997); *see also Lant Pritchet on Poverty, Growth, and Experiments*, EconTalk (May 22, 2017), www.econtalk.org/archives/2017/05/lant_pritchett_1.html. It should be noted, however, that while there is a general consensus among economists that the most effective way to alleviate poverty is through sustained economic growth, the distributional effects of economic growth are still hotly debated and studied. *See* Shahid Yusuf & Joseph E. Stiglitz, *Development Issues: Settled and Open, in* Frontiers of Development Economics: The Future in Perspective 227–268 (Gerald M. Meier & Joseph E. Stiglitz eds., World Bank and Oxford University Press 2000).

2 There is a broad consensus that financial development is an independent variable of economic growth. *See* e.g. Robert G. King & Ross Levine, *Finance and Growth: Schumpeter Might Be Right*, 108 Q. J. Econ 717, 719 (1993); Robert G. King & Ross Levine, *Finance, Entrepreneurship, and Growth: Theory and Evidence*, 32 J. Monetary Econ. 513, 515 (1993); Ross Levine, *Financial Development and Economic Growth: Views and Agenda*, 35 J. Econ. Lit 688, 688 (1997); Ross Levine, *The Legal Environment, and Long Run Economic Growth*, 30 J. Money, Credit, & Banking 596, 598 (1998); Raghuram G. Rajan & Luigi Zingales, *Financial Dependence and Growth*, 88 Am. Econ. Rev. 559, 584 (1998); Ross Levine *et al.*, *Financial Intermediation and Growth: Causality and Causes*, 46 Journal of Monetary Economics 31, 35 (2000); Ross Levine, *Finance and Growth: Theory and Evidence, in* Handbook of Economic Growth 865, 889 (Philippe Aghion & Steven Durlauf eds., Elsevier B.V. 2005); Stephen Haber *et al.*, *Political Institutions and Financial Development, in* Political Institutions and Financial Development 1 (Stephen Haber et al., eds. Stanford University Press 2008); Daren Acemoğlu, *Introduction to Modern Economic Growth* 588 & 726 (Princeton University Press 2009); Sahay et al., IMF Staff Discussion Note, Rethinking Financial Deepening: Stability and Growth in Emerging Markets 5 (SDN/15/08, 2015).

3 The term Entrepreneurial Institutional Theory is inspired by Nee and Opper's book, *Capitalism from Below*. Sonja Opper & Víctor Nee, *Capitalism from Below: Markets and Institutional Change in China* (Harvard University Press 2012) [hereinafter Opper & Nee, Capitalism from Below (2012)].

4 This theoretical view is discussed in Chapter 1.

5 Opper and Nee, *Capitalism from Below* (2012).

6 This theoretical view is presented in Chapter 1.

7 Each theory's model for institutional reform is discussed in Chapter 1 and Chapter 5.

8 Each theory's insights and shortcomings in explaining the case of Afghanistan is discussed in Chapter 5 where, drawing on the lessons from both theories and the case of Afghanistan, this dissertation proposes a new approach for institutional reform for countries like Afghanistan.

9 *See* Islamic Republic of Afghanistan, Afghanistan National Peace and Development Framework 2017–2021 (2016), http://policymof.gov.af/afghanistan-national-peace-and-development-framework-anpdf/ [hereinafter Islamic Republic of Afghanistan, National Peace and Development Framework (2016)]; Islamic Republic of Afghanistan, Afghanistan National Development Strategy 2008–2013 (2008), http://mfa.gov.af/en/page/6547/afghanistan-national-development-strategy/afghanistan-national-development-strategy-ands [hereinafter Islamic Republic of Afghanistan, National Peace and Development Framework (2008)]; Afghanistan Ministry of Commerce and Industries, Ministry of Commerce and Industries Strategic Plan 2016–2020 (2016), http://moci.gov.af/Content/files/stratigic%20plan%202017.pdf [hereinafter Afghanistan Ministry of Commerce and Industries, Strategic Plan (2016)]; Da Afghanistan Bank, Strategic Plan 2017–2021 (2017), http://dab.gov.af/fa/page/media/publications/strategic-plan [hereinafter Da Afghanistan Bank, Strategic Plan (2017)]; Afghanistan Ministry of Economics, Economic Policy of Government of Afghanistan (2013), http://moec.gov.af/Content/files/Policy_National_Economic.pdf [hereinafter Afghanistan Ministry of Economics, Economic Policy (2013)]; Afghanistan Ministry of Justice, Five Strategic Plan: Law and Justice 2014–2018 (2013), http://moj.gov.af/Content/

files/Estrategi.pdf [hereinafter Afghanistan Ministry of Justice, Five Strategic Plan (2013)].

10 These institutions and their effects on access to credit is discussed in Chapter 3.

11 Afghan Government Strategic Policies and their approach to institutional reform is discussed in Chapter 4.

12 Calculated by the author based on Afghanistan Chamber of Commerce Industries, Business Tendency Survey Reports of II-2014, IV-2014, I-2015, II-2015, III-2015, IV-2015, I-2016, II-2016, III-2016, IV-2016, I-2017, II-2017, and III-2017, www.acci.org.af/surveys-and-studies.html [hereinafter Afghanistan Chamber of Commerce Industries, Business Tendency Survey Reports].

13 *Id.*

14 *See* Afghanistan Central Statistics Organization, The National Risk and Vulnerability Assessment: Afghanistan Living Conditions Survey (2005), http://cso.gov.af/en/page/1500/1494/nrav-report [hereinafter National Risk and Vulnerability Assessment (2005)]; Afghanistan Central Statistics Organization, The National Risk and Vulnerability Assessment: Afghanistan Living Conditions Survey (2007–2008), http://cso.gov.af/en/page/1500/1494/nrav-report [hereinafter National Risk and Vulnerability Assessment (2007–2008)]; Afghanistan Central Statistics Organization, The National Risk and Vulnerability Assessment: Afghanistan Living Conditions Survey (2011–2012), http://cso.gov.af/en/page/1500/1494/nrav-report [hereinafter National Risk and Vulnerability Assessment (2011–2012)]; Afghanistan Central Statistics Organization, The National Risk and Vulnerability Assessment: Afghanistan Living Conditions Survey (2013–2014), Qhttp://cso.gov.af/en/page/1500/1494/nrav-report[hereinafter National Risk and Vulnerability Assessment (2014–2015)]; Afghanistan Central Statistics Organization, The National Risk and Vulnerability Assessment: Afghanistan Living Conditions Survey (2016–2017), http://cso.gov.af/en/page/1500/1494/nrav-report [hereinafter National Risk and Vulnerability Assessment (2016–2017)].

15 This is further explained in Chapter 3.

16 This is further explained in Chapter 3.

17 This is further explained in Chapter 2.

18 Calculated by the author based on Afghanistan Central Statistics Organization, Business Establishment Survey 2009 (2010), http://cso.gov.af/en/page/1500/1494/6 [hereinafter Business Establishment Survey (2010)]; Afghanistan Central Statistics Organization, Business Establishment Survey 2015 (2016), http://cso.gov.af/en/page/1500/1494/6 [hereinafter Establishment Survey (2016)].

19 Calculated by the author based on Afghanistan Central Statistics Organization, Afghanistan Demographic Estimates for the Years of 2002/03 until 2017/18, http://cso.gov.af/fa/page/demography-and-socile-statistics/demograph-statistics/3897111 [hereinafter Afghanistan Demographic Estimates for the Years of 2002/03 until 2017/18].

20 *Id.*

21 Calculated by the author based on Afghanistan Supreme Court, Quarterly Judicial Activities Reports for the Years of 2012 until 2017, http://supremecourt.gov.af/fa/page/court-reporting [hereinafter Afghanistan Supreme Court, Judicial Activities Reports for the Years of 2012 until 2017].

22 Calculated by the author as the difference between total of gross bank deposits and total of gross bank loans based on Da Afghanistan Bank, Quarterly Financial Sector Financial Statistics for the period of I-2013 until II-2017, http://dab.gov.af/en/page/financial-supervision/financial-statistics/banks [hereinafter Da Afghanistan Bank, Quarterly Statistics of I-2013 until II-2017].

23 Merchants do not consider these informal credit arrangements as short-term working capital loans or financing because they are most often short-termed and embedded in different transactions such as *hawala* or currency exchange. Therefore, they are not reflected in the statistics of access to finance used in this dissertation.

24 Chapter 4 examines Grounded Institutional Reform in greater detail and also addresses the challenges that the application of this approach poses in the context of Afghanistan.

25 These illustrative examples are examined in greater detail in Chapter 4.
26 These recommendations are discussed in greater detail in the Conclusion and Recommendations.
27 Melanie Birks & Jane Mills, *Grounded Theory: A Practical Guide* 17 (2nd. ed., SAGE Publications Ltd 2015), at 17.
28 *Id.* at 11.
29 Anselm Strauss & Juliet Corbin, *Basics of Qualitative Research: Grounded Theory Procedures and Techniques* 134 (4th ed., SAGE Publications, Inc 2015).
30 *See* Appendix II for the pool of interview questions used for the interviews conducted for this dissertation.
31 *Id.*
32 Calculated by the author based on Business Establishment Survey (2010); Establishment Survey 2015 (2016).
33 Calculated by the author based on Afghanistan Demographic Estimates for the Years of 2002/03 until 2017/18.
34 *Id.*
35 Huquq, which literarily means 'rights' or 'law', is a sub-department of the Department of Justice within Afghanistan's Ministry of Justice.
36 Given that my sample only consisted of men, for the sake of accuracy, I use male pronouns throughout this dissertation.
37 Building Markets, Afghan Women's Economic Participation Survey Report 13 (2013), http://buildingmarkets.org/products-services-/afghan-women-economic-participation.
38 Equality for Peace and Development, Afghanistan Gender Equality Report Card: Evaluating the Government of Afghanistan's Commitments to Women and Gender Equality 67 (2015) (citing Afghanistan Investment Support Agency's (AISA)"Investor Directory" "Investors Directory," AISA, 2013, www.aisa.org.af/directory.php, https://reliefweb.int/report/afghanistan/afghanistan-gender-equality-report-card-evaluating-government-afghanistan-s).
39 *Id.* at 67.
40 The World Bank, Afghanistan National Reconstruction and Poverty Reduction—the Role of Women in Afghanistan's Future 112 (2005), http://siteresources.worldbank.org/AFGHANISTANEXTN/Resources/AfghanistanGenderReport.pdf.
41 Afghan Women's Economic Participation Survey Report. This finding is based on author's interviews with Afghan merchants in five major provinces of Afghanistan (Kabul, Herat, Nangarhar, Balkh, and Kandahar) between March and August 2017, as well as author's personal observations over several years of his work as accountant in Afghanistan's private sector between 2008–2013. In addition, it is supported by the prevalence of cross-border trade discussed earlier in Chapter 1, at 8.
42 78% of businesses owned by women in Afghanistan are small businesses with monthly income of between 30,000 AFN and 50,000 AFN (approx. between 550 USD and 900 USD). *Id.* at 9.
43 *Id.*
44 *See* Appendix I.
45 Douglas C. North, Institutions, Institutional Change and Economic Performance 5 (Cambridge University Press 1990) [hereinafter North, Change and Economic Performance 5 (1990)]; Business Establishment Survey (2010); Establishment Survey (2016), at 4.

References

Afghan Women's Economic Participation Survey Report (2008–2013, 2017)

Afghanistan Central Statistics Organization, The National Risk and Vulnerability Assessment: Afghanistan Living Conditions Survey (2005), http://cso.gov.af/en/page/1500/1494/nrav-report

Afghanistan Central Statistics Organization, The National Risk and Vulnerability Assessment: Afghanistan Living Conditions Survey (2007–2008), http://cso.gov.af/en/page/1500/1494/nrav-report

Afghanistan Central Statistics Organization, The National Risk and Vulnerability Assessment: Afghanistan Living Conditions Survey (2011–2012), http://cso.gov.af/en/page/1500/1494/nrav-report

Afghanistan Central Statistics Organization, The National Risk and Vulnerability Assessment: Afghanistan Living Conditions Survey (2013–2014)

Afghanistan Central Statistics Organization, The National Risk and Vulnerability Assessment: Afghanistan Living Conditions Survey (2016–2017), http://cso.gov.af/en/page/1500/1494/nrav-report

Afghanistan Chamber of Commerce Industries, Business Tendency Survey Reports of II-2014, IV-2014, I-2015, II-2015, III-2015, IV-2015, I-2016, II-2016, III-2016, IV-2016, I-2017, II-2017, and III-2017, www.acci.org.af/surveys-and-studies.html

Afghanistan Ministry of Commerce and Industries, Ministry of Commerce and Industries Strategic Plan 2016–2020 (2016), http://moci.gov.af/Content/files/stratigic%20plan%202017.pdf

Afghanistan Ministry of Economics, Economic Policy of Government of Afghanistan (2013), http://moec.gov.af/Content/files/Policy_National_Economic.pdf

Afghanistan Ministry of Justice, Five Strategic Plans: Law and Justice 2014–2018 (2013), http://moj.gov.af/Content/files/Estrategi.pdf

Afghanistan Supreme Court, Quarterly Judicial Activities Reports for the Years of 2012 until 2017, http://supremecourt.gov.af/fa/page/court-reporting

Anselm Strauss & Juliet Corbin, *Basics of Qualitative Research: Grounded Theory Procedures and Techniques* (4th ed., SAGE Publications, Inc 2015)

Building Markets, Afghan Women's Economic Participation Survey Report 13 (2013), http://buildingmarkets.org/products-services-/afghan-women-economic-participation

Da Afghanistan Bank, Quarterly Financial Sector Financial Statistics for the Period of I-2013 until II-2017, http://dab.gov.af/en/page/financial-supervision/financial-statistics/banks

Da Afghanistan Bank, Strategic Plan 2017–2021 (2017), http://dab.gov.af/fa/page/media/publications/strategic-plan

Dani Rodrik, *One Economics, Many Recipes: Globalization, Institutions and Economic Growth* (Princeton University Press 2007)

Daren Acemoğlu, *Introduction to Modern Economic Growth* (Princeton University Press 2009)

Equality for Peace and Development, Afghanistan Gender Equality Report Card: Evaluating The Government of Afghanistan's Commitments to Women and Gender Equality (2015) (citing Afghanistan Investment Support Agency's (AISA) "Investor Directory" "Investors Directory," AISA (2013), www.aisa.org.af/directory.php, https://reliefweb.int/report/afghanistan/afghanistan-gender-equality-report-card-evaluating-government-afghanistan-s

Islamic Republic of Afghanistan, Afghanistan National Peace and Development Framework 2017–2021 (2016), http://policymof.gov.af/afghanistan-national-peace-and-development-framework-anpdf/

Islamic Republic of Afghanistan, Afghanistan National Development Strategy 2008–2013 (2008), http://mfa.gov.af/en/page/6547/afghanistan-national-development-strategy/afghanistan-national-development-strategy-ands

Lant Pritchet on Poverty, Growth, and Experiments, EconTalk (May 22, 2017), www.econtalk.org/archives/2017/05/lant_pritchett_1.html

Martin Ravallion & Shaohua Chen, *World Bank, What Can New Survey Data Tell Us about Recent Changes in Distribution and Poverty*, 11(2) The World Bank Economic Review 357, 380 (Oxford University Press 1997)

Melanie Birks & Jane Mills, *Grounded Theory: A Practical Guide* 17 (2nd ed., SAGE Publications Ltd 2015)

Raghuram G. Rajan & Luigi Zingales, *Financial Dependence and Growth*, 88 Am. Econ. Rev. 559, 584 (American Economic Association 1998).

Richard H. Adams, Jr., *The World Bank, Economic Growth, Inequality, and Poverty: Findings from a New Data Set* (Policy Research Working Paper 2972, World Bank 2003), http://siteresources.worldbank.org/INTPGI/Resources/14021_WPS_2972_adams.pdf

Robert G. King & Ross Levine, *Finance and Growth: Schumpeter Might Be Right*, 108 Q. J. Econ 717, 719 (The MIT Press 1993a)

Robert G. King & Ross Levine, *Finance, Entrepreneurship, and Growth: Theory and Evidence*, 32 Journal of Monetary Economics 513, 515 (World Bank 1993b)

Ross Levine, *Financial Development and Economic Growth: Views and Agenda*, 35 J. Econ. Lit 688, 688 (American Economic Association 1997)

Ross Levine, *The Legal Environment, and Long Run Economic Growth*, 30 J. Money, Credit, & Banking 596, 598 (Blackwell Publishing 1998)

Ross Levine, *Finance and Growth: Theory and Evidence*, *in* Handbook of Economic Growth 865, 889 (Philippe Aghion & Steven Durlauf eds., Elsevier B.V. 2005)

Ross Levine *et al.*, *Financial Intermediation and Growth: Causality and Causes*, 46 J. Monetary Econo. 31, 35 (Elsevier Science B.V. 2000)

Sahay et al., IMF Staff Discussion Note, Rethinking Financial Deepening: Stability and Growth in Emerging Markets (SDN/15/08, 2015)

Sonja Opper & Víctor Nee, *Capitalism from Below: Markets and Institutional Change in China* (Harvard University Press 2012)

Stephen Haber et al., *Political Institutions and Financial Development*, *in* Political Institutions and Financial Development 1 (Stephen Haber et al., eds. Stanford University Press 2008)

Stiglitz, *Development Issues: Settled and Open*, *in* Frontiers of Development Economics: The Future in Perspective 227–268 (Gerald M. Meier & Joseph E. Stiglitz eds., World Bank and Oxford University Press 2000)

The World Bank, Afghanistan National Reconstruction and Poverty Reduction—the Role of Women in Afghanistan's Future 112 (World Bank 2005), http://siteresources.worldbank.org/AFGHANISTANEXTN/Resources/AfghanistanGenderReport.pdf

1 Background on the Economy and the Problems of Credit Transacting in Afghanistan

This book offers a microlevel analysis of credit transacting in Afghanistan; hence it focuses on actors involved in Afghanistan's credit economy. It explains the behavior of these micro actors insofar as credit transacting is concerned with reference to the prevailing formal and informal institutions that create the incentive structure that they are facing. The first part of this chapter provides an analytical description of actors in Afghanistan's credit economy along with an overview of their socioeconomic and institutional context.

The second part of this chapter focuses on the problems that Afghan merchants have to overcome when forming a credit transaction. This study identifies three main problems: unstable business climate, unsupportive property rights, and uncertain contract enforcement. The problems of credit transacting are central to this study because the ability to overcome these problems is the ultimate test for the existing formal and informal credit institutions as well as different approaches to institutional reforms in Afghanistan.

The Taliban takeover of the country has only worsened the dynamics highlighted; however, its exact effects, beyond the near complete collapse of the formal institutions, are yet to play out.

A General Picture of Afghanistan's Economy under the Islamic Republic

After Afghanistan was invaded by the United States in 2001, it underwent a period of transformation. Afghanistan's GDP quadrupled between 2001 and 2020.[1] Primary school enrollment rose by fourfold.[2] The girls' school formally reopened after being closed by the Taliban (1996–2001), and right before Taliban retook control of the country, girls made up almost 40% of students in school.[3] Thanks to major investment in the health sector, infant mortality was halved[4], far fewer Afghan mothers were dying giving birth,[5] and Afghans, on average, were living eight years longer.[6]

These transformative changes notwithstanding, trends were not positive. Billions of dollars were being pumped into the country—mostly to finance the war against Taliban insurgency—but the poverty was increasing.[7] The economic growth—mostly linked to the foreign military spending in the country—was not

DOI: 10.4324/9781003245476-2

keeping up with the fast population growth.[8] Most Afghans lived in poverty even before Taliban takeover and its concomitant developments triggered a total economic meltdown.

According to the National Risk and Vulnerability Assessment (2007–2008) ("Assessment"), of the five major provinces presented in this study, Nangarhar and Balkh have the highest percentage of the population living under the national poverty line (60%), while Kabul and Kandahar have the lowest percentage with only (23%).[9] Herat falls in between with 39% of the population living under the poverty line.[10]

Almost one-third of the workforce were estimated to be underemployed or unemployed the year before the Islamic Republic collapsed.[11] Afghanistan has an extremely young population; three-fourths of the Afghans are 29 or younger.[12] Unemployment is highest among Afghan youth.

According to the 2007–2008 Assessment of five major provinces, Kandahar has the lowest unemployment rate with 4% unemployment and 22% underemployment, while Kabul has the highest rate of unemployment with 11% unemployment and 19% underemployment.[13] Kabul is closely followed by Herat with 10% unemployment and 52% underemployment. Balkh and Nangarhar fall in between with 8% unemployment each and 29% and 71% underemployment, respectively.

According to the 2005 Assessment, Kandahar and Kabul have the highest share of the employed labor force engaged in commerce (14%), while Nangarhar has the lowest share (7%).[14] Nangarhar is followed by Herat (8%) and Balkh (9%). According to the same data source, of five major provinces, Balkh had the highest share of the employed labor force engaged in crafts and production (5%), while Nangarhar has the lowest (almost 0%). Nangarhar is followed by Kandahar (1%), Herat (2%); Balkh is followed by Kabul (4%).

The data reporting on the distribution of employment across sectors is not consistent. However, the available data from three reporting periods show that employment in agriculture and livestock has decreased from 59% in 2007–2008 to 44% in 2013–2014.[15] Conversely, the employment share of manufacturing has increased by 3% in the same period. Trade has only expanded its share of total employment by 1% for the same period. In the same period, construction and mining have increased their share of total employment by 7%. The public sector has also consistently increased its share in total employment. At the time of Taliban takeover, it was estimated that up to one million Afghans were employed in the public sector (with the security and education sector providing most of the jobs).

Afghanistan has a huge trade deficit.[16] Afghans heavily rely on imports from neighboring countries for consumption. The total annual value of imports is equivalent to half of the country's GDP, and it has been rising while the rise in export stayed has been modest.[17] Afghanistan financed its trade imbalance mostly from international aid and personal remittance from the Afghan diaspora.[18]

Afghanistan has had a very large illegal economy. The size of Afghanistan's illegal economy, taking into account only corruption and opium, could be as high as one-third of the country's GDP.[19] While the illegal economy has helped alleviate the effects of extreme poverty in some parts of the country (e.g. in Kandahar), it hinders the development of the private sector and legal economy.[20] Taliban rise to power blurs the line between illegal and legal economy even though many are hopeful that the corruption in the formal sector would decline under the Taliban government.

Afghan businesses have grown in number, durability, and complexity since 2001; however, their growth has not kept up with the population growth. The private sector growth was hindered by political instability, worsening security conditions, poor infrastructure, and lack of access to finance.[21] Afghanistan has had a very volatile business climate because of unstable political and security conditions.

Afghanistan's formal finance sector has not been effective in pooling savings for investments. Even before sanctions on the Taliban paralyzed the whole financial system, Afghans' endemic distrust of banks was deepened in 2010 when Kabul Bank, Afghanistan's largest private bank, was involved in a one-billion-dollar scandal (approx. 5% of GDP) involving some of the country's top-ranking politicians.[22] Banks in Afghanistan have had an excessive reserve of reaching as high as three billion USD,[23] but they have been able to distribute the deposits they hold in loans because the uncertain investment climate has driven lending interest rates too high, while an inefficient formal property system makes collateralization of loans difficult.[24] The country's formal property right system does not ensure a high enough private return on investment.[25]

Afghan merchants faced high contract enforcement costs. Afghanistan's formal dispute resolution erected post-2001 was burdensome, expensive, and did not reflect the actual business practice of Afghan merchants.[26] Enforcement of court judgments was uncertain.[27] Bankruptcy and limited liabilities were not de facto enforced.[28] The high cost of contract enforcement discouraged the use of formal institutions to structure business relations. Following the Taliban takeover, the formal legal system disintegrated, and it is not clear what kind of institutions will replace them.

Main Types of Actors in Afghanistan's Credit Economy

To help the reader to better follow the analysis of credit transacting in Afghanistan, this section describes the way an archetype of each type of commercial actor would operate in Afghanistan's credit economy. This is a very generalized description and may not apply to every merchant; however, it will help the reader follow along with an analysis of credit transacting in the likely familiar context of Afghanistan. In the next section are three stories offered to illustrate the way archetypes of a buyer/debtor, a seller/creditor, and a *Sarraf* would conduct their business; it brings together typical facts as presented in the data collected for this dissertation.

Buyer/debtor: Ahmad and his sons run a medium-sized supermarket in Herat's food and grain marketplace. Herat's food and grain marketplace is a specialized marketplace that holds a large number of medium-sized supermarkets that sell almost everything a household may need on a daily basis. Ahmad does not own his store; however, he has a *Sar qufli* in the store. This means the owner of the store cannot evict Ahmad and get most of his customers who recognize and trust the store unless s/he pays the market price for the business reputation that Ahmad has generated through his use of the store.

Before opening his store, Ahmad had been working in the same market as an apprentice. Through his time as an apprentice, he learned the business and established relationships with suppliers. He used his savings and the money he made from selling his inheritance to raise enough capital to cover *Sar qufli* and open a supermarket. He stocked the store by buying on credits from suppliers whom he came to know through his years of apprenticeship in the market.

At his store, Ahmad sells almost all the products that a household may need on a daily basis: shampoo, cleaning products, grain, rice, tea, dairy products, beans, etc. Ahmad's customers are ordinary Afghan households who buy their household needs in bulk, for example every month, or as they need to, every day or every week. Most of Ahmad's customers are regulars, and Ahmad knows them personally. They pay for their purchases in cash in Afghani, but Ahmad also accepts foreign currencies such as US dollars and Iranian rial. Ahmad may help out his regular customers sometimes if they do not have the money to pay him right away by letting them pay him back in a week, for example.

Ahmad buys most of his store's supply from a variety of larger merchants who import their products from Iran, Pakistan, China, India, Turkey, and the UAE. Ahmad buys some of his store's supplies, such as beverages, yogurt, milk, chicken meat, and snacks, from domestic manufacturers and producers. Ahmad has an ongoing relationship with all his suppliers. He knows them, and they know him and his business too. Ahmad does not pay for his purchases in cash when he buys them; rather he has an account with his suppliers. He purchases products from his suppliers with no payment, or some payment at the time of purchase, adding debt to his account. His suppliers send their employees at the end of each week to collect an installment on Ahmad's outstanding total. Ahmad collects the money he receives from his customers to make weekly payments to his suppliers. Ahmad has to make these payments if he wants to continue to receive products from his suppliers. However, if Ahmad has not been able to sell or has sold very little of the products that he has bought from a supplier, he may share that fact with the supplier and make a small weekly payment or avoid paying for that week entirely. Ahmad almost always owes money to his suppliers unless he or a supplier does not wish to work with him anymore, in which case he has to settle his account. The amount of this residual debt depends on the size and rate of turnover of his account with that supplier. These residual debts help Ahmad run his store with less capital than he would otherwise need.

Because of these weekly payments, Ahmad does not accumulate much cash. Nor does he withdraw much money from his store. After making his weekly payments, Ahmad uses most of the remaining income of his store to pay his business expenses (his biggest business expense is usually rent) and family expenses (which includes his employee sons' families too). If he has some extra cash after making weekly payments and covering personal and business costs, he usually uses it to expand his store or save it to pay for large family expenses, like a son's wedding or a large personal purchase, such as a house, car, or jewelry.

Seller/creditor: Mahmud and his sons run a commercial company, *Mahmud and Sons Ltd*, in Herat. He imports shampoo and soaps from Iran. He has an office and a warehouse in another specialized marketplace that mostly hosts merchants who import cleaning products. In addition to his sons, he has four other employees who do bookkeeping, cleaning, managing the warehouse, and collect his receivables from the market. His sons help him with managing the business.

After being a retailer in the same market for a while, Mahmud uses his family's wealth and his savings to import shampoo and soaps rather than just sell households' needs on a retail basis. Mahmud had some connections with Iranian businesses from the time he was a refugee in Iran; he also made several trips to Iran to talk to several Iranian exporters before starting his import business. Mahmud starts importing shampoo and soap by paying in advance in Iranian rial for each shipment via *Sarraf*'s international *hawala*s. However, now that he has established a relationship, he can occasionally post-pay some of the money for a shipment, for example for a week, to keep the import and distribution process smooth.

Mahmud sells the shampoo and soaps that he imports to many different retailers in the market, but he does not receive immediate payment for these sales; rather his customers have a revolving account with him. Mahmud has to wait until retailers sell his products to their customers so they are able to make payments to him. To collect the money from sales of the products he has sold to the retailers, he sends his employees to the retailers' store at the end of each week to collect weekly payments. While Mahmud can be reasonably sure that he will collect some money at the end of each week, how much money he collects will depend on how much of his products have been sold in that given week and on the liquidity of his customers.

To make sure the currency exchange rate fluctuations (AFN/rial and AFN/USD) do not negatively affect his business, Mahmud deposits the money he collects each week (which are mostly in Afghanis) with a *Sarraf*. By doing so, he also wishes to build credibility with a *Sarraf*, in case he needs to send a *hawala* to his Iranian supplier, but he has not collected enough money from his domestic customers. Mahmud will often import a shipment every other month and pay for it in Iranian rial by two international *hawala*s, which he will execute via his *Sarraf*.

If Mahmud is struggling because the market is slow, he cannot make payments to his foreign suppliers and/or to his *Sarraf*s for the *hawalas* that his *Sarraf* had executed for him on credit. Mahmud may decide to raise capital by putting his house under *Gerawee*—especially if he thinks the market is going to improve. Mahmud may also decide to put his house under *Gerawee* to raise capital when the market is good, and he needs capital to expand and import other products so he can capture more market share. If he puts his house under *Gerawee*, he may have to pay monthly rent so he can keep living in his house, or he may forego the rent he was receiving from his property in exchange for a large sum of money he receives under *Gerawee*.

Mahmud will use the income that his business generates to cover his business costs (three big expense items are usually rent for warehouse and office, salaries, transportation, and customs costs of the imported goods), and to cover his personal expenses (which includes his sons' and their families too). When the market is doing well and sales are high, Mahmud's business generates extra income that he can use to expand his business, for example, import other products or enter another sector, maybe produce shampoo and soaps, or buy large assets, for example, house or land.

***Sarraf*:** Zubair is a *Sarraf*. Zubair and his sons run a *Sarrafi* store in Herat's *Sarraf* market, where all other *Sarrafs* are located too. Zubair does not own the store but has a *Sar qufli* on the store. Zubair's sons, his brothers, and his brothers' sons work in his *Sarrafi* with him.

Zubair spends most of his day recording and executing *hawalas* and currency exchanges that he makes. He receives money to *hawala* (to transfer) to other places inside and outside the country, or to exchange in other currencies, or to keep in a client's account to be exchanged or transferred later. He gives out money for the *hawalas* that have been issued against him and accounts for withdrawals by his merchant-clients. Zubair spends most of his days on the phone or online talking to his network of *Sarrafs* in other provinces and other countries to transfer *hawalas*. He also talks to other *Sarrafs* in the market, so he has a sense of what the prevailing exchange rates are and the directions of their possible fluctuations.

Before opening a *Sarrafi* store, Zubair used to buy and sell one or two currencies in the hallway of the *Sarrafi* market or on the street adjacent to the *Sarrafi* market. Zubair also had spent some time as an apprentice in an established *Sarraf*'s store. After he learned the business, Zubair used the money he had saved and his family's wealth to partner with a friend to pay for *Sar qufli* of a small store in the *Sarrafi*'s market. Zubair and his partner amicably split after they each established themselves as respectable *Sarrafs* in the market.

Zubair's *hawala* clients are mostly merchants who send, receive, and exchange currencies related to their business. Zubair's merchant-clients send, receive, and exchange currencies frequently and in large amounts. Zubair has a relationship with his merchant-clients and knows their businesses. Afghans working and living abroad and their families inside Afghanistan are the second customer group of Zubair's business. The second group sends, receives, and exchanges currencies, but less often and in smaller amounts. Zubair has a more limited number of merchant-clients compared to the personal users of *hawala* (the second group).

In his *Sarrafi* business, Zubair handles a lot of money on daily basis and has access to a large portfolio of different currencies. He may hold some of this money in multiple safes in his store. Some of this money is distributed in Zubair's *hawala* networks to other *Sarrafs* located inside and outside Afghanistan with whom he has accounts and executes *hawalas*. Zubair keeps some of this money in demands-accounts in several commercial banks inside and outside Afghanistan.

Zubair uses his large portfolio of currencies to execute *hawala* for his merchant-clients to keep their *hawala* and currency-exchange business when they do not have sufficient funds to pay for a shipment or to pay for customs clearance of a shipment. He uses some of this money to start his own business or to partner in a business, for example, open a UPVC factory. Zubair may use his access to this money to build shopping and business centers that he can sell, lease, transfer in *Sar qulfi*, or sell. Or Zubair may use his access to this money to buy and sell oil.

An Analysis of Businesses in Afghanistan

The data on the type, size, and the number of business entities in Afghanistan are very scattered and inconsistently collected.

As a general rule, businesses wishing to engage in import and export or contract with a government and/or NGOs incorporated their businesses, most often as LLCs.[29] The World Bank's database contains the data on the number of new LLCs registered annually across Afghanistan in 2006 and 2018.[30] The World Bank data suggests a correlation between the number of new LLCs registered and GDP growth in Afghanistan, in a sense that, the trend in the number of registered LLCs roughly tracks the GDP trends.

The author was also able to secure data from the Afghanistan Central Business Registry ("Business Registry") on the number of incorporated businesses—LLCs and other legal forms—registered in five major provinces: Kabul, Herat, Nangarhar, Balkh, and Kandahar between 2014/15–2016/17.[31] Business Registry data do not include incorporated businesses that are only registered as manufacturing and processing business entities. However, almost all manufacturing and processing business entities are registered as commercial business entities as well because they most often engage in import and export, which requires registration as a commercial business.[32] The World Bank and Business Registry data are comparable because an overwhelming majority of the incorporated commercial businesses entities in Afghanistan are registered as LLCs.[33]

The Afghanistan Central Statistics Office has conducted two nationwide surveys of business establishments ("Business Survey") in 2009 and 2015.[34] The Business Survey defines an establishment as "an enterprise or part of an enterprise situated in a single location and in which only a single productive activity was carried out or in which the principal productive activity accounted for most of the value-added."[35] The Business Survey covers all nonagricultural establishments, whether owned by the government or the private sector.[36] The Business Survey employs the most inclusive definition of business, which covers all income-generating business activity units.[37] It counts each business establishment separately, even if they are owned and operated by the same corporation.[38]

In Afghanistan, as a general norm, only those businesses that engage, or expect to engage, in import, export, or contract with a government and/or NGOs will incorporate (and therefore would be reflected in the World Bank and/or Business Registry data source).[39] Businesses engaging in these activity types are not necessarily required by law to be incorporated; however, the rules favor incorporated entities over non-incorporated entities. The overwhelming majority of large businesses in Afghanistan engage in one or several of these activities and therefore are incorporated. The majority of incorporated businesses in Afghanistan are members of the Chamber of Commerce and Industries ("Chamber") in their province.[40] Manufacturers and producers in major provinces have founded a separate organization, the Union of Manufacturers and Producers ("Union") and have overlapping membership in both the Union and the Chamber.[41] There is also a national Chamber of Commerce[42] and a National Union of Manufacturers and Producers in Kabul as well.[43]

Chambers and Unions act as special interest groups in Afghanistan.[44] They represent Afghan merchants and advocate for favorable policies and regulations. Also, local Chambers and Unions play a very important role in the resolution of disputes among their members (discussed in Chapter 3).

If a person wishes, however, to open a store or place of business in the market without forming a corporation, he is allowed to do so but must first obtain a license.[45] A person engaging in most forms of business activities requires a store or a place of business in the market; thus, the overwhelming majority of businesses, at least in the cities, obtain a form of license. Unincorporated businesses may obtain a business license from the local municipality. Unincorporated businesses tend to engage in retailing, craftsmanship, and provision of smaller services and often form professional unions and associations. These unions and associations are often marketplace-wide, that is, membership is based on having a store or a place of business in the same marketplace, or profession-wide, that is, membership is based on being a member of a profession or a craft.[46] In some provinces, for example Herat, the members of these independent market-wide and profession-wide unions have formed a province-wide association, the Craftsmen/Traders Union.[47] There is a National Union of Craftsmen/Trade Union in Kabul as well.[48] The Craftsmen/Traders Union acts as a special interest group in Afghanistan, although their influence is far more limited than the Chambers and Unions.[49] Business unions, associations, and local Craftsmen/Traders Unions, in provinces where they exist, play an important role in the resolution of disputes among their members (see Chapter 3).

Business Registry Data on Business Registry and Initial Capital Investment in Five Major Provinces

The Business Registry data from 2014–2015 to 2016–2017 covers five major provinces: Kabul, Herat, Balkh, Kandahar, and Nangarhar. These five provinces represent half of Afghanistan's economy, one-third of Afghanistan's total population, and almost 80% of its urban population.[50]

Business Registry data suggested, at least for the period reported, that Kabul and Herat had much more competitive markets, while Balkh had the least competitive market—assuming per capita business registry ("registry/capita") is used as a measure of ease of entering the market. Business Registry data show, at least for the period between 2014–2015 and 2016–2017, Kabul had the highest registry/capita by 13.59 commercial business registration per 10,000 persons. Kabul was closely followed by Herat with 11.42 per 10,000 persons. The remaining three provinces had much lower registry/capita. Kandahar was third with 6.64 registration per 10,000 persons followed by Nangarhar and Balkh with 3.25 and 2.84 commercial business registered. Balkh's low registry/capita, despite being one of the most secure provinces, supports the hypothesis developed in Chapter 3 that asserts Balkh has suffered the most from macroeconomic slowdown because it has the least competitive market, which has reduced the incentive for provision of trade credit and the development of its *Sarrafi* market.

Business Registry data also included the amount declared by businesses as their initial capital at the time of registry. Most merchants exaggerate their initial capital at the time of registry because it is recorded on the license, which can be observed by other potential transaction partners (these licenses are public).[51] These prospective transaction partners may consider the stated initial capital on the business license as an indicator of creditworthiness.

Businesses tend to exaggerate their capital to the Business Registry. This practice is enabled by the fact that there is no mechanism to check the accuracy of stated initial capital commitment, and exaggerating has no tax implications.[52] A higher stated capital commitment at the time of registration has two main consequences. First, it results in a higher one-time registration fee, which usually does not amount to a significant sum.[53] Second, and most importantly, it will determine the cap of each shareholders' liabilities if the corporation becomes bankrupt.[54]

Higher stated capital commitment at the time of registration means shareholders will have a greater personal liability in case of bankruptcy.[55] Each shareholder is responsible for his share of the stated capital of the corporation in the case of bankruptcy.[56] In the case of bankruptcy, each shareholder is required to pay up to his/her share of the stated capital if he/she has not already done so.[57] However, in Afghanistan, formal bankruptcy proceedings were extremely scarce; therefore, the bankruptcy effect of the stated capital commitment is not considered by most merchants.[58] The public signaling effect of the stated capital commitment is most visible: if a corporation bids for a 1 million USD contract and the business license it provides for bidding shows the corporation's capital to be 100,000 USD, it is not likely to win the bid.[59] As a result, merchants continue to exaggerate their capital to the Business Registry at the time of registry. Consequently, in case of bankruptcy, assuming the current halt is lifted, the rules of the LLC will provide very limited protection for the shareholders. As the chief judge of Kabul's Primary Commercial Court said, "Corporations do not go bankrupt."[60] Shareholders go bankrupt because they do not have sufficient funds to meet the stated capital commitment. However, according to the decision of Afghanistan's Supreme Court, effectively, individuals could not avail themselves of bankruptcy protection when they are unable to pay for a judgment entered against them.[61] This results in final court judgments that are pending until assets are found or a payment schedule is agreed to.[62]

The institutional incentives of exaggerating a corporation's capital commitment hold regardless of the place of registration. Businesses face similar incentives nationwide; therefore, they are equally likely to exaggerate their initial capital commitment no matter where they are. As a result, Business Registry data still can be useful for understanding the provincial variation of business capital—despite the effect of exaggeration. Later the Afghan government introduced a number of reforms in the Business Registry process that were bringing more accountability in the stated capital at the time of registry, but those reforms don't affect the data reported here.

Business Registry data show that at least between 2014–2015 and 2016–2017, commercial businesses registered in Kabul have the highest mean of stated initial capital commitment: 33,000 USD. Kandahar follows Kabul with a mean initial capital commitment of 30,000 USD. Balkh and Nangarhar both come third with a mean of 22,000 USD. Herat came last with a mean of 19,000 USD.

Business Registry data on the capital commitment and registry/capita show that Kabulis are most likely to register a business, and they, on average, report the highest initial capital commitment. Heratis follow Kabul in the likelihood of registering a business, but they have the lowest mean declared initial capital commitment.[63] Kandaharis are the third most likely to register a business but report, on average, the second-highest mean initial capital commitment. Balkhis and Nangarharis, on average, declare the same mean initial capital commitment, while Balkhis are less likely to open a business. This study draws on this data to identify the varying effects of provincial institutions.

The Business Survey Data on Business Establishments in Afghanistan

The Business Survey data show that between the period 2005 and 2009, the number of business establishments in the country increased by 71%. The primary driver for this growth was the increase in the number of trade and repairing establishments. Between 2005 and 2009, more than 300,000 new trade and repair establishments were created. According to Business Survey data, between 2009 and 2010, business establishments (1) have grown in size; (2) have increased longevity; (3) are more likely to be owned by more than one person; (4) are more likely to be incorporated; and (5) have higher average value added.

Business Survey data indicates that the size of business establishments, measured by the number of employees, has considerably increased. In 2009, only 10% of the business establishments had more than five employees, but in 2015 half the business establishments included in a sample of 1,943 firms had more than 18 employees. Similarly, the longevity of business establishment, according to Business Survey data, has also increased in the same period. In 2009, almost half of all business establishments were four years old or younger, 20% had been in existence for five to nine years, 22% of the business establishments were between ten and nineteen years old, and only 5% had run for twenty years or longer. Between 2009 and 2015, the share of business establishments that had been in existence for four years or less decreased by almost 20% while the share of the businesses running between five to nine years increased by 17%. However, the share of businesses that had been in existence for ten to nineteen years or more stayed roughly the same. Business Survey data also suggest that business establishments have increased their value added by an average of 50% between 2005 and 2009, for which the data exists.

An Overview of the Social Context of Afghanistan's Economy

Islam and ethnic tensions, arguably, are two defining features of Afghanistan's sociocultural context. Although the overwhelming majority of Afghans are Muslim, they do not share the same understanding of what Islam entails in every context. More than 90% of Afghans are Muslims, the majority of whom follow the Hanafi school of jurisprudence (in Arabic called *madhab*), which is the biggest school of jurisprudence in Sunni Islam.[64] A sizable minority of Afghans are Shi'a who follow the Jafari school of jurisprudence.[65] For example, as discussed later in Chapter 3, merchants of different provinces, as well as merchants and non-merchants in the same province, hold different views on what transactions violate the Islamic prohibition of interest. Taliban are staunch adherents of Hanafi maddhab and have stated their intention to enforce the preferred rulings recorded in classical books of Hanafi maddhab as the law in Afghanistan. However, what such a legal attitude would mean for the economy remains unknown.

In addition to being a Muslim-majority country, Afghanistan is an ethnically diverse country with no single dominant ethnic group. Major ethnic groups in Afghanistan are (1) Pashtuns, (2) Tajiks, (3), Hazaras, and (5) Uzbek.[66] Since the 18th century, when Afghanistan was reformed as a unified territory, Afghan rulers have come from the Pashtun ethnic group.[67] Since the 20th century, the balance of power has changed among ethnic groups in Afghanistan. In the 20th century, the dominance of Pashtuns was challenged by Tajiks, whose influence increased as the size of government grew.[68]

Conflicts in the second half of the 20th century have shifted power away from Pashtuns to Tajiks, Hazaras, and Uzbeks, all of whom played important roles in the conflicts.[69] The Taliban reign reasserted the Pashtun sovereignty.[70] The overthrow of the Taliban by the United States with the partnership of the Northern Alliance (predominantly a non-Pashtun military and political coalition) shifted the power from Pashtuns to non-Pashtun groups even further.[71] Over the last few years, however, the trend is being reversed, and Pashtuns have been increasing their power.[72] Taliban retaking of the country and enlisting a caretaker government that is more than 90% from the Pashtun ethnic group further complicates the relationship between Pashtun and non-Pashtuns in Afghanistan. These shifts in the relative power of ethnic groups and the fact that no ethnic group has enjoyed full dominance have created continued and rising ethnic tensions in all spheres of Afghan lives.[73] Research conducted for this study, however, shows that ethnic tensions have had no discernible negative impact on the economy and businesses in sectors where the government influence is limited—whereas impacts in areas where government influences are high, such as formal property right system, are visible.

A Brief Overview of Institutional Context of Afghanistan's Economy[74]

Afghan merchants struggle with significant challenges even before the devastating effect of Taliban takeover occurred. They face a very uncertain environment characterized by poor infrastructures, poor and volatile security conditions, political instability, social tensions, and unreliable transnational trade routes, an environment that has its roots in ethnic tensions, and a prolonged period of civil conflicts and foreign invasions. Formal institutions have low capacity and very limited reach. Corruption plagued formal institutions.

Afghanistan's economy was heavily dependent on foreign aid and the demand generated by the presence of international forces, which is now gone. More than half of the Afghan economy was based on the service industry (e.g. logistics, construction, and transportation), the major demand for which was generated by international forces. The dependence on foreign aid and the presence of international forces made Afghanistan's economy very unstable.

Property rights have generally been insecure. Afghan investors fear that powerful individuals inside and outside the government can be taken away from their properties. Trade-in assets and collateralization of assets are constrained by the uncertainty of formal property rights and the absence of a property registry.

Even before the Taliban takeover poses an existential thread to the financial system, most Afghans distrusted banks, which means that banks were less effective in pooling savings for investment purposes. Banks have difficulty financing investments using the deposits they hold. The highly uncertain investment environment of Afghanistan means that interest rates charged to borrowers are higher and repayment terms are shorter. Given high-interest rates and short repayment terms, most Afghan merchants say bank loans are impractical because the return on investment simply cannot cover the capital cost. When an investment opportunity can cover the capital cost, given the scarcity of reliable formal deeds and lack of well-developed formal property rights, merchants have difficulties providing sufficient collateral for bank loans. This is why banks in Afghanistan were generally liquid, but they could not distribute in loans.[75]

Afghans resolve commercial disputes and enforce contracts through informal bilateral and multilateral reputation-based mechanisms. These informal mechanisms are effective at resolving most commercial disputes and have limited exclusionary effects for Afghans. Despite a highly uncertain business environment, a formal property rights system that cannot be used to securitize credit transactions and generally ineffective formal dispute resolution mechanisms, the Afghan economy is largely a credit-based economy. Most dealings are conducted on credit. Despite the constraints they face, Afghans have managed to fashion financial markets (*Sarrafi*, supply chain, and real estate markets), intermediaries (*Sarrafs*, sellers/creditors, and Realtors), and financial arrangements (e.g. trade credit, *Sarrafs*' working capital loans, *Sar qufli*, and *Gerawee*) to support a largely credit-based economy.

Afghans effectively resolve most common commercial disputes through bilateral and multilateral mechanisms, like business collectives, *ad hoc shuras*[76], and *jirgas*.[77] The informality of the contract enforcement mechanism does not significantly limit the merchants' pool of transaction partners for Afghans; however, it puts outsiders at a disadvantage.

Faced with a highly uncertain environment and formal institutions that are unable to facilitate credit transactions in a way that effectively works in the Afghan context, Afghans have developed financial arrangements, markets, and intermediaries to support a credit-based economy. Sellers/creditors finance supply chains through trade credit and flexible risk-sharing arrangements to maximize sales. *Sarrafs* issue working capital loans to sellers/creditors which create a buffer against cash flow interruptions. Afghan developers and their customers have developed informal property rights based on future business reputation to recover construction costs of shopping centers and business centers for businesses where reputation is closely tied to the place of business. Afghans have developed informal mortgage-like transactions (*Gerawee*) to raise capital against the value of their houses.

Supply chains are financed by sellers/creditors who act as financial intermediaries through risk-sharing and flexible repayment agreements. Sellers/creditors have easy access to working capital loans from *Sarrafs*. They can pay back these loans under flexible repayment terms as they receive payments from buyers/debtors. *Sarrafs* can make these loans using the deposits they hold for Afghan merchants. *Sarrafs* issue these loans because they have lower information costs and because these are short-term, low-risk loans.

A highly competitive business environment animates the provision of trade credit and short-term working capital loans. Herein lies the feedback loop: lower barriers to entry create market competition, which animates the provision of trade credit and short-term working capital loans while easing access to trade credit and short-term working capital loans, which lower the barriers to entry (Diagram 1.1). These existing informal institutional solutions allow Afghan merchants to finance supply chains despite a highly volatile business climate. However, they create inefficiency by locking merchants into existing supply chains. They also cannot be used to finance investments.

Developers can recover capital costs required to construct shopping centers and business offices through the creation and sale of a property right in the future business reputation of shops or offices—called *Sar qufli*—where business reputation is tied to the place of business. *Sar qufli* has developed outside the formal legal system; however, the increased use of this method and increased demand by the users for courts to resolve disputes concerning *Sar qufli* has caused it to be sanctioned by commercial courts. *Sar qufli* is an example of effective synergies between formal and informal institutions achieved through the judiciary without legislation. Although *Sar qufli* is not mentioned in Afghanistan statutory laws, currently, a majority of disputes that are decided by commercial courts pertain to the *Sar qufli*. This is because court judgments are both necessary and effective for the protection of *Sar qufli*. The Afghanistan Supreme Court of Islamic Republic invoked the historical precedent of practice in Islamic countries and the general principle of commercial law, which privileges commercial agreements and commercial

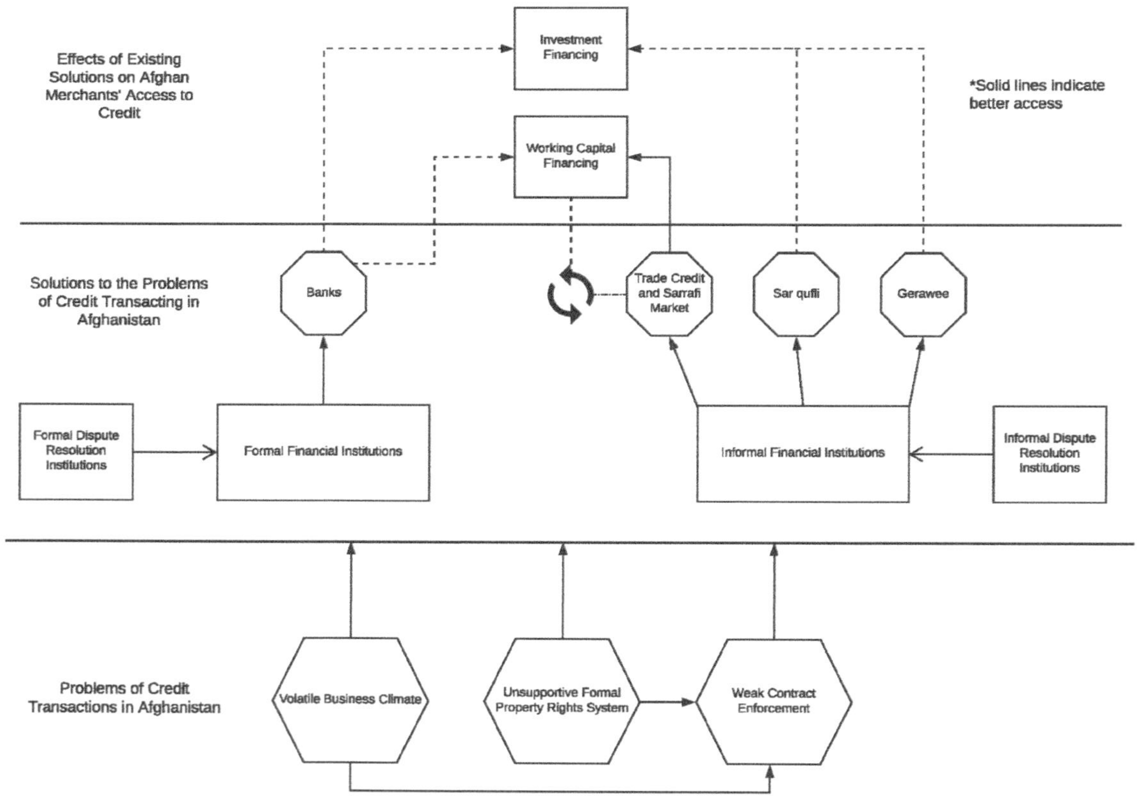

Diagram 1.1 Overview of Afghanistan's Credit Institution

practices as the paramount source of commercial law to justify the recognition and enforcement of *Sar qufli*. Afghan judges under the Islamic Republic relied on a number of Supreme Court decisions, parties' contractual agreements, and local customs to resolve *Sar qufli* disputes.

Afghan merchants can raise capital against the value of their houses through a mortgage-like transaction called *Gerawee* that has developed completely outside the formal legal system, called *Gerawee*. Conservative rough estimates suggest that in the year 2016–2017 in Herat alone, the total amount of capital raised through *Gerawee* was roughly 120 million USD, which was almost triple the total value of outstanding bank loans in Herat for the same year. *Gerawee*, on the other hand, has not been effectively linked to formal institutions although court judgements are, arguably, both necessary and effective in *Gerawee* disputes. This is because *Gerawee* is understood to violate the prohibition of interest in Islamic law. *Gerawee* is not considered a commercial transaction. One party to a *Gerawee* transaction is almost always a non-merchant, and the subject of the transaction is most often a house. The transaction is often fashioned as a sale with a right of repurchase. The noncommercial characteristics of *Gerawee* means a different set of formal laws, actors, and attitudes shape the interaction between *Gerawee* and formal institutions. While interest-bearing transactions in the commercial sector were generally accommodated in formal institutions under the Islamic Republic, they were less tolerated in noncommercial contexts.

Despite the prevalence of ethnic tensions, cross-ethnic business transactions are the norm in Afghanistan. Afghans have managed to, for the most part, isolate the business world from the negative effects of ethnic tensions in sectors of the economy where government influence is limited. However, in the sectors where the government is influential, such as construction and logistic sectors or formal property rights systems, ethnic and political tensions have impacted business relations as well.

Afghans have managed to reduce, but not eliminate, the effects of a highly uncertain environment and inefficient formal institutions. *Sarrafs*' working capital loans cannot be used to finance investment and long-term assets because *Sarrafs* have limited capabilities to pool savings and diversify risk. *Sarrafs*' working capital loans cannot be used to finance high-risk-high return investments like start-up financing. *Sarrafs* cannot pool savings for investment purposes because they make a profit from *hawala* and currency exchange not pooling savings for investment purposes. Trade credit locks sellers/creditors and buyers/debtors in existing supply chain relationships, causing the inefficient allocation of resources.

The previous government's inability and unwillingness to formalize *Gerawee* means that creditors enjoy very limited protections, and the market is vulnerable to fraud and misuse. This means that engaging in *Gerawee* as a creditor involves a lot of risks. These risks have seriously circumscribed the expansion of the *Gerawee* market. Afghan merchants can only raise a fraction of the value of the property they put under *Gerawee* in the market (e.g. they can only raise 6,000 USD for a property worth 30,000 USD). *Gerawee* cannot be used to pool savings for investment because it is a direct transaction between an individual saver, who often has housing needs, and an entrepreneur who needs financing. *Sar qufli* is only effective when the business reputation is closely tied to the place of business. It cannot be used to cover the capital cost of other types of construction projects.

Informal dispute resolution mechanisms generally put outsiders at a disadvantage and do not allow for risk-diversification because they do not recognize the principle of limited liability. The informal contract enforcement mechanism also has a negative effect on the depersonalization of business relations in Afghanistan.

Fundamental Problems of Credit Transactions in Afghanistan

Fundamental problems of credit transacting in Afghanistan determine the prevailing transaction cost and have led to the emergence of informal institutions. To reduce the problem of endogeneity, this study describes the historical roots and the causes of the problems of credit transacting in the Afghan context. The three main problems of credit transacting are the volatility of business climate, an unsupportive formal property right system, and ineffective formal dispute resolution. These three problems are not necessarily independent of each other. In fact, two major reasons for the ineffectiveness of the formal dispute resolution are the underdevelopment of the formal property right system and the high rate of insolvency, which is partly due to the instability of the business climate. However, each of these three problems has direct and distinct effects on the prevailing transaction costs and the emergent informal institutions; hence, this study considers their effects separately.

The analysis presented here focuses on the period before Taliban takeover; however, these problems either endure or have worsened since the takeover.

Afghanistan Has a Volatile Business Climate

Afghanistan has a volatile business climate. Poor security conditions, political tensions, poor infrastructure, and import and aid dependency are the main factors contributing to the instability of Afghanistan's business climate. The volatility of business climate poses problems for credit transactions because they are intertemporal transactions. For example, the instability of the business climate makes it difficult for Afghan merchants too, *ex ante*, adherence to a fixed, inflexible payment schedule. It also increases investment risks and the cost of borrowing. Formal credit institutions have failed to adapt to the volatility of Afghanistan's business context. Informal institutions, on the other hand, have managed to provide credit despite these environmental uncertainties.

The fluctuating judgment of Afghan merchants on the state of business in the country illustrates the volatility of the business climate in Afghanistan. The Business Climate Report is a quarterly report of Afghan merchants' perception of Afghanistan's business climate. The Business Climate Report is based on a periodic phone survey of 300–500 company managers, in five major provinces, working in manufacturing, construction, service, and trade sectors. The survey asks managers about their judgment on their present business situations and their business expectation for the next six months. The indicator values range from 0 (meaning: normal) up to a possible maximum of +100 for a positive climate, and from 0 to a possible minimum of -100 for a negative climate. The business climate is the mean of the situation and the expectations.

The Business Climate Report is a reliable and valid measure of Afghanistan's business climate. The Business Climate Report for the period between the second quarter of 2014 (II-2014) and the second quarter of 2020 (III-2017) traces the decline in GDP growth. The Business Climate Report data, tracing the GDP growth, show Afghan businesses' judgments on their present and future situations have been trending toward negative starting from the end of 2014.

While the overall business climate score, by virtue of being an average score, may obscure the level of volatility in Afghanistan's business climate, the regional breakdown of the Business Climate Report data shows a high level of volatility. The graph representing Business Climate Report data for any of the five major provinces shows that Afghan businesses experience high volatility (Figure 1.2).

The Business Climate Report data ranks the average business climate in five major provinces studied here, from worst to best, for the period II-2014 to II-2020 as follows: Kabul, Balkh, Herat, Kandahar, and Nangarhar (Figure 1.1). Of the five major provinces, Kabul, the capital, received the bulk of major terrorist attacks, and is affected the most by political instability; therefore, its climate was expectedly ranked the worst by the Business Climate Report data.[78] The situation in Balkh is less clear. Balkh was ranked the second-worst, on average, in this period. Balkh was one of the safest and most stable provinces in Afghanistan.[79] However, it possesses the least developed *Sarrafi* market, and cash sales are the norm of business in Balkh. Therefore, there is a correlation between the prevalence of cash sale and the undeveloped *Sarrafi* market, on the one hand, and being affected the most by worsening of macroeconomic conditions.[80]

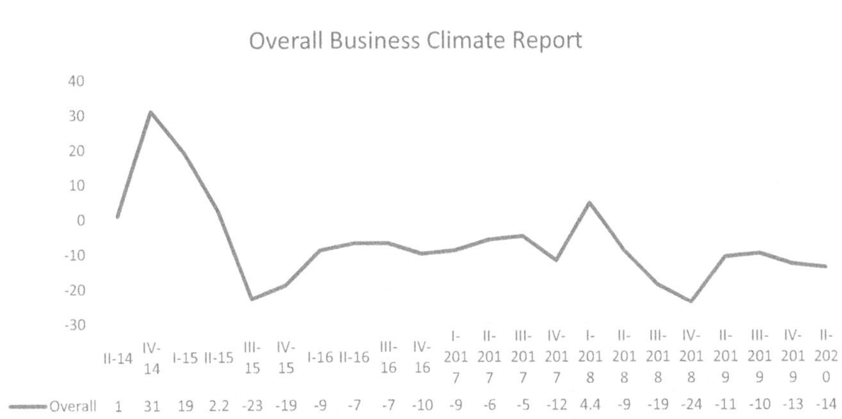

Figure 1.1 Afghanistan's Overall Business Climate Report (II 2014–III 2020)

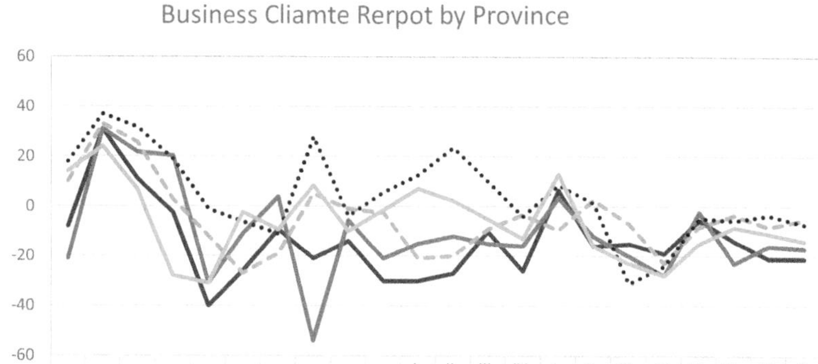

	II-14	IV-14	I-15	II-15	III-15	IV-15	I-16	II-16	III-16	IV-16	I-2017	II-2017	III-2017	IV-2017	I-2018	II-2018	III-2018	IV-2018	II-2019	III-2019	IV-2019	II-2020
Kabul	-8	31	11	-2.5	-40	-26	-9.3	-21	-14	-30	-30	-27	-10	-26	6.5	-16	-15	-19	-5.5	-14	-21	-21
Balkh	-21	31	21.7	20.2	-31	-11	3.89	-54	-5.6	-21	-15	-12	-15	-16	3.5	-12	-20	-28	-2.4	-23	-16	-17
Kandahar	10	33	25.6	2.75	-12	-27	-19	5	-1.1	-2.6	-21	-20	-9.2	-3.4	-9.6	2.7	-7	-23	-8.3	-3.6	-8.3	-5.3
Nangarhar	18	37	31.7	18.9	-1.1	-6.1	-11	27.8	-3.9	5.65	12.6	23.5	10	-4	8.7	1.3	-31	-24	-4.8	-5.6	-3.5	-7.1
Herat	14	24	6.7	-28	-31	-2.4	-9.4	8.33	-10	-1.5	7	2.2	-5.1	-13	12.9	-16	-23	-28	-15	-8.5	-11	-14

Figure 1.2 Afghanistan's Business Climate Report by Province (II 2014–II 2020)

Despite being the most politically stable and safest of five major provinces, Balkh has the most volatile business climate.[81] Of the five major provinces, Balkh's business climate has experienced the most volatility. Balkh's business climate has a standard deviation of 18.8, while the standard deviations for Kabul, Herat, Kandahar, and Nangarhar are, respectively, 15.7, 14.67, 14.54, and 17.18. The absence of a well-developed *Sarrafi* market and prevalence of cash sales may explain the instability of business climate in Balkh, even though it is the safest and politically most stable province (this argument is developed further in Chapter 3).

Herat has one of the most developed *Sarrafi* markets and the most pervasive credit-based supply chains and has the second-best business climate in this period, according to the Business Climate Report. The share of small businesses likely explains why Herat's business climate is less stable compared to Kandahar. Herat has the highest share of small businesses—indicated by the lowest mean of initial capital reported by businesses at the time of registry and the second-highest per capita business registry among the five major provinces. Small businesses are affected the most by the worsening of macroeconomic conditions, according to the Business Climate Report data. The number of small businesses can explain why Herat is ranked the second-best business climate and Kandahar the best. Kandahar has the lowest share of small businesses.

Nangarhar has performed well in the overall business climate but not in business climate stability. Nangarhar also has one of the lowest per capita commercial court use in the country.[82] Nangarhar could be suffering from the overall decline in the share of Afghanistan-Pakistan during this period since it does most of its

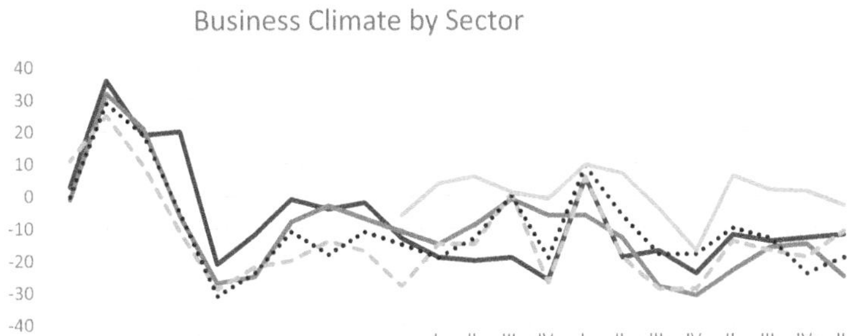

	II-14	IV-14	I-15	II-15	III-15	IV-15	I-16	II-16	III-16	IV-16	I-2017	II-2017	III-2017	IV-2017	I-2018	II-2018	III-2018	IV-2018	II-2019	III-2019	IV-2019	II-2020
Manufacturing	3	36	19	20	-21	-12	-1	-4	-2	-13	-19	-20	-19	-26	5.7	-19	-17	-24	-12	-14	-13	-12
Trade	-1	32	21	-6	-27	-25	-8	-3	-7	-11	-15	-9	-1	-6	-6	-13	-28	-31	-23	-16	-15	-25
Construction	11	25	9.5	-11	-29	-22	-20	-14	-17	-28	-15	-15	0.7	-27	5.9	-19	-29	-29	-14	-17	-19	-11
Service	0	29	19	-5	-31	-24	-11	-18	-11	-15	-19	-13	0.1	-19	9.3	-6	-18	-18	-10	-13	-24	-19
Agriculture										-6	3.8	5.9	1.1	-1	9.6	6.9	-4	-17	6.2	1.8	1.4	-3

Figure 1.3 Afghanistan's Business Climate Report by Sector (II 2014–II 2020)

cross-border trade with Pakistan.[83] Of the five major provinces, Nangarhar has the smallest manufacturing base,[84] and according to the Business Climate Report data, the manufacturing sector has been affected the least by the worsening of macroeconomic conditions.

According to the Business Climate Report data, between II-2014 and II-2020, the manufacturing sector has experienced the least slowdown, while construction and trade have experienced the most negative climate; the latter is likely linked to the COVID, crisis and the former is linked to the drawdown of foreign forces in the country. The service sector has also been affected by a shrinking foreign footprint in the country (e.g. low demand for logistical services) but still has had a solid domestic demand (e.g. telecommunication, banking, and media). Agriculture has been least affected because it's least connected to foreign presence and also starts from a very low point.

The Business Climate Report data show that smaller businesses have consistently been affected the most by worsening of macroeconomic conditions. This is expected because smaller businesses usually have the least capital and are the least diverse businesses.

Security Conditions in Afghanistan Destabilized the Business Climate

The main source of environmental uncertainty in Afghanistan was the deteriorating security condition that culminated in the Taliban takeover of the country. Poor security conditions have a direct and negative effect on the business climate in Afghanistan. A high level of insecurity rendered Afghanistan's business climate very unstable. Afghan security conditions, measured by the number of civilian deaths, trended toward worsening from the beginning, reaching a record high right before Taliban takeover in 2021, marking a bloody end to a long-drawn conflict over the control of the country.[85]

The 2015 Business Survey data shows that more than a quarter of surveyed business establishments reported lack of security was the biggest problem they had faced within the last year of their operation.[86] Comparing Business Survey data from 2009 to 2015 suggests that lack of security has become a more serious problem for businesses between 2009 and 2015 (rising from 7% to 26%) as security conditions in the country deteriorated.[87] Since the security condition has been on a downward trend post-2015, it can be safely assumed that security conditions have become even more of a serious problem for businesses since 2015. Of the five provinces studied here, measured by the number of terrorist attacks, Kabul is the least secure, while Herat and Balkh are the most secure.[88] Kandahar and Nangarhar fall in between.[89]

With Taliban in complete control of the country, the fight over the country ended and the high level of violence, which dropped to a historically low level (at least for now). ISKP, high crime rate, and the prospect of armed resistance in the warmer seasons still haunt the fragile negative peace that has emerged. While the insecurity might have dropped as a measure destabilizing factor, the consequences of Taliban takeover of the country—such as loss of foreign aid, sanctions, and (human and monetary) capital flight—have nullified any potential dividend from the negative peace for the business sector so far.

Political Instability Creates Volatility for Businesses

Political instability was another source of environmental uncertainty in Afghanistan, having a direct and negative effect on the business climate. A high level of political instability renders Afghanistan's business climate unstable. Afghanistan is one of the world's least politically stable countries. In 2017, the World Bank gave Afghanistan's political stability its lowest score of -2.80 ranking Afghanistan 193 out of 194 countries only before Yemen.[90] Afghanistan score only marginally improved until the year 2020, the last year for which data is available.[91]

The year 2017 marked the height of one of the worst cases of the country's frequent electoral crisis. Unable to determine the winner of the election due to rampant corruption, in 2015, following a period of intense political turmoil, a National Unity Government was brokered by the United States Secretary of State suspending the constitutionally mandated process of government succession.[92] Under the National Unity Government Agreement, a power-sharing agreement was reached between the two candidates with the highest votes: Muhammad Ashraf Ghani assumed the presidency, and Abdullah Abdullah assumed the extra-constitutionally-created position of chief executive of the government.[93] Since its inception, the National Unity Government dealt with a string of political crises, culminating in the refusal of the Balkh's strong governor, Atta Muhammad Noor, to vacate the governorship after President Ghani ordered his replacement in December 2017.[94] In March 2018, after three months, the National Unity Government was able to reach a deal ending the Balkh's governorship crisis in exchange for several high governmental positions to be filled by Atta's allies and members of Jamiat-e-Islami, the political party of Atta and Abdullah.[95]

This example is illustrative of the political instability that was compounding the security challenges in the country, hurting the business climate. A high level of sustained political instability in Afghanistan creates an unstable business climate, especially for credit transactions and investment. For example, according to Balkh's Chamber of Commerce and Industries, the political crisis of Balkh's governorship has caused investment in Balkh to decrease by 30%.[96]

With Taliban rise to power, political instability persists. Taliban caretaker government announced soon after they resumed control of the country is yet to be recognized by any country or international organization. The caretaker government—which is comprised of almost exclusive Pashtun, Talib men—suffers from a deep crisis of domestic and international legitimacy.

Poor Infrastructure Creates an Unstable Business Climate and Fragments the Domestic Markets

Afghanistan has a poor and unreliable infrastructure, which precipitates an uncertain Afghanistan business and investment climate. Poor infrastructure is a nationwide and sector-wide problem. According to the 2015 Business Survey, almost half of surveyed business establishments reported unreliable access to electricity was the biggest problem they had faced within the last year of their operation.[97]

However, the Business Climate Report data show significant variation in the regional distribution of business-reported infrastructure problems.[98] According to the average percentage of businesses that reported infrastructure problems, for the period between 2013 and 2016, of the five major provinces, Kandahari businesses have the most infrastructural problems (89%), followed by Nangarhari businesses (87%), followed by Kabul (74%). Herati and Balkhi businesses reported the lowest percentage of infrastructural problems, 64% and 65%, respectively. These findings are not surprising because electricity is the number one infrastructural problem reported across the country, and these findings correlate to the provinces with the electricity problems. Herat and Balkh have the best access to electricity in the country, while Kandahar, Nangarhar, and Kabul, in that order, have the least access to electricity.

There is no significant variation in the sectoral distribution of infrastructural problems. However, the Business Climate Report data suggest that the infrastructure problems associated with sewage and waste disposal and telecom have actually decreased between 2013 and 2016.[99] Infrastructural problems concerning water declined in 2014 and 2015, however, it has made a comeback in 2016 because of droughts.[100]

Afghanistan imports more than 70% of its electricity from neighboring countries. With Taliban in charge, the country has been facing difficulty paying its electricity bill. The exporting countries have so far decided not to cut the power as a gesture of goodwill as they are trying to work with the Taliban government, but there have been occasional interruptions often caused by tensions between the countries and at times caused by the failing power transfer infrastructure inside the country.

Afghanistan's Economic Structure Was a Source of Volatility

The structure of Afghanistan's economy was a cause of volatility in the business climate. Half of Afghanistan's economy, measured by contribution to the rGDP, was comprised of the service sector.[101] The other half was almost equally divided between agriculture and industry.[102] The main source of demand for the service sector was generated by the presence of foreign forces; this was highly unsustainable.[103] This means half of Afghanistan's economy was driven by the highly unpredictable level of foreign commitment and presence of foreign countries. This risk was actualized in 2021 as the US withdrew its forces, following a deal reached with Taliban in Doha, and Taliban gradually took over by force, causing a rapture between Afghanistan economy and its donors.

Since 2002–2003, the service sector has consistently expanded its share of the GDP. Agriculture's share has consistently shrunk, and the industrial share has roughly stayed the same.[104] In 2002–2003, agriculture had accounted for 43.2% of the country's GDP. By 2016–2017, agriculture's share reduced by almost half, accounting only for 23% of Afghanistan's rGDP. In the same period, the share of industry as a percentage of rGDP also failed to increase, decreasing slightly from 21.4% in 2002–2003 to 21.1% in 2016–2017. The service industry expanded its share as a percentage of rGDP in the same period, increasing from 34.1% of rGDP in 2002–2003 to 51.6% in 2016–2017. Within that service sector, transport, communication, producers of government services, wholesale trade, and retail trade, in that order, were responsible for the increased contribution of the service sector to Afghanistan's GDP.

Examining each sector's monetary contribution to Afghanistan's GDP, between 2002–2003 and 2016–2017, of Afghanistan's three economic sectors, the service sector experienced the highest growth, while agriculture experienced the lowest growth. The service sector contribution to GDP increased from 1.54 billion USD in 2002–2003 to 3.93 billion USD In 2016–2017, adjusted for inflation. Within the service sector, finance and insurance, transport and telecommunication, producers of government services, restaurant/hotel, wholesale services, and retail services, in that order, contributed the highest growth.

After the service sector, the industrial sector accounted for the most growth. In 2002–2003, the industrial sector had contributed 0.97 billion USD to the GDP. In 2016–2017, the contribution of industry, adjusted for inflation, rose to 1.8 billion USD. Within the industry sector, mining and quarrying, construction, electricity and gas and water, and manufacturing, in that order, experienced the highest growth.

The agricultural sector showed negative overall growth during this period due to the declining value of the Afghani against the US dollar. In 2002–2003, the agricultural sector contributed roughly 1.95 billion USD/87.42 billion AFN to the GDP. In 2016–2017, the contribution of agriculture to the GDP in US dollars, adjusted for inflation, dropped to 1.7 billion USD, while in Afghanis it increased by 31% reaching 114.6 billion AFN. This is because the AFN/USD exchange rate increased by a higher percentage of 51% in that period.[105]

The high share of the service sector in Afghanistan's economy introduced a new source of instability. The demand for the service industry, which was dominated by logistics and construction, was highly dependent on the presence of foreign forces.[106] This means half of Afghanistan's economy was heavily reliant on the unpredictable level of commitment of foreign countries.[107] While the data is not available yet, but Taliban takeover is almost bound to trigger a painful structural adjustment.

Agriculture, a quarter of Afghanistan's economy, is also highly dependent on the change in climate patterns. Almost half of Afghanistan's workforce is employed in agriculture (although the service industry constitutes half of Afghanistan's economy, it only accounted for 11% of employment).[108] Agriculture in Afghanistan is predominately subsistence agriculture employing traditional farming technology.[109] As a result, agricultural output in Afghanistan is highly dependent on the patterns of rainfall. This introduces an additional source of uncertainty to Afghanistan's business environment.

Afghanistan Relies Heavily on Imports from Unreliable Trade Routes

Afghanistan relies on imports for most of its consumption. Afghanistan is a landlocked country and has to rely on transit routes through its neighboring states for trade. Afghanistan conducts more than half of its trade with its six neighboring countries: Pakistan, Iran, Tajikistan, Turkmenistan, Uzbekistan, and China.[110] Afghanistan has active trade ports with all its neighbors with the exception of China, which is connected to Afghanistan through an impenetrable mountainous corridor, *Wakhan*. Afghanistan has multiple trade ports with Pakistan and Iran, which constitute the country's main trade routes. However, Afghanistan has politically complicated relationships with its neighbors. Taliban's rise to power has not necessarily eliminated these complications.

There are several examples of the tension between trade and politics. Before Taliban recaptured power, the Islamic Republic of Afghanistan accused Pakistan of supporting the Taliban and other insurgent groups within Afghanistan, while Pakistan accused Afghanistan of hosting Baloch separatists and Pakistani Taliban with the support of India.[111] Pakistan often used the threat or actual blockage of its border with Afghanistan as a tool of pressure between the two countries' ongoing political and economic disputes over support of terrorist proxies.[112] The closure of Pakistan-Afghanistan trade routes, which on average happened at least once a year over the last twelve years, causes prices to rise in Afghanistan.[113] The Republic was pursuing an active policy to diversify its imports and its trade routes. As a result, since 2014–2015, Iran replaced Pakistan as Afghanistan's largest trading partner.[114] However, the Afghan Republic relations with, although much better than the Afghanistan-Pakistan relationship, was politically complicated as Afghanistan continuously accused Iran of supporting the Taliban within Afghanistan and meddling in the western side of the country.[115]

In addition to expanding its trade with Iran, Afghan Republic established air corridors with India and Kazakhstan.[116] It was also pursuing air corridors with a number of other countries.[117] These air corridors are generally used to export Afghanistan's agricultural products, predominantly fruits.[118] The Afghan Republic also established a trade route that connects India to Afghanistan via the Persian Gulf and Chabahar Free Trade Zone in Iran.[119] With the hope of expanding and diversifying its transnational trade, Afghanistan acceded to the World Trade Organization in December 2017.[120] The Afghan Republic was working in the context of the Regional Cooperation Conference on Afghanistan to establish a railroad that would connect Iran to Tajikistan, Turkmenistan, and China through Afghanistan.[121] The Afghan Republic was also working to establish the Lapis Lazuli Route that would connect Afghanistan through on-land and on-sea routes to Turkey and finally the Red Sea via Turkmenistan, the Caspian Sea, Azerbaijan, and Georgia.[122] It was also working toward inclusion in China's One Belt One Road Policy, which would connect Afghanistan to China through Uzbekistan and Kazakhstan.[123] The success of these transit projects was highly dependent on the ability of the Afghan Republic to establish and maintain the security of these routes inside Afghanistan—something that the Republic failed to do.

The Taliban's rise to power has not necessarily improved the connectivity of Afghanistan. The relationship with India, a major economic partner of the toppled Afghan Republic, has virtually vanished. The relationship with Pakistan has improved, but the border disputes over the colonial line of Durand continue to plague the relationship, and the border closures have not necessarily decreased. Taliban's hope of Chinese major economic commitment to the country has not been borne out either. While there have been increased activities on Afghan-China cooperation under Taliban, nothing tangible has occurred yet. China has remained aloof so far. China has not provided major aid to Afghanistan either, for example.

The Taliban-Iran relationship also remains complicated. On the one hand, since both Taliban (albeit not the entire jurisdiction of Afghanistan) and Iran are subject to US sanctions, Afghanistan has increased its share of fuel import from Iran, instead of central Asian republics. On the other hand, Iran remains concerned about the plight of Shia minorities in Afghanistan under Taliban rule as well as a boost to narco business and spread of anti-Shia terrorism in the region. Water rights and illegal immigrations also continue to cause tension between the two countries. The relationship with Central Asian republics is also complicated with a range of concerns, chief among them spread of terrorism. In short, the dividend from improvement in security inside Afghanistan in terms of the country's ability to be a source of regional connectivity has not materialized yet, and formidable obstacles remain. Until those obstacles are removed, Afghanistan's heavy reliance on imports from unstable trade routes perpetuates Afghanistan's unstable business climate.

Afghanistan's Imports, Exports, and Cross-Border Trade

Afghans rely on imports for most of what they consume. Afghanistan's annual legal imports were trending upwards before Taliban took over. The data on illegal imports is unavailable; however, given the country's limited control over its border, illegal imports are expected to be substantial.

In 2007/08, when the Afghan Republic started regularly reporting imports data, Afghanistan had imports valued at a total of 3.02 billion USD in 2007/08.[124] Imports reached their height in 2012/13, valued at 8.93 billion USD.[125] Since then, imports have experienced some decline, dropping to 6.53 billion USD in 2016/17 but then shooting up to 8.57 billion USD in 2019.[126]

Food and beverages have been Afghanistan's number one legal import based on the total value imported taken from a decade of trade data (2007/08–2016/17). After food and beverage, oil products constituted Afghanistan's second-largest import category, including petrol, gasoline, diesel, airplane fuel, lubricant, and paints. Construction materials, which include iron, glass, cement, and pipes, are the third import category. Uncategorized imports, marked as "others" in the government statistics, are the fourth-largest import of Afghanistan, followed by vehicles and vehicles' parts. The latter category includes the import of cars, construction vehicles, motorcycles, tricycles, bicycles, and their parts. Clothes, fabrics, yarn, and footwear (soft goods) are the sixth-largest import category in Afghanistan. The foregoing six categories (food and beverages, oil products, construction materials, others, vehicles and vehicles parts, and clothes and footwear) account for approximately 85% of Afghanistan's total imports over the past decade. The remaining ten categories, in order of total contribution, are machinery and its parts, household and office items, electronics, medicine and medical equipment, electricity, household appliances, cigarettes, agricultural medicine and fertilizer, livestock, and gold. These collectively account for only 15% of total imports over the last decade. This indicates a trend of import dependence because the latter groups include items that are important for productive economic activities, such as machinery agricultural medicine and fertilizer. This means Afghans are consuming more, but they are not producing more of what they consume.

Afghanistan's legal exports, in terms of the total value, consists of agricultural products, handicrafts, livestock products, minerals, and industrial products. The annual value of Afghanistan's legal exports stayed roughly the same for the period between 2008/09 and 2016/17 with a total annual export value of 0.5 billion USD. Thanks to the air corridors, Afghanistan exported experienced growth since 2016/17 reached a high value of almost 1 billion at its highest before the collapse of the Republic.[127]

Afghanistan conducts more than half of its legal trade with its six neighboring countries in order of total volume of trade (based on one decade of government trade data 2008/09–2017): Pakistan, Iran, China, Uzbekistan, Turkmenistan, and Tajikistan. Between 2008/09 and 2017, Afghanistan obtained 61% of its imports from these six countries. In the same period, the same six countries accounted for 52% of Afghanistan's exports. Imports from these six countries consistently increased over a decade from 58% in 2008/09 to 67% in 2016/17. Exports to these six countries have been declining as Afghanistan started to export to more countries (especially India); exports to these six countries have dropped from 56% in 2008/09 to 33% in the second quarter of 2017.

Cross-border trade plays a large role in Afghanistan's economy. Four of its five major provinces (Herat, Nangarhar, Balkh, and Kandahar), representing one-third of Afghanistan's economy, are border provinces. Herat borders Turkmenistan and Iran, while Nangarhar and Kandahar border Pakistan, and Balkh borders Uzbekistan and Tajikistan.

Afghanistan has a negative trade. Afghanistan's negative trade balance has been growing because Afghanistan's legal imports have steadily increased at a much higher rate than the country's legal exports. For example, in 2008/09 Afghanistan legally exported 0.54 billion USD while it imported 3.02 billion USD.[128] Eight years later, in 2016/17, the total value of exports marginally increased to 0.6 billion USD, while the total value of imports increased to 6.53 billion USD. Toward the end, in 2019, Afghanistan imported 8.56 billion USD, while it only exported 0.87 billion USD; that is a 7.69 billion USD trade deficit.

Afghanistan was only able to run such a high trade deficit because it relied on foreign aid. According to the World Bank data, between 2001 and 2015, Afghanistan received 61.84 billion USD in net official development assistance and official aid.[129] However, development assistance and foreign aid were on decline since 2010[130] and came to a complete stop when Taliban took over the country. Afghanistan's foreign aid dependency was another source of volatility in Afghanistan's economy as the flow of foreign aid was much less predictable than domestic revenue.[131]

After development assistance and foreign aid, personal remittances are Afghanistan's largest source of financing the country's massive trade deficit. Accurate data on the value of personal remittances are scarce. The current estimates are inconsistent. According to the World Bank data, the total value of personal remittances received in Afghanistan between 2008 and 2016 was 2.22 billion USD.[132] However, in a report released in 2018, the World Bank estimated that the money Afghans working outside Afghanistan have sent home over the last year could account for up to 10% of the country's gross domestic income (approx. 2 billion USD).[133] According to the same report, 16% of Afghan families have at least one member who is working abroad and sending money home.[134] The Afghan Republic Ministry of Refugee and Repatriation estimated that in one year, Afghans living abroad (including refugees and immigrants) injected 7 billion USD into Afghanistan's economy.[135] United Nations International Funds for Agricultural Development estimated the total value of remittance received in Afghanistan in the year 2006 to be 3.4 billion USD.[136] Unlike development assistance and foreign aid, the contribution of Afghans living abroad was on the rise as outward immigration was increasing even before Taliban takeover. However, the COVID-19 crisis coupled with now sanction-induced difficulties with remitting money into Afghanistan are likely to have negatively impacted remittance as well.

After personal remittances, Foreign Direct Investment was the third source of financing for Afghanistan's massive trade deficit. According to World Bank data, the total Foreign Direct Investment inflow between 2001 and 2015 was 1.64 billion USD.[137] Foreign Direct Investment inflow spiked in 2005 and 2009 but declined from 2009 until 2014, when it started to recover.[138] Foreign Direct Investment inflow in 2015 almost returned to the level it was at in 2009.[139] Foreign Direct

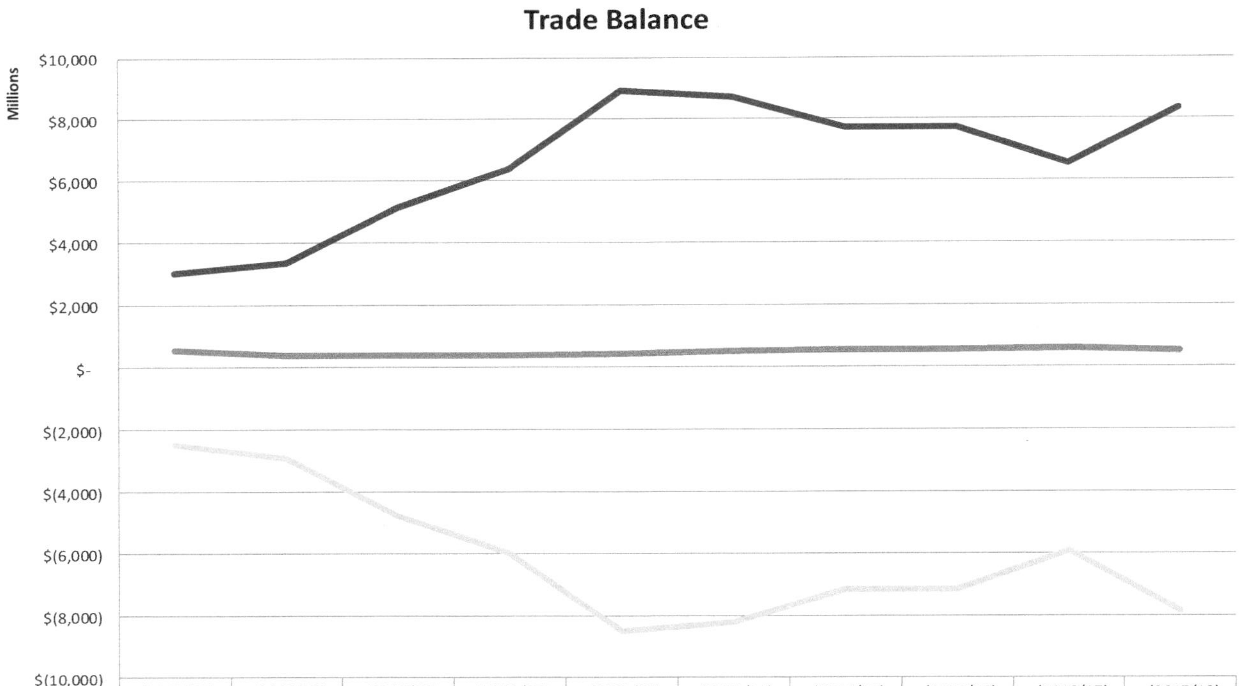

	(2008/09)	(2009/10)	(2010/11)	(2011/12)	(2012/13)	(2013/14)	(2014/15)	(2015/16)	(2016/17)	(2017/18)
Export	$544,561,38	$403,441,00	$388,483,63	$375,850,93	$414,497,88	$514,972,98	$570,534,00	$571,404,96	$596,455,33	$496,676,58
Import	$3,019,860,	$3,336,434,	$5,154,249,	$6,390,310,	$8,932,390,	$8,724,083,	$7,729,168,	$7,722,865,	$6,534,140,	$8,359,725,
Ex-Im	$(2,475,298	$(2,932,993	$(4,765,766	$(6,014,460	$(8,517,892	$(8,209,110	$(7,158,634	$(7,151,460	$(5,937,685	$(7,863,049

Figure 1.4 Afghanistan's Trade Balance (2008/09–2017/18)

Investment outflow from Afghanistan was very scattered. Total Foreign Direct Investment outflow between 2003 and 2016 amounted to 0.36 billion USD.[140] The total of net portfolio investment for the period of 2008–2015 for which we have data is 0.40 billion USD and showed a steady increase.[141]

Formal Property Rights in Afghanistan

The property rights system in Afghanistan poses fundamental problems for credit transacting in Afghanistan. The formal property rights system cannot be used to securitize credit transactions, and it does not incentivize private investment. Afghans have devised informal arrangements to securitize credit transactions (such as *Gerawee* and *Sar qufli*) which do not rely on a formal private property right system.

Property rights in Afghanistan are insecure because of a host of legal and extralegal challenges that have their roots in the country's tumultuous history and corruption. The combination of legal and extralegal challenges has made transacting in properties in Afghanistan very costly.[142] Legal ownership of private property in Afghanistan is uncertain, which makes it difficult to collateralize loans. Due to the limited legal protections, rampant insecurity, and corruption, protection of private property is weak and uncertain, which makes private return on productive activities uncertain and limited. This has reduced incentive for productive activities.[143]

It is yet not clear what the Taliban-in-government would mean for the property right system. Institutionally, the formal legal institutions of the Afghan Republic collapsed on the eve of Taliban takeover. Taliban have been slow to restaff the legal institutions, and when they did, they have appointed almost exclusively Talibs with traditional Islamic training in the legal positions. This signals a complete institutional rapture. The status of laws are more complicated, however. The Taliban have treated the existing laws of the country as valid as long as they are consistent with their understanding of the classical Hanafi School of jurisprudence, they equivocate. No specific announcement has been made about property laws yet. In effect, however, there are reports of non-Talibs, especially from minority communities, being forced to leave their property as Taliban try to reward their supporters and reverse some of the previous transfer of land that they (sometimes) rightly considered illegitimate.

Legal Problems of Formal Property Rights in Afghanistan

Formal protection of property rights in Afghanistan is limited. The legal problems are most acute in the case of immovable property, while the extralegal challenges affect movable property as well. The formal private property system in Afghanistan suffers from both measurement and enforcement problems. Because of problems that have their roots in history, Afghanistan does not have a working titling system which makes transacting in immovable property very costly.[144]

It is very costly to ascertain who owns the immovable property and what are its economically important descriptions.[145] Afghanistan has not developed a unified system of measurement for land due to the fact that the land registry efforts in Afghanistan's history were met with failure.[146] The documents to prove and measure land that do exist are scattered and use local and heterogonous measurements that are not standardized or easily convertible.[147] As a result, the information cost of property transactions is very high.

In addition to the high information cost, legal protection of the immovable property is very uncertain for four interconnected reasons: legal ownership and rules of determining ownership are unclear, the majority of properties are owned and transferred informally, actual possession is not a strong evidence of ownership, and property rights of inheritors go unassigned for generations. Each of these factors is explained in greater detail in the following sections.

Legal Ownership and Rules of Determining Legal Ownership in Afghanistan Are Unclear

Several attempts at redistribution of land by different regimes in Afghanistan history, coupled with unclear rules of determining legal ownership, have created real uncertainty as to who can legally claim ownership of property in Afghanistan. Several past regimes have attempted land reforms, distributing and redistributing private and public lands. However, the subsequent regimes have explicitly or implicitly refused to recognize the legality of the ownership rights that those land reforms sought to create.[148] Taliban recent actions are just a continuation of this historical trend. This, in effect, has caused a legal limbo, which has created legal uncertainty as to who legally owns property in the country. Despite several attempts since 2001, the Afghan Republic failed to create clear rules to facilitate the process of determining legal ownership, reducing uncertainty, and moving toward creating a uniform/unified system of titling.[149] As a result, protection of property rights is insecure not only because information of legal ownership is inaccessible but also because the rules of determining legal ownership are uncertain.

It is very difficult to prove land ownership in Afghanistan because, over the past 30 years, a piece of land could have been compulsorily purchased; expropriated, or redesignated as public land; transferred to another individual by a decree or a statute; privately transferred between private individuals formally or informally; abandoned by its owner; illegally occupied; inherited; or voluntarily or coercively sold, exchanged, or gifted to others.[150] As a result, protection of property rights is insecure not only because information about legal ownership is inaccessible but also because the rules of determining legal ownership are uncertain.

Afghans have been paying taxes on their properties since the 1880s.[151] The records of these tax payments are still preserved in Afghanistan's Ministry of Finance.[152] The Books of Ownership and records of tax payment are still continued to be used to prove ownership in courts today.[153] Throughout the 19th and 20th centuries, before the communist regime took over in Afghanistan, the rulers had often granted ownership of public (and often private) lands to different individuals and groups of people through presidential and royal decrees.[154] These special decrees were intended to buy political support, engineer ethnic composition of different regions of the country, or reward loyalty. The records of these degrees are also still used as proof of ownership in courts today.[155]

Afghanistan first attempted to survey and register land ownership in the 1960s.[156] Land Survey and Statistics Law of 1965 created a Department of Cadastral Survey to conduct a nationwide land survey.[157] The survey also recorded the coordinates of the land, its owner, and its legal status.[158] The survey was aimed to improve tax collection, create a unified legal system for land ownership, which until then had been held under a mixture of customary, religious, and legal rules.[159] It was also hoped by achieving more legal certainty of the legal ownership, it would make it easier for landowners to use their land as collateral to receive loans.[160]

The policy proved extremely costly and difficult to implement and only produced partial results. To reduce costs, a survey of land by cadastral personnel was replaced with self-reporting and confirmation of local government officials.[161] As a result, under the 1960s Land Survey and Ownership Registration Policy, a set of Books of Ownership were produced, and one-third of the country's total land and one-fifth of the country's arable land were surveyed and registered.[162] However, some contemporary experts questioned the accuracy of the data collected especially concerning legal ownership of the land.[163]

In the 1970s and 1980s, two different land redistribution policies were introduced in Afghanistan—the first by President Daud and the second by the communist regime. Under Daud's land redistribution policy, enacted in the Law Concerning Land Survey and Registration of Settlement ("the Decree"), a ceiling of 20 hectare was instituted, and the excess land was required to be distributed to landless farmers who would only obtain full ownership after compensating the former landowner, in installments, based on a fair price set by the government.[164] The Decree also sought to prevent private sales of redistributed lands without official permission and attempted (again) to determine the precise boundaries of all public and private land in Afghanistan.[165] In actuality, the process of implementation of the Decree was slow, and only some properties were actually redistributed under Daud's land reform.[166]

In the 1980s, a communist regime took power in Afghanistan through a military coup. The communist government suspended Daud's land reform policy and instituted a more radical land redistribution policy, setting a land ownership ceiling of six hectares, under the Land Reform Decree of 1980 ("the 1980 Decree").[167] The regime also attempted to conduct a complete survey of lands in the country.[168] The government attempted to expropriate and redistribute the excess private lands without compensation.[169] Under the 1980 Decree, failure to register land, under communist government decree, was to result in confiscation, and attempt to destroy land or property was to be met with severe punishment.[170]

The communist land policy provoked considerable backlash and was a main cause of the subsequent popular revolt. In actuality, due partly to these revolts, the redistribution and survey of the land was only implemented in a limited part of the country.[171] In 1987, when the popular Islamic resistance against the communist regime had grown powerful, President Najib, in an attempt to appease the opposition against the communist government, formally suspended the land redistribution policy.[172] A presidential decree promised that expropriated land would be restored to original owners, and in cases where restitution was not possible, former owners would be compensated.[173] This presidential decree was never in effect implemented.[174]

In 1992, the Mujahedeen government seized Kabul, and a new constitution was drafted but never enacted, which restored the protection of private property under Islamic law.[175] However, the Mujahedeen government failed to overcome its internal divisions, and a civil war ensued. The country descended into lawlessness. During this period, and the period of conflict before it, reportedly, people were forced out of their lands or were forced to hand over their documents of ownership to powerful local commanders or warlords.[176]

It was partly in response to this state of lawlessness that the Taliban emerged and finally took power in Afghanistan the first time around. The Taliban of the 90s suspended the formal laws and created Islamic Courts, which were supposed to apply Shari'ah or Islamic Law. The Taliban of the 90s, reportedly motivated by ethnic reasons, committed mass land seizures in some parts of the country.[177] However, they also issued a number of decrees that were aimed to restore land ownership to their pre-communist revolutionary holder.[178] Similar restoration policies have also been followed by the post-2001 Karzai and Ghani governments.

In 2008, Karzai's government enacted new legislation, the Law of Managing Ownership Affairs.[179] This new legislation created a provincial-level commission headed by the governor to reattempt to survey land, identify its legal owner, and refer disputes to the court.[180] This legislation, and the commission created under it, had very limited achievements.[181] The last government of the Republic headed by President Ghani generally followed the same policy of creating special tribunals and commissions to untangle the complex mess of land ownership in Afghanistan. However, as recently as February 14, 2018, the Afghanistan government inaugurated a new land survey program: Development of Land Ownership System of Afghanistan ("Land Ownership System"). According to President Ghani's statement delivered in its inauguration ceremony, under the Land Ownership System, a complete land survey was going to be conducted in Afghanistan.[182] According to President Ghani, the program was going to retrieve usurped land in Afghanistan and pave the way for legal distribution of public land to farmers and Afghan repatriates.[183] The Land Ownership System was based on Turkey's land reform program.[184] Given the political and economic power of current land usurpers in Afghanistan, and the legal difficulty of determining land ownership in the country, the success of the Land Ownership System was suspect. While the program had some achievements, it did not succeed in making a dent in the complete mess of the property rights system in Afghanistan.

Although the majority of the historical land reforms have focused on rural lands where large landowners reside, they have serious consequences for urban real estate property as well. Since 2001, Afghanistan has gone through a period of rapid population growth and urbanization, which has significantly expanded the boundaries of cities.[185] Consequently, the legal uncertainty created by land reform policies has not been contained to rural areas. As a result of the unclear status of different historical land reforms and the enormous political consequences of formal property rights reform, the rules of determining legal ownership in Afghanistan have largely remained obscure. This lack of clarity renders the creation of an integrated formal property system that would position a property owner and its property into a transparent formal grid impossible. The absence of such a formal property system means Afghans cannot rely on formal property rights to securitize credit transactions, and Huquq Departments cannot identify parties' assets easily to enforce judgments.

The Majority of Property Ownership Transfers in Afghanistan Are Conducted Informally

An overwhelming majority of the transfer of property ownership in Afghanistan is conducted informally and, arguably, illegally.[186] It was estimated that 90% of land ownership in rural areas and 70% of land ownership in urban areas of Afghanistan are held informally.[187] The formal requirements for the legal transfer of ownership are burdensome and costly; therefore, most Afghans opt to transfer ownership informally.[188] Informal transfer of property is less expensive because the parties do not have to pay taxes or spend time and resources to go to different government offices.[189] Informal transfer of property is less burdensome because it relies on verbal confirmation of neighbors to verify ownership.[190]

A main reason for this formal burdensome process of transfer of ownership is the first-order problem of determining whether the person who wants to transfer the ownership is actually the legal owner. This first-order problem stems from the uncertainty of ownership and rules of determining ownership in Afghanistan, as well as the lack of a complete land survey and registry in Afghanistan. As a result, most transfers of ownership occur without complying with mandatory legal rules of transfer of immovable property. In effect, the uncertainty of ownership and the rules of determining legal ownership have caused a decoupling between mandatory legal rules of transfer of ownership and the de facto practice of transfer of ownership forcing courts to recognize the informal transfers of ownership when deciding ownership disputes.[191] This has perpetuated and complicated the creation of uniform legal rules of determining ownership and a common system of property registration. This is a vicious cycle. The complexity of determining legal ownership compels Afghans to transact and transfer property outside the legal framework, making it even more difficult to determine legal ownership.

Formal transfer of property in Afghanistan involves up to ten steps, depending on how one defines each step, and it can take months—even if the transferor holds a formal deed and the transferor's ownership rights are not contested.[192] The steps involve verification of ownership by courts, land authorities, and land archive, which requires a site visit, an archive search, and testimony. If verification is successful and a formal deed is located and verified, the next step is an appraisal, which involves multiple assessments from different Realtors verified by the local municipality and site visits by officials. After the appraisal is completed, the third step is paying the transfer tax, which is 3% for the properties whose value exceeds 2 million AFN (approx. 30,000 USD) and 2% if the value of the property is lower than 2 million AFN. The fourth step is the issuance of the deed, which requires bringing several contract witnesses to the court and paying for the deed form (which costs about 3 USD). This is the process if the person who is transferring the land holds a formal deed. But it is estimated that only 10% of rural property and 30% of urban property owners have official deeds given by the court or government.[193] Most of these deeds are old and do not reflect the current owners of the land.

If a person does not hold a formal deed, the process is even more complicated and involves using several property and legal documents to prove the chain of transmission of ownership from the person who registered the formal deed to the person seeking transfer of ownership.[194] If the land is subject to dispute, which is often the case because of Afghanistan's turbulent history, there needs to be a trial where courts are tasked to determine, from a multitude of often conflicting legal and property documents, who the legitimate owner is.[195] After determining the legal owner, courts have to address the longitudinal question of chain of title transmission by relying most often on customary documents of transfer or testimony—a practice which is against the *de jure* rules of transfer of immovable properties set in Afghanistan's Civil Code.[196] Courts have to rely on customary documents because an overwhelming majority of ownership transfer occurs informally.[197] Formal legal rules do not recognize the use of customary documents for the transfer of property.[198] This has created a decoupling between formal legal rules and the practice of court necessitated by the reality of life in Afghanistan. The formalization of customary practice is difficult because it may validate coercive and improper transfers. As a result, formal legal ownership has continued to remain in a legal limbo. It is unclear how the Taliban, now again in power, will tackle this issue.

Actual Possession Is Not a Useful Presumption of Ownership

Afghanistan's prolonged period of conflict has caused significant internal displacement and outward immigrations, creating a situation where the actual possession of property is not a strong indicator of legal ownership. As such, the conflict not only increases the number of ownership disputes but also makes it harder to determine legal ownership.

By the end of 2020, the estimates of internally displaced Afghans ranged from 2.9 to 3.5 million.[199] Four decades of conflict means Afghans also make up one of the world's largest refugee population. UNHCR estimates that there are more than 2.6 million Afghan refugees mostly living in Iran and Pakistan.[200] This means, at very least, more than 6 million Afghans are living away from their immovable properties without being able to return to or control their properties. According to the Norwegian Refugee Council, usurpation of personal property is a cause of immigration and a barrier to return for a large percentage of Afghan refugees.[201]

Inheritance Goes Undivided for Generations

The common practice of not dividing inheritance for generations has created further legal uncertainty of individual ownership of property. Although traditional Islamic law requires the estate to be divided into fixed shares,[202] Afghan families most often do not divide the inheritance, to avoid upsetting family harmony, and/or to prevent the division of agricultural land, and/or to preserve the durability of a family business.[203]

The formal process of dividing up inheritance is also burdensome and complicated. Furthermore, some families evade the formal inheritance procedures as a way to avoid giving the female heirs their share of inheritance as required by state law and Islamic law.[204] As a result, inheritance disputes are the second most common property disputes, after the usurpation of personal property, before Afghan courts.[205] This is discussed further in Chapter 3 in the context of family-owned businesses in Afghanistan.

Extralegal Challenges of Property Rights in Afghanistan

Aside from the legal problems, Afghans fear a multitude of other extralegal threats to their properties stemming from poor security conditions and corruption. These can include expropriation of their land by powerful individuals inside and outside the government, among other threats. Although Afghan laws set forth fair procedures for the taking of the privately owned by the government,[206] powerful individuals inside and outside the government often have used their power to usurp personal and public property. The usurpation of property in Afghanistan was rampant throughout Afghanistan's prolonged period of conflict. However, rather than decreasing since 2001, it has even accelerated.

According to the statistics of the Afghan Republic Independent Land Authority in 2017, 3,200 square kilometers of public land have been usurped by ordinary and powerful individuals inside and outside the government in Afghanistan (this is roughly equivalent to three-fourths of the total area of Kabul province).[207] According to an Afghanistan Freedom House report released in 2016,[208] an estimated 1,800 square kilometers of private property has been usurped in Afghanistan (this is roughly equivalent to half of the total area of Kabul province).[209]

Before the takeover of the whole country, Afghans were facing arbitrary taxes and expropriation by different groups who, according to the Special Inspector's report, control 30% of the country.[210] Taliban were the main group. There were multiple reports of the Taliban collecting taxes from businesses, business cargos, and agricultural products as an insurgency.[211] Merchants in major urban centers were less often targeted by these extralegal taxes; however, their shipments were often taxed by the Taliban.[212]

The Afghan government's weak control of transit routes inside Afghanistan meant Afghan merchants' cargo was often taxed by the Taliban or corrupt highway officials.[213] The insecure domestic trade routes, coupled with poor road infrastructure, created a fragmented domestic market.[214] As a result, businesses in Afghanistan tend to be regional or province-specific; fragmentation of Afghanistan markets has increased costs for national businesses. The fragmentation of the domestic market hindered specialization because high transportation costs disincentivize regional specialization. Relatedly, a low level of domestic market integration privileges cross-border trade at the expense of in-country trade, further driving the import-dependency of Afghanistan's economy.

Afghans also face high rates of property theft, ransom, and protection money. Powerful individuals inside the government also extract rents from businesses. Afghans pay up to 3 billion USD in bribes each year.[215] Most wealthy Afghans devote resources to protect themselves and their families. It is not uncommon for wealthy Afghan merchants to move around major urban centers in effectively armored motorcades. Wealthy Afghans hire multiple bodyguards, pay protection fees, and remove their families from Afghanistan.[216] *Sarraf*'s unions organized multiple strikes in response to armed robbery and kidnapping of *Sarraf*s in different provinces.[217]

It is unclear how the security environment and corruption will evolve with Taliban in power. There are indications that corruption may decline and that the internal connectivity may improve now that roads are not threatened by insurgency. However, the prospect of universal poverty triggered as a consequence of Taliban takeover of an economy heavily dependent on foreign money complicates the hopes for any dividend from the fragile negative peace and toppling of a government that was seen as corrupt by supporters and enemies alike.

Formal Commercial Dispute Resolution in Afghanistan

Dispute resolution mechanisms are a main determinant of enforcement costs. Which mechanism dominates is thus a factor that has a direct effect on the type and volume of credit transactions that take place in a country. In Afghanistan, formal dispute resolution mechanisms have been expensive, uncertain, and ineffective.[218] Thus, they caused fundamental problems for credit transacting in Afghanistan. Most merchants choose to resolve their disputes outside of the formal dispute resolution institutions. This has had a dynamic effect on depersonalization and economic growth in Afghanistan. Informal dispute resolution institutions are discussed in Chapter 3.

This section also describes the rules of jurisdiction in Afghanistan to explain why *Sar qufli* falls under the jurisdiction of commercial courts while *Gerawee* does not. Given the marked difference in attitudes, laws, and actors involved in commercial and noncommercial formal dispute resolution under the toppled Afghan Republic, the jurisdictional rules are very significant for the development of business-friendly judicial jurisprudence and hence the synergies between formal and informal institutions.

The formal dispute resolution in Afghanistan virtually disintegrated upon Taliban return to power. Taliban caretaker government has made some appointments in the legal sector, virtually all Talibs with only classical Islamic training, but the Taliban legal system is yet to take shape. As such, I describe the formal dispute resolution in Afghanistan before Taliban takeover and analyze why and when merchants most often opted to use them. I describe the laws and procedures in present tense because they are still formally the laws of the country as Taliban are yet to replace them.

How a Formal Commercial Dispute Begins

There is a primary commercial court in each province's capital city.[219] Primary commercial courts hear all disputes arising from a commercial transaction at the first level.[220] In provinces where a primary commercial court has not yet been established, commercial disputes are tried in the civil division of the primary court.[221] There are two ways that a commercial dispute can find its way to a court in Afghanistan:

(1) **Huquq Department.** The plaintiff can file a complaint with the Huquq Department, which is a part of the Ministry of Justice.[222] There is a Huquq Department in each province's capital city as well as at each district. Commercial claims are filed with the Huquq Department in each province's capital city.[223] Upon receipt of a complaint, specialists at the Huquq Department will subpoena the defendant. Specialists first attempt to mediate between the parties to help them reach an amicable resolution of their disputes.[224] If the successful mediation is successful, they will record the agreement, which will end the proceedings.[225] If the mediation proves to be unsuccessful, the specialists will attempt to identify the points of contention and record the parties' claims and possible evidence to be sent to a court so the court proceedings can be expedited.[226] The court has the discretion to consider the records produced by Huquq Department or to ignore them completely.

(2) **Commercial Courts.** Nothing in the law requires a plaintiff to file his complaint at the Huquq Department prior to going to court. Therefore, a plaintiff can bypass the Huquq Department and file a complaint directly at a primary commercial court.[227] However, the court may decide to refer the case back to the Huquq Department or begin its own proceedings. After a final judgment is rendered in a commercial case (or any other noncriminal case), the judgment will be sent to the Huquq Department for enforcement.[228]

Jurisdiction of Commercial Courts

There were marked differences in attitudes, laws, and actors involved in commercial and noncommercial formal dispute resolution under the toppled Afghan Republic. Therefore, the jurisdictional rules were very significant for the development of business-friendly judicial jurisprudence and hence the synergies between formal and informal institutions.

When a case is sent to a primary commercial court by a Huquq Department, or a complaint is filed directly at a primary commercial, the primary commercial court must first determine if it has jurisdiction over the case. Concerning subject matter jurisdiction, according to Article 1 of Usul Muhakimat Tijrati (Principles of Commercial Procedure) ("Commercial Procedure") enacted in 1965, any dispute arising from a commercial transaction falls under the jurisdiction of commercial courts.[229] Concerning personal jurisdiction, Commercial Procedure Articles 6–14 states that a primary commercial court has personal jurisdictions over a defendant if it the court sits in the domicile of the defendant,[230] or the principal of business of the defendant,[231] or a place of business of the defendant that has nexus with the case,[232] or the place of formation or place of execution of the contract, provided that the defendant or its representative is present at that place at the time the complaint is filled with the court.[233]

A commercial transaction is defined in another piece of legislation, Usulnameh on the Commercial Law of Afghanistan (Principles of Afghanistan Commercial Law) ("Commercial Law") enacted in 1955. Commercial Law is the core of Afghanistan's current substantive commercial law.[234] Commercial Law's first chapter enumerates different sources of binding rules applicable to commercial transactions, and their hierarchy[235] defines which transactions qualify as commercial transactions,[236] defines who qualifies as a merchant,[237] and sets forth the fundamental rights and obligations of a merchant.[238]

Commercial Law Article 8 defines a merchant as anyone, whether an individual or a corporation, who possesses legal capacity and habitually engages in one or more commercial transactions in his own name.[239] Commercial Law introduces three categories of commercial transactions: (1) primary commercial transactions, (2) inherent commercial transactions, and (3) auxiliary commercial transactions.

Primary commercial transactions are the main commercial transactions. If a person conducts these transactions habitually, under the law, that person is considered a merchant, and that person's transactions will be presumptively regulated by commercial laws, and any disputes arising from those transactions will fall under the jurisdiction of commercial courts.[240] However, if a person engages in primary commercial transactions incidentally and/or infrequently, that person is not considered a merchant under the law, and that person's transactions are not regulated by commercial laws;[241] therefore, any dispute that may arise does not fall under the jurisdiction of commercial courts.

Inherent commercial transactions, on the other hand, are regulated by commercial laws and are subject to the jurisdiction of commercial courts regardless of the status of the parties concerned.[242] Auxiliary commercial transactions are those transactions that normally do not qualify as commercial transactions and do not confer the status of merchant onto the parties concerned even if conducted habitually. The latter transactions may nonetheless fall under the purview of commercial laws and jurisdiction of commercial courts if conducted by a person who, otherwise, is legally considered a merchant.[243] If a transaction is considered commercial only with regards to one party, commercial laws still apply to the obligations arising from the transactions and any dispute arising from that transaction where the merchant-party is the defendant will be tried in a commercial court.[244]

Primary commercial transactions include three main categories: (1) if a person purchases movable property with the intention of sale or lease to other persons in original or altered form, the sale or lease of such properties is considered a commercial transaction;[245] (2) if a person leases movable property to someone who intends to lease it to others, the original and subsequent lease are considered commercial transactions;[246] (3) it is considered a commercial transaction if a person employs other persons for the purpose of providing services.[247]

Under Afghanistan law, the sale of agricultural products and livestock by farmers is not considered a commercial transaction; therefore, it does not fall under the jurisdiction of a commercial court, unless a permanent industrial establishment is set up to change the agricultural products and livestock to be sold.[248]

According to the Afghan Republic Supreme Court, ownership disputes do not fall under the jurisdiction of commercial courts.[249] Therefore, a transaction concerning the transfer of ownership of a non-fungible property (real estate by its nature is non-fungible) is not a commercial transaction, and disputes arising from that transaction fall outside the jurisdiction of commercial courts. The Supreme Court, however, has decided that transactions concerning the benefits of a non-fungible property can be a commercial transaction if it falls within one of the categories of commercial transactions.[250] Therefore, disputes arising from a commercial transaction concerning the benefits of a non-fungible property does fall under the jurisdiction of commercial courts.

The Supreme Court has decided that if a person leases a store, or gives a store to *Sar qufli*, for commercial purposes, disputes arising from the lease and *Sar qufli* fall under the jurisdiction of commercial courts.[251] This is because, according to Afghanistan Supreme Court's jurisprudence, *Sar qufli* and commercial leases are transactions relating to the benefit of non-fungible properties rather than its ownership.[252] The subject of transaction in *Sar qufli* and commercial lease is the right to benefit from a non-fungible property (e.g. a store or a warehouse), not its ownership. Therefore, these transactions fall under the jurisdiction of the commercial court. *Sar qufli* and commercial lease make up the most common disputes in Afghanistan commercial courts. *Gerawee*, on the other hand, does not fall under the jurisdiction of commercial courts because according to the Afghanistan Supreme Court, the *Gerawee*, or its formal legal form, *Bai al-Wafa* (the sale with the right of repurchase), or a sale with a repudiation condition, constitute a transaction concerning the ownership of a non-fungible property (e.g. a house, a store, or a piece of agricultural land), and therefore fall outside the jurisdiction of commercial courts.[253] The jurisprudence of Afghanistan courts with regards to *Gerawee* and *Sar qufli* are discussed in greater detail in Chapter 3.

Regional Distribution of Commercial Disputes in Afghanistan Commercial Courts

According to data from the Quarterly Judicial Activities Reports of now toppled Afghan Republic ("Judicial Report"), primary commercial courts and commercial dewans of appeal courts in Afghanistan's five major provinces (Kabul, Herat, Nangarhar, Balkh, and Kandahar) account for roughly 90% of commercial cases received and decided by commercial courts at primary and appellate levels nationwide.[254] Even though these five provinces only represent half of Afghanistan's economy[255] and one-third of Afghanistan's population.[256] However, this does not necessarily mean that the merchants who do reside in the 29 other Afghan provinces, representing the other half of Afghanistan's population do not utilize commercial courts. Instead, as interview data reveal, businesses in Afghanistan tend to be regional, and these five provinces are regional hubs; also, commercial courts have very expansive rules of personal jurisdiction. Therefore, it is very easy for a commercial dispute involving merchants doing business in a number of neighboring provinces to gravitate to primary commercial courts in regional hub cities where courts are more competent, and rule of law is stronger.

Commercial Court Procedure

Commercial court procedures disincentivize the use of courts because they are burdensome, and the rules of evidence are incongruent with the prevailing business practices in the country.[257]

After a primary commercial court decides it has jurisdiction over a case, it commences its proceedings. However, before the primary commercial court hears preliminary motions, it advises the parties to consider mediation.[258] If the parties agree, the court will ask each party to choose a mediator.[259] The court records the name of the mediators, but the mediators conduct the mediation completely separate from the court.[260] Pretrial mediation is not mandatory; parties or a party may refuse mediation.[261] Mediation is not "court-annexed": the mediators work completely independently from the court. If the mediation is successful and parties reach an amicable resolution, the court will incorporate their agreement in its judgment as it stands without any modification,[262] and that will be the end of the proceedings. If mediation is unsuccessful, the mediators may submit their opinion to the court. However, this report does not have any evidentiary or binding value under the law.[263] Parties to the dispute can return to the mediation at any stage of the proceedings if they choose.[264] However, the court will only advise the parties to resort to mediation once.[265]

If parties refuse to try mediation or if a mediation fails, the primary commercial court begins its proceedings by inviting parties to file their preliminary motions.[266] After these motions are decided on, the court requests parties to file their briefs and present evidence.[267]

Commercial Law Article 2 sets forth the source of binding rules applicable in commercial disputes:

> Commercial disputes are to be settled in accordance with legally binding agreements and their absence, disputes are to be determined and settled by reference to the meaning and implication of existing commercial laws. In the absence of a law, local and special customs (those that are commonly recognized, consented to, and used) are applied. Local customs and practices are preferred to general custom. In the absence of any other of the above-mentioned methods any other laws which might apply to the dispute are used.[268]

Parties may use any of the following as evidence in a commercial court: (1) witness testimony (Articles 131–143 Commercial Procedure);[269] (2) expert witness (Article 143–155 Commercial Procedure);[270] (3) written documents (Articles 156–199 Commercial Procedure);[271] (4) confession (Article 200–203 Commercial Procedure);[272] and (5) commercial books (Article 79 Commercial Law).[273]

Under Commercial Law Article 65, "[e]very merchant must keep three books—a book showing his capital, a ledger, and a journal."[274] Under Commercial Law Article 68,

> The books kept according to Article 65 are to be taken personally by the merchant or his agent to the local registration office [i.e. Provincial Departments of Ministry of Finance] for marking and sealing.[275] The registration should mark all the pages with ink and seal them. Then the office will note the total sheets of each book on its first and last pages. After nothing the date besides the seals of the first and last pages, the registration office should also include there a certified signature.[276]

Only if this requirement is met, under Commercial Law Article 79, "during a dispute between two merchants over commercial transactions, the legal commercial books could be used [as evidence]."[277] If a book is kept according to the legal requirements, it can be used against or for the advantage of the possessor.[278] In practice, however, merchants do not avail themselves of this evidentiary advantage because doing so would require them to put their entire dealings under the review of the tax authorities.[279]

The process of accepting witness testimony in commercial courts is more expedient than in civil courts. In civil disputes, witnesses must be secretly and publicly vetted.[280] In the secret vetting, the court sends letters to those who have knowledge of the character and affairs of the witness (e.g. employer).[281] In the public vetting, two individuals attend a court session to testify to the reliability and character of the witness.[282] Only if the two-step vetting process is successful will the witness testimony be accepted.[283] In commercial court procedure, however, according to the Afghanistan Supreme Court, this two-step vetting process is not required.[284] Commercial judges hear witness testimony and assess their credibility unless they have a reason to inquire about the reliability and character of the witness.[285] This is a very important procedural advantage of commercial courts which increases the value of jurisdictional rules.

A panel of three judges at the primary commercial courts hear the case, and the decision at the primary level is made by the majority of the three judges that preside over the case.[286] After the primary court reaches its decision and the primary commercial court's decision is announced to the parties, either party has the right to appeal the case to the court of appeals. The decision of the primary commercial court is binding and enforceable upon announcement. However, in certain cases, the decision of the primary commercial court will also be final. Under Article 53 of the Laws on Organization and Jurisdiction of Judiciary, in the following scenarios the decision of the primary commercial court is final: (1) parties accept the decision as final; (2) the time for filling an appeal runs out, and an appeal is not filed; (3) the value of the subject of the decision does not exceed 100,000 AFN (i.e. roughly 2,000 USD).[287] If none of these conditions are satisfied, the decision of the primary commercial court can be appealed as a matter of right to the commercial dewan of the court of appeal.

Commercial disputes which are appealed to the court of appeal will be decided by the commercial dewan of the court of appeal.[288] Under Afghanistan law, a panel of three judges at the commercial dewan of the court of appeal will rehear the case in its entirety and render a decision by the majority.[289] The decision of the commercial dewan of the court of appeal is binding and enforceable after it is announced to the parties.[290]

Decisions of the commercial dewan of court of appeal are reviewed by the commercial dewan of Afghanistan Supreme Court.[291] Two justices, advised by judicial advisors, review and decide the cases at dewans of Afghanistan Supreme Court.[292] Dewans of the Afghanistan Supreme Court only review the application of law in a case.[293] Dewans of the Afghanistan Supreme Court do not rehear the case or decide on a question of fact.[294] A dewan of the Afghanistan Supreme Court may affirm, break and remand, correct, or annul a decision of a lower court that has been appealed to it.[295] If a dewan of the Afghanistan Supreme Court affirms the decision of the lower court, that decision becomes final.[296] If a dewan of the Afghanistan Supreme Court determines that the decision of the lower court contains an error in application or interpretation of the law, it breaks the decision and remands the case to the same court for a new decision.[297] If a dewan of the Afghanistan Supreme Court finds the error to be inconsequential in the outcome of the case, it corrects the decision without remanding it to the court of appeal.[298] If the commercial dewan of the Afghanistan Supreme Court finds that the decision of the court of appeal lacks a fundamental condition for a dispute or it contains a gross violation of procedure, it annuls the decision and remands to the court of appeal to be re-decided by a new panel of judges.[299]

Enforcement of Commercial Courts' Decisions

Under now toppled Afghan Republic, the enforcement of the commercial courts' decisions was generally uncertain, which made use of commercial courts ineffective. The most likely outcome was a payment schedule; this could be long and requires continued supervision of courts and the Huquq Department (see Figure 1.5). Merchants can usually achieve a similar, or even better, solution outside the courts.[300] However, non-fungible properties (especially immovable non-fungible properties) are an exception to this rule.

If a party obtains a final judgment in an ownership dispute concerning a non-fungible property (e.g. a store or a house), and the property is located in an area where the government has control, the judgment will most likely be enforced. It is because the subject of this judgment is an identifiable specific property. Under Afghanistan's rules of civil and commercial procedures, precise description of the specific property is a fundamental requirement of lawsuits.[301]

Sar qufli and lease disputes relate to, by virtue of their subject, an immovable non-fungible property, falling within this category. This explains why parties most often resort to courts for *Sar qufli* and commercial lease disputes.[302] A court judgment is both effective and necessary when it comes to *Sar qufli* and lease disputes. It is because, in *Sar qufli* and lease disputes, the lawsuit is brought against a party that has actual possession of an immovable property in an attempt to forcefully regain possession.[303] Therefore, the subject of the judgment is permanent, and the remedy requires the use of force. This is the reason why *Sar qufli* and lease disputes make up the majority of the case load of commercial courts.[304]

Under Afghan law, the department of Huquq is in charge of enforcing the judgments issued by commercial courts.[305] The following analysis of the enforcement of commercial court judgments focuses on the judgments concerning fungible property and monetary claims and is based on the interview conducted by the author with a judgment specialist at the Herat Huquq Department.[306] The enforcement of judgments concerning fungible properties and monetary claims has paramount importance because due to the nature of commercial transactions, non-fungible properties and monetary claims are the most common subject of disputes among merchants. Although disputes concerning non-fungible properties (e.g. lease of a store or warehouse) dominate the formal court cases, they constitute a small parentage of commercial disputes. In Afghanistan, after an enforceable judgment is rendered, the judgment will be sent to the Huquq Department for enforcement.[307] The Huquq Department will notify the losing part of the fact that a final and enforceable judgment has been rendered against him or her.[308] At this point, there are five possible outcomes:[309]

(1) If the losing party complies voluntarily, the Huquq Department will save the file, and the proceedings end.
(2) If the losing party rejects the court's judgment and refuses to comply, the losing party will be considered in contempt of court and will be referred to the prosecution office. The prosecutor will issue an indictment and the public security dewan of the court will convict him. The court usually starts with a six-month conviction. If the losing party does not comply and repeats the contemptuous behavior after the end of his sentence, he can be indicted and convicted of an increased sentence. Theoretically, this process can be repeated until the losing party complies.
(3) If the losing party accepts the court's judgment but claims that he does not have the assets to pay for the judgment, the Huquq Department will suggest setting up a payment schedule. If the judgment-holder agrees, the Huquq Department will submit the payment schedule to the provincial governor's office. If the governor grants approval, the court with jurisdiction over the case will issue an order against the losing party requiring him to pay the judgment per the payment schedule. If the losing party violates the payment schedule, he is found in contempt of the court. He will be referred to the prosecution office and will be tried for contempt.

While a provision of the law states that the payment schedule cannot exceed nine months, and Afghanistan Supreme Court has reaffirmed this limit,[310] "another provision says that the courts determine the length according to the losing party's financial status. Some courts have taken this to mean the court can approve a payment schedule that exceeds 9 months if the financial status of the losing side warrants it."[311] The amount of each installment is determined in the following manner: the court determines the monthly income of the losing side (e.g. a daily wage of the simple laborer) then subtracts the losing side's essential expenses and require him to pay the remaining amount to the winning side to satisfy the judgment.[312] According to Kamal, a judgment enforcement specialist at Herat Huquq Department, most payment schedules consist of four to nine monthly payments.[313]

(4) If the losing party accepts the court's judgment but refuses to pay, claiming that he does not have the assets to pay for the judgment, or if either the losing side cannot pay the judgment in installments or the prevailing side does not accept the installments, claiming that the losing side has sufficient assets and should not need a payment schedule, the Huquq Department, on the recommendation of the prevailing side, will send letters to the municipality, district, banks, or other places where the losing side's assets can be identified to obtain a report on the possible assets. If any asset is identified, the Huquq Department will ask a court to order the confiscation (e.g. if it is a bank account) or auction (e.g. if it is real estate or car) of the identified assets so the prevailing party can be paid from the money that is received from the auction or confiscation.

(5) If no assets can be found and the losing side cannot pay the judgment in installments, that is, he does not make enough money, the Huquq Department will require the losing side to procure a guarantor—someone who will ensure that the loser will pay the judgment as soon as his financial status improves. After receiving a guarantee, the Huquq Department will defer enforcement of the judgment until such time as the losing party's financial status improves so he can pay in installments or in whole or until such time that the winner can identify any assets of the losing side against which the judgment can be enforced.

Currently, there are no formal bankruptcy proceedings in Afghanistan. According to the decision 307–369 (2007) of the High Council of Afghanistan Supreme Court,[314] courts are ordered not to initiate bankruptcy proceedings in commercial or noncommercial cases.[315] The courts are instead required to enter into judgments and determine the obligation of the losing side.[316] If the winner can show that the loser has assets, the judgment will be enforced.[317] If the winner cannot show that the loser has assets, and the loser does not have assets, enforcement will be delayed until such time when the winner can show that defendant has assets that can be used to satisfy the judgment.[318]

Figure 1.5 provides rough estimates of judgment enforcement outcomes for different provinces (excluding the judgment concerning the non-fungible properties detailed in Section 2.6.3.5) as provided by the Huquq Department Judgment Specialists:

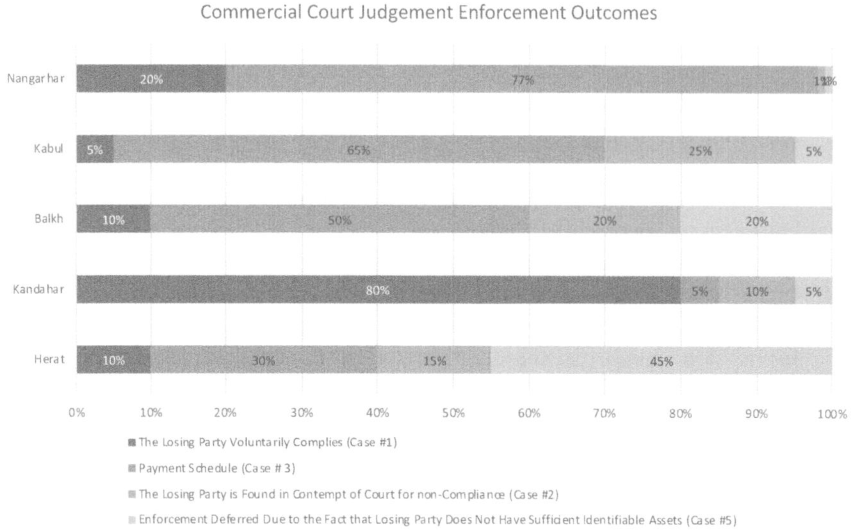

Figure 1.5 Afghanistan's Commercial Courts' Judgment Enforcement Outcomes by Province for the Last Hijri Year

According to these rough estimates, scheduled payments were the most common outcome of a commercial court's judgment. This is not surprising because defendants who have assets will usually pay before a final judgment is rendered. They know that their assets will be sold for a lower price in court-ordered auctions; therefore, only those who do not have identifiable assets wait until after the formal judgment is rendered. This also explains why court remedies are so unpopular. Creditors usually can reach an agreement for a better payment schedule, considering the time and money that the litigation process takes, without going to courts.

However, there are two outliers in the enforcement of judgments. Commercial judgements are most often deferred in Herat province because the losing party does not have sufficient and identifiable assets, while Kandahar is the province where the losing party is most likely to voluntarily comply with a court judgment. These outliers can be explained if one takes into account the number of commercial judgements per year rendered in these five provinces adjusted for population: per every million people, the average annual number of commercial judgements rendered in the major provinces in the past six years are as follows: Kabul (258), Herat (204), Balkh (125), Kandahar (48), and Nangarhar (32).[319]

Herat has the highest rate of enforcement deferral because Heratis are much more likely to use the courts, making it more likely for a judgment to be rendered against a party with insufficient identifiable assets. In addition, Herat has the largest portion of small businesses. These are the most frequent court-users and most likely not to have sufficient funds.[320] Kandahar, on the other hand, has very low court-usage coupled with the lowest portion of small businesses, which could explain why most judgements are voluntarily enforced. Nangarhar, on the other hand, while having a low court-usage rate, has a much larger portion of small businesses, which can explain why it diverges from Kandahar when it comes to the prevalence of schedule payments.

The sharp difference between the number of commercial judgements per million people for Kandahar (48) and Nangarhar (32), which are predominantly Pashtun and the most ethnically homogenous provinces, compared to Kabul, Herat, and Balkh, which are more ethnically heterogeneous and/or are dominated by the Tajik ethnic group, suggests ethnic homogeneity and Pashtun institutions of *jirga* are likely responsible for making the out-of-court dispute settlement more effective, reducing the court-use rates. This hypothesis is supported by the comparison between per capita business registry and court use between Balkh, Kandahar, and Nangarhar. Balkh has a higher court-use rate (almost double) compared to Nangarhar and Kandahar while Kandahar and Nangarhar both have higher per capita business registries. The prevalence of small businesses cannot explain this pattern because while Kandahar has a low number of smaller businesses, Nangarhar has a large number of small businesses.

In addition to the formal rules of enforcement, there are two other features of court procedures that have a direct effect on the popularity of the courts among merchants: judgment tax and nonacceptance of verbal contracts. It seems that the tax on final judgment is an important deterrent against the use of formal courts. The tax ostensibly is designed to do three things; however, it is not clear if it has achieved its goals: (a) cover the court's costs, (b) deter frivolous lawsuits, and (c) encourage amicable resolution of disputes outside the courts.

If a court enters a judgment against the plaintiff, the plaintiff has to only pay 1% of the value of the judgment to the government.[321] However, if a court enters a judgment against a defendant, the defendant is required to pay 10% of the value of the judgment. If parties reach an amicable solution outside the courts and want their agreement to be incorporated into a court's judgment, each side has to pay 5%. The lower rate for the plaintiff seems to be designed to encourage the use of formal courts; the higher rate for the defendant seems to be designed to encourage a settlement. However, the court can only formally approve the settlement only if the parties pay 5% each. This last provision seems to penalize parties using the formal court system to effectuate an amicable resolution, which seems to be at odds with the government's policy to encourage the use of the formal court system. Additionally, this tax is collectible upon issuance of the first court's verdict despite the fact that the judgment can be appealed as a matter of right to the second and third courts.

It is interesting that very few interviewees mentioned the judgment tax as a reason why they do not use the formal court system. The most common reasons for not using the formal court system cited by interviewees were corruption and the ineffectiveness of the court. Few may have mentioned the judgment tax because merchants don't use the courts often, so they don't experience the judgment tax.

Afghan courts generally do not enforce verbal contracts.[322] This is despite the fact that an overwhelming majority of the business dealings in Afghanistan are conducted verbally.[323] In talking with judges in five major Afghan provinces that collectively handle 90% of commercial disputes in Afghanistan, it appeared that hostility toward verbal contracts stem from their uncertainty and non-specificity.[324] Verbal contracts are not invalid under Afghanistan commercial laws. Therefore, most judges do not claim that a verbal contract is *ipso facto* invalid. However, the commercial judges interviewed for this study have cited reasons such as the difficulty of proving the formation of a verbal contract, its content, and its terms to explain why they base most of their decisions on written contracts.[325] This study hypothesizes that it is a formalist approach to the law and conservative attitudes of judges that are stopping commercial judges from enforcing verbal contracts rather than a legal obstacle.

THE CAUSES OF UNCERTAINTY ABOUT COURT JUDGMENT ENFORCEMENT

A confluence of multiple factors—which are fundamentally related to the high volatility of Afghanistan's business climate and underdeveloped formal property rights—render enforcement of commercial courts' judgment uncertain.

The first factor is the difficulty in identifying the losing party's assets. In absence of an inclusive formal property right system, information pertaining to the losing party's assets is hard to locate. As explained in Section 2.6.2., the existing property rights system in Afghanistan is highly fragmented. There is no central property registry for formal property rights and more than 80% of the property is held informally.[326] Judgment enforcement officials are not optimally positioned to access the information about the losing party's assets held informally (compared to local business associations, for example). Judgment enforcement officials have to rely on limited formal property recording, self-reporting, and the information provided by the winning party to identify assets against which a judgment can be enforced.[327] The uncertainty of rules to determine ownership further complicates judgment enforcement.

The difficulty in identifying the losing party's assets is precisely the rationale behind the Afghanistan Supreme Court decision to halt the use of formal bankruptcy proceedings in Afghanistan. Given the scarcity of property information, the Afghanistan Supreme Court ostensibly worries that the losing parties will misuse the bankruptcy proceedings by hiding their assets. As a result, genuinely insolvent merchants cannot avail themselves of the protection of bankruptcy proceedings. This institutional failure disincentivizes merchants from taking risks, which means they are less likely to expand or invest in new businesses.

The second reason for the low enforcement rate is the type of disputes that find their way to courts. Most often court disputes are end-of-business and end-of-relationship disputes among smaller and medium-sized merchants who are non-cooperative (compared to the disputes that are resolved outside of court).[328] As a result, commercial disputes in courts most often are rendered against judgment-proof and obstructionist parties. This will be discussed further in Chapter 3. The third factor is the high insolvency rates caused by high business climate volatility. Commercial court judgments are hard to enforce partly because losing parties are more likely to be insolvent, rendering them judgment-proof. Afghan merchants are more likely to be bankrupt because Afghanistan has a very volatile business climate.

The final factor is underdeveloped security rights. High insolvency rates in Afghanistan mean that security rights are of paramount importance for securitizing credit transactions. The fact that merchants do not have enough assets to satisfy court judgments means determining who has priority over the existing assets is crucial. However, outside formal mortgage laws, security rights are very underdeveloped in Afghanistan. Afghan laws and Afghan courts do not often recognize contractually created security rights.[329] This means informal credit transactions cannot be securitized.[330] In common cases of insolvency, a majority of creditors, given the very low rate of formal mortgage law users, have limited protection—even if they have entered into a transaction based on the confidence of a certain asset.

ENFORCEMENT OF BANK LOANS

Despite the challenges enumerated previously, under the toppled Afghan Republic, Afghan judges and Afghan laws were not the primary impediments or reasons why Afghan merchants have trouble accessing bank loans. Government Strategic Policies assumed enacting mortgage and negotiable documents law based on international best practices and training judges in applying them would improve enforcement of formal credit contracts, expand bank-provided formal credit, and improve access to credit for Afghan merchants.[331] This study suggests that the problem of formal credit in Afghanistan was related to low demand, not weak enforcement. Specifically, Afghan merchants do not use formal credit devices because bank-provided credit has not overcome the problems of credit transactions in Afghanistan. Chiefly, banks have difficulty collecting on defaulted loans primarily because of a volatile real estate market, unreliable formal property right systems, not an uncooperative judiciary.

Under the Afghan Republic, Afghan judges and Afghan laws were not the main impediments to the enforcement of bank loans. Then Afghan Supreme Court emphasized the primacy of the rights of banks, holding formal mortgages over other creditors.[332] According to the rules of commercial procedure, authorization of the sale of the collateral does not require a trial and upon verification of registry of formal collateral, the court may issue an injunction (*qarar*) authorizing auction of the collateral.[333]

The interest-bearing nature of bank loans did not stop Afghan judges from enforcing bank loans. All commercial judges interviewed stated they enforce bank loans according to Afghan laws despite the interest-bearing nature of the transaction.[334] As the chief judge of the Primary Commercial Court in Balkh explained, "This is the law. I do think interest is prohibited under Islamic law, but I will enforce a bank loan because it is the law. The responsibility lies with the people who made the law not me."[335] This suggests that formalism of Afghan judges may be, at least partly, due to the incongruity between the morality of judges and the morality of the laws.

Interview data reveals that, in case of default, courts could be relied on to enforce bank loans by selling the collateral if certain conditions are present.[336] The enforcement of bank loans most often was hindered, according to commercial judges, for several reasons. First, given the complexity of determining legal ownership, sometimes when a bank seeks to sell a mortgage, other parties claim ownership of the collateral; this requires courts to determine ownership before authorizing the auction.[337] Second, there are multiple liens on the collateral.[338] According to Afghan mortgage laws, a property can be used as collateral for multiple loans if the new mortgagee is informed of the existing liens.[339] In such a case, liens will be enforced in the order of registry.[340] Sometimes banks accept collaterals that are already subject to a lien, in which case, the courts will have to ascertain whether the mortgagee knew about the existing lien and determine the priorities of enforcement.[341] As a result, banks may not be able to collect on a nonperforming loan. Third, volatility in the real estate market means the value of the collateral may depreciate below the amount of the debt, rendering it impossible for the banks to satisfy the debt by the sale of the collateral.[342] In such a case, banks will be treated as an unsecured debtor and may have to pursue collection through a trial or join other possible creditors in court to collect the remaining debt. Lastly, banks will only enforce a security right if the collateral is fully and precisely specified in the loan contract and the mortgage registration documents.[343] According to Afghan commercial judges of the Afghan Republic, a common problem in enforcing a mortgage claim is that the property is not fully specified because banks did not diligently specify the mortgage in the loan contract and/or mortgage registration.[344]

Afghan judges, and to a lesser degree, Afghanistan mortgage laws, were not the main impediment to the enforcement of bank loans. Although this opposes the premise of most institutional reform policies,[345] it was the volatile real estate market, prevailing property rights system, and failure of the banks to diligently comply with the legal requirements that impede the enforcement of banks loans.

In 2009, Pvalovic and Charap researched the variation in lending practices of banks in Afghanistan by interviewing top management of eight commercial banks in Afghanistan.[346] According to Pavlovic and Charap, bank executives expressed reservations about the legal system.[347] Banks that have used the formal legal system to collect loans opinioned that it was time-consuming, difficult, and highly bureaucratic.[348] Bank executives expressed a preference for use of nonconventional enforcement methods, such as blacklisting.[349] Bank executives also expressed reservations about the use of collateral. The issues that reportedly impeded the use of collateral included as follows:

> (1) a 6% collateral registration fee, (2) invalid title deeds, (3) multiple title deeds held over the same property, and (4) ". . . using bribes or connections to get hold of property titles filed in other banks . . . [to] bring the titles to . . . [ask] for loans."[350]

Given the expressed dissatisfaction with the use of land as collateral, bank executives, according to Pavlovic and Charap, did not attach so much weight to the collateral. Instead, they assigned priority to a borrowers' reputation, business relations, and personal contacts when deciding to issue a loan.[351] This practice, which foreign bank executives whose banks did not engage in domestic lending, has been derogatorily described as "relationship banking."[352]

It is difficult to determine whether this kind of relationship banking still continues in Afghanistan—especially after the Kabul Bank scandal and the increased regulatory oversight that ensued. It is quite possible that domestic private banks, which are virtually the only banks issuing loans to the private sector in Afghanistan, continue to substitute and/or complement formal legal recourse and risk-assessment procedures with proactive business information gathering and private contract enforcement mechanisms. It should be noted that at the time of Pvalovic and Charap's research in 2009, it appeared that almost 100% of bank loans in Afghanistan were performing.[353]

The reported attitudes of bank executives support the proposition put forward in this study. Bank executives did not say that Afghan judges or Afghanistan laws do not enforce collaterals. Instead, they believed that formal dispute resolution is more time-consuming and expensive than reputation-based enforcement and that Afghanistan's formal property right system renders collateral unreliable. These two propositions are valid and in congruence with the argument put forward here; namely, it is property rights system, not Afghan judges or Afghan mortgage laws, that impede the enforcement of bank loans in Afghanistan.

After August of 2021, the Taliban as the de facto government of Afghanistan have generally worked within the financial laws of the Republic, most likely because the sanctions against Taliban posed an existential threat to the financial system, making all other concerns secondary. However, with time, it is likely that the Taliban would enact reforms to bring the financial laws of the country more in line with their understanding of Islamic law. Moreover, the Talib judges who now make up the entire judiciary are much less likely to enforce interest-bearing loans.

Formal Arbitration and Mediation

There was no legally binding arbitration in Afghanistan until the very end because the Afghan laws failed to define a clear mechanism for enforcement of an arbitral award. Faizy, head of Afghanistan Commercial Dispute Resolution Center (the "Center"), stated in June of 2017, "although Afghanistan has passed an arbitration law, there is no arbitration in Afghanistan because there are no arbitration rules, and also there is no procedure or authority by which an arbitrator's license can be issued."[354] The Center only provides mediation, which is completely nonbinding. Mediation services provided by the Center are not very popular. According to Faizy, there have been only 13 mediations held by the Center in the last three years (2014/15–2016/17) with most of them being held last year.

Faizy said, "The difference between our mediation and *jirgas* is that we use written documents and follow the law." While Faizy saw this as a positive point, the formality of the Center-provided mediation may be the reason for its unpopularity. This hypothesis is supported by the fact that according to Faizy, members of the board of the Chamber conduct informal dispute resolution without referring disputes to the Center. This is despite the fact that the Center is a part of the Chamber.

Since 2017, the Arbitration field experienced some progress in Afghanistan. The Center enacted arbitration rules, certified a number of arbitrators who issued a number of awards as well. However, the Center and the broader business community did not succeed in reforming the laws of the country to mandate the Huquq Department, the primary department responsible for enforcement of commercial court judgments, to enforce the arbitral awards as well.

Herat's Chamber of Commerce and Industries ("Herat Chamber") is the only chamber in Afghanistan operating a formal dispute resolution center.[355] Herat's Center is a party to an agreement that allows it to jointly operate with a chamber of commerce in Mashhad, Herat's neighboring province in Iran. According to the president of Herat Chamber, the Center provides binding arbitration as well as mediation services. However, legally binding arbitration has not yet been used. The Center in Herat handles four to five cases each year, the majority of which, according to the president of the Herat Chamber, consist of disputes between Herati merchants and Irani merchants. The Herat Chamber is a party to a joint chamber of commerce between Herat and Mashhad. Disputes between Irani and Herati merchants who are a member of the Mashhad Chamber and the Herat Chamber, respectively, can be resolved through the dispute resolution committee of the joint chamber. These services are used to resolve a few cases each year, according to the president of the Herat Chamber.

The low user rate of the centralized and formalized mediation, in contrast with the use of localized and informal dispute resolution conducted by unions and/or *ad hoc* group of merchants, suggest Afghan government strategies should focus on policies that support the informal dispute resolution rather than attempt to formalize and centralize the resolution of commercial disputes using ADR center models.

Credit transactions in Afghanistan pose a number of fundamental problems. These problems have their roots in Afghanistan's history of conflict and the failure of state buildings in the Afghan context. Afghanistan's highly volatile business climate makes credit transactions costlier while rendering adherence to fixed repayment terms, *ex ante*, challenging. Formal property rights are underdeveloped, and formal deeds are scarce; as such, formal property rights cannot be used to securitize credit transactions. The underdevelopment of formal private property rights and a highly volatile business climate make it difficult to hold debtors accountable using formal dispute resolution institutions. To overcome these problems, a number of informal institutions have emerged to facilitate credit transactions among Afghan merchants. Thus, the fundamental problems of credit transacting have determined the emergence of informal credit and dispute resolution to which this dissertation will turn in the next chapter. The inability of formal institutions to adapt to the context of Afghanistan and provide credit in a way that works for the Afghan context is primarily responsible for the low demand for formal credit in Afghanistan, a subject to which this dissertation turns in Chapter 4.

Notes

1 The World Bank, World Bank Development Indicators, GDP at Constant Price from 2015 in USD, Afghanistan's GDP at Constant Price from 2015 in USD for the Years of 2001 until 2020 (January 29, 2022), https://data.worldbank.org/indicator/NY.GDP.MKTP.KD?end=2020&locations=AF&start=2001.

2 The World Bank, World Bank Development Indicators, School Enrollment by primary Gross Percentage, Afghanistan's School Enrollment by primary Gross Percentage for the Years of 2001 until 2019, https://data.worldbank.org/indicator/SE.PRM.ENRR?end=2019&locations=AF&start=2001.

3 UNICEF, UNICEF Global Database on adjusted Net Attendance Rates (Apr. 2021), https://data.unicef.org/wp-content/uploads/2021/04/Adjusted-net-attendance-rate_2021-1.xlsx.

4 The World Bank, World Bank Development Indicators, Mortality Rates for Infants per 1,000 Live Births, Afghanistan's Mortality Rates for Infants per 1,000 Live Births for the Years of 2001 until 2019, https://data.worldbank.org/indicator/SP.DYN.IMRT.IN?end=2019&locations=AF&start=2001

5 The World Bank, World Bank Development Indicators, Maternal mortality ratio for modeled estimate, per 100,000 live births, Afghanistan's Maternal mortality ratio for modeled estimate, per 100,000 live births for the Years of 2000 until 2017, https://data.worldbank.org/indicator/SH.STA.MMRT?end=2017&locations=AF&start=2000

6 The World Bank, World Bank Development Indicators, Life expectancy at birth up to total years, Afghanistan's Life expectancy at birth up to total years for the Years of 2000 until 2019, https://data.worldbank.org/indicator/SP.DYN.LE00.IN?end=2019&locations=AF&start=2001

7 The World Bank, World Bank Development Indicators, Poverty headcount ratio at national poverty lines For the Percentage of population, Afghanistan's Poverty headcount ratio at national poverty lines For the Percentage of population for the Years of 2007 until 2016, https://data.worldbank.org/indicator/si.pov.nahc?locations=af

8 The World Bank, World Bank Development Indicators, GDP Growth by Annual Percent, Afghanistan's GDP Growth by Annual Percent 2003–2016, https://data.worldbank.org/indicator/NY.GDP.MKTP.KD.ZG?locations=AF.

9 *See* The National Risk and Vulnerability Assessment (2007–2008); National Risk and Vulnerability Assessment (2005).

10 *Id.*

11 www.ilo.org/shinyapps/bulkexplorer12/?lang=en&segment=indicator&id=EAP_DWAP_SEX_AGE_RT_A

12 *Id.*

13 The statistics in this paragraph is based on National Risk and Vulnerability Assessment (2007–2008).

14 The statistics in this paragraph are based on National Risk and Vulnerability Assessment (2005).

15 The statistics in this paragraph are calculated by the author based on the National Risk and Vulnerability Assessment: Afghanistan Living Conditions Survey 2007–2008, National Risk and Vulnerability Assessment (2007–2008); National Risk and Vulnerability Assessment (2011–2012); National Risk and Vulnerability Assessment (2013–2014).

16 Calculated by the author based on Afghanistan Central Statistics Organization, Afghanistan Import and Export Annual Data for the Years of 2008/09 until 2016/17, http://cso.gov.af/fa/page/economy-statistics/6323/annual-trade. [hereinafter Afghanistan Central Statistics Organization, Annual Data for the Years of 2008/09 until 2016/17].

17 Calculated by the author based on *Id.* and Afghanistan Current GDP by Sector for the Years 2002/03 until 2016/17, http://cso.gov.af/fa/page/ict/11328/888 [hereinafter Afghanistan Central Statistics Organization, GDP by Sector for the Years 2002/03 until 2016/17].

18 This will be discussed further later in this chapter in the context of problems of credit transacting.
19 Calculated by the author based on United Nations Office on Drugs and Crime, Afghanistan Opium Survey 2015: Cultivation and Production, www.unodc.org/documents/crop-monitoring/Afghanistan/_Afghan_opium_survey_2015_web.pdf [hereinafter United Nations Office on Drugs and Crime, Afghanistan Opium Survey], Integrity Watch Afghanistan, National Corruption Survey 2016: Afghan Perceptions and Experiences of Corruption (2016), https://iwaweb.org/national-corruption-corruption-survey-2016/ [hereinafter Integrity Watch Afghanistan, National Corruption Survey (2016)], and Afghanistan Central Statistics Organization, GDP by Sector for the Years 2002/03 until 2016/17.
20 Richard Ghiasy et al., International Council of Swedish Industry, Afghanistan's Private Sector: Status and Ways Forward 5 (SIPRI and NIR 2015), www.sipri.org/publications/2015/afghanistans-private-sector-status-and-way-forward [hereinafter Ghiasy et al., Afghanistan's Private Sector (2015)].
21 *See* e.g. *Id.*
22 *See* Matthew Rosenberg, *Audit Says Kabul Bank Began as 'Ponzi Scheme,'* N.Y. Times (November 26, 2012), www.nytimes.com/2012/11/27/world/asia/kabul-bank-audit-details-extent-of-fraud.html.
23 Calculated by the author based Da Afghanistan Bank, Quarterly Statistics of I-2013 until II-2017.
24 The formal financial system is discussed further in Chapter 4.
25 Afghanistan's property rights system is discussed later in this chapter.
26 Afghanistan's formal dispute resolution system is discussed later in this chapter.
27 *See* Section 2.6.3.
28 *See* Section 2.6.3.
29 This finding is based on author's interviews with Afghan merchants in five major provinces of Afghanistan (Kabul, Herat, Nangarhar, Balkh, and Kandahar) between March and August 2017, as well as author's personal observations over several years of his work as accountant in Afghanistan's private sector between 2008 and 2013.
30 https://data.worldbank.org/indicator/IC.BUS.NREG?locations=AF.
31 Business Registry Data for the Years of 2014/15 until 2016/17 for Kabul, Herat, Kandahar, Balkh, and Nangarhar. Received by the author from Afghanistan Central Business Registry's Directory through head of office of Business Registry at Afghanistan Ministry of Commerce (Received on September 23, 2017) [hereinafter Business Registry Data for the Years of 2014/15 until 2016/17 for Kabul, Herat, Kandahar, Balkh, and Nangarhar (2017)].
32 This finding is based on author's interviews with Afghan merchants in five major provinces of Afghanistan (Kabul, Herat, Nangarhar, Balkh, and Kandahar) between March and August 2017, as well as author's personal observations over several years of his working as an accountant in Afghanistan's private sector between 2008 and 2013.
33 *Id.*
34 *See* Business Establishment Survey (2010); Establishment Survey (2016).
35 Establishment Survey (2016), at 4.
36 *Id.*
37 *Id.*
38 *Id.*
39 This finding is based on author's interviews with Afghan merchants in five major provinces of Afghanistan (Kabul, Herat, Nangarhar, Balkh, and Kandahar) between March and August 2017, as well as author's personal observations over several years of his work as accountant in Afghanistan's private sector between 2008 and 2013.
40 *Id.*
41 *Id.*
42 *See* Afghanistan Chamber of Commerce and Industries, www.acci.org.af/.

43 Author's interview with the president of Afghanistan's National Union of of Manufacturers and Producers at Kabul (June 2017).
44 Author's interview with the president of Afghanistan's National Union of of Manufacturers and Producers at Kabul (June 2017); *see also* Afghanistan Chamber of Commerce and Industries, www.acci.org.af/ [hereinafter Afghanistan Chamber of Commerce and Industries].
45 Municipality's directives require those who wish to open a store or an office in the city to obtain a license. The requirements for a license vary depending on the profession and/or the business the applicant wishes to engage in.
46 This finding is based on author's interviews with Afghan merchants in five major provinces of Afghanistan (Kabul, Herat, Nangarhar, Balkh, and Kandahar) between March and August 2017, as well as author's personal observations over several years of his work as accountant in Afghanistan's private sector between 2008 and 2013.
47 Author's interview with the president of Herat Craftsmen/Traders Union at Herat (Apr. 2017).
48 *Id.*
49 *Id.*
50 According to the 2015 Business Survey, these five provinces account for almost 40% of business establishments, 60% of average value added by business establishments, 53% of gross fixed capital owned by the business establishments, and 40% of the employees employed by business establishments in the whole country. Calculated by the author based on business establishment survey (2010); establishment survey (2016).
51 This finding is based on author's interviews with Afghan merchants in five major provinces of Afghanistan (Kabul, Herat, Nangarhar, Balkh, and Kandahar) between March and August 2017, as well as author's personal observations over several years of his work as accountant in Afghanistan's private sector between 2008 and 2013.
52 *Id.*
53 *Id.*
54 *See* Qanun Sherkathai Sahami va Mahdud Al-Masuliat Afghanistan [Corporation and Limited Liabilities Law of Afghanistan] (Law No. 913, 1385 [2006]).
55 *Id.*
56 *Id.*
57 *Id.*
58 This is discussed further later in this chapter and Chapter 3.
59 This finding is based on author's interviews with Afghan merchants in five major provinces of Afghanistan (Kabul, Herat, Nangarhar, Balkh, and Kandahar) between March and August 2017, as well as author's personal observations over several years of his work as accountant in Afghanistan's private sector between 2008 and 2013.
60 Author's interview with the chief judge of Kabul Primary Commercial Court in Kabul (June 2017)
61 This is discussed further in this chapter and also in Chapter 3.
62 *See* Section 3.5. and in Chapter 3.
63 *Id.*
64 *See* Central Intelligence Agency World Factbook: Afghanistan, www.cia.gov/Library/publications/the-world-factbook/geos/af.html.
65 *Id.*
66 *Id.*
67 *See generally* Richard S. Newell, *The Politics of Afghanistan* (1972) (stating that Pashtuns have ruled Afghanistan over the past two centuries with limited interruptions) [hereinafter Newell, *The Politics of Afghanistan* (1972)].
68 *Id.*
69 *See generally* Amin Saikal, *Modern Afghanistan: A History of Struggle and Survival* (2004) (arguing that Afghanistan's years of conflict has increased the political power of

minorities in Afghanistan) [hereinafter Saikal, *Modern Afghanistan* (2004)]; *See also* Gilles Dorronsoro, *Revolution Unending: Afghanistan, 1979 to the Present* (John King trans.) (2005) (making a similar argument about the rise of influence of minorities in Afghanistan because of conflicts which helped them organize and form political and military organizations) [hereinafter Dorronsoro, *Revolution Unending* (2005)].

70 *See* Saikal, *Modern Afghanistan* (2004) (noting the ethnic elements of Taliban); Dorronsoro, *Revolution Unending* (2005) (similarly discussing the ethnic politics of Taliban).

71 *Id.*

72 This is based on the current perception of non-Pashtun population of Afghanistan as assessed by the author.

73 For an analysis of the influence of ethnic tensions over Afghanistan's politics and political institutions, *see* Mohammad Bashir Mobasher, *Understanding Ethnic-Electoral Dynamics: How Ethnic Politics Affect Electoral Laws and Election Outcomes in Afghanistan*, 51 Gonz. L. Rev. 355 (2015–2016).

74 This section is intended as an overview. It briefly summarizes the main descriptive findings of the research presented in this dissertation. Each of these findings is discussed and proven separately elsewhere in this dissertation.

75 Calculated by the author based on Da Afghanistan Bank, Quarterly Statistics of I-2013 until II-2017.

76 *Shura*, which literarily means consultation or congregation, is an Islamic concept which drives from the Quranic command, "Those who hearken to their Lord, and establish regular Prayer; *who (conduct) their affairs by mutual Consultation*; who spend out of what We bestow on them for Sustenance" (emphasis added), The Holy Quran (Abdullah Yusuf Ali, trans, Wordsworth Classics of World Literature 2001) 42:38. In context of this dissertation, *shura* refers to a congregation of varying level of permanence and/or institutionalization that often consist of merchants or other respected individuals gathered with the aim of either consulting on an issue or making a collective decision or helping resolve a dispute.

77 *Jirga* is a cultural institution of Pashtuns. It consists of a congregation of autonomous Pashtun men who gather with the aim of either consulting on a public issue or making a public decision or resolving a dispute. For more information on the institution of *Jirga* within Pashtun culture, *see* Thomas J. Barfield, United States Institute for Peace, Afghan Customary Law and Its Relationship to Formal Judicial Institutions 9 (2003), www.usip.org/sites/default/files/file/barfield2.pdf. [hereinafter Barfield, Afghan Customary Law and Its Relationship to Formal Judicial Institutions (2003)].

78 *See* e.g. provincial breakdown of civilian causalities for the year 2017, which is 1,831 for Kabul, 862 for Nangarhar, 716 for Kandahar, 495 for Herat, and 129 for Balkh. United Nations Assistance Mission in Afghanistan, Protection of Civilians in Armed Conflict 2017 Annual Report 67 (2017), https://unama.unmissions.org/sites/default/files/afghanistan_protection_of_civilians_annual_report_2017_final_6_march.pdf. [hereinafter United Nations Assistance Mission in Afghanistan, Protection of Civilians in Armed Conflict Annual Report (2017)].

79 *Id.*

80 *See* Chapter 3.

81 *Id.*

82 Calculated by the author based on Afghanistan Supreme Court, Judicial Activities Reports for the Years of 2012 until 2017.

83 Calculated by the author based on Afghanistan Central Statistics Organization, Annual Data for the Years of 2008/09 until 2016/17.

84 Measured by the number of people employed in manufacturing sector. *See* National Risk and Vulnerability Assessment (2005).

85 Special Inspector General for Afghanistan Reconstruction, Quarterly Report to the United States Congress 87 (October 30, 2017) www.sigar.mil/pdf/quarterlyreports/2017-04-30qr.pdf.

86 Lack of security followed temporary cutting of electricity (43%) and was followed by lack of infrastructure facilities (15%), lack of laborers (5%), and disagreement of partners (3%). Eight percent of surveyed business establishments named other problems as the main problems they had faced within the last of their operation. *See* establishment survey (2016).
87 Calculated by the author based on business establishment survey (2010); establishment survey (2016).
88 See United Nations Assistance Mission in Afghanistan, Protection of Civilians in Armed Conflict Annual Report 67 (2017).
89 *Id.*
90 *See* The World Bank, World Bank Development Indicators, Political Stability Index, Afghanistan's Political Stability Score for the Years of 1996 until 2020, www.theglobaleconomy.com/afghanistan/wb_political_stability/. The World Bank compiles and summarizes information from over 30 existing data sources to produce its index.
91 *Id.*
92 *See* the full text of the "government of national unity deal" as emailed to the journalists by the US Embassy on September 21, 2014, at the Afghanistan Analyst Network's website; articles of the Constitution cited in the agreement were given after the text by the Afghanistan Analyst Network, www.afghanistan-analysts.org/miscellaneous/aan-resources/the-government-of-national-unity-deal-full-text/.
93 *Id.*
94 *See* Matin Sahak, *Powerful Afghan Governor Defying President Ghani Agrees To Go*, Reuters (March 22, 2018), www.reuters.com/article/us-afghanistan-governor/powerful-afghan-governor-defying-president-ghani-agrees-to-go-idUSKBN1GY1PU.
95 *Id.*
96 *See* Karim Amini, *Ongoing ARG-Jamiat Rift Affects Investment in Balkh*, TOLO News (February 02, 2018), www.tolonews.com/afghanistan/ongoing-arg-jamiat-rift-affects-investment-balkh.
97 *See* Establishment Survey 2015 (2016).
98 The data reported in this paragraph is based on Afghanistan Chamber of Commerce Industries, Business Tendency Survey Reports.
99 Calculated by the author based on Afghanistan Chamber of Commerce Industries, Business Tendency Survey Reports.
100 *Id.*
101 Calculated by the author based on Afghanistan Central Statistics Organization, Sectoral Contribution to the GDP for the Years of 2002/03 until 2016/17, http://cso.gov.af/fa/page/ict/11328/11332 [hereinafter Afghanistan Central Statistics Organization, Sectoral Contribution to the GDP].
102 Calculated by the author based on Afghanistan Central Statistics Organization, Sectoral Contribution to the GDP.
103 For a similar analysis, see Ghiasy et al., Afghanistan's Private Sector (2015).
104 The data on the sectoral contribution of different sector to Afghanistan's economy reported in the following paragraphs is calculated by the author based on Afghanistan Central Statistics Organization, Sectoral Contribution to the GDP.
105 Calculated by the author based on Da Afghanistan Bank, Currency Hijri Monthly Average USD For the Years of 1385 Hijri Until 1396 Hijri, http://dab.gov.af/en/page/monetary-policy/rates-statistics/currency-hijri-average [hereinafter on Da Afghanistan Bank, Monthly Average USD For the Years of 1385 Hijri Until 1396 Hijri].
106 For a similar analysis, *see* Ghiasy et al., Afghanistan's Private Sector (2015).
107 *Id.*
108 Calculated by the author based on National Risk and Vulnerability Assessment (2005); National Risk and Vulnerability Assessment (2007–2008); National Risk and Vulnerability Assessment (2011–2012); National Risk and Vulnerability Assessment (2014–2015); National Risk and Vulnerability Assessment (2016–2017).

109 Comparing the data on productivity of agricultural production from the country's two different time period separated by almost fifty years (1967–1968 and 2016–2017) reveals that agricultural productivity has stayed roughly the same over the last half a century. *See* Maxwell J. Fry, The Afghan Economy 52 (1974) and Afghanistan Central Statistics Organization, Agricultural Survey Data for the Years of 2008 until 2017.

110 Calculated by the author based on Afghanistan Central Statistics Organization, Annual Data for the Years of 2008/09 until 2016/17.

111 For an analysis of current state of relationships between Pakistan and Afghanistan, *see* Mujib Mashal and Salman Masood, *Cutting Off Pakistan, U.S. Takes Gamble in Complex Afghan War*, N. Y. Times (January 5, 2018), www.nytimes.com/2018/01/05/world/asia/pakistan-aid-afghan-war.html.

112 For an example of recent blockages, *see* Staff Report, *Pakistan Reopens Key Afghan Trade Route for Trial Run*, Daily Times (Mar. 10, 2018), https://dailytimes.com.pk/212864/pakistan-reopens-key-afghan-trade-route-for-trial-run/.

113 *Id.*

114 Calculated by the author based on Afghanistan Central Statistics Organization, Annual Data for the Years of 2008/09 until 2016/17.

115 *See* e.g. *Ra'is Amniat Melli Afghanistan: Iran va Russia ta hududi be Taliban kumak mikonan [The Head of Afghanistan's Intelligence Agency: Iran and Russia Help Taliban to Some Extent]*, BBC Persian (February 4, 2018), www.bbc.com/persian/afghanistan-42937425.

116 *See* Anjana Pasricha, *India and Afghanistan Open Air Freight Corridor to Bypass Pakistan*, VOANews (June 21, 2017), www.voanews.com/a/india-afghanistan-air-freight-corridor-opens/3909537.html; *Start of Export via Kabul-Almaty, Kazakhstan by Kam Air Airline*, Afghanistan Chamber of Commerce and Industries (February 21, 2018), ACCI.org, www.acci.org.af/da/component/content/article/38-news/1313-n.html.

117 *See* e.g. Indonesia, Turkey, and Dubai, UAE, *see* Zarmina Mohammadi, *Afghanistan-Indonesia To Open Air Corridor*, TOLONews (February 6, 2018), www.tolonews.com/index.php/business/afghanistan-indonesia-open-air-corridor; *BAZAR: Afghanistan-Turkey Air Corridor Discussed*, TOLONews (May 13, 2018), www.tolonews.com/business/bazar-afghanistan-turkey-air-corridor-discussed; *Kabul to have air corridors with Ankara, Dubai*, 1TVNews.af (Apr. 28, 2018), www.1tvnews.af/en/news/afghanistan/34318-kabul-to-have-air-corridors-with-ankara-dubai.

118 *See* e.g. *Kabul to have air corridors with Ankara, Dubai*, 1TVNews.af (Apr. 28, 2018), www.1tvnews.af/en/news/afghanistan/34318-kabul-to-have-air-corridors-with-ankara-dubai ("The country's chamber of commerce said that dried fruits and herbal products were ready to be exported to Ankara and Dubai through air corridors.")

119 *See* Ministry of Foreign Affairs of Afghanistan, *Counting down the hours now to RECCA VII (Ashgabat, November 14–15, 2017)!*, Video Clip Posted on Facebook (Jan. 2018), www.facebook.com/mfa.afghanistan/videos/1551999691524672/ [hereinafter Ministry of Foreign Affairs of Afghanistan, *Counting down the hours now to RECCA VII (2018)]*.

120 *See* Accession: Afghanistan, World Trade Organization, www.wto.org/english/thewto_e/acc_e/a1_afghanistan_e.htm (last visited June 4, 2018).

121 *See* Ministry of Foreign Affairs of Afghanistan, *Counting down the hours now to RECCA VII (2018)*.

122 *Id.*

123 *Id.*

124 All the data discussed in this section, unless otherwise specified, are calculated by the author based on Afghanistan Central Statistics Organization, Annual Data for the Years of 2008/09 until 2016/17.

125 https://wits.worldbank.org/CountryProfile/en/Country/AFG/StartYear/2015/EndYear/2019/TradeFlow/Import/indicator/MPRT-TRD-VL.
126 https://wits.worldbank.org/CountryProfile/en/Country/AFG/StartYear/2015/EndYear/2019/TradeFlow/Import/indicator/MPRT-TRD-VL.
127 https://wits.worldbank.org/CountryProfile/en/Country/AFG/StartYear/2015/EndYear/2019/TradeFlow/Export/indicator/XPRT-TRD-VL.
128 The statistics on the Afghanistan trade balance reported in this paragraph is calculated by the author based on Afghanistan Central Statistics Organization, Annual Data for the Years of 2008/09 until 2016/17.
129 *See* the World Bank, World Bank Development Indicators, Net official development assistance received in current USD, Afghanistan's Net official development assistance received in current USD for the Years of 1960 until 2015, https://data.worldbank.org/indicator/DT.ODA.ODAT.CD?locations=AF.
130 *Id.*
131 *See* Ales Bulir and A. Javir Hamann, International Monetary Fund, Volatility of Development Aid: An Update 727, 728 (IMF Staff Papers 54, 2007).
132 Calculated by the author based on the World Bank, World Bank Development Indicators, personal remittances received in current USD, Afghanistan's personal remittances received in current USD for the years of 2008 until 2016, https://data.worldbank.org/indicator/BX.TRF.PWKR.CD.DT?end=2016&locations=AF&start=2008.
133 Robert Holzmann, World Bank, Managed Labor Migration in Afghanistan: Exploring Employment and Growth Opportunities for Afghanistan 12 (2018), http://documents.worldbank.org/curated/en/746891516915310370/pdf/122987-WP-P158055-PUBLIC-SummaryReportFINALonline.pdf [hereinafter Holzmann, Managed Labor Migration in Afghanistan (2018)].
134 *Id.*
135 *Id.*
136 International Fund for Agricultural Development, Sending Money Home: Worldwide Remittance Flows to Developing Countries 10 (2007), https://publications.iadb.org/handle/11319/1072.
137 Calculated by the author based on the World Bank, World Bank Development Indicators, Foreign Direct Investment Net Inflows in current USD, Afghanistan's Direct Investment Net Inflows in current USD for the years of 2001 until 2015, https://data.worldbank.org/indicator/BX.KLT.DINV.CD.WD?end=2016&locations=AF&start=2001.
138 *Id.*
139 *Id.*
140 *See* the World Bank, World Bank Development Indicators, Foreign Direct Investment Net Outflows in current USD, Afghanistan's Direct Investment Net Outflows in current USD for the years of 2001 until 2016, https://data.worldbank.org/indicator/BM.KLT.DINV.CD.WD?end=2016&locations=AF&start=2003.
141 *See* the World Bank, World Bank Development Indicators, Net Portfolio Investment in current USD, Afghanistan's Net Portfolio Investment in current USD for the years of 2008 until 2016, https://data.worldbank.org/indicator/BN.KLT.PTXL.CD?end=2016&locations=AF&start=2008.
142 This includes transfer of property as well as use of personal property as collateral.
143 This finding is based on author's interviews with Afghan merchants in five major provinces of Afghanistan (Kabul, Herat, Nangarhar, Balkh, and Kandahar) between March and August 2017, as well as author's personal observations over several years of his work as accountant in Afghanistan's private sector between 2008 and 2013.
144 *See generally* Conor Foley, *Norwegian Refugee Council, a Guide to Property Law in Afghanistan* 32 (2nd ed., 2011), www.nrc.no/globalassets/pdf/reports/a-guide-to-property-law-in-afghanistan.pdf [hereinafter Foley, *A Guide to Property Law in*

Afghanistan (2011)]; Liz Alden Wiley, Afghan Research and Evaluation Unit, Land Rights in Crisis: Restoring land tenure to Afghanistan 1 (2003), https://reliefweb.int/report/afghanistan/land-rights-crisis-restoring-tenure-security-afghanistan [hereinafter Wiley, Land Rights in Crisis (2003)]; Liz Alden Wiley, Afghan Research and Evaluation Unit Putting Rural Land Registration in Perspective: The Afghanistan Case 1 (2004), http://citeseerx.ist.psu.edu/viewdoc/download?doi=10.1.1.521.8602&rep=rep1&type=pdf [hereinafter Wiley, Putting Rural Land Registration in Perspective (2004)]; Tres Thompson et al., Stanford Law School, Afghanistan Legal Education Project, An Introduction to the Property Law of Afghanistan 46 (2015), https://www-cdn.law.stanford.edu/wp-content/uploads/2016/05/ALEP-Property-Law-1st-Ed_English.pdf [hereinafter Thompson et al., An Introduction to the Property Law of Afghanistan (2015)].

145 *See* Foley, *A Guide to Property Law in Afghanistan* (2011), at 32; Thompson et al., An Introduction to the Property Law of Afghanistan (2015), at 44; Wiley, Land Rights in Crisis (2003), at 9.

146 *See* Foley, A Guide to Property Law in Afghanistan (2011), at 34; Wiley, Land Rights in Crisis (2003), at 3.

147 *Id.*

148 *See* Foley, A Guide to Property Law in Afghanistan (2011), at 28; Thompson et al., An Introduction to the Property Law of Afghanistan (2015) at 89; Wiley (2003), Wiley, Land Rights in Crisis (2003), at 16.

149 *See* Foley, A Guide to Property Law in Afghanistan (2011), at 44; Wiley, Land Rights in Crisis (2003), at 39.

150 Foley, A Guide to Property Law in Afghanistan (2011), at 34.

151 Wiley, Putting Rural Land Registration in Perspective (2004), at 10.

152 *Id.*

153 Foley, A Guide to Property Law in Afghanistan (2011), at 34.

154 *Id.* at 30.

155 *Id.* at 35.

156 Foley, A Guide to Property Law in Afghanistan (2011), at 35; Wiley, Land Rights in Crisis (2003), at 43.

157 Qanun Survey va Ehsaya Arazi [Land Survey and Statistics Law] 1344 [1965] Arts.13–17.

158 Wiley, Land Rights in Crisis (2003), at 41.

159 *See* Foley, A Guide to Property Law in Afghanistan (2011), at 32.

160 *See* Liz Alden Wily, Afghanistan Research & Evaluation Unit, Looking for Peace on the Pastures: Rural Land Relations in Afghanistan 80 (2004), https://areu.org.af/wp-content/uploads/2015/12/437E-Looking-for-Peace-on-the-Pastures-Rural-Land-Relations-in-Afghanistan-SP-web.pdf. [hereinafter Wily, Rural Land Relations in Afghanistan (2004)].

161 *See* Wiley, Land Rights in Crisis (2003), at 42.

162 *Id.*, at 35.

163 *See* Foley, A Guide to Property Law in Afghanistan (2011), at 33.

164 Qanun Survey Arazi va Sabt Survey Sakenin [The Law Concerning Land Survey and Registration of Settlement Survey] 1355 [1976].

165 *Id.*

166 *See* Foley, A Guide to Property Law in Afghanistan (2011), at 32.

167 Farman Eslah Arazi [Land Reform Decree] (No. 8, 1359 [1980]) art. 31 [hereinafter Land Reform Decree, (1980) art. 31].

168 *Id.*

169 *See* Foley, A Guide to Property Law in Afghanistan (2011), at 32.

170 Land Reform Decree, (1980) art. 31.

171 *See* Foley, A Guide to Property Law in Afghanistan (2011), at 33.

172 *See* Qanun Assasi Afghanistan [Afghanistan Constitution] 1366 [1987], arts. 29 and 30.

173 *See* e.g. Farman Rayees Jumhur Afghanistan dar bara Isterdad Amval That Malikiat Duwlat [The Decree of the President of Republic of Afghanistan with regard to Return of the Properties under the Control of the Government to their Owners] (Law No. 715, 1369 [1991]).
174 *See* Foley, A Guide to Property Law in Afghanistan (2011), at 34.
175 *See* Shamshad Pasarlay, *Islam and the Sharia in the 1993 Mujahideen—Draft Constitution of the Islamic State of Afghanistan: A Comparative Perspective*, 3 Indon. J. Int'l & Comp. L. 183, 202 (2016).
176 *See* Foley, A Guide to Property Law in Afghanistan (2011), at 31.
177 *Id.*
178 *See* Qanun Zamin [Law on Land] (No. 783, 1376 [1997]); Qanun Tanzim Umur Zamindari Emirat Islami Afghanistan [Islamic Emirate of Afghanistan's Land Management Law] (No. 795, 1381 [2001]) [hereinafter Land Management Law (2001)]; Qanun Estimlak Zamin [Law of Land Expropriation] (No. 794, 1380 [2000]).
179 *See* Qanun Tanzim Umur Malikiat [Law of Managing Ownership Affairs] 1387 [2008].
180 *Id.*
181 *See* Foley, A Guide to Property Law in Afghanistan (2011), at 31; and Section 2.6.2.1.3.
182 *See* BBC Afghanistan Division, *Land Management Development Program Has Begun in Afghanistan*, BBC Persian (February 15, 2018), www.bbc.com/persian/afghanistan-43073751.
183 *Id.*
184 *Id.*
185 *See* Afghanistan Demographic Estimates for the Years of 2002/03 until 2017/18.
186 In 2005, in Kabul, for example, 60% of the land transfers were not legally registered. *See* David Stanfield, Jonathan Reed, and M. Yasin Safar, Emerging Markets Group, Description of Procedures for Producing Legal Deeds to Record Property Transactions in Afghanistan 12 (2005), www.terrainstitute.org/pdf/Description%20of%20Procedures.pdf.
187 Liz Alden Wily, Afghanistan Research and Evaluation Unit, Land, People and The State of Afghanistan: 2002–2012 22 (2013), www.areu.org.af/Uploads/EditionPdfs/ [hereinafter Wily, People and The State of Afghanistan (2013)].
188 *See* Thompson et al., An Introduction to the Property Law of Afghanistan (2015), at 60;
189 *Id.* at 61.
190 *Id.*
191 *Id.*, at 59.
192 The description of process of formal property transfer reported in this paragraph is based on written communication between the author and head of district court for the District of Enjil, Herat via Facebook Messenger (November 10, 2017); *see also* Thompson et al., An Introduction to the Property Law of Afghanistan (2015), at 54–64.
193 Wily, People and The State of Afghanistan (2013), at 22.
194 *See* Thompson et al., An Introduction to the Property Law of Afghanistan (2015), at 44;
195 *See* Foley, A Guide to Property Law in Afghanistan (2011), at 35.
196 Land Management Law (2001), the following are considered property and legal documents for the purpose of proving ownership: (1) documents of the legal court are based on purchase, ownership, donation, patrimony, distribution of patrimony, land exchange, waiver, settlement, document of irrevocable decision, which is issued based on the previous documents of property, which include the following terms: (a) should be registered within the judicial bureau; (b) its dissolvent should not exist; (c) the land registered in the legal document, if taxable, should be registered in Tax Office. (2) Decree of the State/Government (prime minister) and the document of land purchasing from the state ownership should include the following terms:

(a) should be issued by an authorized office; (b) its dissolvent should not exist; (c) if taxable, should be registered in Tax Office. (3) Documents of tax payment which should include the following terms: (a) its dissolvent should not exist, (b) should be registered in the property/land registry original books, and (c) should have tax bill dated before 15/Assad/1354 (Solar Year). [1975]; (4) [. . .]. (5) Customary documents are legal based on the following terms: (a) vendor of the land should have a legal document; (b) the conventional document should have been arranged before 15/Assad/1354 (Solar Year), and the vendee of the land should have filled out the land-title form before 1357 (Solar Year) and after the confirmation of neighbors of the plot, handed into the relevant office. In areas where the land-title forms were distributed or not, but the land registry office was removed somehow, and there is no claim for the land, the purchase of the land and the possession taking of the vendee by the neighbors should be approved. (6) The legal documents of the land which should include the following terms: (a) the legal document should exist, (b) the document should be issued after legal clearance of the land, (c) should be registered in the property/land registry original book and Tax Office, and (d) there should be no claim for the land. (7) Document of the land ownership (land-title) which include the following terms: (a) the document should be arranged and issued via relevant court after legal clearance of the land and (b) should be registered in the property/land registry original book and Tax Office.

197 *See* David Stanfield et al., Terra Institute, Description of Procedures for Producing Legal Deeds to Record Property Transactions in Afghanistan (2005), www.terrainstitute.org/pdf/Description%20of%20Procedures.pdf.

198 *See* Qanuni Madani [Civil Code] 1355 [1977], art. 1222, which states, "Ownership of real estate and other real rights, on which the conditions stated by law on registration of documents are not observed, shall not transfer." [hereinafter Civil Code (1977)].

199 https://reporting.unhcr.org/sites/default/files/Afghanistan%20Situation%20Emergency%20Update%201%20September%202021.pdf and www.internal-displacement.org/countries/afghanistan.

200 https://data2.unhcr.org/en/situations/afghanistan#_ga=2.113765831.1722129200.1642082286-1358251986.1642082286.

201 *See* Foley, A Guide to Property Law in Afghanistan (2011), at 8.

202 For a comparative study of Islamic law of inheritance, *see* Hamid Khan, The Islamic Law of Inheritance (2008) [hereinafter Khan, The Islamic Law of Inheritance (2008)].

203 *See* 3.1.8.

204 *See* e.g. Nouchine Yavari d'Hellencourt et al., Ministry of Urban Development and Housing and UN-Habitat, Preliminary Study of Land Tenure Related Issues in Urban Afghanistan With special reference to Kabul City (2002).

205 Calculated by the author based on Afghanistan Supreme Court, Judicial Activities Reports for the Years of 2012 until 2017.

206 Qanun Assasi Afghanistan [Afghanistan Constitution] 1382 [2014], art. 14 (No one's property shall be confiscated without the order of the law and decision of an authoritative court. Acquisition of private property shall be legally permitted only for the sake of public interests and in exchange for prior and just compensation.) [hereinafter Afghanistan Constitution (2014)].

207 *See* Samira Zafari, *One Million and Six Hundred Thousand Jarib of Public Land Has been Usurped in Afghanistan*, ArianaNews.AF (December 21, 2017), https://ariananews.af/%DB%8C%DA%A9-%D9%85%DB%8C%D9%84%DB%8C%D9%88%D9%86-%D9%88-%D8%B4%D8%B4-%D8%B5%D8%AF-%D9%87%D8%B2%D8%A7%D8%B1-%D8%AC%D8%B1%DB%8C%D8%A8-%D8%B2%D9%85%DB%8C%D9%86-%D8%AF%D9%88%D9%84%D8%AA%DB%8C-%D8%AF/?lang=fa.

208 *See* BBC Afghanistan Division, *Freedom House: More than One Million and Two Hundred Thousands Jaribs Are Grabbed in Afghanistan*, BBC Persian (February 21,

2016), www.bbc.com/persian/afghanistan/2016/02/160221_k05_landgrab_house_of_freedom_report [hereinafter BBC Afghanistan Division, *More than One Million and Two Hundred Thousands Jaribs Are Grabbed in Afghanistan* (February 21, 2016)].

209 Afghanistan Freedom House reports lower figure of the area of public land usurped in Afghanistan, 2400km^2. *See* BBC Afghanistan Division, *More than One Million and Two Hundred Thousands Jaribs Are Grabbed in Afghanistan* (February 21, 2016).

210 *See Taliban Collect Taxes in Farah*, 8am.af (September 13, 2017), http://8am.af/1396/10/10/ghazni-has-become-the-talibans-tax-area/; http://8am.af/1396/07/22/the-taliban-collect-taxes-in-farah/; *New Findings Reveal Taliban Collect Tax in Ghazni*, TOLO News (January 10, 2018), www.tolonews.com/afghanistan/new-findings-reveal-taliban-collecting-tax-ghazni; Ahmad Hanayesh, Yaqubi: T*aliban Collect Taxes from People in The Districts of Kapisa Where They Have Control*, Radio Azadi, https://da.azadiradio.com/a/28560065.html; *Nimrooz Authorities: Taliban Collect Taxes from Merchants on Khashrood—Delaram High Way*, Radio Azadi (January 1, 2018), https://da.azadiradio.com/a/28958957.html.

211 *Id.*

212 *Id.*

213 *Id.*

214 This finding is based on author's interviews with Afghan merchants in five major provinces of Afghanistan (Kabul, Herat, Nangarhar, Balkh, and Kandahar) between March and August 2017, as well as author's personal observations over several years of his work as accountant in Afghanistan's private sector between 2008 and 2013. In addition, it is supported by the prevalence of cross-border trade discussed earlier in this chapter.

215 *See* Integrity Watch Afghanistan, National Corruption Survey (2016).

216 For example, while in Afghanistan for this research, I witnessed a TV interview on TOLONews with a Kabuli *Sarraf* whose nephew was kidnapped for ransom (kidnappers asked for 4 million USD), where he said that he had to hire 20 bodyguards to protect himself and his family.

217 *See* Khairullah Rasooli, Saraffan dar Sarasar Afghanistan emrooz a'etesab kari kardan [Sarrafs in Afghanistan Staged a Nationwide Strike Today], VOADari (December 29, 2017), www.darivoa.com/a/Afghan-money-changer-union-made-a-strike-across-Afghanistan/4182373.html.

218 *See* e.g. Afghanistan Ministry of Commerce and Industries, Strategic Plan (2016).

219 Qanun Tashkil va Salahiat Quva Qazaiee [Laws on Organization and Jurisdiction of Judiciary] (No. 851, 1384 [2005]), art. 61 [hereinafter Laws on Organization and Jurisdiction of Judiciary (2005)].

220 *Id.*

221 Laws on Organization and Jurisdiction of Judiciary (2005), art. 65.

222 Qanun Usul Muhakimat Madani [Law of Civil Procedure] (No. 722, 1369 [1990]), art. 12(2) [hereinafter Law of Civil Procedure (1990)].

223 *See* Qanun Tarz Tahsil Huquq [Law of Enforcement of Rights] (No. 786, 1377 [1999]) [hereinafter Law of Enforcement of Rights (1999)].

224 *Id.*

225 *Id.*

226 *Id.*

227 Law of Civil Procedure (1990), art. 12.

228 *See* Law of Enforcement of Rights (1999).

229 Usul Muhakimat Tijrati [Principles of Commercial Procedure] (No. 1–4, 1343 [1965]) [hereinafter Principles of Commercial Procedure (1965)].

230 *Id.* art. 6.

231 *Id.* art. 12.

232 *Id.* art. 11.

233 *Id.* art. 8.

234 Commercial Law consists of five books: (1) General Regulation, (2) Partnership and Corporations, (3) Commercial Documents, (4) Commercial Agreements. Currently, only the first book of Commercial Law is in effect. Different legislations have mostly replaced the last three chapters. However, Commercial Law's first chapter is still a critical piece of legislation in area of commercial law. Asulnama Tijarat [Principles of Commercial Law] 1336 [1958] [hereinafter Principles of Commercial Law (1958)].

235 *Id.* arts. 1–3.

236 *Id.* arts. 14–23.

237 *Id.* art. 8.

238 *Id.* arts. 24–84.

239 *Id.*

240 *Id.* arts. 8 and 23; Principles of Commercial Procedure (1965), art. 1.

241 Principles of Commercial Law (1958), art. 10.

242 According to Commercial Law Article 19, inherent commercial transactions are as follows: (a) working for commission; (b) brokerage; (c) bill and draft transactions (whether recorded in the name of a person or a bearer); (d) money exchange transactions; (e) transactions made by private and public (special and general) banks; (f) transaction relating to current accounts and agreements thereof; (g) transactions relating to mortgage documents and receipts existing against goods placed in commercial general storehouses; (h) Establishment of commercial companies and buying and selling of shares; (i) contraction of contracting for any kind of insurance for all risks whether for fees or for reciprocal terms. *Id.*

243 *Id.* art. 20.

244 *Id.* art. 21.

245 *Id.* art. 14.

246 *Id.* art. 15.

247 The following types of transaction are also considered primary commercial transactions (Article 18): (a) agreement to provide any kind of movable property and accept any kind of activities and products; (b) establishment of a power plant or press, photography, printing, and selling of books; (c) establishment of theaters, movies, parks and public places, for example, hotels, business compounds, restaurants and the like, employment offices, and auction places; (d) transportation of passengers, animals, and goods via land, air, and water; (e) distribution of water, gas, electricity and the establishment of telephone communication. *Id.* art. 16.

248 "If a landowner, farmer, or a cattle-raiser sells his products or changes them to other forms before selling them, such action should be considered as normal or ordinary activities [not a commercial transaction]. Similarly, if a farmer with agricultural and industrial machines or plants exchange his product—or if a professional person or his employee (or his machines) produces his professional product and sells them; [. . .] But if a person for the purpose of changing his agricultural product opens a permanent establishment possessing the qualities of an industrial business, this is considered a commercial transaction." *Id.* art. 17.

249 Afghanistan Supreme Court, Judicial Seminar 190 (1395 [2017]) [hereinafter Afghanistan Supreme Court, Judicial Seminar (2017)].

250 *Id.*

251 *Id.*

252 *Id.*

253 *Id.*

254 Calculated by the author based on Afghanistan Supreme Court, Judicial Activities Reports for the Years of 2012 until 2017.

255 Calculated by the author based on business establishment survey (2010); establishment survey (2016).

256 Calculated by the author based on Afghanistan Demographic Estimates for the Years of 2002/03 until 2017/18.
257 *See* e.g. Afghanistan Ministry of Commerce and Industries, Strategic Plan (2016), at 12.
258 *See* Principles of Commercial Procedure (1965), and Section 2.6.3.1.
259 *Id.*
260 *Id.*
261 *Id.*
262 *Id.* art. 40.
263 *Id.*
264 *Id.* art. 37.
265 *Id.* art. 40.
266 *Id.*
267 *Id.*
268 Principles of Commercial Law (1958).
269 Principles of Commercial Procedure (1965).
270 *Id.*
271 *Id.*
272 *Id.*
273 Principles of Commercial Law (1958).
274 *Id.*
275 *Id.*
276 *Id.* art. 68.
277 *Id.*
278 *Id.* art. 80.
279 This finding is based on author's interviews with Afghan merchants in five major provinces of Afghanistan (Kabul, Herat, Nangarhar, Balkh, and Kandahar) between March and August 2017, as well as author's personal observations over several years of his work as accountant in Afghanistan's private sector between 2008 and 2013.
280 *See* Law of Civil Procedure (1965).
281 *Id.*
282 *Id.*
283 *Id.*
284 Afghanistan Supreme Court, Judicial Seminar (2017), at 180.
285 *Id.*
286 Laws on Organization and Jurisdiction of Judiciary (2005), art. 6(3)(1).
287 *Id.*
288 There is one court of appeal located in each provincial capital, which decides all the cases from that province at the second level. A chief judge heads court of appeal in each province. Court of appeals, in most provinces, consist of six dewans: (1) General Criminal Dewan, (2) Public Security Dewan, (3) Dewan of Crimes Against Internal and External Security, (4) Dewan of Civil and Personal Affairs, and Public Rights, and (5) Commercial Dewan. *Id.* art. 32.
289 *Id.* art. 6(3)(2).
290 *Id.* art. 35.
291 Afghanistan Supreme Court is the highest judicial organ in Afghanistan and heads the judicial branch. Afghanistan Constitution (2014), art. 116. The high judicial council, which consists of all nine members of the Afghanistan Supreme Court, is the highest judicial body within the Afghanistan Supreme Court. Laws on Organization and Jurisdiction of Judiciary (2005), art. 17. The Afghanistan Supreme Court has five judicial dewans, each of which is headed by a justice: (1) General Criminal Dewan, (2) Public Security Dewan, (3) Civil and Public Rights Dewan, (4) Dewan of Crimes Against Internal and External Security and Military Crimes, (5) Commercial Dewan.

The decision of each of these dewans will be enforced under the authority of the High Council of Afghanistan Supreme Court. Laws on Organization and Jurisdiction of Judiciary (2005), art. 18.

292 Laws on Organization and Jurisdiction of Judiciary (2005), art. 6(3)(3).

293 *Id.* arts. 26–27.

294 *Id.*

295 *Id.*

296 *Id.* art. 28.

297 *Id.* arts. 26–27.

298 *Id.*

299 *Id.* art. 27.

300 This finding is based on author's interviews with Afghan merchants in five major provinces of Afghanistan (Kabul, Herat, Nangarhar, Balkh, and Kandahar) between March and August 2017, as well as author's personal observations over several years of his work as accountant in Afghanistan's private sector between 2008 and 2013.

301 Law of Civil Procedure (19), art. 13.

302 *Sar qufli* and lease disputes are the most common disputes resolved by commercial courts in Afghanistan; calculated by the author based on Afghanistan Supreme Court, Judicial Activities Reports for the Years of 2012 until 2017.

303 Author's interview with the chief judge of Kabul Primary Commercial Court (June 2017).

304 Calculated by the author based on Afghanistan Supreme Court, Judicial Activities Reports for the Years of 2012 until 2017.

305 *See* Law of Enforcement of Rights (1999).

306 Author's interview with a judgment enforcement specialist at Herat Huquq Department (April 2017).

307 *See* Law of Enforcement of Rights (1999).

308 Author's interview with a judgment enforcement specialist at Herat Huquq Department (April 2017).

309 The facts concerning different enforcement outcome reported in the following paragraphs is based on author's interview with a judgment enforcement specialist at Herat Huquq Department (April 2017).

310 Afghanistan Supreme Court, Judicial Seminar (2017), at 129.

311 Author's interview with a judgment enforcement specialist at Herat Huquq Department (April 2017).

312 *Id.*; Afghanistan Supreme Court, Judicial Seminar (2017), at 190.

313 Author's interview with a judgment enforcement specialist at Herat Huquq Department (April 2017).

314 Afghanistan Supreme Court, Mutahadulmal [Decision] (No. 307–369, 1385 [2007]).

315 *Id.*

316 *Id.*

317 *Id.*

318 *Id.*

319 Calculated by the author based on Afghanistan Supreme Court, Judicial Activities Reports for the Years of 2012 until 2017.

320 The data reported in this paragraph is calculated by the author based on Business Registry Data for the Years of 2014/15 until 2016/17 for Kabul, Herat, Kandahar, Balkh, and Nangarhar (2017).

321 The facts reported in this paragraph is based on author's interview with the head of Kabul's Primary Commercial Court (June 2017).

322 Author's interviews with commercial judges of five major provinces of Afghanistan (Kabul, Herat, Balkh, Nangarhar, and Kandahar between March and August 2017).

323 This finding is based on author's interviews with Afghan merchants in five major provinces of Afghanistan (Kabul, Herat, Nangarhar, Balkh, and Kandahar) between

March and August 2017, as well as author's personal observations over several years of his work as accountant in Afghanistan's private sector between 2008 and 2013.

324 Author's interviews with commercial judges of five major provinces of Afghanistan (Kabul, Herat, Balkh, Nangarhar, and Kandahar between March and August 2017).

325 For example, a primary commercial court judge in Balkh said, "We do not enforce verbal contracts because it is very difficult to determine its terms and content." Author's interview with a Primary Commercial Court judge in Balkh (May 2017).

326 Wily, People and The State of Afghanistan (2013), at 22.

327 Author's interview with a judgment enforcement specialist at Herat Huquq Department (April 2017).

328 This is why increased use of commercial courts in Afghanistan is correlated with worsening of macroeconomic conditions. This finding is based on author's interviews with Afghan merchants in five major provinces of Afghanistan (Kabul, Herat, Nangarhar, Balkh, and Kandahar) between March and August 2017, as well as author's personal observations over several years of his work as accountant in Afghanistan's private sector between 2008 and 2013.

329 *See* Chapter 3 in context of judicial attitudes toward *Gerawee*.

330 *Id.*

331 *See* e.g. Afghanistan Ministry of Commerce and Industries, Strategic Plan (2016), at 12.

332 Afghanistan Supreme Court, Judicial Seminar (2017), at 173.

333 *Id.*

334 Author's interviews with commercial judges of five major provinces of Afghanistan (Kabul, Herat, Balkh, Nangarhar, and Kandahar between March and August 2017).

335 Author's interview with the Chief Judge of Balkh's Primary Commercial Court (May 2017).

336 Author's interviews with commercial judges of five major provinces of Afghanistan (Kabul, Herat, Balkh, Nangarhar, and Kandahar between March and August 2017).

337 *Id.*

338 *Id.*

339 *See* Qanun Rahn Amwal Manqul dar Mua'amalat Banki [Law on Use of movable Properties as Collateral in Banking Transactions] (No. 990, 1387 [2009]) [hereinafter Law on Use of movable Properties as Collateral in Banking Transactions (2009)]; Qanun Rahn Amwal Qair-Manqul dar Mua'amalat Banki [Law on Use of immovable Properties as Collateral in Banking Transactions] (No. 990, 1387 [2009]) [hereinafter Law on Use of immovable Properties as Collateral in Banking Transactions (2009)].

340 *Id.*

341 Afghanistan Supreme Court, Judicial Seminar (2017), at 185.

342 Author's interviews with commercial judges of five major provinces of Afghanistan (Kabul, Herat, Balkh, Nangarhar, and Kandahar between March and August 2017).

343 *See* Law on Use of movable Properties as Collateral in Banking Transactions (2009); Law on Use of immovable Properties as Collateral in Banking Transactions (2009).

344 Author's interviews with commercial judges of five major provinces of Afghanistan (Kabul, Herat, Balkh, Nangarhar, and Kandahar between March and August 2017).

345 *See* e.g. Afghanistan Ministry of Commerce and Industries, Strategic Plan (2016), at 12.

346 Joshua Charap and Jelena Pavlovic, IMF Middle East and Central Asia Department, Development of the Commercial Banking System in Afghanistan: Risks and Rewards 18 (IMF Working Paper WP/09/150, 2009), www.imf.org/external/pubs/ft/wp/2009/wp09150.pdf

347 *Id.*

348 *Id.* at 17.

349 *Id.* at 18.

350 *Id.*

351 *Id.*
352 *Id.* at 19.
353 *Id.* at 18.
354 The following facts about the Center is based on author's interview with the head of Afghanistan Commercial Dispute Resolution Center at Afghanistan Chamber of Commerce and Industries (Kabul, June 2017).
355 The following facts concerning Herat Chamber of Commerce is based on author's interview with the president of Herat's Chamber of Commerce and Industries (Herat, April 2017).

References

Accession: Afghanistan, World Trade Organization, www.wto.org/english/thewto_e/acc_e/a1_afghanistan_e.htm (last visited June 4, 2018)

Afghanistan Analyst Network, www.afghanistan-analysts.org/miscellaneous/aan-resources/the-government-of-national-unity-deal-full-text/

Afghanistan Central Statistics Organization, Afghanistan Current GDP by Sector for the Years 2002/03 until 2016/17, http://cso.gov.af/fa/page/ict/11328/888Afghanistan Central Statistics Organization

Afghanistan Central Statistics Organization, Afghanistan Import and Export Annual Data for the Years of 2008/09 until 2016/17, http://cso.gov.af/fa/page/economy-statistics/6323/annual-trade

Afghanistan Central Statistics Organization, Agricultural Survey Data for the Years of 2008 until 2017

Afghanistan Central Statistics Organization, Business Establishment Survey 2009 (2010), http://cso.gov.af/en/page/1500/1494/6

Afghanistan Central Statistics Organization, Business Establishment Survey 2015 (2016), http://cso.gov.af/en/page/1500/1494/6

Afghanistan Central Statistics Organization, The National Risk and Vulnerability Assessment: Afghanistan Living Conditions Survey (2005), http://cso.gov.af/en/page/1500/1494/nrav-report

Afghanistan Central Statistics Organization, The National Risk and Vulnerability Assessment: Afghanistan Living Conditions Survey (2007–2008), http://cso.gov.af/en/page/1500/1494/nrav-report

Afghanistan Central Statistics Organization, The National Risk and Vulnerability Assessment: Afghanistan Living Conditions Survey (2011–2012), http://cso.gov.af/en/page/1500/1494/nrav-report

Afghanistan Central Statistics Organization, The National Risk and Vulnerability Assessment: Afghanistan Living Conditions Survey (2013–2014)

Afghanistan Central Statistics Organization, Sectoral Contribution to the GDP for the Years of 2002/03 until 2016/17, http://cso.gov.af/fa/page/ict/11328/11332

Afghanistan Chamber of Commerce and Industries, www.acci.org.af/

Afghanistan Chamber of Commerce and Industries, www.acci.org.af/

Afghanistan Chamber of Commerce Industries, Business Tendency Survey Reports of II-2014, IV-2014, I-2015, II-2015, III-2015, IV-2015, I-2016, II-2016, III-2016, IV-2016, I-2017, II-2017, and III-2017, www.acci.org.af/surveys-and-studies.html

Afghanistan Demographic Estimates for the Years of 2002/03 until 2017/18, http://cso.gov.af/fa/page/demography-and-socile-statistics/demograph-statistics/3897111

Afghanistan Supreme Court, Judicial Seminar 190 (1395 [2017])

Afghanistan Supreme Court, Mutahadulmal [Decision] (No. 307–369, 1385 [2007])
Afghanistan Supreme Court, Quarterly Judicial Activities Reports for the Years of 2012 until 2017, http://supremecourt.gov.af/fa/page/court-reporting
Ahmad Hanayesh, *Yaqubi: Taliban Collect Taxes from People in The Districts of Kapisa Where They Have Control* (Radio Azadi), https://da.azadiradio.com/a/28560065.html
Ales Bulir & A. Javir Hamann, *International Monetary Fund*, Volatility of Development Aid: An Update 727, 728 (IMF Staff Papers 54, 2007)
Amin Saikal, *Modern Afghanistan: A History of Struggle and Survival* (I B Tauris 2004)
Anjana Pasricha, *India and Afghanistan Open Air Freight Corridor to Bypass Pakistan*, VOANews (June 21, 2017), www.voanews.com/a/india-afghanistan-air-freight-corridor-opens/3909537.html
Asulnama Tijarat [Principles of Commercial Law] 1336 [1958]
BAZAR: Afghanistan-Turkey Air Corridor Discussed, TOLONews (May 13, 2018), www.tolonews.com/business/bazar-afghanistan-turkey-air-corridor-discussed
BBC Afghanistan Division, *Freedom House: More than One Million and Two Hundred Thousands Jaribs Are Grabbed in Afghanistan*, BBC Persian (February 21, 2016), www.bbc.com/persian/afghanistan/2016/02/160221_k05_landgrab_house_of_freedom_report
BBC Afghanistan Division, *More than One Million and Two Hundred Thousands Jaribs Are Grabbed in Afghanistan* (BBC Persian February 21, 2016)
BBC Afghanistan Division, *Land Management Development Program Has Begun in Afghanistan*, BBC Persian (February 15, 2018), www.bbc.com/persian/afghanistan-43073751
Business Climate Survey report (June 2020), https://harakat.af/uploads/publications/1599117511Business%20Climate%20Survey%20Report.pdf
Business Registry Data for the Years of 2014/15 until 2016/17 For Kabul, Herat, Kandahar, Balkh, and Nangarhar, Received by the author from Afghanistan Central Business Registry's Directory Through Head of Office of Business Registry at Afghanistan Ministry of Commerce (September 23, 2017)
Central Intelligence Agency World Factbook: Afghanistan, www.cia.gov/Library/publications/the-world-factbook/geos/af.html
Conor Foley, *Norwegian Refugee Council, a Guide to Property Law in Afghanistan* (2nd ed., 2011), www.nrc.no/globalassets/pdf/reports/a-guide-to-property-law-in-afghanistan.pdf
Da Afghanistan Bank, Currency Hijri Monthly Average USD For the Years of 1385 Hijri Until 1396 Hijri, http://dab.gov.af/en/page/monetary-policy/rates-statistics/currency-hijri-average
Da Afghanistan Bank, Quarterly Financial Sector Financial Statistics for the Period of I-2013 until II-2017, http://dab.gov.af/en/page/financial-supervision/financial-statistics/banks
David Stanfield, Jonathan Reed, & M. Yasin Safar, Emerging Markets Group, Description of Procedures for Producing Legal Deeds to Record Property Transactions in Afghanistan (2005), www.terrainstitute.org/pdf/Description%20of%20Procedures.pdf.
David Stanfield et al., Terra Institute, Description of Procedures for Producing Legal Deeds to Record Property Transactions in Afghanistan (2005), www.terrainstitute.org/pdf/Description%20of%20Procedures.pdf
Farman Eslah Arazi [Land Reform Decree] (No. 8, 1359 [1980])
Farman Rayees Jumhur Afghanistan dar bara Isterdad Amval That Malikiat Duwlat [The Decree of the President of Republic of Afghanistan with regard to Return of the Properties under the Control of the Government to their Owners] (Law No. 715, 1369 [1991])
Gilles Dorronsoro, *Revolution Unending: Afghanistan, 1979 to the Present* (John King trans.) (C Hurst & Co Publishers Ltd 2005)

Hamid Khan, *The Islamic Law of Inheritance* (Oxford University Press 2008)

The Holy Quran (Abdullah Yusuf Ali, trans, Wordsworth Classics of World Literature 2001)

Integrity Watch Afghanistan, National Corruption Survey 2016: Afghan Perceptions and Experiences of Corruption (2016), https://iwaweb.org/national-corruption-corruption-survey-2016/

International Fund for Agricultural Development, Sending Money Home: Worldwide Remittance Flows to Developing Countries (2007), https://publications.iadb.org/handle/11319/1072

Joshua Charap & Jelena Pavlovic, *IMF Middle East and Central Asia Department, Development of the Commercial Banking System in Afghanistan: Risks and Rewards* 18 (IMF Working Paper WP/09/150, 2009), www.imf.org/external/pubs/ft/wp/2009/wp09150.pdf

Kabul to have air corridors with Ankara, Dubai, 1TVNews.af (April 28, 2018), www.1tvnews.af/en/news/afghanistan/34318-kabul-to-have-air-corridors-with-ankara-dubai.

Karim Amini, *Ongoing ARG-Jamiat Rift Affects Investment in Balkh*, TOLO News (February 02, 2018), www.tolonews.com/afghanistan/ongoing-arg-jamiat-rift-affects-investment-balkh

Khairullah Rasooli, *Saraffan dar Sarasar Afghanistan emrooz a'etesab kari kardan [Sarrafs in Afghanistan Staged a Nationwide Strike Today]*, VOA Dari (December 29, 2017), www.darivoa.com/a/Afghan-money-changer-union-made-a-strike-across-Afghanistan/4182373.html

Liz Alden Wiley, *Afghan Research and Evaluation Unit, Land Rights in Crisis: Restoring Land Tenure to Afghanistan* (AREU 2003), https://reliefweb.int/report/afghanistan/land-rights-crisis-restoring-tenure-security-afghanistan

Liz Alden Wiley, *Afghan Research and Evaluation Unit Putting Rural Land Registration in Perspective: The Afghanistan Case* (AREU 2004), http://citeseerx.ist.psu.edu/viewdoc/download?doi=10.1.1.521.8602&rep=rep1&type=pdf

Liz Alden Wily, *Afghanistan Research & Evaluation Unit, Looking for Peace on the Pastures: Rural Land Relations in Afghanistan* (AREU 2004), https://areu.org.af/wp-content/uploads/2015/12/437E-Looking-for-Peace-on-the-Pastures-Rural-Land-Relations-in-Afghanistan-SP-web.pdf

Liz Alden Wily, *Afghanistan Research and Evaluation Unit, Land, People and The State of Afghanistan: 2002–2012* (AREU 2013), www.areu.org.af/Uploads/EditionPdfs/

Matin Sahak, *Powerful Afghan Governor Defying President Ghani Agrees To Go*, Reuters (March 22, 2018), www.reuters.com/article/us-afghanistan-governor/powerful-afghan-governor-defying-president-ghani-agrees-to-go-idUSKBN1GY1PU

Matthew Rosenberg, *Audit Says Kabul Bank Began as 'Ponzi Scheme*,' N.Y. Times (November 26, 2012), www.nytimes.com/2012/11/27/world/asia/kabul-bank-audit-details-extent-of-fraud.html

Maxwell J. Fry, *The Afghan Economy* (Cambridge University Press 1974)

Ministry of Foreign Affairs of Afghanistan, *Counting down the hours now to RECCA VII (Ashgabat, November 14–15, 2017)!* Video Clip Posted on Facebook (January 2018), www.facebook.com/mfa.afghanistan/videos/1551999691524672/

Ministry of Foreign Affairs of Afghanistan, *Counting down the hours now to RECCA VII (2018).*

Mohammad Bashir Mobasher, *Understanding Ethnic-Electoral Dynamics: How Ethnic Politics Affect Electoral Laws and Election Outcomes in Afghanistan*, 51 Gonz. L. Rev. (Washington International Law Journal 2015–2016)

Mujib Mashal & Salman Masood, *Cutting Off Pakistan, U.S. Takes Gamble in Complex Afghan War*, N. Y. Times (January 5, 2018), www.nytimes.com/2018/01/05/world/asia/pakistan-aid-afghan-war.html

New Findings Reveal Taliban Collect Tax in Ghazni, TOLO News (January 10, 2018), www.tolonews.com/afghanistan/new-findings-reveal-taliban-collecting-tax-ghazni

Nimrooz Authorities: Taliban Collect Taxes from Merchants on Khashrood—Delaram High Way, Radio Azadi (January 1, 2018), https://da.azadiradio.com/a/28958957.html

Nouchine Yavari d'Hellencourt et al., *Ministry of Urban Development & Housing and UN-Habitat, Preliminary Study of Land Tenure Related Issues in Urban Afghanistan with Special Reference to Kabul City* (Routledge 2002)

Qanun Assasi Afghanistan [Afghanistan Constitution] 1366 [1987]

Qanun Assasi Afghanistan [Afghanistan Constitution] 1382 [2014]

Qanun Estimlak Zamin [Law of Land Expropriation] (No. 794, 1380 [2000]).

Qanun Rahn Amwal Manqul dar Mua'amalat Banki [Law on Use of movable Properties as Collateral in Banking Transactions] (No. 990, 1387 [2009])

Qanun Rahn Amwal Qair-Manqul dar Mua'amalat Banki [Law on Use of immovable Properties as Collateral in Banking Transactions] (No. 990, 1387 [2009])

Qanun Sherkathai Sahami va Mahdud Al-Masuliat Afghanistan [Corporation and Limited Liabilities Law of Afghanistan] (Law No. 913, 1385 [2006])

Qanun Survey va Ehsaya Arazi [Land Survey and Statistics Law] 1344 [1965] Arts.13–17

Qanun Survey Arazi va Sabt Survey Sakenin [The Law Concerning Land Survey and Registration of Settlement Survey] 1355 [1976]

Qanun Tanzim Umur Malikiat [Law of Managing Ownership Affairs] 1387 [2008]

Qanun Tarz Tahsil Huquq [Law of Enforcement of Rights] (No. 786, 1377 [1999])

Qanun Tashkil va Salahiat Quva Qazaiee [Laws on Organization and Jurisdiction of Judiciary] (No. 851, 1384 [2005])

Qanun Usul Muhakimat Madani [Law of Civil Procedure] (No. 722, 1369 [1990])

Qanun Zamin [Law on Land] (No. 783, 1376 [1997]); Qanun Tanzim Umur Zamindari Emirat Islami Afghanistan [Islamic Emirate of Afghanistan's Land Management Law] (No. 795, 1381 [2001])

Qanuni Madani [Civil Code] 1355 [1977]

Ra'is Amniat Melli Afghanistan: Iran va Russia ta hududi be Taliban kumak mikonan [The Head of Afghanistan's Intelligence Agency: Iran and Russia Help Taliban to Some Extent] BBC Persian (February 4, 2018), www.bbc.com/persian/afghanistan-42937425

Richard Ghiasy et al., *International Council of Swedish Industry, Afghanistan's Private Sector: Status and Ways Forward* (SIPRI and NIR 2015)

Richard S. Newell, *The Politics of Afghanistan* (Cornell University Press 1972)

Robert Holzmann, *World Bank, Managed Labor Migration in Afghanistan: Exploring Employment and Growth Opportunities for Afghanistan* (2018), http://documents.worldbank.org/curated/en/746891516915310370/pdf/122987-WP-P158055-PUBLIC-SummaryReportFINALonline.pdf

Samira Zafari, *One Million and Six Hundred Thousand Jarib of Public Land Has been Usurped in Afghanistan*, ArianaNews.AF (December 21, 2017), https://ariananews.af/%DB%8C%DA%A9-%D9%85%DB%8C%D9%84%DB%8C%D9%88%D9%86-%D9%88-%D8%B4%D8%B4-%D8%B5%D8%AF-%D9%87%D8%B2%D8%A7%D8%B1-%D8%AC%D8%B1%DB%8C%D8%A8-%D8%B2%D9%85%DB%8C%D9%86-%D8%AF%D9%88%D9%84%D8%AA%DB%8C-%D8%AF/?lang=fa

Shamshad Pasarlay, *Islam and the Sharia in the 1993 Mujahideen—Draft Constitution of the Islamic State of Afghanistan: A Comparative Perspective*, 3 Indon. J. Int'l & Comp. L. 183 (2016)

Special Inspector General for Afghanistan Reconstruction, Quarterly Report to the United States Congress (October 30, 2017) www.sigar.mil/pdf/quarterlyreports/2017-04-30qr.pdf

Staff Report, *Pakistan Reopens Key Afghan Trade Route for Trial Run*, Daily Times (March 10, 2018), https://dailytimes.com.pk/212864/pakistan-reopens-key-afghan-trade-route-for-trial-run/

Start of Export via Kabul-Almaty, Kazakhstan by Kam Air Airline, Afghanistan Chamber of Commerce and Industries (February 21, 2018), ACCI.org, www.acci.org.af/da/component/content/article/38-news/1313-n.html

Taliban Collect Taxes in Farah, 8am.af (September 13, 2017), http://8am.af/1396/10/10/ghazni-has-become-the-talibans-tax-area/; http://8am.af/1396/07/22/the-taliban-collect-taxes-in-farah/

Thomas J. Barfield, United States Institute for Peace, Afghan Customary Law and Its Relationship to Formal Judicial Institutions (2003), www.usip.org/sites/default/files/file/barfield2.pdf

Tres Thompson et al., Stanford Law School, Afghanistan Legal Education Project, An Introduction to the Property Law of Afghanistan (2015), https://www-cdn.law.stanford.edu/wp-content/uploads/2016/05/ALEP-Property-Law-1st-Ed_English.pdf

UNICEF, UNICEF Global Database on adjusted Net Attendance Rates (April 2021), https://data.unicef.org/wp-content/uploads/2021/04/Adjusted-net-attendance-rate_2021-1.xlsx

United Nations Assistance Mission in Afghanistan, Protection of Civilians in Armed Conflict 2017 Annual Report (2017), https://unama.unmissions.org/sites/default/files/afghanistan_protection_of_civilians_annual_report_2017_final_6_march.pdf

United Nations Office on Drugs and Crime, Afghanistan Opium Survey 2015: Cultivation and Production, www.unodc.org/documents/crop-monitoring/Afghanistan/_Afghan_opium_survey_2015_web.pdf

Usul Muhakimat Tijrati [Principles of Commercial Procedure] (No. 1–4, 1343 [1965])

The World Bank, World Bank Development Indicators, GDP Growth by Annual Percent, Afghanistan's GDP Growth by Annual Percent 2003–2016, https://data.worldbank.org/indicator/NY.GDP.MKTP.KD.ZG?locations=AF

The World Bank, World Bank Development Indicators, Foreign Direct Investment Net Inflows in current USD, Afghanistan's Direct Investment Net Inflows in current USD for the Years of 2001 until 2015, https://data.worldbank.org/indicator/BX.KLT.DINV.CD.WD?end=2016&locations=AF&start=2001

The World Bank, World Bank Development Indicators, Foreign Direct Investment Net Outflows in current USD, Afghanistan's Direct Investment Net Outflows in current USD for the Years of 2001 until 2016, https://data.worldbank.org/indicator/BM.KLT.DINV.CD.WD?end=2016&locations=AF&start=2003

The World Bank, World Bank Development Indicators, GDP at Constant Price from 2015 in USD, Afghanistan's GDP at Constant Price from 2015 in USD for the Years of 2001 until 2020 (January 29, 2022), https://data.worldbank.org/indicator/NY.GDP.MKTP.KD?end=2020&locations=AF&start=2001

The World Bank, World Bank Development Indicators, Life expectancy at birth up to total years, Afghanistan's Life expectancy at birth up to total years for the Years of 2000 until 2019, https://data.worldbank.org/indicator/SP.DYN.LE00.IN?end=2019&locations=AF&start=2001

The World Bank, World Bank Development Indicators, Maternal mortality ratio for modeled estimate, per 100,000 live births, Afghanistan's Maternal mortality ratio for modeled estimate, per 100,000 live births for the Years of 2000 until 2017, https://data.worldbank.org/indicator/SH.STA.MMRT?end=2017&locations=AF&start=2000

The World Bank, World Bank Development Indicators, Mortality Rates for Infants per 1,000 Live Births, Afghanistan's Mortality Rates for Infants per 1,000 Live Births for the Years of 2001 until 2019, https://data.worldbank.org/indicator/SP.DYN.IMRT.IN?end=2019&locations=AF&start=2001

The World Bank, World Bank Development Indicators, Net Official Development Assistance Received in Current USD, Afghanistan's Net Official Development Assistance Received in Current USD for the Years of 1960 until 2015, https://data.worldbank.org/indicator/DT.ODA.ODAT.CD?locations=AF

The World Bank, World Bank Development Indicators, Net Portfolio Investment in Current USD, Afghanistan's Net Portfolio Investment in Current USD for the Years of 2008 until 2016, https://data.worldbank.org/indicator/BN.KLT.PTXL.CD?end=2016&locations=AF&start=2008

The World Bank, World Bank Development Indicators, Personal Remittances Received in Current USD, Afghanistan's Personal Remittances Received in Current USD for the Years of 2008 until 2016, https://data.worldbank.org/indicator/BX.TRF.PWKR.CD.DT?end=2016&locations=AF&start=2008

The World Bank, World Bank Development Indicators, Political Stability Index, Afghanistan's Political Stability Score for the Years of 1996 until 2020, www.theglobaleconomy.com/afghanistan/wb_political_stability/

The World Bank, World Bank Development Indicators, Poverty headcount ratio at national poverty lines For the Percentage of population, Afghanistan's Poverty headcount ratio at national poverty lines For the Percentage of population for the Years of 2007 until 2016, https://data.worldbank.org/indicator/SI.POV.NAHC?locations=AF

The World Bank, World Bank Development Indicators, School Enrollment by Primary Gross Percentage, Afghanistan's School Enrollment by primary Gross Percentage for the Years of 2001 until 2019, https://data.worldbank.org/indicator/SE.PRM.ENRR?locations=AF

Zarmina Mohammadi, *Afghanistan-Indonesia to Open Air Corridor*, TOLONews (February 6, 2018), www.tolonews.com/index.php/business/afghanistan-indonesia-open-air-corridor.

2 Informal Financial and Dispute Resolution Institutions in Afghanistan

Afghans have developed a number of credit institutions to support credit transactions despite Afghanistan's highly uncertain environment and formal institutions that are unable to facilitate credit transactions in a way that works for the Afghan context. These institutions are not a substitute for good formal institutions. However, they have been able to provide access to working capital finance and to a lesser extent investment financing while the formal institutions have failed to offer credits on terms that Afghan merchants can use.

Sellers/creditors finance supply chains through trade credit and flexible risk-sharing arrangements to maximize sales. *Sarrafs* issue working capital loans to sellers/creditors which create a buffer against cash flow interruptions. A highly competitive business environment animates the provision of trade credit and short-term working capital loans. A feedback loop exists: lower barriers to entry create market competition, which animates the provision of trade credit and short-term working capital loans, while easing access to trade credit and short-term working capital loans lower the barriers to entry. These existing institutional solutions allow Afghan merchants to finance supply chains despite a highly volatile business climate. However, they create inefficiency by effectively locking merchants into existing supply chains. They also cannot be used to finance investments. In addition to supply chain financing, Afghan developers and their customers have developed a property right in future business reputation to recover construction cost of shopping and business centers for businesses where reputation is closely tied to the place of business. Afghans have also developed informal mortgage-like transactions, known as *Gerawee*, to raise capital against the value of their houses.

Supply Chains and Trade Credit

> If you walk to a store in Jalalabad [capital city of Nangarhar] you can see 30,000 USD worth of capital even though store owner doesn't even have 10,000 USD of his own capital.[1]
>
> (A Nangarhari merchant)

In the four provinces studied in this research, with the exception of Balkh, credit sale is the norm of business. In Afghanistan, sellers/creditors import products in

DOI: 10.4324/9781003245476-3

cash from other countries. They then sell them, mostly on credit, to buyers/debtors using a weekly payment system, which in most of the country it is called *ugraee*.

Contracts are not a tool for *ex ante* allocation of risk; rather they are flexible risk-sharing arrangements forming the basis of an ongoing business relationship. Credit sales are the norm in Afghanistan even though delays in payment, but not nonpayment, are very common. Buyers/debtors commonly fail to make scheduled payments or underpay. Sellers/creditors strategy of response is wait and follow-up.

In Afghanistan, sellers/creditors bear the cost of capital and market uncertainties. If a buyer/debtor is not paid for a product he has bought on credit, he is excused from paying the seller/creditor on the agreed due date. This creates a veil between personal assets and business assets and, to a lesser extent, between personal assets and assets used for different business purposes. Therefore, a merchant with sizable assets is often excused from paying for a purchase until he has been paid for the sale of a product he has bought on credit—even if he entered *ex ante* into a written commitment to pay for the purchase on a specific date.

Under this arrangement, a contract is not a tool for the allocation of risk. A buyer/debtor only pays when he is paid for the product he purchased on credit; this means creditors receive irregular payments based on prevailing market conditions. As a merchant in Herat said, "I am owed a million dollars by people in the market, but I cannot be sure if I can collect 1,000 USD this week from the market!"[2]

Sellers/creditors cannot use contracts to allocate market risks because buyers/debtors are not willing to accept fixed payment terms even in exchange for a discounted price. As a manufacturer in Herat explained, "People would not pay in cash even if I give them big discounts. Everyone wants to buy on credit."[3] Buyers/debtors are not willing to bear the market risk because the Afghanistan business climate is so uncertain, and profit margins are low because retail markets are very competitive. Therefore, in most sectors, bearing market risk by committing to an inflexible payment schedule requires significant capital or market power. If a buyer/debtor has sufficient capital, he moves up in the supply chain and becomes a seller/creditor, as often happens when a buyer/debtor accumulates enough capital.

No single variable can explain the supply and demand for trade credit. In the trade credit literature, the following are suggested as the main determinants of trade credit: weak legal system (weak contract enforcement and weak property rights), lack of access to bank loans, competitive market, and corruption.[4] In the case of Afghanistan, market competition combined with the risk-sharing features of the prevailing trade credit structure is the primary determinant of the supply and demand for trade credit. Lack of access to banks likely plays a role as well. However, it is impossible to know the role of access to bank loans because it would require observing Afghan merchants' behavior in an institutional environment where they had better access to bank loans.

Market competition animates the provision of trade credit in Afghanistan. A seller/creditor sells on credit because if he does not do so, he loses market share. When asked about the reason he sells on credit despite complaining about payment delays, a Nangarhari merchant said, "If I don't sell on credit, I won't sell."[5]

Afghan markets are highly competitive because it is far easier for newcomers to access trade credit than it is to access start-up financing. This means newcomers crowd in and rise within existing markets, increasing the internal competition within already existing supply chains. In the trade credit literature, it is generally accepted that trade credit puts start-ups at a disadvantage because they are less likely to have established reputations.[6] In Afghanistan, however, start-up status is not as important as the sector that a start-up enters. Newcomers can easily obtain trade credit even with minimum reputation, but they can only do so as distributors of the existing sellers/creditors. Start-ups cannot access credit to implement a new idea or create new markets.

The most appealing feature of trade credit for Afghan merchants, which has caused its popularity, is that it facilitates a risk-sharing system where the debtor/buyer can pass market uncertainty and capital cost to sellers/creditors, who are better positioned to bear the burden of risk. Given Afghanistan's highly volatile business climate, the risk-sharing feature of trade credit allows larger firms (sellers/creditors) to act as financial intermediaries improving access to credit for smaller firms (buyers/debtors) while maximizing their sales. This process is perpetuated by market competition.

Ge and Qiu differentiate between trade credit as a transactional tool, that is, short-term and less-overdue debt, and trade credit as a financing tool, that is, longer-term and more overdue debt.[7] According to their research in China, empirical firm-level data suggest that for non-state-owned enterprises, trade credit is a way for suppliers to help their customers with financing who have limited access to bank loans.[8] In Afghanistan, my research suggests that trade credit is a financing tool as well, but risk-sharing has a prominent role. In trade credit literature, however, risk-sharing is not a salient function of trade credit.

The hypothesis that trade credit is a way for suppliers to finance their customers (e.g. to keep them in business) is contradicted by the observation that large, established suppliers also receive trade credit and most often receive more and better trade credit (compared to capital-poor businesses). This is because large buyers have more market power, but it is interesting that they do not use their market power to obtain discounted prices as much as they do to obtain trade credit. Klapper and his colleagues suggest the reason for this may be because untrusted suppliers need to extend trade credit to provide a guaranty for the quality of their products.[9] Menichini, on the other hand, posits that trade credit may be a way for a business to hedge its receivables.[10] It also may be because a business has problems collecting the debt from its customer, so it delays paying its suppliers.[11]

In Afghanistan, manufacturers, producers, or service providers who buy some of their input from domestic suppliers receive trade credits on better terms compared to smaller businesses. The main reason for this is market power. Larger businesses present less risk, as selling to a large manufacturing business poses less risk of nonpayment and delays in payment compared to a smaller business. Most merchants would prefer to have a capital-intensive large manufacturing business as debtor/buyer than a smaller business. This gives large businesses market power which they use to extract better credit terms but not necessarily discounted prices since profit margins are already slim for seller/creditors. The reasons why larger businesses opt to extract better credit terms rather than discounted prices are the hedging and guaranty functions of trade credit.

In Afghanistan, the use of trade credit as a hedging tool is clearly observable. Research interviews reveal that businesses, large or small, will demand trade credit because they have to offer it to their customers. Merchants want to be sure that if they are not paid for their receivables, they can pass a part of that burden on to their suppliers by not paying their payables. Therefore, most buyers/debtors opt for trade credit even when offered good discounts for a cash purchase. However, sellers/creditors who import their products do not have this option because they do not have access to trade credit when they purchase from suppliers located outside of Afghanistan. I later discuss Afghan merchants' access to trade credit from suppliers located outside Afghanistan.

The use of trade credit as a guaranty of quality finds empirical support in Afghanistan as well. New producers and importers start by offering very good trade credit terms to get buyers/debtors to sell their products in their stores, whereas more established products do not have to be as generous with their credit terms because buyers/debtors will have to buy their products as consumers demand them.

The research presented here does not show a correlation between weak contract enforcement and an increase in trade credit. As explained in Chapter 2, weak contract enforcement is not a main reason banks do not issue bank loans in Afghanistan. The weak system of property rights, however, impedes the collateralization of bank loans and, therefore, contributes to the prevalence of trade credit by reducing the bank loan supply. Lack of a strong property rights system, such as clear and reliable titles, is limiting the issuance of bank loans and increasing the need for trade credit. Similarly, the current property rights system also impedes the enforcement of court judgments, reducing the effectiveness of formal dispute resolution in enforcing credit transactions.

Afghanistan has been plagued with corruption; however, the research presented in this study does not suggest a direct connection between corruption and the widespread use of trade credit in Afghanistan. Instead, market competition causes the supply of trade credit, and the risk-sharing-enabling drives the demand for it in Afghanistan. This finding shows that the relationship between corruption and market monopoly is not a necessary relationship. While in the literature corruption is found to reduce market competition, and therefore, the supply of trade credit, in Afghanistan, despite highly corrupt formal institutions, corruption has not reduced market competition in most major provinces and, therefore, has not impeded the provision of trade credit. This divergence is likely due to the risk-sharing-enabling feature of trade credit, which reduces the barriers to entry in the supply chains, making trade credit most prominent in the supply chains in Afghanistan. Corruption does impede competition in the public procurement sector, however.

Market Competition and Provision of Trade Credit

Afghan merchants can easily access credit inside Afghanistan. Sellers/creditors provide trade credit because buyers/debtors have more market power. Interviewed sellers/creditors indicate that the reason they have to sell on credit, even though payments are often delayed, is market competition.[12] This finding is unexpected because in the literature, it is often argued that in places where informal institutions prevail, high barriers to entry lead to better access to credit for insiders by solving the problem of credible commitment.[13] However, in Afghanistan, interview data suggest that in places where barriers to entry are lower, because of geographical location and/or the presence of a well-developed *Sarrafi* market, credit sales are more common.[14] Highly competitive supply chains give buyers/debtors more market powers in provinces with lower barriers to entry, forcing sellers/creditors to supply trade credit and bear the risk of an uncertain business climate to retain customers.

In Afghanistan, most consumers are very poor; therefore, it is difficult for Afghan merchants to distinguish their products by a factor other than price and credit. This may explain why the competitiveness of the market has not caused fierce competition for innovation and an increase in quality. Instead, it has mostly caused competition toward price-cutting and providing better-credit terms. Cash sales are associated with the markets with higher barriers to entry. Interview data suggest that only those sellers who have a quasi-monopoly in their respective markets can require their buyers to pay in cash without experiencing fewer sales. For example, a tire cap producer in Herat said that he only sells on cash.[15] "I can sell on cash without losing customers because I am the only producer of this product."[16]

The hypothesis that market competition is the main cause of an increase in credit sales is supported by the observation that credit sales are the norm in each of the five research sites with the exception of Balkh. As explained in Chapter 2, Balkh has the most monopolistic economy of the five major provinces studied here (measured by per capita business registry). Balkh has an underdeveloped *Sarrafi* market, which means there is a higher capital requirement for sellers/creditors. Balkh also borders with the Central Asian countries. It is harder for sellers/creditors to establish relationships with suppliers located in Central Asian countries. Due to the history of communism in those countries, states still have large control in the market, and competition is very low (Turkmenistan, Uzbekistan, and Tajikistan). This means only a limited number of Afghan creditors/sellers have the capital and connections to establish business relations and import products from Central Asian countries. In contrast, Herat, Nangarhar, and Kandahar are located on the border of either Iran or Pakistan, where, for reasons which I examine later, it is easier for Afghan sellers/creditors to establish business connections and import products. In short, barriers to entry are lower in Herat, Kandahar, Nangarhar, and Kabul compared to Balkh due to their different geopolitical and geo-economic positioning, as well as their access to a well-developed *Sarrafi* market. I return to the case of Balkh in the discussion of *Sarrafi* markets.

Weekly Payment System (*Ugraee*)[17]

Sellers/creditors are paid for their credit sales through a weekly payment system, *ugraee*. *Ugraee* is basically a system of payment and a revolving line of credit.

Under the *ugraee* system, a buyer/debtor purchases a product without immediate payments in exchange for a promise to make weekly payments that are made on a certain date at the end of every week (Diagram 2.1). Buyers/debtors need to make weekly payments to receive further sale credit. However, justified short-term delays are common and often excused. When either party, seller/creditor or buyers/debtors, exists in the markets, however, weekly payments are often discontinued, and disputes are likely to arise.

When a seller/creditor exits the market, the buyers/debtors do not have an incentive to continue making weekly payments as the supply of the product is discontinued. Additionally, the buyer/debtor will have to redirect weekly payments to a new supplier or another extant supplier to ensure continued supply of the product. If a buyer/debtor exits the market, the seller/creditor does not have a reason to excuse delays because the sellers/creditors do not expect further sales to existing buyers/debtors. Additionally, existing buyer/debtors pose a greater risk of nonpayments due to their diminished incentive to pay (they no longer value the relationship). Thus, the prevailing supply chain structure locks parties into existing supply chains, creating market inefficiency.[18]

Ugraee is a tool that imposes financial discipline on the buyers/debtors. As a weekly payment system, *ugraee* has the following objectives: (1) to reduce the time lag between when a product is sold and when the seller/creditor is paid so the buyer/debtor is not able to use the money for other purposes, (2) to reduce the amount of each weekly installments to a manageable amount so that the buyer/debtor is able to pay, (3) to stay informed of the financial status and solvency of the buyer/debtor—collecting these weekly payments most often means that the seller/creditor or his agent visit the buyer/debtor place of business every week. This way if a seller/creditor notices that the buyer/debtor has sold the products, but he is not paying him to make payments to other sellers/creditors, or because he is about to go bankrupt or exit the market, the seller/creditor may discontinue his sales to the buyer/debtor or, in rare cases, repossess his products. In short, for sellers/creditors, *ugraee* is a tool to impose financial discipline on the buyers/debtors.

Ugraee is a very pervasive system; most interviewees said they operate under the *ugraee* system. However, the system is most visible within supply chains. The weekly payment system is so pervasive that it has conditioned the whole economy, even in the sectors where it is not necessarily used. For example, it has become a norm that creditors cannot expect repayment of debts early in the week because it normally takes several days for the money, coming from cash sales to consumers, to get channeled through retailers and wholesale distributors, where it is accumulated and paid to importers and producers. This weekly payment system is part of the reason why *Sarrafs* need to give their clients short-term working capital loans—although they are not called loans—so they can meet their financial requirements to the suppliers located outside of Afghanistan, where the flexible weekly payment system is not in place. These short-term working capital loans are often paid back using the weekly payment system.

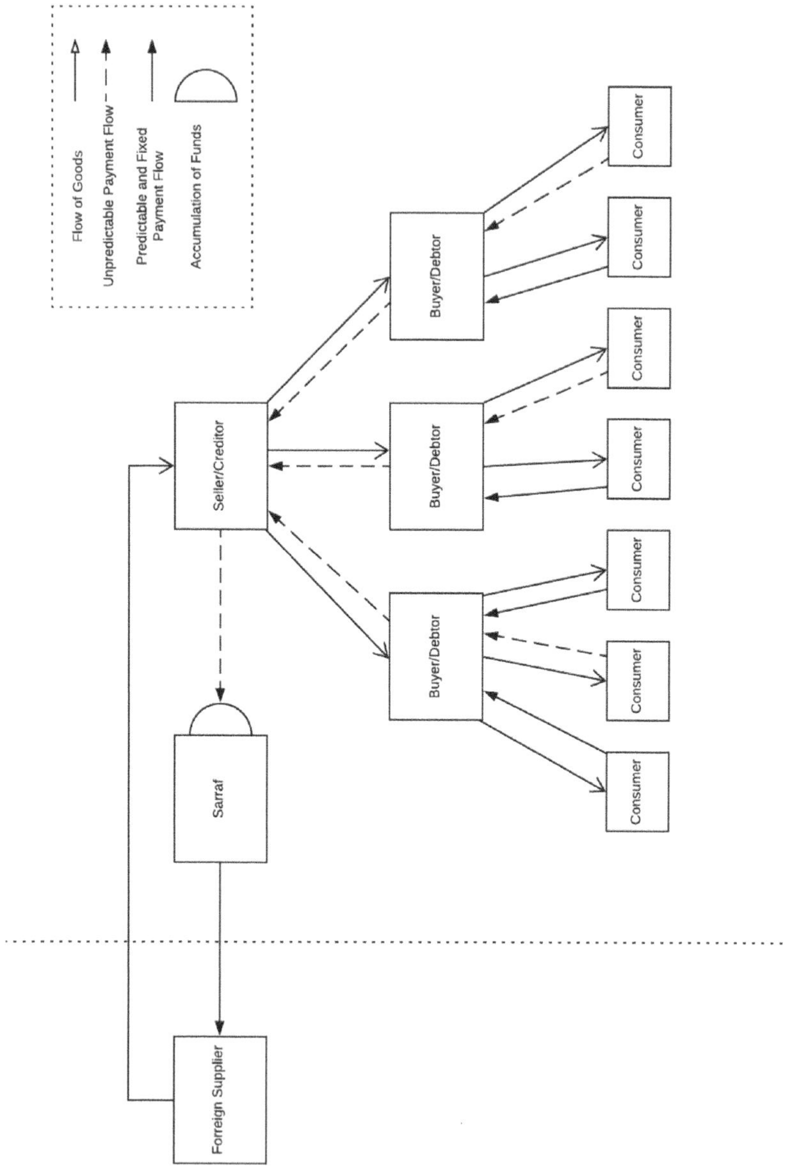

Diagram 2.1 Supply Chain Financing in Afghanistan

How Businesses Come to Trust Credit Sales in Afghanistan

It is not hard for a debtor/buyer to obtain trade credit inside Afghanistan (it is also not hard for sellers/creditors to obtain working capital loans from *Sarraf*s). Most dealings in Afghanistan are conducted based on *shenakht*, that is, knowing. It means a buyer/debtor can receive credit if the seller/creditor thinks that he can be trusted. There are several ways that *shenakht* can be established. A buyer can start buying in cash and establish a relationship. Or a buyer has a personal link to the seller, that is, they are friends, related, neighbor, part of a *qawm* (an imagined community of people with a common ancestor), etc., which enables a buyer to establish *shenakht* based on an existing relationship. Most commonly, however, it suffices that a buyer owns or runs a store or a place of business in a local marketplace. Buyer may also establish a relationship by using *wasata*, or an intermediary, to make the connection with the seller.

Although all four means of acquiring *shenakht* are used in the five regions studied, there is variation among cases. When asked how they determine to sell to someone on credit, interviewees in Nangarhar attributed greater weight to the fact that the buyer/debtor has a presence in the marketplace, meaning usually that the buyer/debtor has a store or a place of business in the market.[19] This implies a much more physical conception of market and business partners. Interviewees in Herat and Kabul talked about credit relations in a much more abstract way.[20]

When asked about problems with payment, most interviewees in Nangarhar responded that they were concerned primarily with the end-of-business nonpayment.[21] They assumed that the only occasion when a debtor/buyer will not pay is when he has left the market, for example, has sold his store and his house (again a much more physical sense of market and credit relationship). They assumed that the person could not refuse to pay and still be active in the market. Because of this assumption, when they were asked under which conditions, they would go to courts, they listed only nonpayment and cases of insolvency. This is consistent with the data on the use of commercial courts discussed in Chapter 2. Of five major provinces, as discussed in Chapter 2, Nangarhar has one of the lowest rates of court use.

The fourth means of establishing *shenakht* is *wasata*. *Wasata* literally means the middle one, or connector, or intermediary, and it refers to the practice whereby a person uses his *shenakht* with a seller/creditor to vouch for a buyer/debtor who does not have a direct *shenakht* with that seller/creditor. The use of *wasata* allows people to get access to each other's social and business networks. Customarily this intermediary does not guarantee the payment; however, *Sarraf*s, when acting as *wasata*, sometimes do guarantee the payment. Although the intermediary does not usually promise to make the payment if the debtor/buyer fails to pay, the *wasata* will be called upon to locate and pressure the buyer/debtor if the buyer/debtor delays a payment or defaults. The assumption is that the buyer/debtor values his relationship with the *wasata* enough that the buyer/debtor would pay to avoid embarrassing the *wasata*. If the buyer/debtor fails to pay, the *wasata* will lose his credibility in the market and his standing in his social circle. In other words, the intermediary extends his reputation and social status to the buyer/debtor, so the actions of the buyer/debtor reflect on the *wasata* as well.

Sarrafs are the most reliable *wasata*—mostly because they are believed to be capital-rich and very protective of their reputation—arguably their most important asset. *Sarrafs* provide *wasata* services using soft and hard methods. In soft methods, they, like most other *wasata*, just call up a seller/creditor to make an introduction. In the hard method, *Sarrafs* guarantee the payment. They issue written guarantee letters—these are usually in form of postdated checks. When the economy was booming, these postdated checks could have been discounted to obtain cash at any moment, but as the market slowed down, the discounting of *Sarrafs*' checks became less common, and in some markets, it has been banned.[22]

Interview data suggest that *Sarrafs*' checks are used more often to guarantee payments among parties that cannot secure a credible relationship using *wasata*, past dealings, or personal relations and do not operate in the same marketplace.[23] This means *Sarrafs*' checks are most common in sectors that involve one-time large deals between non-repeating parties. *Sarrafs* rely on their extensive nationwide networks to facilitate credit dealings between businesses that do not have direct relationships with each other. They provide devices that are comparable to a domestic letter of credit.

Written guarantees—*which would be a legally enforceable guaranty in courts*[24]—are not common in Afghanistan. With the exception of *Sarrafs*' postdated checks, in Afghanistan's context, it is most common for a guarantor, for example, a *wasata*, to verbally vouch for a debtor/buyer. Most guarantees are conducted verbally, in local vernacular called *lafzy* (adj. *lafzy*; noun *lafz*). *Lafz* literarily means "word," but it has a stronger connotation akin to the English phrase of "giving your word" as a promise to someone.

Kabul interview data suggests that the use of written guaranty is also sector-variant.[25] Construction companies are required to provide a letter of guarantee issued by a bank to the government or international organization which solicit most of the construction contracts. Construction companies, in turn, require the subcontractors to provide them with written guarantees, as one Kabuli construction company owner said.[26] The same interviewee also mentioned that they require major subcontractors to deposit cash as a guaranty.[27] The use of cash as a guaranty shows the ineffectiveness of other forms of guarantee that require extra steps, either judicial or nonjudicial before enforcement can be achieved.

Construction companies can require written and/or cash guarantees because they have considerable market power in relation to their subcontractors. To acquire a construction deal as the main contractor requires substantial resources and strong connections—competition is low given that the procurement sector is rife with corruption. The number of construction companies that can secure large construction deals are limited. The market for large construction and logistics deals is essentially an oligopoly (mostly dominated by well-connected players). The subcontracting market, on the other hand, is very competitive. It is much easier to enter into the subcontracting market for logistic and construction contracts. This creates a situation where large construction companies have a lot of leverage against subcontractors and can demand terms that are very favorable toward them.

Therefore large construction companies can demand cash deposits as guaranty before giving out a subcontract deal.

Interview data suggest that ethnicity, *qawm* (i.e. an extensive network of imagined blood relations), and *madhab* (i.e. belonging to Shi'a or Sunni religious grouping) differences are *not* impeding trade in Afghanistan.[28] Inter-ethnical, inter-*qawm*, and inter-*madhab* dealings are the norm of business in all research sites. Ethnicity, *qawm*, and *madhab* not only fail to constrain trade, but they also actually facilitate trade.[29] They facilitate credit transactions by providing *shenakht*.[30]

Non-Afghans are Disadvantaged as Credit Transaction Partners[31]

Institutions supporting credit transactions in Afghanistan are effective and inclusive for those who are part of Afghan society. Afghan buyers/debtors have easy access to trade credit from sellers/creditors located inside Afghanistan if buyers/debtors are part of Afghan society. A buyer/debtor does not have to be an insider with relation to a certain market, a certain ethnic group, or a certain province to obtain trade credit. My research suggests it is not difficult for a buyer/debtor to draw on a cross-section of personal, social, economic, and/or financial networks of *Sarrafs* to obtain credit from a seller/creditor that occupies a distant social, ethnic, or even geographical position inside Afghanistan.[32] Conversely, if a debtor/buyer is not part of Afghan society, for example, a debtor/buyer who is a non-Afghan doing business in Afghanistan, he would be at a disadvantage.

A non-Afghan's disadvantage stems from his higher information costs and his lack of credibility. A non-Afghan merchant can partly remedy his informational disadvantage by residing in Afghanistan. However, he can only partly solve the problem because some sources of information stem from a range of social relations that even a resident non-Afghan cannot access (e.g. familiar connections). If a non-Afghan has a significant presence in Afghanistan, he will have more access, and some of his disadvantages will be reduced. However, because institutions supporting credit transactions in Afghanistan rely heavily on social connections and the rich inflow of information that stems from those connections, a resident non-Afghan is still at a disadvantage.

Under this system, a non-Afghan is simply a less credible credit-transaction partner. The informal institutions that support credit transactions in Afghanistan rely on a stable connection between a debtor/buyer and a locality within Afghanistan. They assume that an Afghan buyer/debtor cannot just leave the whole social system; however, a non-Afghan can. This reduces the ability of a non-Afghan to credibly commit. Formal contracts may help reduce the problem of credible commitment for a non-Afghan, however, it can only partially do so. Several interviewees in Kabul[33] and Kandahar mentioned that they were owed by foreigners doing business in Afghanistan.[34] The foreign debtor left the country without paying, and they had no recourse against them. One interviewee said, "[former] Afghan government was no help. I tried to sue him in Turkey, but it did not work."[35] In short, institutions supporting credit transactions in Afghanistan are most often only effective and inclusive for those who are part of Afghan society.

A non-Afghan seller/creditor is similarly at a disadvantage because he does not have full access to the institutions that ensure the enforcement of credit transactions. A non-Afghan can remedy his outsider status through a partnership with a local Afghan merchant. This way a foreigner can gain access to the networks of the local partner and remedy his outsider status. Therefore, it is common for foreigners to form a partnership with local Afghans. This often facilitates the transfer of know-how in Afghanistan.

While some countries require foreign investors to form joint ventures as a condition of entering their domestic markets (a rule designed to facilitate technology and know-how transfer),[36] in Afghanistan the same effect is achieved through informal means. The informality of Afghan business forces foreigners to do business in partnership with local merchants, which results in the transfer of know-how and technology. Most often Afghan partners split from the foreign investors and create their own business or force out the foreign investors and gain control of the joint business. (I personally worked for several Afghan businesses as an accountant, and this is exactly what those businesses did.)[37] This dynamic points to the negative effect of the informality of the Afghan market when it comes to foreign investors: they have very limited power in relation to their domestic partners, and it disincentivizes entrance into Afghan markets by foreign investors. As such, Afghanistan needs to improve the legal protection of foreign investors to incentivize foreign investment in Afghanistan. This is another reason that the improvement of formal dispute resolution institutions and depersonalization of business relations are necessary for long-term economic growth in Afghanistan.

Outsourcing of Buyers/Debtors' Vetting and Debt Collection

This study shows sellers/creditors in Afghanistan do not outsource debt collection and vetting of buyers/debtors.[38] Sellers/creditors could outsource debt collection by using independent sale representatives who would vet buyer/debtor, collect the weekly payments, and bear the risk of irregular payments and/or nonpayments, in exchange for a commission fee. This way, theoretically, sellers/creditors would be able to receive regular payments in predictable amounts in exchange for a premium. However, sellers/creditors in Afghanistan do not outsource vetting and debt collection.

There is a market gap here. Given the high cost of collecting debt and the prevalence of the *ugraee* payment system in Afghanistan, one would expect sellers/creditors to be eager to outsource debt collection and vetting of buyers/debtors. Sale representatives could arguably operate with lower marginal cost, taking advantage of the economies of scale and pooling of information. One would expect to see a great market for debt collection in Afghanistan, but that market has not developed yet. There was only one company, Bamsa, which collected debt and vetted buyers/debtors as an independent business.[39] However, this company was established with foreign aid funding, and it works only with consumer-buyers who are mostly government employees.[40] They ensure repayments of the debt by reaching an agreement with the governmental departments to subtract the payments from the buyers' salaries.[41]

A small percentage of sellers/creditors do use sales representatives who work on commission for marketing and sales. Only three interviewees mentioned that they use sales representatives to sell their products, one in Kabul, one in Kandahar, and one in Balkh.[42] But these sale representatives do not bear the risk of irregular and/or nonpayments.

There may be several reasons why debt collection markets have not developed in Afghanistan. One reason for the absence of a debt collection market in Afghanistan is the personal nature of the debt. The debt is not easily transferable in Afghanistan, either legally or practically. Legally, it is complicated to transfer debt under Afghan laws.[43] But as this study has shown, the law does not have much bearing on how businesses operate. Practically, buyers/debtors establish relationships with the sellers/creditors. This relationship is more like a risk-sharing and cooperation arrangement without a strict allocation of risk. This creates a problem for assigning the debt to someone else because, in this context, debt is not a strict monetary claim against the debtor but rather an uncertain financial interest. Furthermore, credit relationships are very personal. People care very much about with whom they work, to whom they owe money, and who comes to their place of business to collect the debt. As a Herati merchant stated, "Our customers do not like anyone showing up at their place of business asking for payment."[44]

Use of Written Contracts

Another institutional feature of business in Afghanistan which facilitates credit transactions is written contracts. Interview data reveal the following about the use of written contracts in Afghanistan's business context. First, putting things in writing has an important symbolic significance. It could be surmised from interview data that making people sign a written document invokes a higher internal commitment. Afghans seem to take their written commitments more seriously. It is an interesting way of solving the problem of credible commitment. Merchants can often obtain trade credit that they otherwise would not have access to by signing a written paper saying that they will make payments on time.

The internal and symbolic force of written commitments is reinforced with an external enforcement mechanism as well. Interview data suggest the reason merchants sometimes put their dealings in writing is to make the transaction verifiable. Therefore, merchants are more likely to use written contracts when they believe they will likely need to prove the transaction to a third party. This third party may be but is not necessarily a court. In fact, when it comes to commercial disputes, most often the third party to which the merchants will refer their dispute is another merchant or a group of merchants who are willing to mediate the dispute.

Merchants are more likely to use written documents if they do not know the other party well enough, when the contract is complicated and is for a long time, and if the other person's financial status is a concern. Similarly, interview data show that it is common practice for a creditor to obtain a written certification of the debt after default in exchange for a discount or extension on the term of debt as part of intraparty negotiations. This is because the creditor is expecting that he will need to prove the debt and default in front of a third party at that point, whether a court or a union or a *jirga*, so having a written certificate will be useful.

There is variation among cases studied here when it comes to the use of written contracts. Kabulis, Heratis, and Balkhis are more likely to use written contracts.[45] Kandaharis and Nangarharis are less likely to write down their agreements.[46] There is an aversion to the use of written contracts in Nangarhar. Unlike Kabul, Herat, and Balkh, where the use of written agreements—such as written contracts, receipts, or checks—is common, in Nangarhar there seems to be a unanimous aversion to the use of written contracts.[47] As one Nangarhari merchant said, "People do not like to sign papers here. I cannot ask a customer to even sign the invoice, let alone a contract."[48] Based on interview data, I hypothesize it is because the use of written contracts implies distrust and suspicion, which is more strongly frowned upon in Pashtun culture—the dominant culture in Nangarhar, which is a predominantly Pashtun province. This would also explain why Kandaharis, who are also predominately Pashtun, exhibit a similar aversion—although not to the same degree.[49]

The low rate of use of written and signed documents in Kandahar and Nangarhar, which is instrumental informal dispute resolution proceedings, can also explain why these two provinces have a considerably lower rate of per capita use of the court. I return to the low court-use rate in Kandahar and Nangarhar later.

It should also be noted that the worsening of market conditions and increased risk of disputes affect the willingness of merchants to use written contracts. Interviewees reported that the use of written contracts has increased in the market because the economy has slowed down, and credit dealings entail a higher risk. As the owner of a construction company in Kabul said, "In the past, we only worked verbally [i.e. *lafzy*] but some people denied that we gave them marble. For example, we had sent three shipments they said they only received two. Now, we use written contracts where we specify the time of payment and number of the shipment."[50] He added, "Written contracts are better. You are surer when you have a written contract. We wouldn't use it in courts but when there is a written contract the other party fears and complies. Also, if we decided to go to a third party it is easy to prove the other party cannot deny it." He further stated, "We also add to the contract the condition for termination of the contract. That helps too." He expressed, "If you have only a verbal contract, there is nothing you can do."

Trade Credit Versus Bank Loans

The trade credit literature generally argues that sellers/creditors are better positioned, compared to banks, to issue credit because they have access to better information, and they have lower liquidation costs. Because sellers/creditors operate in the same market as their debtors/buyers, they have access to low-cost information about the financial status of their debtors/buyers and can resell the products should the buyers/debtors default. The former is true in Afghanistan; however, the latter is not. Sellers/creditors in Afghanistan have continued interaction with debtors/buyers through *ugraee*. They also receive reputation information faster and cheaper since they operate in the same marketplace and the same sector as their debtors/buyers. Compared to banks, sellers/creditors have access to better and lower-cost information on the financial status of debtors/buyers and their prospect of payments (as explained previously, banks try to remedy their informational disadvantage by resorting to "relationship banking"). Conversely, in Afghanistan, lower liquidation costs cannot explain the difference between the ability of sellers/creditors and banks to evaluate debtors. This is because, according to interview data, repossession of sold goods is rare.[51] In Afghanistan, a seller/creditor cannot expect to be paid if the product has not been sold. This means that as long as a product is in the possession of a buyer/debtor, that is, it is not sold, the creditors/sellers cannot expect to be paid. Therefore, repossession is not a remedy for default; instead, it is a precondition for payment.

Yano and Shiraishi argue that trade credit is efficient because profitability is more strongly linked with trade credit than with bank loans.[52] Their research corroborated Fisman and Love's findings[53] that smaller firms have more difficulty obtaining trade credit because they have not established yet a reputation; however, they found that profitability and access to trade credit are more strongly linked for medium and small firms compared to large firms.[54] This means that credit helps with the entrance and survival of small- and medium-sized firms. Medium-sized firms are most helped with trade credit because they also have the reputations.

The case of Afghanistan confirms Yano and Shiraishi's findings that trade credit is helping small- and medium-sized firms, which are buyers/debtors, to enter the market and survive. On the relative profitability of beneficiaries of trade credit and banks' loans, the data is not conclusive in Afghanistan. However, the data suggests that large businesses, who are the borrowers of banks' loans, are more profitable than smaller businesses in Afghanistan, businesses that are receivers of trade credit.[55] Therefore, in Afghanistan, bank loans may be more strongly correlated with profitability. This is expected because banks are very discriminating in the issuance of bank loans in Afghanistan. In China, on the other hand, banks are inclined to issue loans to state-owned enterprises, which are less productive compared to private enterprises, which rely on trade credit.[56]

Cull, Xu, and Zhu, in their research of formal finance and trade credit during China's economic transition, found that state-owned enterprises as well as profitable private firms did lend-on part of the loans they received from banks to their customers, which made the allocation of resources by banks more efficient. However, according to their research, the size of this lend-on was not significant enough to explain Chinese economic growth.[57] Other institutions, either formal or informal, must have played more important roles, they concluded.[58] In Afghanistan, lend-on does not seem to be as important given the small share of bank loans as a source of capital.

Demirgiiu-Kunt and Maksimovic studied the role of firms as financial intermediaries.[59] They found that from a policy standpoint, lend-on is important because the use of trade credit decreases as a legal system improves, meaning that lend-on is a way to make up for a weak legal system where a sizable banking market is present.[60] In the case of Afghanistan, this analysis does not hold because Afghanistan does not possess a strong banking sector.[61] In addition, although this research has not collected data on the temporal variation in the use of trade credit, most interviewees reported that over the last few years, the demand for trade credit has increased while its supply has decreased.[62] While the quality of the legal system arguably improved over the same period (if one takes the number of judges as a measure), it did not cause the decline in the supply of trade credit in Afghanistan. Rather the decrease in the supply of trade credit in Afghanistan has been caused by worsening of market conditions. Worsening of macroeconomic conditions has decreased the willingness of the sellers/creditors to invest (so they do not import or distribute as much) while increasing the risk of debtors/buyers' default. Therefore, the positive correlation in Afghanistan between improvement of the formal legal system and increase in trade credit is spurious.

The research on the relationship between financial crises and bank loans, on the one hand, and trade credit supply and demand, on the other hand, has yielded contradictory findings. Garcia-Appendini and Montoriol-Garriga argued that during the 2007–2008 US financial crisis, cash-rich firms provided liquidity to their customers, as bank loans contracted, in the form of trade credit because their opportunity cost decreased.[63] There are other studies that suggest, during financial crises and bank loan contraction, trade credit supply decreases as trade credit demand increases and that net trade credit is positively correlated with bank loans.[64] Whether trade credit is a supply-driven dynamic, as shown by the decrease of supply, or a demand-driven dynamic, as shown by the increase of trade credit demand at the time of bank loan contraction, is still an open question.

Inasmuch as the relationship between trade credit and financial crisis is concerned, Afghanistan was going through a period of economic slowdown at the time of my field research, which has continued until today. However, the dynamic of Afghanistan's economic slowdown is not comparable to those of a developed economy. Afghanistan's economic slowdown is mostly caused by an increase in insecurity, political instability, and a decrease in the inflow of foreign aid. It would be impossible to draw a correlation between contraction of banks loans and economic slowdown as banks play a limited role in the capital market to begin with. However, interview data suggests that as the economy slows down, buyers/debtors demand more trade credit, while sellers/creditors contract the provision of trade credit.[65] In the meantime, it seems that seller/creditor demand for working capital loans from *Sarrafs* increase so they can continue to provide trade credit albeit at a lower rate.[66]

The pervasiveness of trade credit in Afghanistan means that the Afghan economy is very vulnerable. Trade credit, compared to bank loans, is not well diversified because buyers/debtors are the customers of sellers/creditors.[67] If a sector experiences slowdown, there will be a ripple effect through the whole economy affecting buyers/debtors, sellers/creditors, and *Sarrafs*. This makes the Afghan economy very vulnerable to sectoral shocks.

Sources of Initial Capital to Start a Business

Almost all interviewees reported that they use the revenue from their previous business ventures as initial capital for their current business.[68] Merchants start small, most often as a retailer, which requires little capital, and then if successful, they grow by reinvesting their earnings and by increasing their debt-capital ratio. This suggests that businesses grow along very narrow market paths. For example, a successful businessman runs a store where he sells shampoo bought on credit from a seller/creditor. Next, he expands and becomes a wholesale distributor who distributes shampoo bought on credit from domestic sellers/creditors wholesale. Next, he becomes an importer of shampoo, and in rare cases, he may advance to become a shampoo producer. This means that existing markets become highly competitive, and new markets do not get created. It is very difficult to find someone to finance a new idea. Similarly, it is extremely difficult to secure a long-term loan to enter a new market.

Bank loans were very difficult to secure without valuable real estate with a formal deed, and as seen in Chapter 2, formal deeds are scarce in Afghanistan, even before the Taliban takeover threatened the survival of the financial system.[69] Although the law provides for the use of movable property as collateral for banks' loans,[70] de facto, banks in Afghanistan only accept real estate as collateral.[71] Afghanistan has created an online registry for the registration of immovable property as collateral, but the project has generally been unsuccessful.[72]

Banks only accept real estate as collateral because it is easier to collect against real estate. Once it is formally registered as collateral, banks, in the event of default, can bring an action to liquidate the real estate regardless of which person has possession. The purchase of real estate under the name of a business is not common in Afghanistan—with exception of the purchase of land for a factory. Manufacturers can only purchase land in an industrial town as a corporation. The fact that most businesses in Afghanistan do not own real estate means that to receive a bank loan, a person must put down his personal property as collateral. This represents a high degree of risk. In addition, in a business with multiple equity partners, it would require one partner to accept higher risk—this is what a Kabuli merchant said.[73]

Even if a business or an equity partner owns real estate and is willing to use it as collateral, banks only accept it if the owner has a formal deed. As explained in Chapter 2, in Afghanistan, formal deeds are scarce. Afghanistan lacks a property registry.[74] Most real estate is bought and sold informally without registration. Several decades of civil war and immigration mean that those who possess property may not be the actual owner. It is common for estates to go several generations without being divided and distributed among inheritors. In short, it is very difficult to verify someone's title over a real estate; therefore, reliable formal deeds are scarce. Even if someone could secure a formal deed, the interest rate and the terms of payment rendered bank loans unappealing, according to interviewees.[75] *Sarrafi* long-term interest-bearing loans are easier to obtain, but the interest rates are even higher.[76]

There is an added difficulty when it comes to borrowing from banks: banks require merchants to adhere to inflexible repayment schedules backed by the threat of formal legal actions. Merchants sell on credit and take in highly unpredictable payments. It is very difficult for them to adhere to an inflexible repayment schedule.

Therefore, they prefer trade credit and *Sarrafs*' loans.[77] Trade credit is the most flexible; however, *Sarrafs*' loans payments are more flexible than bank payments.

Interview data also confirms that low financial literacy among the owners of Afghan businesses is impeding their access to bank loans.[78] A Kabuli merchant said, "The reason Afghan merchants do not take bank loans but have no problem taking loans from *Sarraf* is poor management. They cannot work with banks, but *Sarrafs* use old-fashioned accounting and relation-based business, so Afghans are more comfortable working with *Sarrafs*."[79]

Afghan businesses are also less likely to hire trained accountants. This may be the reason that they are not equipped to work with banks in terms of producing the required financial and business documents and reports. Poor financial management within Afghan businesses, in turn, makes it difficult for banks to assess loans applicants and/or measure risk. Compounding the problem is that, according to several reports, Afghan banks have the limited institutional capacity to assess loan applicants and measure risk.[80] In addition, Afghan banks lack sufficient qualified staff that could review and assess loan applications and measures risk.[81] The low capacity on the side of applicants, along with the limited capacity on the side of banks, is a further constraint on the issuance of bank loans in Afghanistan.

Prevailing Institutions in Afghanistan Disincentivize Destructive Innovation and Creative Destruction

Schumpeter identified creative destruction as a solution to the problem of diminishing return and an important source of sustained economic growth.[82] The probability of a destructive innovation in Afghanistan is very low because those who have the capital are invested in maintaining the existing supply chains, and those who do not have the necessary capital cannot obtain financing except within existing supply chains.

The easiest way to start a business in Afghanistan is to enter the supply chain as a retailer.[83] Newcomers have to move up within existing supply chains because they can only rely on trade credit to start a business and to grow. Suppliers are willing to extend credit so they can sell already existing products in already existing markets. It is very hard to break through narrow market paths. Therefore, most merchants in Afghanistan, and many Afghans, complain that "businessmen just copy each other, and no one has a new idea."[84]

Established businesses that have sufficient capital also have an incentive to stay within existing supply chains because, as sellers/creditors, a significant portion of their capital is locked in within the existing supply chains. Some interviewees claimed that almost half of their capital was locked in their receivables.[85] The rough median estimate was one-third.[86] A decision to move out of a supply chain would make it difficult to recover preexisting receivables because the prospect of discontinuity of supply means that buyers/debtors have reduced incentives to pay. Buyers/debtors would need to replace their suppliers, which means they have to stop or reduce making weekly payments to the existing suppliers to make payments to a new supplier.

When a seller/creditor exits the market, the buyers/debtors have no incentive to continue making weekly payments because the supply of goods will be discontinued. Additionally, the buyer/debtor will have to redirect weekly payments to a new supplier or another extant supplier to ensure the continued supply of the goods. If a buyer/debtor exits the market, the seller/creditor does not have a reason to excuse delays because sellers/creditors do not expect to be able to make additional sales to existing buyers/debtors. Additionally, existing buyers/debtors pose a greater risk of nonpayments because they have diminished incentive to pay (they do not value the relationship any longer.)

Nevertheless, business expansion and diversification does happen, as you can see from the list of interviewees. Large businesses (most often sellers/creditors) do engage in multiple markets and sectors.[87] However, business expansion and investing in new ideas happen at a lower rate in Afghanistan. The probability of a destructive innovation in Afghanistan is very low because those who have the capital are invested in maintaining the existing supply chains, and those who do not have the capital cannot obtain financing except within existing supply chains. The Afghan institutional settings do not incentivize innovation because they lock both sides into a web of interrelated credit networks. Afghanistan's institutional settings disincentivize productive investments and are bound to lead to an economic slowdown.

Interview data suggest that most producers are former traders and/or importers of the products they produce.[88] Ease of access to trade credit domestically on the one hand and the difficulty of access to credit outside of Afghanistan on the other favors domestic production. However, it has not resulted in the flourishing of the Afghan manufacturing industry. This is because most raw materials have to be imported. Most Afghan manufacturers produce low value-added products: the difference between the final product value and the manufacturing input is not very high. Although domestic producers can easily buy their inputs domestically on credit, most of the necessary inputs are not available in the domestic market.[89]

Furthermore, the larger amount of initial capital required for manufacturing cannot be raised using the Afghan capital market. Manufacturing businesses require a lot of initial capital that the afghan financial market cannot provide. Banks' and *Sarrafs*' long-term loans are very expensive and hard to secure.[90] In addition to these institutional failures, Afghanistan's manufacturing industry is plagued with corruption and poor infrastructures.[91] In addition, ease of access to credit inside Afghanistan is usually limited to trade credit and working capital loans, not investment financing.[92] These are the reasons why Afghan manufacturers usually only produce products that, if imported, would carry high tariffs and transportation costs or products that do not require a lot of imported raw materials—such as beverages, dairy products, dried fruits.

Agency Costs Limit Business Expansion

Merchants can decide to expand their operations horizontally through the distribution of labor, for example, outsourcing debt collection or subcontracting a construction project, or vertically by expanding their business organization, that is, hiring people to collect a debt or perform a construction project and monitoring them. Agency cost refers to the monitoring cost of ensuring the agent acts in the interest of the principal.[93] Therefore, agency cost is a useful concept to analyze the pattern of horizontal and vertical business expansion and their relations with prevailing institutions in Afghanistan.

According to economists, the institutions that underpin trade credit transactions determine the cost of horizontal expansion. However, they also affect the choice to use these institutions or internalize their objective operation by expanding a business organization. In short, prevailing institutions will determine whether a business decides to use market institutions (horizontal expansions) or hierarchical organizations (vertical expansion). Coase and Williamson's theories are concerned with explaining this choice.[94]

Afghan businesses face high agency costs because the informality of business relations in Afghanistan means business decisions do not easily lend themselves to external evaluation. In Afghanistan, most agents who are entrusted with financial authority in a business are relatives or people who have been made equity partners.[95] This is caused by high agency costs. The only way a principal can be sure that an employee, at the management level with significant financial authority, would work in the principal's interest is to choose the employee from among current equity partners or to make that employee an equity partner. This is because financial decisions in the Afghan context do not easily lend themselves to objective evaluation.

It is difficult to hold a managerial employee accountable for a decision, for example, a decision to sell to someone on credit, if payments are inherently uncertain and unpredictable. In this way, the Afghan business context provides ample opportunity for shirking and collusion. Sellers/creditors counter this risk by giving this financial authority to someone who has an equity interest. This is a reason why the separation of management and ownership is rare in Afghanistan.

High agency costs and the personal nature of the business also contribute to the low number of national businesses in Afghanistan. (The other main reason is the poor transport infrastructure, as discussed in Chapter 2). Most businesses are limited to a single province or a region. Multi-provincial businesses usually have a direct personal presence in multiple provinces. For example, an equity partner or a very close friend or relative heads the business in another province. This may be because businesses need personal and direct knowledge of the other market to be able to work in a credit-based market without impersonal institutions.

Family Businesses in Afghanistan

The research presented here shows that in Afghanistan, most large sellers/creditors, who make up the majority of the sample of interviewees, are family businesses. Virtually all businesses in the sample are family businesses, meaning that equity owners are members of a single family.[96] Family, for the purpose of a family business, generally includes first- and second-degree male family members, that is, father, father's brothers (uncle), and their sons, brothers, and sons. Being a family business has several capital and survival advantages in Afghanistan. Family businesses can more easily pool capital. The literature on the capital market in China suggests borrowing money from friends and family is also a main way to raise capital and start a business in China.[97] In Afghanistan, raising capital from friends and families takes the form of equity financing, not debt financing. Members of a family commonly pool their capital to start or expand a business, and they all become equity partners.

Relatedly, family businesses last longer because, in the case of the death of an equity partner, his share will transfer to other equity partners (who are each other's inheritors). In Afghanistan, often family businesses are started by one family member, commonly a father or a brother. A father or a brother will make his sons and brothers equity partners to ensure the continuation of the business after he dies. This is critical for two reasons. First, Afghanistan adopts Islamic rules of inheritance, which are very egalitarian and anti-capital-accumulation.[98] This means that after an equity partner or founder of a business dies, his estate will be distributed among multiple inheritors. Second, in Afghanistan, separation of ownership and management rarely exists (partly because of high agency cost and informality of economic relations). Most businesses in Afghanistan are manager-owned LLCs; therefore restructuring of ownership, most often, means dismantling the business.

For example, if a merchant dies who has three sons, two daughters, a father, and a mother, they all will inherit a share of his estate according to mandatory rules (this family size is common in Afghanistan). Family businesses ensure the longevity of the business by making all inheritors de facto equity partners. While the legal rights of all family members are not often specified, most inheritors de facto have some ownership share in the business.

The third advantage of a family business in Afghanistan is related to agency cost. Family businesses in Afghanistan have lower agency costs because they have access to a pool of agents: equity partners and their families (nephews, nieces, etc.), who are invested in making the business thrive. After all, they either own equity shares or expect to inherit equity shares in the future. Given the advantages of family businesses, large sellers/creditors in Afghanistan are most often family businesses.

In family businesses, women are not generally active equity partners. Most often, women's share of the inheritance is paid from nonbusiness assets (e.g. house or land) or they become silent equity partners. In the latter case, they receive a share of business revenue—most often a smaller share—through irregular payments, but they are not directly involved in the running of the business. Sometimes, women can become active equity partners through their husbands, most commonly when their husband is already part of a family business as a managerial employee or an equity owner (e.g. when they marry a cousin from their father's side).

The positive correlation between being a family business and longevity and growth of a business explains why virtually all interviewees in the sample said that they were from a merchant family.[99] Given this research mostly comprises sellers/creditors, it can be argued that being a business family, success and longevity of a business are positively correlated in Afghanistan.

Trade Credit from Suppliers Located Outside Afghanistan

Afghan merchants can easily obtain trade credit from sellers/creditors located inside Afghanistan; however, access to trade credit from suppliers located outside of Afghanistan is much more challenging. The many ways that businesses can obtain credit inside Afghanistan (discussed earlier in this chapter) show that Afghan businesses have easy access to trade credit inside Afghanistan. However, when it comes to foreign business sellers/creditors, Afghan businesses face many challenges obtaining credit.

Sellers/creditors in Afghanistan who import products from outside the country must pay on the spot. There are two exceptions to this norm: Pakistan and Iran. Sellers/creditors that have a strong presence in either Pakistan or Iran—i.e. those who have lived and done business there or already have companies in those countries—are able to secure short- to medium-term trade credit from Pakistan and Iran. This is mostly because many Afghans have a long history of living and working in Pakistan and Iran. In the case of Pakistan, Afghan merchants can only access trade credit in sectors, and with businesses, with which they have established personal relations. This means that they are not able to secure credit from large Pakistani businesses. They can only secure credit from small- and medium-sized Pakistani businesses, which conduct their dealings based on personal relations.

In the case of Iran, only those who have an Iranian checkbook can obtain trade credit. This is because, in Iran, checks are the main instrument that is used to back trade credit dealings, according to interviewees.[100] Acquiring a checkbook in Iran requires strong ties and a long and significant presence in Iran. This is probably why Kandaharis have a hard time obtaining credit from Iran, while Heratis and Balkhis are better positioned for it. Herat sits on the border with Iran, and Balkh has a large Shi'a population. Iran, a Shi'a state, provides preferential treatment for Afghan Shi'as.[101]

Even when Afghan sellers/creditors receive trade credit from a foreign business, it is not the same kind of trade credit they issue inside Afghanistan. Credit from foreign businesses is based on a contract that strictly allocates market risk. Afghan sellers/creditors are required to pay for the product that has been imported, regardless of whether the product has been sold or not. This is in direct contrast to the way that domestic credit sales work. In domestic credit sales, a seller/creditor is most often paid if and only if the buyer/debtor has sold the products and has been paid for them.

Interview data suggest that the combination of credit-based business in Afghanistan and the inability of most Afghan sellers/creditors to obtain credit outside the country creates a barrier to entry for import-based businesses, which make up the majority of large businesses in Afghanistan.[102] In Afghanistan, the capital required to operate an import-based business is high because importers have to either buy in cash or on inflexible credit terms and sell in the domestic market on uncertain credit terms. As one Kabuli medicine merchant puts it, "If you want to do business in this market, you need three times the capital that you would need if the market was more cash-based. You have to have 100,000 USD to pay the advance for an order to the Indian supplier, you need an extra 100,000 USD to give credit in the domestic market, and you must have an extra 100,000 USD of inventory in your warehouse so you can fill orders. This way you need to have 300,000 USD where under another model 100,000 USD would be enough because you are buying in cash and selling on credit."[103]

Sarrafs play a vital role in mitigating the burden of buying cash from suppliers located outside of Afghanistan and selling in the domestic, uncertain credit-based market. I return to the topic of the *Sarrafi* market.

Is the Solution Curbing Credit Sales?

Would reducing reliance on credit sales help Afghanistan create sustainable economic growth? The answer is likely no. Contraction of credit sales or imposition of fixed payment terms, theoretically, could reduce merchants' reliance on *Sarrafs* and could improve a merchant's ability to commit to the inflexible repayment terms required by bank loans. However, most Afghans lived below the poverty line at the time of my fieldwork, and now with Taliban in power, Afghans are facing the prospect of universal poverty.[104] The only way to maximize sales is to sell on credit. That is why merchants are doing it. Credit sales help merchants maximize their sales and profits. Curbing credit sales would hurt Afghanistan's economy by reducing sales and increasing prices. It would reduce market competition by increasing the capital required to enter the supply chain, thus, increasing prices. Therefore, curbing credit sales is neither desirable nor possible.

Curbing credit sales is likely impossible in Afghanistan because merchants cannot shift toward cash sales or credit sales with more inflexible repayment terms. This is because Afghanistan espouses a free market economy and has highly competitive retail markets. If a seller/creditor decided to reduce credit sales, he would lose his market share to another seller/creditor who is willing to offer better credit terms. Arguably, to transition toward a less-uncertain credit model of business would require coordinated actions by all sellers/creditors. Such coordinated actions would be impossible since Afghanistan espouses a free market economic model.[105] Taliban have also generally espoused a free market mentality except when they have strong practical incentives; in which case, Taliban have adopted temporary anti–free market measures in certain locales.[106]

Transitioning to a more certain credit model would mean that retailers and smaller businesses would need to take more risks as retailers—as opposed to the current model, where the sellers/creditors who have the most capital bear most of the market risk. Such reallocation of risk would mean that to enter the supply chain, a merchant would need more capital. This would result in less competitive markets and higher prices.

Such a reallocation of risk would, in theory, improve access to credits by allowing businesses to borrow from banks, which would counter increased capital requirements. One could argue that such a transition would improve the overall capital market and access to credit in Afghanistan. However, such a position is premised on the assumption that banks can effectively allocate resources if merchants are more willing to commit to inflexible payment requirements. The data does not seem to support this assumption even before the current sanction-induced crisis. First, as long as Afghanistan does not have a property registry and has not reformed the way formal titles are recorded and verified, it would be very difficult to collateralize a bank loan (even though banks do currently have 3 billion USD excessive reserves).[107] Second, formal financial institutions in Afghanistan have limited reach and capacity.[108]

Sarrafs and *Sarrafi* Markets

Sarrafs were estimated to conduct 90% of financial transactions in Afghanistan even before sanctions handicapped the formal financial sector.[109] *Sarrafs* are the main providers of financial services to Afghan merchants. They provide a wide range of financial services: deposit-keeping, domestic and international money transfer (*hawala*), currency exchange, speculative trade of currencies, *Sarraf*'s check, short-term working capital loans, medium- and long-term interest-bearing loans, and equity financing. Sellers/creditors generally deposit their money with *Sarrafs* and use *Sarrafs*' short-term working capital loans, while sellers/creditors and buyers/debtors use *Sarrafs*' interest-bearing loans. Merchants (sellers/creditors and buyers/debtors) use *Sarraf*'s check. Both merchants and non-merchants use *Sarrafs*' domestic and international *hawala* services, as well as currency exchange services. *Sarrafs* are generally the only parties that engage in speculative trade in currencies.

Sarrafs make their profit from fees they charge on domestic and international *hawalas*, the difference between buying and selling price of a currency, return from equity investments, interest income from medium- and long-term loans, income from speculative currency trade, and arbitraging the price difference in currencies in across locations.[110] *Hawala* fees and currency exchange fees are the main source of income for most *Sarrafs* followed by equity investments.[111] Medium- and long-term loans, speculative trade, and currency arbitrage make up a small portion of *Sarrafs*' profits.[112]

The profit-makeup of *Sarrafs* explains why they are very ineffective at pooling savings. *Sarrafs* generally do not accept deposits from non-merchants. *Sarrafs* make most of their profits from *hawala* and currency exchange business generated by their merchant-clients because merchant-clients conduct the most currency exchange and *hawala* transactions. Non-merchants do not have frequent, large *hawala* and currency exchange needs. *Sarrafs* do not make money from holding more deposits; they earn more from the *hawala* and currency exchange business. The main reason they offer short-term working capital loans is to retain merchants as their clients in a competitive market. That is why they generally do not charge interest on working capital loans.

Sarrafs cannot act as financial intermediaries to pool savings for investment purposes because they make most of their profits from *hawala* and currency exchange business and only offer short-term working capital loans to retain the merchants as clients who are the main source of *hawala* and currency exchange business. Most *Sarrafs* do not generally issue medium- and long-term loans for the same reasons banks have difficulties issuing loans: the Afghanistan business climate is very uncertain, which increases the risk of long-term investment, and it is difficult to secure long-term credit transactions.[113] Banks are better positioned to offer long-term loans because they have more capital, they are better at pooling savings, and they have better access to legal collateralization tools.[114] This is why banks, not *Sarrafs*, are the main provider of investment loans. *Sarrafs* issue a very small percentage of investment loans.[115]

Sarrafs cannot substitute for banks in mobilizing savings for investments. Afghanistan needs to improve the formal banking system to facilitate the mobilization of savings for investment and induce sustainable economic growth. However, *Sarrafs* do reduce the capital requirements for sellers/creditors by providing them low-cost working capital loans. These short-term working capital loans allow sellers/creditors to finance supply chains and bear the risk of market uncertainties.

Most merchants surveyed in this research said they trust banks more than they trust *Sarrafs*—this was before the Taliban takeover instigated bank runs in 2021.[116] *Sarrafs* are more likely to go bankrupt than banks. Therefore, the preference to use *Sarrafs* instead of banks for deposit-keeping and other financial services is not determined by culture or attitude but rather by the incentive structure that merchants face. Low demand for bank loans is not caused by the stickiness of informal financial institutions; it is caused by the inability of formal institutions to solve the problems of credit transacting in Afghanistan.

Deposit-Keeping

Sarrafs generally only accept deposits from merchants. However, sometimes non-merchants keep their money with *Sarrafs* for safekeeping.[117] *Sarrafs* do not pay interest on these deposits. *Sarrafs* are not interested in receiving deposits from non-merchants because their profits come from other services they provide to merchants.[118]

Merchants deposit their money in *Sarrafs* for several reasons. Most merchants in Afghanistan work with foreign currencies, which makes them vulnerable to fluctuations in exchange rates of different currencies. To protect themselves against exchange-rate fluctuations, merchants keep reserves of different currencies with *Sarrafs* where they can readily convert them. Relatedly, merchants expect that they may need short-term working capital loans to make inflexible payments to their foreign suppliers since cash flow from receivables is highly unpredictable. Merchants deposit their money with *Sarrafs* so they will have good standing should they need short-term working capital loans. Even if a business does not deposit money with *Sarrafs*, *ex ante*, they can do so ex post. Merchants can compensate a *Sarraf* for a short-term working capital loan by effectively exchanging a loan for a loan: a *Sarraf* will give a merchant 50,000 USD for a month with the implicit expectation that the merchant will deposit 100,000 USD at his *Sarrafi* and leave it for a couple of months after the immediate financial difficulties are satisfied, as a Kabuli merchant said he has done. This model seems to fit with the *Sarraf*'s model of business in Afghanistan. Unlike banks, which collect the money from savers to loan them to investors and businesses, *Sarrafs* collect the money from merchants and loan them to merchants or use them for their own businesses, so they are willing to accept a loan (usually a larger future loan) in exchange for a loan.

Merchants need to transfer money domestically and internationally. Even before the current crisis, banks in Afghanistan did not have a presence in most of the country,[119] while *Sarrafs* have networks that reach even remote corners of the country. For international money transfers, merchants prefer to use *Sarrafs* whenever they can because *Sarrafs* require no documentation. When using *Sarrafs*, merchants do not need to have documents like invoices or contracts, so they can manipulate contracts and invoices, or use fake ones, for the purpose of taxation and tariffs. As a Kabuli merchant put it, "Banks ask for formal documents, *Sarrafs* don't. So if you want to put a lower price on your customs documents, you need to work with *Sarrafs*."[120] Merchants provide *Sarrafs* with domestic and international *hawala* (as well as currency exchange) to ensure they will receive short-term working capital loans when needed. This is because *Sarrafs* most often issue short-term working capital loans to retain the *hawala* (and currency exchange) business of a merchant. Additionally, short-term working capital loans are most often excused in the form of an international *hawala*.

Merchants who are involved in the illegal economy also need to work with *Sarrafs*. *Sarrafs* do not record or maintain information on the source of deposits or depositors.[121] *Sarrafs*, similarly, do not maintain or record information about the individuals to whom funds are transferred from a certain account. *Sarrafs* operate in a very nontransparent manner, which makes them very appealing to those who would like to keep their financial dealings secret. I discuss this in greater detail in Chapters 4 and 5, including Da Afghanistan Bank's efforts to regulate *Sarrafs* and impose reporting obligations against *Sarrafs*.

Sarrafs facilitate depositing money in banks and transfer of funds via banks by pooling deposits and funds.[122] *Sarrafs* pool their clients' funds and money transfers. However, they may use banks to keep the funds safe to transfer the funds. Therefore, depositing money in a *Sarrafi* does not usually remove the money from the banking system.[123] *Sarrafs* keep the majority of their funds in multiple personal bank accounts.[124] *Sarrafs* often transfer money inside Afghanistan and internationally using banks.[125] This is because holding money and physically transferring money is very dangerous in Afghanistan. *Sarrafs* try to reduce security risks by using banks to store and transfer money. This is also the reason that the current crisis in the banking sector is negatively affecting *Sarrafi* markets as well.

However, *Sarrafs* do physically transfer money because sometimes it is necessary (banks do not have a presence in large areas of Afghanistan).[126] It may be less expensive to physically transfer money, and sometimes the physical transfer of money helps *Sarrafs* profit from the difference in currency exchange rates prevailing in different countries (arbitrage).[127] *Sarrafs* pool their clients' funds and money transfers then use banks to keep the funds safe or transfer the funds.

*Domestic Money Transfer (***Hawala***)*

As discussed previously, *Sarrafs* have networks that reach every corner of the country where banks are not accessible. *Sarrafs* charge a reasonable commission fee for money transfers. *Sarrafs* execute *hawalas* via phone in real time. Once a sender deposits a sum of money with a *Sarraf* to be transferred to a receiver in another location, *Sarrafs* give the sender a number of *hawala*, which usually corresponds to a serial number in the *Sarraf*'s book of *hawala*. To receive the money, the receiver has only to go to an affiliated *Sarraf* in the destination and present the serial number to receive the money. Merchants do not often collect *hawala* personally; instead, the transferred money is collected to their account in the *Sarrafi*. In *hawalas* involving non-merchants, the cell phone number of the receiver is also recorded. When the receiver goes to the affiliated *Sarraf* in the destination location, the affiliated *Sarraf* will call the number and check that it is the number of the receiver. Thus, *Sarrafs* use phone numbers as identification (70% of Afghans have cellular subscriptions).[128]

Sarrafs usually relay *hawala* serial numbers every hour via phone or email or in real time via online chat services. Sometimes sender-*Sarraf* and receiver-*Sarraf* are branches of the same *Sarrafi*; however, most often they are independent *Sarrafs* that have *hawala* arrangements. To run a successful *Sarrafi* and to attract clients and their deposits, *Sarrafs* must be able to meet the *hawala* needs of their clients. Therefore, inter-*Sarrafi hawala* arrangements are crucial and mutually beneficial to *Sarrafs*. However, this does not mean every *Sarraf* needs to have a *hawala* arrangement with another *Sarraf* in every corner of the country (or the world). In fact, no individual *Sarraf* has such an all-encompassing network; however, they are still able to successfully execute *hawala* as they do. *Sarrafs* are able to execute *hawala* to every corner of Afghanistan because they are part of a thick *hawala* network. If a *Sarraf* does not have a *hawala* arrangement with a *Sarraf* in Baghlan, for example, that *Sarraf* can use a fellow *Sarraf* affiliate in Baghlan. *Sarrafs* execute other *Sarrafs*' *hawala* frequently; this is how each *Sarraf* can provide one-stop *hawala* services to his clients. This process is easily facilitated because *Sarrafs* are concentrated in a small number of connected buildings and operate in very close physical proximity to one another. This means each *Sarraf* knows all other *Sarrafs* and has repeated and continuous personal and business interactions with other *Sarrafs*. In the *hawala* system, each *Sarraf* functions as a hub immersed in a network of other hubs that run to every remote corner of the country.

The current financial crisis has increased the demand for *hawala* services. *Sarrafs* have also increased the *hawala* fees given higher demands and difficulties in the transfer of funds even domestically following the sanction-induced banking crisis in the country.

*International Money Transfer (*Hawala*)*

Sarrafs execute international *hawalas* in basically the same way as domestic *hawalas* using *hawala* serial numbers and very short delays. The users of international *hawalas* fall into two different categories: those who use international *hawalas* for personal remittance (16% of Afghan families have been estimated to rely on these remittances for their income;[129] the number must have increased given the loss of domestic income most families have experienced following Taliban takeover), and those who use international *hawala* for business purposes.

The former use *Sarrafs* because they charge lower fees (especially for small amounts, which is common for remittances) compared to banks or international money transfer businesses, for example, Western Union, and because they can transfer the money to any location within Afghanistan. The size of the Afghanistan *hawala* market, including both domestic and international *hawala*, was estimated to be between 5.6 billion USD and 6.1 billion USD in 2004–2005.[130] All the evidence suggests that that number has only increased since then.

Merchants use international *hawalas* to make payments to their foreign suppliers. Merchants use *Sarrafs*' international *hawalas* as opposed to bank money transfer services, which are often cheaper in a business context, for two main reasons. First, *Sarrafs* do not require documents, so merchants do not have to produce accurate invoices or other documents, which would subject them to taxation and tariffs, to justify a *hawala*. Banks are subject to money laundering reporting regulations, so they require extensive documents to transfer money internationally. Da Afghanistan Bank's efforts to impose anti-money laundering regulations against *Sarraf* would have seriously undermined their appeal as a provider of *hawalas* for Afghan merchants (which is responsible for a large share of their profit), so *Sarrafs* fiercely resisted these regulations.[131]

Second, often an international *hawala* is a credit *hawala*. This occurs when a *Sarraf* executes a *hawala*, that is, a transfer of money to a merchant's foreign supplier when a merchant does not have sufficient funds with the *Sarraf*. The merchant will then pay back the *Sarraf* as he collects the money from his domestic receivables. In effect, often international business *hawalas* are a synthesis of a *hawala* and a short-term working capital loan.

Sarrafs' networks of international *hawala* is not as wide as their network of domestic *hawalas*. *Sarrafs* make strategic decisions to set up offshore branches or to form a network with *Sarrafs* in other countries based on the distribution of the Afghan diaspora, who are the source of personal remittances, and the location of suppliers of imported products, who receive business *hawalas*. At the time of this research, *Sarrafs* were able to execute *hawalas* to Pakistan, Iran, India, UAE, China, Singapore, and Germany, to name a few.[132] *Sarrafs*' offshore branches are not often *Sarrafi* as different countries have very different, and often strict, regulations on the operation of a *Sarrafi*; instead, they may be import/export corporations that facilitate money transfers.[133]

When Taliban took over control of Da Afghanistan Bank, sanctions on Taliban, in effect, had rendered the entire Afghan banking system blacklisted. In such an environment, iNGOs and even foreign governments had turned to the *Sarrafi* markets to send money to the country and distribute money domestically (the former happened less frequently than the latter). A similar strategy was used in 2001, when Afghanistan had no banking sector.

Currency Exchange

The use of foreign currency permeates the Afghan economy. It is not an exaggeration to say that Afghanistan is a de facto multi-currency economy. And it was before the Taliban takeover greatly devalued Afghan currency and ushered in a deep liquidity crisis. Merchants, most often, either use foreign currencies for their domestic dealings or set the price for their products based on the prevailing currency exchange rate because most products are imported. Merchants, to protect themselves against fluctuation in currency exchange rates, convert the revenue they receive in Afghanis into foreign currencies regularly. Merchants maintain reserves of foreign currencies with *Sarraf*s. In some parts of the country, a foreign currency is the de facto currency in circulation instead of Afghanis. For example, in Nangarhar, the Pakistani rupee is the currency used even for small and everyday transactions (e.g. when visiting Nangarhar for this research, I used Pakistani rupee to buy fruit as I was given Pakistani rupees as change when I paid for a taxi). In the province of Nimrooz, located on the border with Iran, the Iranian rial is the de facto currency in circulation.[134] Anywhere in Afghanistan, a person can pay for goods or services, small or large, in virtually any currency. Some international organizations pay the salary of their local staff in US dollars.[135] Most large transactions (e.g. purchasing a car or a house) are done using US dollars or at the very least priced based on USD. However, a person can pay for anything in Afghanis too, but the other party will calculate the price and accept equivalent Afghanis in accordance with the prevailing exchange rate. Since Afghanistan is, de facto, a multicurrency economy. Therefore, currency exchange is a very large business.

Currency exchange is the proto-*Sarrafi* service. *Sarraf*s often start out as mobile *Sarraf* by buying and selling currencies in the *Sarrafi* market before they accumulate capital and open a *Sarrafi* store and expand their services.[136] Currency exchange is still a large source of revenue for *Sarraf*s, small or large.[137] *Sarraf*s make their profit from the difference between the purchase and sale price of a currency product. For example, at the time of writing, USD/AFN is bought at 104.20 AFN and sold for 104.30 USD/AFN in the Herat *Sarrafi* market. A medium-sized established *Sarraf* exchanges a few hundred thousand dollars a day making up to 1,000 USD a day from USD/AFN exchange alone. Iranian rial and Pakistani rupee generate even more profit for *Sarraf*s because the difference between their buy-and-sell price is higher, and their values fluctuate more.

*Sarraf*s' medium- and long-term loans are often executed in the form of a currency sale. For example, a borrower may buy 100,000 USD for a significantly higher price than the prevailing market price in exchange for deferred payment of Afghanis in the future.

*Speculative Trade in Currencies (*Sita*) and Public Auctions (*Booli*)*

Some *Sarraf*s engage in speculative trade of currencies, called *sita*. *Sita* operates like an option contract. *Sita* can be performed using a call option or a put option. When a call option is selected, a *Sarraf* (the buyer of the option) who thinks that USD/AFN will appreciate in value enters into an agreement with another *Sarraf* (seller of the option) to buy a certain amount of USD/AFN on a certain date in the future for a price lower than predicted price. On the due date, if the prevailing market price is lower than the price option price, the buyer of the option will pay the difference to the seller of the option, or he can buy USD/AFN for the market price. If the prevailing market price is higher than the option price, the seller of the option will pay the difference to the buyer of the option or deliver USD/AFN for the prevailing market price.

Sita is most often conducted with respect to a volatile currency. For example, according to an interviewee in Herat, "*Sarraf* market is usually largely based on one or two currencies. It used to be USD, then Pakistani rupee, but now it is Iran rial [the rise of Iran rial may be because Afghanistan has recently reduced its trade with Pakistan and increased its trade with Iran[138]]. Rial is very volatile, so *sita* based on market changes can be very profitable."[139]

Sita is a very risky practice, which is why most *Sarrafi* unions have banned it. It does continue today, but it is not very common. The *Sarraf* union's decision to ban the practice was motivated by a desire to protect the collective reputation of *Sarrafs* because reputation is a form of common asset.[140] According to the president of the *Sarrafi* union in Herat, "So many *Sarrafs* used to go bankrupt or default on their payments because they had lost money practicing *sita. We had to stop the practice or people would not trust the Sarrafs anymore*"[141] (emphasis added).

Sita is also considered to violate the Islamic prohibition of interest (*riba*). *Sarrafi* unions also cite Islamic prohibitions as the impetus behind a crackdown on the *sita*.[142] Since the doctrine of *riba* existed long before the crackdown took place, however, the crackdown was more likely about protecting the collective reputation of the *Sarrafi* market rather than upholding Islamic law that animated the action against *sita*.

At times when currency exchange rates are very volatile and a foreign currency is scarce, like now that USD is very scarce, *Sarrafs* may conduct *Booli* to set the exchange rate. Under this practice, a *Sarraf* can publicly auction off the USD he holds in the *Sarrafi* market, a crowded physical marketplace. This way the prospective buyers would compete for the limited available USD. The process determines the prevailing market price of USD in the *Sarrafi* market. As it should be apparent, the practice tends to cause the value of the auctioned currency to increase, which benefits the seller but causes inflation since the price of almost everything in Afghanistan is correlated with the prevailing currency exchange rate of popular currencies, like USD. As such, Taliban have reportedly banned the practice to curb inflation.

Sarraf's *Checks*

Sarrafs issue checks for their clients to guarantee future payments. These are usually postdated checks. *Sarrafs* issue these checks on the assumption that the client on whose account the check is issued will supply the necessary funds before the due date. In cases where the funds are present, the merchants use *Sarraf*'s checks to ensure they have access to the funds until the payment becomes due.

These checks contain the name, logo, and address of the *Sarrafi* that issued them. They may record the name of the payee, or they may be payable to the carrier. The amount and date of payment are also recorded on the check. *Sarrafs*' checks are often used to facilitate credit sales between merchants who do not have a direct relationship with each other. *Sarraf* checks are most often local, meaning they are only payable at a certain location, that is, the place of business of the issuer. However, *Sarrafs* sometimes rely on their networks to obtain a check from another *Sarraf* located in another location for their client.

Sarraf checks are negotiable documents. They can be easily transferred by endorsement or exchange of the check. *Sarraf* postdated checks can be discounted at the market, and they can ensure the liquidity of debts. However, currently, the practice of discounting the check is less common because the economic slowdown has increased the default risk, and *Sarrafs* have less capital and fewer reserves.[143] This is a reason why Afghanistan needs to improve its formal bank system to improve liquidity.

In addition, *Sarraf* checks enjoy very high creditability. They are usually the most reliable guaranty of payment one can produce in Afghanistan (with the exception of using cash deposits as a guaranty). Nearly all interviewees stated they accept *Sarrafs*' checks.[144] It is common for a merchant to ask the *Sarraf*-issuer to verify the check before accepting it. Once a check is verified by the issuer, the check is payable on the due date. According to the norms of the market, *Sarrafs* are required to pay the specific amount on the check on the due date without any defense that may relate to the underlying transaction. *Sarrafs* undertake a large risk by issuing a check.

Sarraf unions have tried to curb the use of *Sarraf*'s checks because they are very risky instruments. According to *Sarraf* unions, numerous *Sarrafs* have gone bankrupt because a number of clients on whose account they issued a check did not supply sufficient funds before the due date, and the *Sarrafs* were unable to honor their checks.[145] Defaulting on a check will undermine a *Sarraf*'s most valuable asset, his reputation, and will diminish the collective credibility of *Sarrafs*. If a *Sarraf*'s financial commitments cannot be trusted, a *Sarraf* cannot work in the market. Therefore, a default on a check most often means the end of business for a *Sarraf*.

While they are treated as informal negotiable instruments, *Sarraf*'s checks are not formal negotiable documents under Afghanistan laws. Under Afghanistan's Negotiable Documents Law ("Negotiable Documents Law"), the issuer of a check has to be a bank, and a check must possess a number of formal requirements to qualify as a formal negotiable document.[146] Moreover, checks, under Afghan laws, are not an instrument of credits, and they cannot be legally postdated. The Negotiable Documents Law does not recognize a formal check as an instrument that can guarantee future payment; therefore, no formal law protects postdated checks.[147] A formal check is payable upon presentation, and a term that makes a check payable only on a future date is void.[148] Under the Negotiable Documents Law, the negotiable documents that can be used to guarantee a future payment must either take the form of a draft or a promissory note.[149] *Sarraf*'s checks do not meet the formal requirements of either a draft or promissory note.

Although the *raison d'être* of *Sarraf*'s checks is to guarantee future obligations, they do not comply with the formal legal requirements of a check, draft, or promissory note; therefore, *Sarraf*'s checks do not legally qualify as a formal negotiable document. In court cases, *Sarraf*'s checks have been given the same legal status as any other written proof of debt. However, they do not avail the holder of preferential procedural and substantive protections accorded to formal negotiable documents. *Sarraf*'s check avails its holder of the same procedural and substantive protection as any other written proof of debt. For example, a defense concerning the underlying transaction can be used to excuse payment because the *Sarraf*'s check is not a formal negotiable document.

These legal handicaps of a *Sarraf*'s checks are not relevant for merchants. This is because failure to honor a check is most often a death sentence for a *Sarraf*'s ability to function in the *Sarrafi* market. Therefore, check users know that if a *Sarraf* has the funds, he will honor the check. If he does not have the funds, a court judgment will not be of much help.

In the past, according to the president of the Herat *Sarrafi* Union, the union would endorse a *Sarraf*'s check upon request. Therefore, in case of a default, other *Sarrafs* would help pay the amount.[150] This process was in place to safeguard *Sarraf*'s collective assets, that is, *Sarraf*'s reputation. *Sarrafs* share this reputation. Merchants and people trust the name of *Sarrafs* and accord great weight to the fact that a *Sarraf* has a store in the *Sarrafi* market. If a *Sarraf* defaults on a check, it diminishes the reputation of all *Sarrafs*. After the economic slowdown, however, the Herat *Sarraf* union discontinued the practice of endorsing *Sarrafs*' checks. To protect the collective reputation of *Sarrafs*, *Sarraf* unions have pressured their members to either refrain from issuing checks or only issue them to highly creditworthy clients. Some unions have banned the practice entirely.

Short-Term Working Capital Loans

Sarrafs are the primary source of working capital loans in Afghanistan. Sellers/creditors rely on these short-term working capital loans to protect themselves against interruptions in cash flow caused by the unpredictability of receivables payments. When sellers/creditors need to make a payment to a supplier located outside of Afghanistan and they do not have sufficient funds, *Sarraf* usually transfer the money (credit *hawala*). Sellers/creditors will pay back the money as they collect their receivables from the debtors/buyers using the *ugraee*.[151] It usually does not take more than a month for a seller/creditor to pay the *Sarrafs* for these short-term working capital loans.

In addition to paying foreign payables, another common use of *Sarrafs*' short-term working capital loans is customs expenses. A seller/creditor needs to pay a large sum of money to buy from a foreign supplier. When the product arrives at the border, most sellers/creditors have difficulty finding enough cash to pay tariffs and customs clearance costs. These sellers/creditors often rely on *Sarrafs*' short-term capital loans to pay for tariffs and customs clearance costs. Sellers/creditors will pay these loans as they collect their receivables from the domestic buyers/debtors using the *ugraee* system.

Working capital loans present limited risk to the *Sarrafs*; therefore, they are the easiest for a merchant to secure. Short-term working capital loans present a limited risk to *Sarrafs* because (1) they are short-term loans, and (2) they are attached to real products. *Sarrafs* issue working capital loans in the form of credit *hawala* to pay a foreign supplier for a purchase of a product or to clear a shipment from customs. Therefore, the loan is secured by real products. *Sarrafs* are confident that they are going to be paid as the product is sold.

Sarrafs help merchants bridge the gap between their inflexible financial commitments to their foreign suppliers and their flexible and uncertain financial payments from their domestic customers. As a Kabuli cell phone merchant put it:

> When you sell in Afghanistan using a weekly payment system whilst buying in China, where you have to pay in cash, you have to work with *Sarrafs*. You need *Sarrafs* to give you credit so you can make the large payments. Then you can pay *Sarrafs* as you collect the money throughout weeks when you are paid by your domestic customers in Afghanistan. *Sarrafs* allow you to bridge the gap between a cash-based market and a credit-based market . . . we use *Sarrafs* despite the fact that Bank's TT [transfer of money via banks] is cheaper.[152]

Sarrafs generally do not charge interest for the short-term working capital loans that they provide for their clients, which are most often executed in the form of a credit *hawala*. They do not charge interest for the same reason major businesses sell on credit: market competition. If a *Sarraf* charges interest on short-term working capital loans, the client will go to another *Sarraf* who would not, and there is no shortage of *Sarrafs*. Thus, if a *Sarraf* charges interest on short-term working capital loans, it risks losing *hawala* and currency-exchange business generated by merchant-clients.

However, in some cases, *Sarrafs* may charge interest. Some short-term capital loans may bear interest. The way the interest is usually charged is through higher *hawala* fees for credit *hawalas* or a higher currency exchange rate. *Sarrafs* may charge higher *hawala* fees or higher exchange rates when the client does not have the sufficient funds.

There is variation among cases when it comes to access to interest-free short-term working capital loans. In Nangarhar and Balkh, compared to Herat and Kabul, *Sarraf*'s short-term working capital loans are less likely to be free of interest.[153] In Herat, interviewees were more likely to say that they received short-term working capital loans from *Sarrafs*.[154] This may be due to the fact that Herat's market is bigger than Nangarhar's market, so the *Sarrafi*'s financing model is able to provide credit at a lower marginal cost in Herat.

The interview data from this study shows that the use of *Sarraf*'s short-term working capital loans has become more common in the market recently (post-2015), likely because the market has been slow.[155] "Everyone needs and uses these credit *hawalas*," as one Herati merchant stated.[156] This supports the hypothesis that *Sarrafs* have helped reduce the negative impact of the economic recession in Afghanistan. Balkh, arguably, was hit worse by the economic slowdown because it did not have a well-developed *Sarrafi* market.[157]

Merchants do not consider this funding as working capital loans or financing because they are most often short-termed and embedded in different transactions, such as *hawala* or currency exchange. Therefore, they are not reflected in the statistics of access to finance.

Medium- and Long-Term Sarrafi *Loans*

Merchants sometimes use *Sarrafs*' medium- and long-term loans. Like short-term working capital loans, *Sarraf*'s medium- and long-term loans are working capital loans, meaning they are not used to buy long-term assets, invest, start a business, or expand a business. Rather they are used often to pay account payables. These loans are usually given for a duration of between a month and a year.

Interest rates on these loans are so high that a merchant would only take them if he had no other choice, according to a Herati *Sarraf*.[158] These loans are a last resort, often used to keep a business from failing. The clients for *Sarrafs*' interest-bearing loans may be struggling sellers/creditors or debtors/buyers. The borrowers are those merchants who do not have access to bank loans because they do not have the necessary collateral. The borrowers also do not have access to short-term working capital loans because they cannot pay back the loan in a short period of time, or they cannot secure an interest-free short-term working capital loans because they do not generate enough *hawala* or currency-exchange business.

Sarraf interest-bearing loans, most often, differ from bank loans in two ways: (1) the *Sarrafs*' borrowers are more likely capital-poor, so they would not qualify for a bank loan because they do not have the necessary formal collateral; (2) *Sarrafs*' loans are working capital loans while bank loans are more commonly used to buy long-term assets, invest, or expand a business. This is because banks' borrowers are merchants who are, most often, in a good financial position—they have to be otherwise they would not qualify for a bank's loan[159]—while the *Sarrafs*' borrower are in a relatively poor financial condition; otherwise they would not agree to such high-interest rates.

The Survey for Afghanistan Capital Markets Assessment of large businesses conducted in 2010 found that businesses that borrow from banks have a much larger capital investment compared to the average capital investment of the survey.[160] The average capital investment of the survey was 2.6 million USD, while the average capital investment of the businesses borrowing from banks was 10.4 million USD.[161]

Sarrafs' medium- and long-term loans come with very high interest. A Herati *Sarraf*, for example, said, "*Sarrafs* charge 25–30% annual interest rate on their medium and long-term interest-bearing loans."[162] It is because *Sarrafs* do not require collateral for their loans, and also, those who take on these loans are high-risk borrowers because they are facing harsh financial conditions. Therefore, these loans present a very high risk that needs to be compensated with very high-interest rates.

As explained previously, these loans are often executed in the form of a future currency sale. Most of *Sarraf*'s interest-bearing loans are executed in the form of a *hawala* or deferred money exchange, or a transaction involving transfer or exchange of currency. This way, it seems, they are trying to avert the immediate impression of *riba*-based transactions (prohibition against interest in Islamic law). In Herat and Nangarhar, the use of these transactional techniques is more common compared to Balkh, where merchants openly admit to using simple interest-bearing loans.[163] This may be due to the varying degree of permanence of religious norms in different provinces. Similarly, merchants in Balkh, compared to Herat and Nangarhar, are much less likely to mention the doctrine of *riba* as the reason why they have not taken a loan from a bank or a *Sarrafi*.[164] Interestingly enough though, this welcoming attitude toward interest-bearing loans has not resulted in a noticeable increase in the use of banks or *Sarrafi*'s loans among interviewees. Similarly, this pro-interest attitude has not resulted in the development of the financial market in Balkh; in fact, the opposite is the case.[165]

Interview data show although it is *not* common for an entrepreneur to use a *Sarraf*'s loan to start a business or expand his existing business, *Sarraf*'s line of short-term loans do help entrepreneurs start a business with less initial capital than otherwise would have been needed to overcome interruptions and delays in payments.[166] *Sarrafs* enable businesses to sell on credit and stay competitive. It appears that in provinces with well-developed *Sarrafi* markets, *Sarrafs* enable sellers/creditors to bear more market risk by providing them with a buffer against cash flow interruptions. *Sarrafs* thus help sellers/creditors in Afghanistan handle a very high level of market uncertainties.

Sarrafs lending decisions mirror the criteria a seller/creditor uses when deciding to sell on credit, that is, a combination of personal relations, *wasata*, business place, and past dealings. However, seller/creditors cannot obtain a *Sarraf*'s loan, or a *Sarraf*'s check, without a history of past dealing, whereas a buyer/debtor can obtain trade credit for his first purchase. This is because *Sarrafs*' loans are often provided to retain clients. They attempt to be a one-stop financial shop, so they provide their clients with credit services. A *Sarraf* would not offer credit services to a non-client. Past dealing is important with interest-bearing loans because those are risky; without a history of past dealing, a *Sarraf* does not trust a merchant with an interest-bearing loan.

A merchant's ability to secure credit from a *Sarraf*, either through a working capital loan or medium- and long-term interest-bearing loans, is directly related to the amount of capital and *hawala* and currency business that that merchant brings to the *Sarraf*. This means that larger and more successful businesses have better access to credit, while smaller and start-up businesses have less access.

Sarrafs' medium- and long-term loans are considered loans by Afghan merchants because they have longer terms and often bear interest. Therefore, they are reflected in the survey answers concerning access to finance.

Equity Financing

Sarrafs use the funds they hold for their clients to invest in existing businesses or to start a new business. A *Sarraf*'s equity portfolio typically contains three main types of investments. First, *Sarrafs* use their funds to invest in ventures that have a fast and safe return. *Sarrafs* used to invest in oil deals, real estate deals, and construction deals when those markets were booming, but all these markets have slowed down. Many *Sarrafs* who had invested in those areas went bankrupt. Currently, *Sarrafs* do not invest in those fields. Second, *Sarrafs* may use their funds to buy equity shares in different businesses. Most *Sarrafs* are either silent or active equity partners in multiple businesses. *Sarrafs* may invest in their clients' businesses since they have good information on the financial state of their client's businesses. Finally, *Sarrafs* most often use their funds to start a business. Most *Sarrafs* own multiple businesses. In the last two cases, *Sarrafs*, like most other businesses in Afghanistan, will rely on a family model of business to invest in businesses or start a new business by investing in their family members' businesses or by providing start-up capital for a family member to start a new business.

The Case of Balkh's **Sarrafi** *Market*

The case of Balkh highlights the importance of the *Sarrafi* market in Afghanistan. Research for this dissertation suggests that Balkh's *Sarrafi* market is the least developed among the five research sites,[167] and Balkh has suffered the most from worsening of macroeconomic conditions.[168] I argue that the underdevelopment of *Sarrafi* markets has made Balkh more vulnerable to worsening of macroeconomic conditions.

Balkh's *Sarrafs* do not have an exclusive marketplace. They share their marketplace with other businesses. They do not own their marketplace, so Balkh's *Sarraf* union has much less control over who can open a *Sarrafi* in the market. They are more likely to do other things besides *Sarrafi* in their stores, for example, cell phone top-up credit or airline tickets. There are fewer *Sarrafs* in the market. They are less busy. And their market is much less vibrant and crowded. They do not have the same reputation of credibility as *Sarrafs* in other provinces. As one *Sarraf* put it, "I am sometimes ashamed to say what my profession is."[169] Balkh *Sarrafs* have less capital of their own and handle much less capital of the Balkh market. They are less likely to invest in business ventures.

Although worsening macroeconomic conditions at the time of the fieldwork caused merchants to reduce their credit sales and other credit transactions in all five of the studied provinces, credit transactions were more severely impacted in Balkh.[170] Businesses in Balkh engage in credit transactions significantly less than their counterparts in other research sites.[171] They are less likely to sell on credit, have a revolving credit account with a *Sarraf*, have access to interest-free short-term working capital loans from a *Sarraf*, or buy their supply on credit.[172]

The Business Climate Reports show that Balkh has been more severely impacted by Afghanistan's economic slowdown, and it has the most unstable business climate.[173] The Business Climate Reports data show Balkh, despite being a very safe and stable province, has the most unstable business climate, and also it has the second-worst overall business climate.[174] Balkh also is the most monopolistic economy of the five major provinces, measured in the number of business registries/capita.[175] Given that Balkh has the least developed *Sarrafi* market among the five major provinces of Afghanistan, this dissertation argues that the underdeveloped *Sarrafi* market has made Balkh more vulnerable to worsening of macroeconomic conditions.

Sarrafs help sellers/creditors supply trade credit despite unpredictable receivable payments by providing working capital loans that protect sellers/creditors against cash flow interruptions. Balkh merchants have limited access to these protections; therefore, they are less likely to supply trade credit, and they are more likely to suffer if the market slows down. *Sarrafs* distribute market risk by pooling their clients' funds and providing working capital loans to protect their clients against cash flow interruptions. Thus, they soften the blow of macroeconomic slowdown by spreading the market risk. In effect, short-term working capital loans function as a system of cross-insurance, where *Sarrafs*' clients contribute to a common pool by keeping deposits in a *Sarrafi*; these deposits are used to provide relief in the form of working capital loans to the same clients should they need it. Merchants in Balkh are less likely to have access to short-term working capital loans; therefore, they are more affected by macroeconomic slowdowns, and Balkh's business climate is less stable.

On the issue of causal ordering, the availability of data on how the Balkh's market has responded to worsening macroeconomic conditions helps eliminate the possibility that underdeveloped *Sarrafi* markets are not the cause but rather an effect of bad economic conditions. If causal ordering ran the opposite way, Balkh would have developed better *Sarrafi* markets when the Afghan economy was doing better. In this case, we would not see these effects when the macroeconomic conditions turned for worse.

There are two possible hypotheses as to why Balkh has not developed a strong *Sarrafi* market:

(1) **Neighbor-effect hypothesis.** Balkh has not developed a strong *Sarrafi* market because it sits on the border with Central Asian countries,[176] where credit sales are much less common due to the fact that governments exercise more control over exports. As a result, it is much harder for Balkhi sellers/creditors to obtain credit from and establish relations with suppliers located in these neighboring Central Asian countries. Since they do not engage in cross-border credit transactions as often as merchants in Nangarhar and Herat, there has been reduced demand for *Sarrafi* services, so Balkh's *Sarrafi* market has remained underdeveloped.

(2) **The political-effect hypothesis.** Balkh has not developed a strong *Sarrafi* market because Atta Noor, the long-lasting governor of Balkh (he was the governor for almost fourteen years, from 2004–2018),[177] had a relatively strong grip over the economy in this province, which has reduced competition and increased barriers to entry. Less competition means fewer sellers/creditors and more capital-rich sellers/creditors active in the market, which means less demand for *Sarraf*'s financial services.

The low rate of credit sales is also unexpected from the point of view of the literature. The literature suggests that in places where informal credit institutions prevail, the smaller the size of the economy, the better access to credit is expected because information costs are lower in smaller economies.[178] However, I posit that in Afghanistan, Balkh, which is a smaller economy compared to Herat and Kabul, has poor credit conditions because it does not have well-developed informal financial institutions.

The case of Balkh also discredits the hypothesis that it is the stickiness of informal institutions that is stopping formal institutions from gaining traction with Afghan merchants. In Balkh, a convergence of exogenous factors has reduced market competition, causing Balkh to diverge from the credit-based supply chain structure pervasive in other major provinces. As a result, credit sales are less common in Balkh than in other major provinces. However, the absence of pervasive informal supply chain institutions has not resulted in increased use of formal institutions. This is despite the fact that Balkhis merchants have expressed the least religious reservation when discussing bank loans when interviewed. Despite having the fewest reservations about *riba*, Balkh's merchants have not been more likely to use bank loans.[179] This study argues that the failure of formal financing to expand in Balkh shows that the reason Afghan merchants do not use formal credit institutions is not the stickiness of existing credit institutions but instead it is due to the failure of formal institutions to solve the credit transaction problems that Afghan merchants face.

Religious Prohibition of Interest and Access to Finance

The case of Balkh also suggests that an interest-friendly attitude has not led to the development of either a bank- or *Sarrafi*-based financial market. Balkh has the least-developed financial market, while Balkhis have the most welcoming attitudes of merchants in five major provinces toward interest-bearing loans.[180] Herat, Nangarhar, and Kabul have developed *Sarrafi*-based financial markets where *hawala* and currency-exchange-based transactions are often used to execute transactions that compensate *Sarrafs* for time-value of the money, while merchants in those provinces express stronger religious objections to the use of interest-bearing loans.[181] This shows religious objections to the use of interest-bearing loans are not a major impediment to the development of the financial market.

Islamic banks were proposed by the Afghan Republic's Da Afghanistan Bank and the Ministry of Commerce and Industries as solutions to the problem of the low demand for bank loans based on the idea that religious objection to interest is the main reason behind low demand for bank loans.[182] Taliban caretaker government has also formed a committee on Islamic finance. However, the research presented in this study suggests that merchants do not use bank loans primarily because formal institutions have not overcome the fundamental problems of credit transactions in Afghanistan (highly volatile business climate, inefficient formal property right system, and uncertain formal contract enforcement), not because of their religious objection to the use of interest. This finding is supported by the lack of popularity of existing Shari'ah-compliant financial products.[183]

Many banks in Afghanistan offer Shari'ah-compliant financial products. Afghanistan also has one full-fledged Islamic bank, the Islamic Bank of Afghanistan. However, interviews show that most merchants do not use these products for the same reasons they do not use their conventional counterparts: high cost, the short length of loans, and demanding collateral requirements.[184] These are the same problems as those mentioned about conventional banks. Therefore, it is the failure of formal financial institutions (Islamic and conventional) to overcome the problems of credit transacting in Afghanistan that deter merchants from using banks (either Islamic or conventional) rather than a concern that interest has been prohibited by Islamic law.

This is, however, not to say that if formal financial institutions could supply loans in a way that would work in the context of Afghanistan (i.e. overcome the problems of credit transacting), Afghan merchants, *ceteris paribus*, would not prefer Shari'ah-compliant financing to conventional financing. Most likely they would. After all, Islamic financial institutions use transactional techniques to avoid contravention of religious norms; *Sarrafs* use transactional techniques to achieve the same goals, however, with less doctrinal vigor.

Regional Variations within Sarrafi *Markets*

There are variations in *Sarrafi* markets in five major provinces studied here.

Sarrafs *in Kabul*

Sarrafs handle a significant portion of market capital in Afghanistan. They handle the largest share of market capital in Nangarhar and Herat. They handle the smallest share of market capital in Balkh. Kandahar and Kabul fall somewhere in between.

Kabuli merchants are more likely to say that they work mostly with banks, not *Sarrafs*; however, they use banks only (1) to transfer money to their suppliers in countries with strict financial regulations, which are most countries other than Pakistan, Iran, and UAE (this is the case for merchants across Afghanistan and the reason for it is international money laundering regulations) and (2) to establish checking accounts. When it comes to using short-time working capital loans, most Kabuli merchants said that they have used *Sarraf*'s credit *hawala*, or at least they knew they could if they needed.[185] This higher use of the banking system by Kabuli merchants is likely because there are more large businesses in Kabul. It may also mean that more Kabuli businesses have (1) more capital so less need for *Sarrafs* and (2) more of an international presence, which exposes them to more regulations.

Interviewees in Kabul were more likely to use banks for money transfer and current account services while at the same time keeping their connections with *Sarrafs*.[186] Interestingly, the increased connections with banks have not resulted in an increase in the use of bank loans.[187] Similarly, the underdevelopment of the *Sarrafi* market in Balkh has not caused its banking system to grow as far as the provision of credit is concerned. Balkhi and Kabuli businesses are more likely to say that they work mostly with banks, but they are no more likely to say that they have a bank loan compared to Heratis or Nanagarharis.[188] Therefore, the increased use of banks is not necessarily correlated with a decreased use of *Sarrafs*. Similarly, as previously explained, depositing funds with *Sarrafs* do not necessarily remove the funds from the banking system because *Sarrafs* ultimately store and transfer those funds via banks.

Sarrafs *in Kandahar*

Kandahari *Sarrafs*, compared to their counterparts in three other major provinces, are less involved with other businesses as creditors or investors.[189] *Sarrafs* are not the richest people in Kandahar, while they are often among the richest people in Kabul and Herat.[190] This may be due to the influence of black money. Kandahari *Sarrafs* likely make most of their profit from handling revenue of illegal economy rather than investing in business ventures.

According to Thompson's field research on the *Sarrafs*, *hawala*, and drug money in Afghanistan, of the five provinces studied here, Kandahar has the highest estimated percentage of drug-related funds in provincial markets.[191] According to Thompson's survey, in the years of her field research (2014–2015), 80–90% of *hawala* funds in Kandahar are related to drug money, whereas the figures in Balkh and Herat are only 50% and 30%, respectively.[192]

Gerawee

Trade credit and *Sarrafi* markets are the main source of working capital financing in Afghanistan; they reduce the need for investment financing by reducing the necessary capital to run a business. Trade credit lowers the capital requirement for entry into the supply chain and retail markets, while *Sarrafs*' short-term working capital loans protect sellers/creditors from cash flow interruption, reducing the amount of capital required to become a seller/creditor in Afghanistan. *Sarrafs*' short-term working capital loans also enable risk-sharing trade credit arrangements in Afghanistan by helping sellers/creditors diversify market risk. However, neither can be used to finance investment or buy long-term assets. *Gerawee* and bank loans are the main source of investment financing in Afghanistan. This section focuses on *Gerawee*;[193] bank loans will be discussed in Chapter 4.

Size of Gerawee *Market*

Conservative rough estimates of total values of *Gerawee* in four major provinces suggest *Gerawee* plays a large role in investment financing. According to rough estimates acquired from the president of Real Estate Agent Union, experienced real estate agents, or Huquq Departments, the total value of *Gerawee*, for the year 2017, in Afghanistan's four major provinces is as follows: Herat (120 million USD), Kabul (240 million USD), Balkh (69 million USD), and Nangarhar (0.4 million USD).[194] Estimates for Kandahar were not available.

The estimated value of *Gerawee* for four major provinces indicates *Gerawee* plays a large role in investment financing in Afghanistan. The total value of *Gerawee* contracted within one year in four major provinces amounts to 429.40 million USD (see Figure 2.1). This is almost two-thirds of the total value of outstanding bank loans for the whole country around the same time.[195] If one extrapolates the *Gerawee* numbers to reflect the value of *Gerawee* for the whole country (34 provinces), it could be safely argued that the total value of *Gerawee* in a year exceeds the total value of outstanding bank loans.[196] In Herat alone, conservative rough estimates suggest, in the year 2016–2017, the total value of *Gerawee* was roughly 120 million USD,[197] which was almost triple the total value of outstanding bank loans in Herat for the same year.[198] This comparison suggests that *Gerawee* is likely a more important source of financing investment in Afghanistan than bank loans.

It is difficult, however, to estimate what percentage of the total value of *Gerawee* is used for investment purposes because *Gerawor*s do not necessarily use the transaction to raise capital for investment. A *Gerawor* may use the *Gerawee* to raise money for personal expenses as well (e.g. paying for a wedding ceremony). However, my research shows that merchants commonly use *Gerawee* for investment purposes.[199]

Gerawee sits at the intersection between housing and finance. The supply of *Gerawee* is determined by the need to raise capital, while the demand for *Gerawee* is determined by the need for housing. Therefore, it is hard to explain provincial variations in the distribution of the total value of *Gerawee* in terms of access to investment financing. However, the data suggest that *Gerawee* is more common in Herat and Kabul compared to Balkh and Nangarhar (see Figure 2.1). According to the president of Nangarhar's Real Estate Agents' Union, the unpopularity of *Gerawee* in Nangarhar is due to the belief that the practice violates the religious prohibition of interest (*riba*).[200] According to an experienced real estate

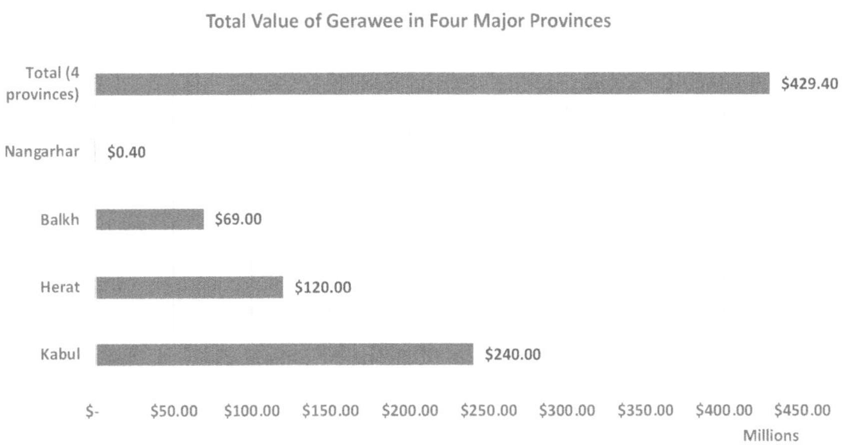

Figure 2.1 Total Estimated Value of Gerawee in Four Major Provinces of Afghanistan within the Year (2017)

agent in Balkh, most property owners prefer to lease their property rather than put it under *Gerawee* because the ratio of rent to *Gerawee*-value is high.[201] This means property owners in Balkh cannot raise enough capital through *Gerawee* to justify foregoing rent by putting the property under *Gerawee*.

If a party wishes to get court enforcement of a *Gerawee* contract, he would have to do so in a regional civil court since commercial courts do not have subject matter jurisdiction on *Gerawee* cases.[202] Despite its prevalence, *Gerawee* has not, to this date, been recognized by the civil courts. This is because judges of the now toppled Afghan Republic believed that it violates the prohibition of interest in Islam.[203] The Taliban appointees are expected to hold similar views given their almost universal classical Islamic law training.

The difference between commercial and noncommercial cases is not caused but helped by formal laws. Afghanistan's commercial law explicitly recognizes interest-bearing transactions, while the noncommercial laws tend to prohibit such transactions.[204] However, the formal laws are not the cause of varied judicial attitudes because civil judges cite religious reasons independent of legal reasons as to why they do not enforce transactions that they think violate the religious prohibition of interest, including *Gerawee*.[205] Commercial judges under the Islamic Republic, while expressing concern about the religious aspects of interest-bearing transactions, accept that in a business context, those transactions are allowed out of economic necessity.[206] The relatively weak formal protection of *Gerawee* has increased the risk to creditors making *Gerawee* less effective as a financing arrangement. This is a reason why users can only raise limited capital through *Gerawee*, often less than one-tenth of the likely sale price,[207] and why the most common form of *Gerawee* is possessory-*Gerawee*.

Gerawee also cannot be used to pool savings because it is a transaction between an individual saver, who often has housing needs, and an entrepreneur who has a financing need. This means that *Gerawee* cannot be used to diversify risk. It also means that *Gerawee* cannot be used to pool savings for investment purposes. As a result, *Gerawee* cannot substitute for a bank-based financial market.

Gerawee *and Its Variations*

This section examines *Gerawee* in the context of Afghanistan, illustrating the various forms of *Gerawee* practices through hypothetical examples. The aim is to highlight the underlying economics of *Gerawee* and demonstrate the nuances of its various practiced forms in Afghanistan.

The following examples introduce the most common variations of *Gerawee* transactions:

Example 1. A, who needs a sum of money (*Gerawor*), may enter into an agreement with B, who is willing to provide him with a sum of money (*Gerawe-ee*). Under the terms of their agreement, B agrees to provide A with an amount of money to be fully repaid at a later date in exchange for the right to live in A's house. The amount of money paid by B usually is much lower than the market value of the house. It is common for the agreement to specify the length of the contract (i.e. the date of repayment); however, B usually will have the right to live in the house until the debt is fully repaid, even if the term of the contract elapses.

Example 2. B agrees to provide A with an amount of money to be fully repaid at a later date in exchange for the right to lease A's house for considerably lower rent than the market price. Like the previous scenario, the amount of money paid by B is usually much lower than the market value of the house. Similarly, it is common for the agreement to specify the length of the contract (i.e. the date of repayment). B usually has the right to retain the lease to the house until the debt is fully repaid, even if the term of the contract elapses.

Example 3. B agrees to provide A with an amount of money to be fully repaid at a later date in exchange for the right to lease A's house to a tenant. Under this scenario, B will receive the rent from the tenant. Like the previous scenarios, the amount of money paid by B usually is much lower than the

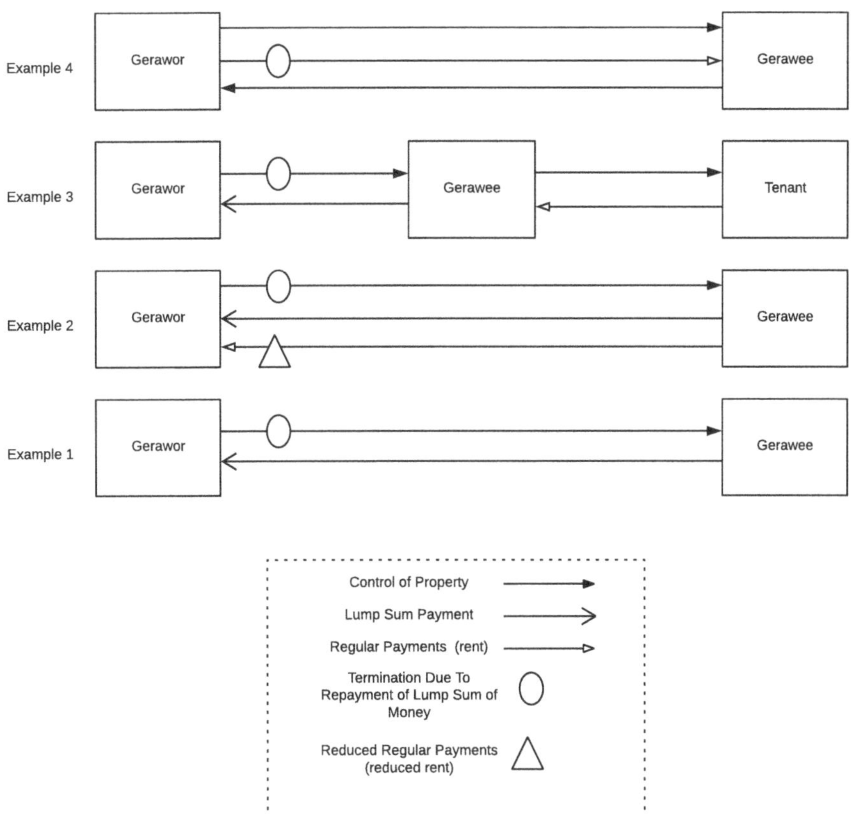

Diagram 2.2 Gerawee and Its Variations

market value of the house. It is common for the agreement to specify the length of the contract (i.e. the date of repayment); however, like the other arrangements described previously, B usually will have the right to receive the rent from the tenant until being fully repaid, even if the term of the contract elapses.

Example 4. Another example of *Gerawee* is an agreement under which B agrees to provide A with an amount of money to be fully repaid at a later date in exchange for the right to lease A's house to a tenant. However, unlike Example 3, B will lease back A's house to A (meaning A will retain the possession of the house). B will receive the rent from A. Like the previous scenarios, the amount of money paid by B usually is much lower than the market value of the house. Similarly, it is common for the agreement to specify the length of the contract (i.e. the date of repayment); however, B usually has the right to receive rent from A until the debt is fully repaid, even if the term of the contract elapses. This scenario is closest to a mortgage contract.

Important Characteristics of the **Gerawee** *Market*

To thoroughly understand the practice of *Gerawee* in its social context, one must be acquainted with the five main characteristics of *Gerawee*. These characteristics illuminate the dynamic of the *Gerawor-Gerawee*-ee relationship. They also show the role local real estate agents play in concluding a *Gerawee* agreement and their economic interests in the continuance of the practice. Real estate agents are therefore important players who have a stake in decreasing the Shari'ah frictions in the practice.

Concerning the subject of a *Gerawee*, houses are the most common subject or property in *Gerawee*; however, stores, warehouses, and agricultural land may also be subjected to the *Gerawee*, although with less frequency. Movable property, on the other hand, is not subject to the *Gerawee*.

Who are the usual *Gerawee* actors? The creditor/*Gerawee*-ee is usually an unsophisticated party. Creditor/*Gerawee*-ee are those who have small- or medium-sized savings but are not capable of conducting their own business venture. They seek *Gerawee* to supplement to their income or, in some cases, provide their sole source of income or a way to save on paying rent. Hence, widows, orphans, elderly, and low-ranking governmental employees are common creditors/*Gerawee*-ee. On the other hand, the debtor/*Gerawor* is usually an entrepreneur or small venture owner who needs financing and can make a profit on the amount of money he receives that exceeds the amount of money he is paying in rent or the amount of rent that he forgoes. However, it is not uncommon for the *Gerawor* to use the money for extra living expenses, such as repaying an overdue debt, paying for a son's wedding, or paying medical expenses.

Because of the imbalance of power between the *Gerawor*, who usually is a business-minded person, and *Gerawee*-ee, who usually is not, as well as the weakness of formal legal protections, misuse is not uncommon in the *Gerawee* market, decreasing its popularity and efficiency. For example, a common form of misuse in *Gerawee* is when a *Gerawor* enters multiple *Gerawee* agreements with multiple *Gerawee*-ee for a cumulative amount of money that exceeds the value of the property. In essence, by engaging in such fraudulent practice, the *Gerawor* is hoping to acquire a disproportionately larger amount of money against the lower-valued property. In another example, the *Gerawor* may refuse to pay back the money owed and stop paying rent after only paying a few installments. In cases like this, a *Gerawor* may pay back money owed after a while but not the unpaid rent. In this way, the *Gerawor* exploits the weakness of the enforcement system when the *Gerawor* is in possession of the property.

The safest form of *Gerawee* for *Gerawee*-ee, which is also the most common form, is possessory *Gerawee* (see Example 1 in the previous section). Under this form of *Gerawee*, the *Gerawee*-ee will retain the possession of the property, continuing to live in the house, until the *Gerawor* pays back the money he received under *Gerawee*. This form of *Gerawee* has been very popular because it provides a solution to the growing needs for housing in urban centers while supplying a source of capital for entrepreneurs. It secures a loan through the transfer of possession, but it does not have the same inefficient consequences of traditional possessory security transactions because the creditor acquires the right to live in the house, solving the need for housing. This form of *Gerawee* has great potential because many Afghan merchants have invested a lot of money in real estate when the economy was booming, so they currently own excessive real estate, and fast-growing urbanization ensures a continued and increasing demand for housing. These two dynamics will continue to sustain and grow *Gerawee* as a twin finance-housing solution and, if correctly managed, can create positive consequences for economic growth by reducing financing constraints on Afghan businesses.

Gerawee agreements are usually concluded through local real estate agents called "*Rahnamya Mua'malat*." Under the law, the sale and lease of real estate must be conducted through a registered real estate agent who will record the agreement on government-issued agreement forms and report them to the finance department for tax purposes.[208] However, it is not uncommon for parties to reach an agreement between themselves without involving a Realtor to avoid paying extra fees and taxes. Local real estate agents have small offices where a *Gerawor* registers the property and *Gerawee*-ee visit to find out about potential *Gerawors* and properties. These agencies are usually small in size and cover a local geographical area. They usually charge both parties for a fee (1% to 2%) of the amount *Gerawee* for their services. The real estate agents draft and keep copies of the *Gerawee* agreements. These agreements are usually standardized and are signed on a government-issued contract form. These real estate agents are licensed by the Department of Justice and have an obligation to report their transactions to the Department of Justice and Department of Finance for tax purposes.

Gerawee-ees rely on verbal confirmation from local real estate agents, neighbors, representative of the neighborhood (in Farsi: wakil *ghuzar*) (in urban centers), and head of a village (in Farsi: *Arbab*) (in villages) to verify ownership. Head of the village and representative of the neighborhood often open real estate agencies often to cash on their information and social standing.

Gerawee can run for years, allowing it to be used as a long-term financing device. A *Gerawee*-ee is entitled to the benefit of the property (live in it, rent it, or receive rent) until the *Gerawor* is able to repay the sum of money paid by *Gerawee*. Depending on the financial status of *Gerawor* and the faith of the investment for which a *Gerawor* has used the money, *Gerawee* can last for several years. Most *Gerawee* last more than a year; however, in some cases, they can last up to ten years. The medium length of *Gerawee* is three years. A *Gerawor* controls the length of *Gerawee*. *Gerawee* can be as long as the *Gerawor* needs it to be. If a *Gerawee*-ee wants to end the *Gerawee*, a *Gerawor* does not have to pay back the money because a *Gerawor* can find another *Gerawee-ee* for the property, given the generally increasing housing demand. It is very common for a *Gerawor* to retain the money and replace several *Gerawee*-ees until he is ready to pay the money and repossess the property or resume receiving its benefits.

In response to objections from local *muftis*, who tend to believe that the practice violates the prohibition of *riba* (and is therefore un-Islamic)[209], real estate agents are increasingly concluding *Gerawee* agreements under the title of *Bai al-Wafa*.[210] This designation is an attempt to justify the legitimacy of the practice under Shari'ah by relying on the Hanafi jurisprudence. As will be discussed subsequently, however, this attempt has had only partial success. In fact, *fatwas* condemning the practice have been increasing. The disapproval of *muftis* cannot explain the divergence of judicial opinions on the formalization of *Gerawee*, on the one hand, and *Sar qufli* and other interest-bearing commercial transactions, on the other, because *muftis* often disapprove of *Sar qufli*. They also vehemently disapprove of interest-bearing commercial transactions of any forms (especially those conducted by *Sarrafs*.)

Bay' al-Wafa: *Sale with a Right of Repurchase*

Rahn (commonly translated into English as "pledge") is the sole formal security mechanism over assets in Islamic law.[211] The *Majalla*[212] gives the following definition of *rahn*: "A pledge [that] consists of setting aside property from which it is possible to obtain payment or satisfaction of some claims. Such property is then said to be pledged, or given in pledge."[213] Under *rahn*, the possession of the property must be transferred to the creditor. According to article 706 of *Majalla*, "If the pledge is not transferred to the effective possession of the pledgee . . . such contract is incomplete and revocable."

Under *Bay' al-Wafa* (sale with right of repurchase), debtor A "sells" an asset to creditor B. Then B "pays a price" for it, $1,000 for example. The contract contains a repurchase condition, which authorizes A to repurchase the asset by paying back the same price (the $1,000) at a later date. Under the sale contract, the title in the property is transferred to B and remains with B during the term of the contract. Thus, B receives the benefit of the property (e.g. by living in the house or renting the house to a tenant) or receives rent from A for the continued enjoyment of the property (e.g. A pays rent in exchange for continuing to stay in the house). B as the owner, that is, holder of formal title, retains a legitimate and justified use of personal property. However, B cannot make any change to the title or the property that would render the repurchase condition ineffective.[214] Thus, the property is, in effect, security for the debt. Some jurists have accepted this kind of contract as valid because of what they deem as "economic imperatives."[215] The *Majalla* acknowledges this position in Articles 396–403.

However, *Bai al-Wafa* has some weakness as a security contract. First, like *rahn*, it is a possessory security: possession of the property must be transferred to the creditor. Second, according to Article 397 of the *Majalla*, the creditor cannot sell the property without the consent of the debtor, even if the time of contract elapses.[216] Finally, because of the resemblance to *riba*, the opinion of the jurists has been widely divided on the question of which party is entitled to the revenue of the assets.[217] Article 398 of the *Majalla* allows the parties to agree that a portion of the revenue goes to the creditor.[218] This version of *Bai al-Wafa*, which allowed for revenue sharing, has been widely practiced in Egypt, Algeria, Turkey, and restrictedly was practiced in Syria and Lebanon.[219]

Gerawee *in* Fatwas *Issued by the Afghan* Muftis

Traditionally *fiqh*[220] has developed in a grassroots bottom-up way. Muslims have referred their concrete questions to the *mufti*, who have been recognized through an informal system of peer-evaluation as competent to answer them.[221] These scholars are called *mufti* (sing.), *Muftis* (plural). *Muftis* then answer those questions in a nonbinding ruling called a *fatwa*.[222] Although nonbinding, these *fatwas* carry significant religious authority for Muslims who try to be faithful to the teachings of their religion.

Taliban have often committed to enforcing *fatwas* of Hanafi *muftis* now that they are in power, so the distinction between state law and the corpse of Hanafi jurisprudence may get more blurred now that the Taliban control the Afghan state again. Taliban, however, have not yet prohibited the practice ostensibly because it would be impractical as many Afghans are dependent on it.

This section explores the reasoning of the contemporary *fatwas* issued by Afghan *muftis*, some of which favor the practice of *Gerawee*, and some of which oppose it.[223] The *fatwas* favoring the practice rely heavily on Hanafi jurisprudence, which has allowed *Bai al-Wafa* and similar transactions on the ground, that the transaction, if formally understood, does not violate the prohibition of interest (*riba*), and that the economic imperatives compel jurists to take a formalistic, not a functional, approach to the understanding of the transaction, allowing it to continue.

Other *fatwas*, on the other hand, oppose *Gerawee*. Specifically, they criticize *Gerawee* arguing that (1) the practice is an obvious ruse to circumvent the prohibition of *riba*; (2) the practice discourages preferable Islamic practices, such as benevolent loans (*qard al-hasana*), *mudaraba* (trust financing contract), and *musharakah* (partnership); and (3) the practice further increases social injustice. This opposition responds to the part of Hanafi tradition that favors the practice by arguing that parties engaging in the *Gerawee* do not have the genuine intention to conclude a sale contract (*bai*). These critics believe that a *bona fide* intention of transfer of title in the property is a salient characteristic of the *bai* (contract of sale) and is key to the legitimization of the practice.

Status of Gerawee *under Afghan Civil Code of 1977*

In addition to Shari'ah-based objection to the *Gerawee*, the practice has ambiguous standing under Afghanistan Civil Law. *Gerawee* as a customary practice does not conform to the Afghan Civil Law. Relevant provisions of the Civil Code of 1977 ("Civil Code") are Articles 1136–1153, which deal with *Bai al-Wafa*.[224] These provisions are reflective of religious concerns with the prohibition of *riba*. In most cases, these provisions are consistent with the arguments of those *muftis* who oppose the practice of *Gerawee*. Article 1136 defines statutory *Bai al-Wafa* as "having the right of taking back the object of sale by seller and that of taking back price by the buyer."[225] The mandatory provisions of statutory *Bai al-Wafa* set forth in the Civil Code contradicts the common practice of *Gerawee* on several points.

According to Article 1137 of the Civil Code, the right of a seller and buyer to "take back" cannot be conditioned and limited to a specific period of time.[226] In particular, the agreement cannot specify that the seller (i.e. debtor/*Gerawee*-ee) cannot take back his property for a period of time. Even if parties agree to such a term, the second clause of the same article states that such an agreement will be void.[227] Furthermore, Article 1151 of the Civil Code explicitly states that, in contracts involving immovable properties, if the parties intend the agreement to be a pledge with the right to use the property (i.e. mortgage), the sale and pledge both are voided.[228] Under this provision, the parties cannot use the statutory *Bai al-Wafa* as a means to secure credit for a loan. The parties must have the intention to transfer the title in the property: they must have the intention of concluding a *bona fide* sale contract.

Civil Code Articles 1136–1153 are a synthesis of provisions of different Arabic countries' civil codes (drafted using al-Sanhuri's methodology, hence, Sanhuri codes). Afghanistan's Civil Code adopts the majority position of Sanhuri civil codes in disallowing *Bai al-Wafa* to be used as a security contract. However, it diverges from the majority position in adopting detailed provisions determining the rights and obligations of the buyer and seller under a non-security *Bai al-Wafa*. In determining parties' rights and obligations, the Civil Code adopts its provisions from the Lebanon Civil Code (1932) Articles 473–486.[229] The Lebanon Civil Code (1932) diverges from the position of the majority of Islamic jurists and the majority of Sanhuri codes by allowing *Bai al-Wafa* to be used as a security contract.[230] The Lebanon Civil Code position is based on the French Civil Code.[231] However, Lebanon shortens the term of validity of the right of repurchase from the French Civil Code's ten years to three years.[232]

Most Sanhuri codes summarily address *Bai al-Wafa* (i.e. Sale with a Right of Repurchase). For example, the Egyptian Civil Code (1948) only has one article on this type of sale: Article 465, which says, "If seller adds a term to the sale contract thereby the seller can repurchase the thing that is being sold within a specified time the sale contract is void."[233] Similarly, the Syrian Civil Code (1949) and the Libya Civil Code (1954) each contain a single article on the sale with the right of repurchase (Article 433 and Article 454, respectively) which are identical to Egyptian Civil Code Article 465.[234] While the Jordan Civil Code (1976) is silent on the issue of Sale with the Right of Repurchase,[235] the Iraq Civil Code (1951) has a single article on *Bai al-Wafa*, Article 1333, which states, "Bai al-Wafa is considered the same as a possessory rahn [pledge]."[236] Iraq Civil Code Article 1333, in effect, states the provisions of the Iraq Civil Code on possessory *rahn* is applicable to *Bai al-Wafa* as well.[237] It should be noted that this approach does not solve the *riba*-problem of use of *Bai al-Wafa* as a security contract because under pledge the ownership remains with the pledgor (seller); therefore, the pledgee's (buyer) use of property raises a *riba*-problem.

Notably, the Lebanon Civil Code (1932) recognizes the validity of a term of repurchase in a sale contract, which is subjected to a specified length of time under the condition that it cannot exceed three years (Article 474).[238] The Lebanon Civil Code sets forth the rights and obligations of buyer and seller under *Bai al-Wafa* within 15 articles (Article 473–486).[239] In effect, the Lebanon Civil Code, following the French Civil Code, and the minority view among Muslim jurists, allows *Bai al-Wafa* to function as a security contract.[240] However, it adopts a shorter time period of three years (compared to the French Civil Code's ten years) for the validity of the right of repurchase.[241]

The Afghanistan Civil Code adopts the majority position of Arabic civil codes and a majority of Muslim jurists by rending the use of *Bai al-Wafa* void as a security device. The Afghanistan Civil Code adopts Lebanon Civil Code's position in that it contains 19 articles setting forth the rights and obligations of the parties under a *Bai al-Wafa*, which is not being used to securitize a loan. Thus, the Afghanistan Civil Code takes on a more moderate stance on *Bai al-Wafa*. It allows the sale contract to include a repurchase clause for a purpose other than securitizing a loan, and it sets forth a series of legal provisions based on Lebanon Civil Code's *Bai al-Wafa*'s provisions that would regulate a non-security *Bai al-Wafa*.

Gerawee *Cases Before Afghan Courts*

Because of the legal and Shari'ah-related uncertainties associated with the customary practice of *Gerawee*, the civil courts, which have jurisdiction over *Gerawee* disputes, have had difficulty adjudicating the legal disputes that arise out of the practice. Hence, the opinions of Afghan courts under the now toppled Islamic Republic varied on the issue of *Gerawee*.

Under the Islamic Republic, Some judges did not recognize the *Gerawee* agreement as valid on the ground that it violates the Qura'nic prohibition of *riba*. They cite to Article 3 of the 2014 Afghan Constitution that reads: "[n]o law shall contravene the tenets and provisions of the holy religion of Islam in Afghanistan."[242] However, they usually compelled the *Gerawor* to repay the amount received based on the notion of fairness. Other judges recognized the *Gerawee* contract as valid, invoking the Hanafi jurisprudence on *Bai al-Wafa* and the provisions of the Afghanistan Civil Code (Article 1137 and 1136).[243] They usually relied on the stipulation of the parties in the agreement, that it is a *Bai al-Wafa*, and refrain from the further inquiry which may render the agreement void.

The judges, however, did not find that *Gerawee* creates a security right. The property under *Gerawee* is not treated as collateral. Courts, both opposing and favoring courts, did order the repayment of the price under *Gerawee*; however, they did not recognize priority for the lender under *Gerawee* if the *Gerawor* is insolvent. The Taliban judicial appointees are likely to continue this practice, but we cannot know.

Sar qufli

Sar qufli is an informally developed institution that is slowly being formalized through judicial decisions without legislation. The practice, in essence, commodifies the future reputation of a business in cases where reputation is closely tied to a place.[244] By commodifying the future business reputation of a place, it improves capital liquidity in the market. *Sar qufli* can be used to raise capital to develop a property (as evident in paradigmatic *Sar qufli* cases, which will be discussed later). It can also be used to raise capital against the value of developed property. Thus, *Sar qufli* relaxes the capital constraints on property development projects.

What is* Sar qufli*?

Sar qufli (which literally means *main lock* or *headlock*), in Afghanistan, has been adopted by merchants and developers as a response to their practical needs outside of formal institutions. As a customary transaction, the specifics of *Sar qufli* transactions may vary across localities. However, in its essence, *Sar qufli* can be best conceptualized as commodification of commercial reputation.

Williamson identifies asset specificity as a transaction problem that can give rise to opportunistic behaviors.[245] Since the reputation value created by the tenant is closely tied to the place of business, meaning it is specific to the property and is not easily transferable, it allows the landlord to extract quasi rent from the tenant by charging higher rents or capturing the reputation value of the place of business by opportunistically evicting the tenant. *Sar qufli* has evolved organically in Afghanistan and other places to curtail the opportunistic behaviors that Williamson argued arise from the problem of asset specificity in commercial lease of immovable property.[246]

Sar qufli is a transaction whereby a lessee protects himself against eviction by paying a lump sum of money to the lessor. By paying a sum of money, the lessee acquires *Sar qufli* in the property. The lessor cannot evict a *Sar qufli*–holder lessee as long as he pays the comparable rent.[247] Lessees use *Sar qufli* to protect the value it creates by the use of the property (a business reputation which is tied to a place and, therefore, is not readily movable). A lessor uses *Sar qufli* to retain ownership of the property while either raising capital to develop the property (e.g. build a shopping center) or raising capital (cashing in) against the value of an already developed property.

It is very common for a developer or owner to offer stores and offices in a commercial building that is being developed or is finished for *Sar qufli*. This way, if someone is interested in using an office or a store in the building, he will pay a lump sum of money, in addition, or without additional regular payments, to obtain a *Sar qufli* over a store or an office in the building.

As the person uses the store/office for his business, the value of the store/office will increase in correlation with the success and popularity of the business. Customers will know that they can go to this address to obtain a certain product or service. Similarly, if the business is successful, customers will trust the service and goods they obtain from that location. This means that rival businesses would be willing to pay a large sum of money for the chance to acquire the location for their own businesses.

Under this system, when the lease term expires, the developer/owner may be tempted to lease the store/office to a rival business or to keep the store/office for himself and launch a similar business. As a result, the developer/owner will, in effect, take the value created by the lessee who had been using the property. *Sar qufli* protects the user of the store/office (i.e. lessee) against appropriation of the reputation-value created through use.

When someone has a *Sar qufli*, he will get to keep using the property, subject to a reasonable increase in rent, unless the owner/developer pays the market price of the value created by the usage, essentially buying back the *Sar qufli*. The owner/developer can only evict the *Sar qufli*–holder lessee by buying back the *Sar qufli*, by paying the *Sar qufli*–holder lessee to hand over his *Sar qufli*. The *Sar qufli*–holder lessee is only willing to hand over the *Sar qufli* for a price equal to or more than the market value of the reputation that has been created through use. The market value, in essence, is determined by how much a *Sar qufli*–holder lessee is willing to accept to vacate the place of business. Therefore, in essence, *Sar qufli* commodifies the reputation value of a place of business. This market price is determined through an open market mechanism, in other words, how much other businesses (or the owner) are willing to pay to obtain the location for their own businesses, that is, demand, and how much the *Sar qufli*–holder lessee is willing to accept to vacate the place of business (supply).

The market value of commercial reputation can be very significant. When a commercial building first opens, it has a low value, but when through use and over time commercial buildings become a hub for a certain market, such as sales from electronics to stationarity or establishment of a *Sarrafi* market, the value of the building and individual store/office can skyrocket. *Sar qufli* is a transaction that allows users of the property, who created the value created through use, to protect their investment and financial interest.

Sar qufli is transferable. The user of a property (a *Sar qufli*–holder lessee) can sell the right to use that property to someone, other than the developer/owner, for a price. However, in this case, the developer/owner has the right of first refusal. *Sar qufli* is also inheritable.

The person who obtains a *Sar qufli* does not obtain ownership of the underlying property. This means that the developer/owner can modify, expand, or renovate the building provided it does not substantially interfere with the right of the person with *Sar qufli* to use the property.

The value of *Sar qulfi* may go down too. If someone obtains a *Sar qufli* for a large sum of money, and that store/office loses its commercial reputation for any reason, he may incur a loss as he is not guaranteed to receive back the money he paid when he obtained the *Sar qufli*. In short, the value of *Sar qufli* fluctuates like a commodity based on supply and demand.

Sar quflis are particularly valuable in Afghanistan because most markets (such as a market where electronics are sold, *Sarrafi* markets, wholesale food markets, oil and gas markets, etc.) are geographically concentrated in a few market-buildings. Therefore, the location of a place of business has a crucial role in its success. For example, it is practically impossible to operate a *Sarrafi* outside a few neighboring *Sarrafi* market-buildings. People associate having a store in the market with being credible. In effect, by buying a store in the *Sarrafi* market-building or buying the right to use a store in the *Sarrafi* market-building, the buyer is buying into a collective reputation. This is why a *Sar qufli* price for a store in the *Sarrafi* market-building can reach up to thousands of dollars.

From a developer/owner perspective, *Sar qufli* is a way to raise or recover the capital without transferring ownership. The developer/owner will remain the owner. This means he enjoys a right of first refusal on the purchase of the reputation value created in the property by the user, and he can expand the property, for example, by adding another floor, while he receives reasonable rent payments.

While the most common subject of *Sar qufli* is a place of business (i.e. store or office), it does not have to be. The subject of *Sar qufli*, legally, can be any leasable property. Given the economic logic of transactions, the *Sar qufli* is used to protect the lessee against forced eviction after the lessee has added to the value of a property. Therefore, it is used for properties for which such protection may be required. For example, a manufacturing business may opt to *Sar qufli*–lease a piece of land, rather than buy it, to erect a factory. This way, the *Sar qufli*–holder lessee can make sure that as long as he pays a comparable rent, the lessor cannot take the erected structure (i.e. factory) by evicting him.

Sar qufli is a transaction developed outside of Afghanistan's formal legal system, but it has come to be recognized by courts. Afghanistan's statutory laws do not mention *Sar qufli*. It is a transaction that was created through practice in the market. As the practice became more and more common, courts were called upon to resolve the disputes concerning this practice. Although Afghanistan has yet to enact statutory laws regarding *Sar qufli*, the courts have responded by enforcing the customary norms that have grown surrounding the practice in the marketplace.

Recognition of Sar qufli *by Commercial Courts*

In Afghanistan, it is common to find transactions outside of the formal legal system. However, what makes *Sar qufli* interesting is the formalization of rules surrounding this practice as courts are used to resolving disputes arising from the practice. The use of courts to resolve disputes involving *Sar qufli* stems from the

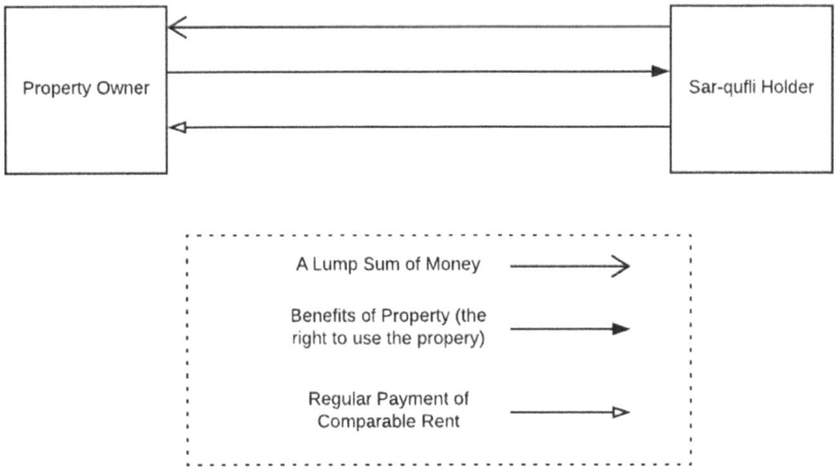

Diagram 2.3 Sar qufli

nature of *Sar qufli* as a claim, or rather a defense, involving an immovable property, most commonly a store or an office.[248]

Most noncriminal cases handled by courts in Afghanistan are disputes involving immovable property. According to the Head of Huquq General Department at the Ministry of Justice, in 2016–2017, Huquq Departments across the country processed 15,867 claims involving immovable properties, 9,966 claims involving monetary claims, and 3,266 involving family and personal affair disputes.[249] This means roughly 55% of requests for noncriminal court proceedings in Afghanistan were related to immovable properties.

Court remedies are both necessary and effective when it comes to immovable property disputes.[250] Court remedies are necessary because immovable property claims are brought against the person who is in actual possession of the immovable property;[251] therefore, coercive action is required to remove the property from that person's actual possession. According to Judge Sediqi, *Sar qufli* disputes often arise when a landlord files a petition to evict a tenant claiming that the term of the lease has either expired or has been violated, and the tenant in response claims that the tenant is not a simple tenant, and he has *Sar qufli* over the immovable property.[252] In response to *Sar qufli* defense, the court would require the tenant to prove the existence of *Sar qufli* to defend himself against an eviction petition.[253]

Court remedies are also effective when it comes to immovable properties. As the interviews show, a major factor that dissuades the merchants from going to courts is that even if they win a case, they are not confident that the judgment can be enforced.[254] For example, in a monetary claim, if the losing party does not have identifiable assets, a judgment against him is useless. Conversely, a judgment recognizing a party's right over an immovable property will almost always be enforced because the property exists, and its possession can be transferred to the winning party. In a *Sar qufli* case, for example, if a tenant is able to prove the existence of a *Sar qufli*, he/she will not be forced to vacate the store.

According to the chief judge of Kabul Primary Commercial Court, no statutory laws recognize or address *Sar qufli*.[255] Under the Islamic Republic, judges across the country, following Afghanistan's Supreme Court's decision, relied on agreement of the parties, a number of decisions made at the Judicial Seminars ("Seminar") and approved by the Afghanistan Supreme Court, and local customs to decide *Sar qufli* disputes.[256] The Seminar is a judicial seminar where chief provincial judges and the justices of the Afghanistan Supreme Court convene, usually every two or three years, to discuss and resolve the most challenging legal questions that face the judiciary. The questions are posed by the judges across countries. The Seminar answers these questions. The Afghanistan Supreme Court High Judicial Council then approves these answers, making them binding for lower courts to follow. Questions about the legality of *Sar qufli* were first posed to the Seminar 1381/2002.[257]

The question of legality and Shari'ah-compliance of *Sar qufli* was raised in Afghanistan because *Sar qufli* limits the rights of the owner indefinitely. The owner cannot forcefully evict a *Sar qufli*–holder lessee indefinitely so long as he holds the *Sar qufli*. The potential for an indefinite constraint of ownership rights made the legality and Shari'ah-compliance of *Sar qufli* suspect in Afghanistan. Therefore, the Seminar was asked to render an opinion on whether the practice of *Sar qufli*, "which is widespread in Kabul," existed in the formative ages of Islam or emerged thereafter. And if it did not exist in the formative period of Islam, who first authorized the practice in Islamic history? And was the practice permissible or not?[258]

In effect, the 2002 Seminar was asked to decide whether the practice was Shari'ah-compliant and therefore legal[259], or whether it violated the Shari'ah and therefore was illegal. The reason the legality of *Sar qufli* was entangled with its Islamic precedents and its Shari'ah-compliance is that the 1964 Constitution, which was in force at the time, mandated judges to, in the absence of pertinent legislation, resolve disputes according to the Hanafi school of Islamic law jurisprudence.[260] The 2004 Constitution has reaffirmed this mandate.[261]

The Seminar rendered the following opinion: (1) *Sar qufli* (which the 2002 Seminar understood to be identical to the practice in Arabic called *khlow hawaniat*) did not exist at the formative age of Islam; (2) classical Sunni jurists did not issue an opinion on the permissibility of the practice; and (3) the practice originated during the reign of Sultan Ghor in the 11th century, when the sultan collected money from his subjects to erect stores on public land with the promise that they would be able to use the stores as long as they paid reasonable rent (paradigmatic case of *Sar qufli*).[262] The practice then spread to the rest of the Islamic world. Muslim scholars, especially Islamic scholars of Cairo, issued *fatwas* approving the Shari'ah-compliance of the practice.[263] Some version of the practice has spread to different parts of the world. The practice is especially common in

Kabul.[264] Therefore, the Seminar concluded the practice was Shari'ah-compliant and, hence, legal, citing several supporting opinions concerning *khlow hawaniat* (which Seminar understands to be the Arabic term for *Sar qufli*) reflected in an authoritative compilation of Hanafi *fatwas* (*al-Mukhtar*) and several exegeses of Majilla as proof that the practice is permissible under the Hanafi school of law.[265] It used these texts, especially *al-Mukhtar*, to elaborate on the rules governing different aspects of the *Sar qufli* in Afghanistan.[266]

The Seminar defined *Sar qufli* as a transaction whereby a lessee, upon payment of a lump sum of money to a lessor, is protected against eviction as long as he continues paying a comparable rent.[267] It answered several legal questions concerning *Sar qufli* (which were presumably raised during the Seminar):

(1) Only receipt of a lump sum of money by the owner of the property creates *Sar qufli*; therefore, if a lessee sublets the property in exchange for a lump sum of money, this does not circumscribe the ownership rights of the owner; therefore, the owner can evict the first or second lessee, and the *Sar qufli* cannot be invoked by either lessee.[268]
(2) Islamic law prohibits excessive uncertainty in transactions (prohibition of *qarar*).[269] Therefore, a developer cannot accept payments from several people in exchange for the promise that he will give them one or two stores if the stores are not specified.[270]
(3) The government can collect payment from different individuals to build a shopping center on public land in exchange for the promise to lease the stores to those individuals.[271] In such a case, those individuals will acquire a *Sar qufli* in the stores. In fact, this was the paradigmatic case of *Sar qufli*.[272]
(4) If the holder of *Sar qufli* leaves the property for a period of time, and then the owner leases the property to someone else in his absence, the holder of *Sar qufli*, upon return, is entitled to receive his *Sar qufli* payment back or evict the current lessee to resume his lease of the property.[273]
(5) *Sar qufli* is a transferable right; therefore, the holder of *Sar qufli* can transfer his right to another person, and this transfer can occur several times.[274] The current holder of *Sar qufli* can invoke *Sar qufli* against the owner as long as the comparable rent is uninterruptedly paid to the owner.[275]
(6) The owner cannot evict the *Sar qufli* holder until a comparable rent is uninterruptedly paid.[276] In case of failure to pay the rent, the owner can evict the *Sar qufli* owner upon payment of the same amount of the money that he has received upon creation of *Sar qufli*.[277]
(7) If a tenant with the permission of the owner performs improvements on the property, the tenant acquires a *Sar qufli* in the property, therefore, cannot be evicted as long as he pays comparable rent.[278] In case he fails to pay the rent, the owner can evict the *Sar qufli* holder upon payment of the value of the improvements.[279]
(8) *Sar qufli* is an inheritable right; therefore, the death of *Sar qufli* holder does not void the *Sar qufli*.[280]

The 1395/2017 Seminar has confirmed that these 2002 Seminar's decisions, along with the agreement of the parties and the local customs, form the legal framework of *Sar qufli* in Afghanistan.[281] The 1395/2017 decisions have especially emphasized the primacy of customs (*'urf*) in commercial matters as a rationale for continued recognition of *Sar qufli* by commercial courts.[282] The 1395/2017 Seminar stated,

> Since *Sar qufli* is common in commercial customs and dealings, and under PCA commercial customs plays an important role in resolution of commercial disputes, and according to the decisions of the High Council of the Afghanistan Supreme Court commercial courts have the jurisdiction to resolve *Sar qufli* disputes, the courts shall decide *Sar qufli* cases in the following manner.[283]

The 1395/2017 Seminar reiterated and specified similar rules decided in the 1381/2002 Seminar.[284] The 1395/2017 Seminar, in particular, instructs the courts to use expert witnesses to determine the prevailing *Sar qufli* customs when deciding *Sar qufli* cases.[285]

The 1395/2017 Seminar, in response to a clarification request, opined that judicial decisions concerning *Sar qufli* are not subject to taxation because the imposition of a tax without legislation is unconstitutional, and there is no legislation concerning *Sar qufli*.[286] This has most likely contributed to the continued use of courts to resolve *Sar qufli* disputes by reducing the cost of use of formal dispute resolution. This suggests reducing the judgment tax (discussed in Chapter 2) likely will improve the popularity of formal dispute resolution in Afghanistan.

A conflict often arises, according to a questioner at the 1395/2017 Seminar, when courts attempt to auction collateral held by banks in case of default, but the collateral is subject to *Sar qufli*.[287] How should this conflict be resolved? In case of a conflict between a security right and a *Sar qufli*, the Seminar opined that the court should accord primacy to the security holder (against *Sar qufli* holder) only if the security owner was unaware of the existence of *Sar qufli* at the time of the creation of security right.[288] If the security right holder was aware of the existence of *Sar qufli* at the time of the creation of the security right, the right of *Sar qufli* holder is not affected by the security right.[289] The Seminar opined that it is a question of fact whether the security right holder had prior knowledge or not, and courts should resolve this question.[290]

According to Judge Sediqi, the majority of commercial judges expressed discontent with the lack of codification on a transaction that makes up the majority of disputes in primary commercial courts and the second most common disputes on appeal.[291] To remedy the situation, some chief commercial judges drafted a directive proposal to be approved by the Afghanistan Supreme Court,[292] but the directive was never adopted. The 1395/2017 Seminar also mandated that a law should be drafted concerning *Sar qufli* which incorporates the judicial jurisprudence.[293] No such law has been enacted at the time of writing. Taliban judicial appointees are likely to keep with the judicial practice of recognizing *Sar qufli* both because of its prevalence and the Islamic justification that the previous judiciary found for it in the Hanafi school of Islamic jurisprudence—the school of jurisprudence from which the Taliban judicial appointee is universally drawn.

The Contrast between Judicial Treatment of **Sar qufli** *and* **Gerawee**

The contrast between judicial attitudes toward *Sar qufli* and *Gerawee* is reflective of the heterogeneous normative attitudes toward informal practices within different sectors of the Afghan judiciary under the Islamic Republic. Judges within the commercial context were more willing to recognize customarily created institutions and interest-bearing transactions than judges in a noncommercial context.[294]

Sar qufli has been judicially formalized despite being an informally created institution concerning an intangible asset, that is, future business reputation, which indefinitely unbundles property rights, that is, the owner of the property is different than the owner of the business reputation connected to that property. Concerning the question of interest, although *Sar qufli* does not raise the same religious concerns as *Gerawee*, commercial judges routinely enforce interest-bearing loan contracts.[295]

The divergent attitudes toward *Gerawee*, on the one hand, and *Sar qufli* and interest-bearing bank loans, on the other, are more interesting when one considers that Afghanistan did not have specialized judges. There was no difference between commercial and noncommercial judges. A criminal judge could get transferred to a commercial court and vice versa.[296]

The difference in attitudes toward formalization of informal practices has great consequences for the creation of efficient formal institutions. De Soto and North both suggest that the remedy for an informal economy is to make the law more user-friendly.[297] They suggest that formally held rights can be incorporated into formal institutions by removing the formal barriers for their inclusion with positive consequences for efficiency.[298] Formal institutions must be made responsive to actual needs of users.[299] Given the heterogeneous attitudes toward formalization, informal practices in commercial and noncommercial contexts, in Afghanistan, the jurisdictional rules, which are amenable to manipulation, could have great efficiency-enhancing potential. Afghanistan still can facilitate formalization of informal financial arrangements through categorizing them as commercial transactions with positive consequences on efficiency and economic growth.

There are multiple reasons for the business-friendly attitudes in Afghanistan's commercial context. One reason has to do with the history of commerce and commercial law in Afghanistan.

Commercial law traditionally has had a unique status in Afghanistan in that it was never an exclusive domain of Shari'ah and religious scholars (*'uluma*).[300] Even before Afghan rulers, notably Amir Abdul Rahman Khan, attempted to centralize the juridical power in the late 19th century, it was generally accepted that commercial disputes could be resolved in special tribunals where commercial customs were the prevailing source of law, and experienced merchants acted as arbiters.[301] For example, the first commercial court in Afghanistan, created by

Amir Abdul Rahman Khan, Panchat, consisted of several non-Muslim arbitrators.[302] Panchat was supposed to resolve commercial disputes based on prevailing commercial customs.[303]

Similarly, although Afghan rulers until the 1980s avoided codifying Islamic law in areas of private law out of fear of public backlash, especially from '*uluma*, major commercial law legislation based on French commercial codes was enacted without arousing backlash in the 1950s.[304] Afghanistan's first bank started issuing interest-bearing loans as early as the 1930s.[305] This is while efforts to centralize the juridical power in other areas of law were met with fierce resistance.[306] This shows that Afghans have generally accepted that commercial laws were subject to different norms.[307] The reason for this discriminating treatment could be because Afghanistan's commercial sector, until the start of a prolonged period of conflict in the 1980s, included a significant number of non-Muslims.[308]

The Afghan financial industry, prior to Nadir Khan almost exclusive, and until the Taliban mostly was run by Hindus and Sikhs.[309] In the 1970s, there were approximately 700,000 Hindus and Sikhs living in Afghanistan; they made up roughly 10% of Afghanistan's population. However, currently, they are estimated to be less than 7,000 (i.e. approximately 0.023% of the population).[310] Jews were active in the financial sector as well.[311] Sikhs, Hindus, and Jews in Afghanistan did not operate under Islamic Law or tribal traditions.[312] In fact, their ability to operate unbounded by the restrictive Islamic financial law doctrines was a reason that they were successful.[313] They could charge interest.[314] Another reason for their success, and perhaps the more important one, was their wide ethnic/religious networks in India and, in the case of Jews, as wide as Europe and the United States. These broad networks allowed them to diversify their portfolios and operate a vast financial sector and far-reaching *hawala* networks without relying on formal legal institutions.[315] Their influence in Afghanistan's commerce was so significant that Panchat, Afghanistan's first formal commercial arbitration court, which was established by Amir Abdul Rahman Khan in the 19th century, included three Hindu arbitrators, who made up almost half of the Panchat's arbitrators.[316] The reason that Amir was so accommodating toward Hindus, Amir Tarzi argues, was to ensure that Indian-Afghan trade would continue, and Hindu merchants would feel protected when they conducted business in Afghanistan.[317]

Another reason for the prevailing business-friendly attitude in Afghanistan's commercial context, even when it comes to interest-bearing transactions, may be that commercial space is a specialized space and does not include the general public. There are different actors who are active in commercial and noncommercial contexts. Noncommercial contexts include non-specialized and non-repeating actors, that is, non-merchants; therefore, they are more sensitive to the general norms of behavior like the prohibition of interest. However, commercial contexts include specialized and repeat actors who are bound together with the aim of making a profit. Therefore, in this specialized space, participating actors, formal institutions, and wider society are willing to carve a space where the general norms of behavior like the prohibition of interest is tweaked by allowing transactional techniques to reduce the barriers to profit-enhancing transactions.

The normative divergence of attitudes within formal institutions concerning commercial and noncommercial contexts, coupled with the efficiency-enhancing potentials of formalizing informal institutions, suggest that Afghanistan could achieve some efficiency-enhancing outcomes by allocating certain transactions to the formal institutions concerned with commercial transactions. For example, the Afghanistan Supreme Court could designate *Gerawee* transactions and disputes arising therefrom, when the *Gerawor* is a merchant, to the commercial courts. This may facilitate the formalization of *Gerawee* and increase the legal protections available to creditors allowing the *Gerawee* market to realize its potential of relaxing the financing constraints on Afghan entrepreneurs.

The Afghanistan Supreme Court under the Republic, while recognizing the need to expand the definition of commercial transactions, and correspondingly the jurisdiction of commercial courts, was resistant against using judicial re-interpretation of commercial laws and jurisdictional rules to expand the scope of commercial laws and commercial courts' jurisdiction.[318] Under the former Supreme Court's jurisprudence, transactions concerning ownership of non-fungible property do not qualify as commercial transactions; therefore, these disputes thereof do not fall under the jurisdiction of commercial courts.[319] Transactions concerning ownership of fungible property and benefits of non-fungible and fungible properties, on the other hand, qualify as commercial transactions; therefore, these disputes do fall under the jurisdiction of commercial courts.[320]

Under this jurisprudence, *Sar qufli* is a transaction concerning the benefit of a non-fungible property (or the right to use the property), while the formal title used to introduce *Gerawee* in courts, *Bay al-Wafa* (sale with the right or repurchase), is a transaction concerning the ownership of a non-fungible property. The court has ruled that *Sar qufli* is a commercial transaction, while *Gerawee* is a noncommercial transaction. As a result, the former falls under the jurisdiction of commercial courts while the latter does not.[321]

The Afghanistan Supreme Court during the era of Republic welcomed legislation to expand the scope of commercial transactions since "commerce has expanded in complexity and scope."[322] However, by deferring the formalization of *Gerawee* (or similar institutions) to the legislature, it removes them from the specialized space of the judiciary. This places the faith of formalization of informal institutions at the hands of the political institutions of legislature, where the normative stance of the broader society holds sway. The Afghan legislature was dominated by representatives who held a conservative, normative stance,[323] and the process of legislation was very political, meaning it was more sensitive to a broader normative stance in the society. Therefore, the deferral of specialized rule-making to the legislature was likely to hinder the formalization of informal institutions, which enabled transactions that did not conform to the broader normative stance in the society to take place in a specialized context of, for example, commerce.

This problem could be remedied by expanding the general scope of commercial transactions and jurisdiction of commercial courts allowing commercial courts to judicially formalize informal institutions like *Gerawee*. For this solution to work, however, the judiciary must take a more proactive role in specialized rule-making. For example, allocating *Gerawee* to the jurisdiction of commercial courts in cases where *Gerawor* is a merchant could allow commercial courts to formalize *Gerawee* as an informal institution based on the prominence of commercial *'urf* (customs) and agreements of the parties in a commercial context rather than relying on the pseudo-category of *Bay al-Wafa*, which does not reflect the *raison d'être* of the *Gerawee* (i.e. the securitization of a loan), to remedy the unfairness of the misuse of *Gerawee* by *Gerawee*-ee.

It is not yet clear how the Taliban overhaul of the judiciary is going to change the judicial attitude regarding *Gerawee* and *Sar qufli*. On the one hand, Taliban have been pragmatic in the business space out of necessity. On the other hand, they are known to subordinate practical consideration for ideologically charged issues. Only time will tell which side will prevail on these issues.

Informal Dispute Resolution Institutions in Afghanistan: Who Uses Them and Why?

The formal dispute resolution system under the now toppled Islamic Republic of Afghanistan was generally ineffective.[324] Contrary to commonly held beliefs, Afghan merchants avoided going to courts, not because of their unchanging aversion to the use of formal, non-reconciliatory dispute resolution rooted in a cultural desire to maintain communal harmony,[325] but because formal dispute resolutions were ineffective. As explained in Chapter 2, court procedures were costly and time-consuming, while enforcement of court judgments was uncertain. The uncertainty in the enforcement of court judgments is due to the difficulty in identifying a person's assets, high rates of insolvency, and absence of clear security rights outside formal mortgage transactions.[326] Most often, court judgments were enforced through repayment schedules that could be, in practice, as long as a few years.[327]

In Afghanistan, the out-of-court dispute resolution options can in most cases deliver the same result as formal court systems in a cheaper and more effective way. Informal dispute resolution institutions, for example, business associations, are often better at identifying a person's assets and dealing with insolvent parties. This is because users of informal institutions tend to be more cooperative (they choose to resolve their dispute there), these institutions have better knowledge of assets to which a person has access (even if he does not legally own those assets), and they are not bound by the formal rules of separation of ownership.

Afghan merchants *did* use courts when it was necessary and effective.[328] For example, commercial courts in Afghanistan handled many *Sar qufli* and commercial lease cases. Merchants used courts for *Sar qufli* and commercial lease cases because these are property right claims brought against the party who is in actual possession of the property. In such cases, the court judgments are both necessary and effective because they provide access to the coercive power of the state to repossess a specific immovable property.

Banks are less likely to have access to informal dispute resolution institutions. If the formal collateral is either insufficient or unreliable, banks are less likely to have access to the rich information about a borrower's assets that informal institutions provide, and if borrowers are insolvent, they generally cannot avail themselves of informal institutions that are generally more effective at the handling of insolvency cases at informal institutions. Afghan courts, however, were generally effective in enforcing formal mortgages held by banks. As long as the market fluctuation did not cause the collateral to significantly depreciate, the collateral was clearly identified at the time of registry, and banks had done their due process to ensure there were not multiple liens on the collateral, Afghan courts could be relied on to auction collateral in the event of default, albeit after a lengthy process.

While informal dispute resolutions are effective in resolving most common disputes among merchants who are part of Afghan society, they put outsiders at a disadvantage. They also create path-dependency. By conflating a person's social reputation and business reputation, informal dispute resolution institutions increase the cost of dissolving business relations, locking parties into the existing business networks. They also hinder the formalization/depersonalization of business relations with possible negative consequences for long-term economic growth. Informal dispute resolution institutions circumvent the application of formal legal rules of bankruptcy, limited liability, and separation of private ownerships; thus, they make it harder for the Afghan economy to formalize.

Afghan Merchants Prefer Informal Dispute Resolution Institutions

My research shows that Afghan merchants have an aversion to the use of courts.[329] In general, they prefer interparty negotiation and compromise and, to a lesser extent, multilateral dispute resolution institutions such as business community unions and associations. However, there are two outliers in the research sample in Herat. Both are well-educated, medium-sized merchants who have a positive view of the formal court system.[330] They resorted to the courts for relatively low-value claims.[331] In most of these cases, the parties against whom these outliers brought claims (defendants) complied before the court could render a final decision.[332] There are three possible explanations for these outliers' views on the court system:

It may be that when claims are of a low value, the defendant feels that going through the formal court procedures will be too costly (mainly because of perception of corruption) and time-consuming; therefore, they comply. In effect, the courts' reputation for ineffectiveness and corruption works in favor of a small number of plaintiffs who go to courts for small claims. Or it may be that courts are generally effective, and it is the false common perception that courts do not work which is keeping merchants from using the courts. The unique background of these two merchants (e.g. being well-educated) may be the reason why they do not share the same false perception. If this is true, one should wonder why the feedback from these few successful cases has not motivated other merchants to use courts. Alternatively, it may be that these two merchants' experiences represent an exception either because of their connections, social status, or some other reason.

Who Uses Formal and Informal Dispute Resolution Institutions in Afghanistan

My research shows consistent attitudes in all research sites; small- and medium-sized merchants are the most common users of courts, while large merchants use courts much less frequently.[333] This finding is unexpected because the dominant position in the literature posits that the size of the business is positively correlated with the use of formal institutions, especially courts.[334] In Afghanistan, small- and medium-sized merchants use courts more often than larger merchants.[335] There are several possible explanations for this. First, I found that in Afghanistan, the use of court is usually an end-of-business occurrence. Smaller businesses, because of their limited capital, are more likely to get involved in such end-of-business disputes, and therefore, they are more likely to use courts. Larger merchants, on the other hand, have a higher tolerance for nonpayment and delays in payment. They can price in nonpayments and other problems. Therefore, they are less likely to use courts. In addition, larger merchants are better connected and more involved in the business community and thus are better positioned to take advantage of out-of-court remedies like unions, chambers, or *jirgas*. Larger merchants are better connected and more involved in the business community; as such, they have better access to out-of-court forums. Similarly, decisions of multilateral dispute resolution forums, such as unions, chambers, or *jirgas*, are most effective against larger merchants because they have more to lose in the form of social status and reputation. Therefore, larger merchants are less inclined to use courts compared to smaller merchants.

This research also shows that the use of threat and force to enforce commercial obligations was rare in all research sites. Therefore, the fact that larger businesses usually are more powerful is less likely to be a reason they do not use courts. This is the case even though larger businesses are also more likely to have more resources to influence formal institutions, through money and political connections. Therefore, the political and social power of larger businesses are not likely a determinant in the choice between formal and informal dispute resolution institutions.

This research also shows that the availability of out-of-court and out-of-chamber solutions determines whether a merchant goes to court or the chamber. Large businesses do not go to courts because they have better access to out-of-court dispute resolution. As an example, Pakistani merchants who do business with Afghan merchants tend to avoid the Kandahar Chamber of Commerce for informal dispute resolution because the Pakistani merchants, by virtue of their ethnic and personal relations, have access to out-of-chamber dispute resolution mechanisms that they trust. For example, they can resort to a *jirga* to resolve their dispute. Iranian merchants who do business in Afghanistan, on the other hand, have less access to out-of-chamber remedies; therefore, as an interview with the vice president of the Kandahar Chamber revealed, Iranian merchants are more likely to resort to the Chamber to resolve a dispute.[336]

Why Merchants Use Informal Dispute Resolution

My research suggests that the effectiveness of court remedies dictates when and if merchants decide to pursue a dispute in court rather than some informal dispute resolution mechanism.[337] Merchants decide to go to court (1) if they determine that the defendant has the assets that could be used to satisfy a possible court verdict and (2) if they determine that the potential court remedy will be superior to anything they can achieve outside the courts using bilateral and multilateral informal schemes. Both are reasons why courts are used to resolve disputes concerning immovable properties.

Formal rules of enforcement of court judgments have a direct effect on a merchant's decision to pursue a court's remedy. As explained in Chapter 2, in Afghanistan, enforcement of court judgment was very uncertain and ineffective (for disputes that did not involve immovable properties). The outcome most often achieved via enforcement of a formal court judgment was a payment schedule.

Court remedies, in effect, compete with out-of-court debt collection remedies. Currently, out-of-court debt collection remedies are generally superior to the formal court system. If the defendant refuses to pay, the out-of-court remedies range from bilateral negotiations to harassment and, in some cases, harsher tools of intimidation. In some cases, the creditors are willing to exchange one debt for another with a discount as a last resort. A Kabuli cell phone merchant said, "When a debtor is unable to pay, the creditor suggests that he buy something like a car on credit and then sell it for a very good price [a high price] to the creditor in exchange for the debt."[338] This way the debtor is able to use his soft capital, that is, his reputation and social connections, to cancel part of the debt by selling the goods for a higher price and/or get an extension on the debt by exchanging one long-delayed debt to another more recent one. This way the debtor gets to stay in business longer.

In multilateral dispute resolution, merchants involve market elders, unions, chambers, or even friends and families in a dispute.[339] In multilateral mechanisms, a group of people (or a person) who are knowledgeable about the customary norms of the relevant market mediate between the disputants so they can reach an amicable resolution. The mediators' incentive is to resolve the dispute in a way that would allow the disputants to continue doing business in the market while upholding the norms of the market. Mediators are not interested in finding the party at fault. They often review the evidence provided by each disputant, but as the vice president of the Kandahar Chamber said, "It is not about evidence. If the evidence were clear or helpful, they [disputants] would not come to us. We are conciliators. We persuade them to compromise."[340] Mediators do make decisions, but mediators' decisions are not binding on the disputants. Disputants can, and sometimes do, decide to go to court after a mediation. Multilateral mechanisms are effective at resolving disputes. An overwhelming majority of disputes that are brought before multilateral mechanisms are resolved.[341]

Multilateral mechanisms are effective because they are often the last resort. According to the same interviewee, "They [disputants] come to us as a last resort. We find a way to end the dispute. If courts were any help, they would have gone to courts."[342] However, it is also true that going to a *jirga*, a *shura*, or a union shows a willingness by all parties to resolve the issue because these forums do not have subpoena power to compel attendance, so a merchant has to decide to go to them.

Informal institutions pressure disputants to resolve their dispute by increasing the social and economic cost of noncompliance. They do so by increasing the number and quality of the people who are aware and involved in a dispute. As disputants refuse to reach an amicable resolution of their disputes, the number and quality of the people who are aware of and involved in the dispute increases. For example, it may start with just a few immediate neighbors of the disputants in the market trying to persuade them to agree on a resolution, then it moves to a market-wide association, then to a province-wide commercial chamber or a union. As the dispute persists, more merchants, who are potential business partners, and more important merchants, who are the main sellers/creditors in the market, become aware of and involved in the dispute. Thus, the increasing reputation cost of the dispute pressures parties to agree on a resolution.

Furthermore, although institutions such as *shura*, *jirga*, or a union are business institutions, they also wield significant social power too. This means that just because a disputant exits a market, as often these disputes are end-of-business disputes, he does not become immune to the social power of these institutions. This also means that the effectiveness of multilateral mechanisms is directly correlated with the social and business status of the disputants in the market. Large businesses and influential members of the market and society care more about their social status and their standing in the market, so they are more likely to comply with a decision of a multilateral institution.

In the context of Afghanistan, multilateral institutions, such as *jirga*s, unions, and *shuras*, enjoy greater social legitimacy compared to the courts.[343] Courts under the Islamic Republic did not enjoy great social legitimacy because they were perceived as corrupt.[344] This means that a disputant might have been more concerned about defying a decision of a *jirga*, *shura*, or a union than a court's judgment. The multilateral institutions in the *Sarraf*'s market are particularly effective because they are backed by a collective desire to protect the reputation of the *Sarrafi* market, which is a form of common assets.[345] The power of the *Sarraf* union to mediate disputes among *Sarraf*s is formalized by the Da Afghanistan Bank's Regulation, which empowers *Sarraf* unions to mediate disputes between *Sarraf*s if *Sarraf*s resort to the union.

Notably, the interviewees express discontent with the decisions of multilateral institutors. Interview data reveal common discontent with the decisions of *jirgas* and business forums. These discontents cumulate around two points: some merchants believe that these *jirgas* are not impartial, and some creditors believe they are pro-debtor. The latter is generally the evidence for the former. As one

Kandahari merchant expressed, "They [*Jirgas*] ask us to accept 100,000 AFN for a 1 million AFN debt or they set up a long repayment schedule. For example, they ask us to accept 100,000 AFN this year and 300,000 AFN next year."[346]

At first, these complaints may appear to be the shortcomings of informal dispute resolution. However, this is only when one compares the informal process to the court proceedings against a solvent defendant. Such a comparison would be misleading. This is because the informal process of *jirgas* and unions most often are invoked when the defendant is insolvent. These cases are end-of-business and end-of-relationship cases. Therefore, the correct comparison would be to compare the informal processes with a bankruptcy proceeding. If one does that, the decisions of informal institutions appear more reasonable and realistic rather than merely conciliatory or pro-debtor.

In Afghanistan, as explained earlier, formal bankruptcy proceedings are seldom invoked.[347] The Supreme Court of the Islamic Republic formally instructed the courts not to initiate bankruptcy proceedings even if the person against whom a judgement was issued claims to have no way to pay for the judgement. This decision was ostensibly made to ensure that the losing party cannot avail himself of the protection of bankruptcy laws by hiding his assets, which he can do relatively easily due to the informality of property ownership in Afghanistan. The courts were required to enter into a judgment and determine the obligation of the losing side; however, the judgment would only be enforced if the defendant has sufficient identifiable assets. If the court cannot identify that the losing party has sufficient assets, and the winner is not able to show that the losing party has sufficient assets, enforcement is delayed until such time when sufficient assets are identified. In effect, because a debtor could not enjoy the benefits of invoking bankruptcy in formal courts, informal forums provide a much-needed relief.

However, the formal suspension of bankruptcy proceedings, coupled with the informal norms of dispute resolution, means that in Afghanistan, the usual protection afforded by limited liability, in effect, do not exist. Informal dispute resolution mechanisms do not recognize the principle of limited liability. They are instead guided by a moral understanding of obligation coupled with a culturally informed notion of fairness. As a result, all of a debtor's assets are considered when settling a debt. The suspension of the principle of limited liability hinders effective risk diversification that would be legally available to a merchant. This dissuades merchants from engaging in risky businesses. This pro-creditor attitude is counterbalanced with the notion of fairness. Under informal dispute resolution institutions, the creditor is often expected, demanded, and advised to provide relief to the debtor based on the culturally informed notions of fairness, forgiveness, and mutual help.

The informal institutions are sometimes effective because they are not bound with the formal rules of property ownership. In an informal institution, all the assets to which the debtor has access are considered a legitimate source for debt collection. While courts could only enforce judgments against property formally held by the losing party, informal institutions can pressure the debtor to use any asset to which he has access (regardless of formal property rules) to repay a debt.

For example, the jewelry of a debtor's wife cannot be used to enforce a court judgment because it is legally owned by the wife; however, in a *shura*, union, or a *jirga*, a debtor cannot claim he does not have sufficient assets to honor his debt if his wife has valuable jewelry.

Variation in the Effectiveness of Informal Dispute Resolution Institutions

My research suggests that there is a significant variation in the ability of business associations, such as unions and chambers, to resolve disputes.[348] The interview data suggests that the ability of an association to effectively resolve a dispute is dependent on a series of factors, which include the geographical concentration of its members, the exclusiveness of the market, the number of players, the profession-type (whether it is a lifetime profession or not), whether the market's collective reputation is a common asset, and whether the structure of the market gives association leader gatekeeping power.[349]

Dispute resolution is more institutionalized in associations like *Sarraf*'s union that represent a market which is concentrated in few buildings, has a limited number of members who interact with each other regularly, and whose members pursue their business as a life career. Additional characteristics of *Sarrafi* unions are that the formal laws give the association some authority over admission and resolution of disputes, and its members share the collective reputation of the *Sarraf* as a common asset.[350]

Chambers are on the other end of the spectrum. Chambers' members are spread across a province, and they do not necessarily have consistent interactions with each other. The members may easily join or exit the chamber. Merchant-members do not share a collective reputation, and the chamber has no influence on who gets to be a merchant. The unions and local associations fall somewhere in between.

There is also regional variation.[351] Dispute resolution is much less institutionalized in Balkh as compared to Herat. In Balkh, there are fewer business unions. The unions that do exist do not engage in dispute resolution. The Balkh Chamber of Commerce, which is the only business association that engages in some dispute resolution practices, does so on an ad hoc basis (there is no dispute resolution board/committee/center) and much less often than Herat. The Balkh Chamber does not offer transnational dispute resolution, whereas Herat Chamber does most of its dispute resolution work in this area. The Balkh Chamber is not part of any transnational or joint chamber with Afghanistan's business partner (e.g. Iran or Pakistan).

Balkh's *Sarrafi* union is similarly less institutionalized. Until very recently, there has been no dispute resolution board/committee/center or administrative body for the *Sarrafi* union. The president of Balkh's *Sarrafi* union only has a very small shop where he supposedly discharges his duties as the president of the union. This is in contrast to Herat, where *Sarraf* union has more space, more administrative staff, and a more developed organizational structure.

Sarrafs in Nangarhar and Herat, compared to Balkh, have exhibited more vigorous self-regulation. This self-regulation seems to be correlated with the development of the local financial market and its credibility and the prevalence of credit sales. For example, in both Nangarhar and Herat, *Sarrafs* said that the union has banned *Sarraf*'s checks because too many *Sarrafs* were going bankrupt due to failing checks, and it was ruining the reputation of *Sarrafs* (which is their most valuable asset). This ban did not stop the practice of issuance of postdated checks entirely, but it helped contain the practice and has evidently helped restore the reputation of *Sarrafs*. Balkh's *Sarrafs* reported dissatisfaction with the ability of the union to safeguard the collective reputation of *Sarrafs*. Interviewee data suggests that *Sarraf* unions in Nangarhar and Herat had more control over who gets to enter the *Sarrafs* market through controlling who can open a store in the physical *Sarrafi* market compared to Balkh's union.

In contrast to Herat and similar to Balkh, in Nangarhar, dispute resolution is less institutionalized in the unions or the chamber. In fact, interestingly enough, most interviewees talked about the union and the chamber as if they were part of the government, and going to them would be similar to going to the government. This may be because of the prevalence of other Pashtun cultural institutions, like *jirga*. In Nangarhar, use of *jirga* is more the norm. *Jirga* is an ad hoc council formed from influential people who have knowledge about the disputants. The *jirga* mediates between the disputants and seems to be very effective in resolving smaller disputes in Nangarhar. Another possible reason for the under-institutionalization of dispute resolution in Nangarhar, at least in regard to the chamber, is due to the proximity of Nangarhar to Kabul. Nangarhar is only a three-hour drive away from the center of Kabul, so most big disputes are referred to and handled there because most large merchants have a presence in Kabul as well. Smaller disputes seem to be handled locally by *jirgas*.

Kandahar follows more closely on the Nangarhar model of merchant dispute resolution. Like Nangarhar, Kandahar is similarly a majority Pashtun province where the use of *jirga* is the norm. However, unlike Nangarhar, in Kandahar *jirga* are institutionalized within the chamber and unions. In other words, Pashtun culture and *jirga* do not seem to be an impediment to institutionalization of dispute resolution. On the contrary, they seem to facilitate institutionalization of dispute resolution in Kandahar.

A sizable group of Kandahari merchants trade dried fruits with Europe and India.[352] Their business partners in those countries are usually from the Afghan diaspora.[353] They use the same model of risk-sharing and flexible contracts to trade with their Afghan counterparts in Europe and India. They employ the institution of *jirga* to resolve disputes with their Afghan counterpart in Europe.[354] The migration of the institution of *jirga* along with the use of flexible, risk-sharing contracts is a very interesting phenomenon which merits further study.

Informal Dispute Resolution and Pashtun Culture

My research suggests that informal dispute resolutions are more effective in Kandahar and Nangarhar.[355] This observation is confirmed by the low rate of per capita court use in these two provinces compared to the other three provinces, which are either more ethnically heterogeneous or dominated by non-Pashtun ethnic groups.[356]

The cultural roots of *jirgas* give them more coercive power in predominately Pashtun provinces, such as Kandahar and Nangarhar. The cultural salience of *jirga* in the Pashtun culture provides a focal point and increases its coercive and persuasive power in predominantly Pashtun provinces.[357] Defying and disrespecting a *jirga* has more severe social consequences in a homogenously Pashtun province. While *shuras* (which have Islamic roots and are generally understood as a generic counterpart to the *jirgas*) and business community unions were common across all research sites and provinces, they did not have the same cultural salience as *jirgas*. This is likely because Pashtuns have a longer history of autonomy and self-regulation in Afghanistan compared to non-Pashtun ethnic groups, who, by the virtue of being minorities, were more reliant on and controlled by the central authority in Afghanistan.[358] For example, Tajiks have historically been more likely to settle in a city (compared to Pashtuns) and to staff the Afghan government's bureaucracy.[359]

As explained earlier in this chapter, Pashtuns' cultural aversion to the use of signed written documents (to avoid offending their customers by doubting their trustworthiness) in the course of their business dealings, for example, in Nangarhar, also contributes to the low rate of court use. Written signed documents are instrumental in court proceedings; it is much harder to win a case before a formal court without written signed documents as evidence. Thus, both the cultural salience of *jirga* in the Pashtun culture and their aversion to the use of signed written documents in the course of business dealings render the use of formal courts both less necessary and more difficult in Kandahar and Nangarhar.[360]

The Use of Force to Resolve a Commercial Dispute

The use of force/threat to collect a debt or to resist debt collection is rare in Afghanistan.[361] It is mostly because business in Afghanistan is based on reputation and relationship. If a merchant uses force to resolve a dispute, it will affect his ability to do business as it will dissuade other merchants from doing business with a merchant who has a reputation of resorting to force/threat. As a Nangarhari merchant said, "If you use force or threat, you cannot work in the market."[362]

Although rare, use of force and threat in commercial settings does occur. Most often, the use of force is exercised by a non-merchant party in a commercial transaction. For example, a non-merchant who is a party in a one-time business deal (e.g. import of oil) may resort to using threats to resolve a dispute. Interviews conducted in Kabul suggest the use of force/threat was more common there.[363] This may be because of two reasons: (1) there were more people with access to power in Kabul; and (2) because there are fewer wide-reaching cultural, ethnic, or social norms constraining power/use of threat due to the increased diversity in Kabul. Kabul's interview data suggest that the use of force/threat is also sector-variant. Some sectors are more prone to the use of threat/force due to their player types.[364] For example, the construction market is dominated with actors who wield significant political power; therefore, they are more prone to use force or threat in a business context.[365]

Kandahar's interview data suggest that *qawm* (a perceived community of people with a common ancestor) is a factor that controls the use of force in both business and other settings in Kandahar.[366] On the other hand, it seems that political connections may be a reason that has empowered Kandahari merchants in certain sectors that rely on political connections.[367] The effect of *qawm* is possibly more felt in Kandahar because it is the least urbanized and least ethnically diverse of the five research sites.[368]

The consequences of Taliban return to power in relation to formal and informal dispute resolution remain unknown. By the time of writing, Taliban had appointed at least two judges for each province and filled several positions in the Supreme Court. In many instances, these appointments formalized the position of Taliban shadow judiciary. On the one hand, Taliban have been often more capable of enforcing their court judgements given their credibility and willingness when it comes to using violence against anyone who challenges their writ. On the other hand, the low number of judicial appointees, necessitated by financial constraints, coupled with their positive attitude toward business associations, their embeddedness in the Pashtun cultural milieu suggests that the privileged position of a multilateral business association in handling disputes may endure under the Taliban rule at least for some time.

Notes

1 Author's interview with a merchant in Nangarhar (May 2017).
2 Author's interview with a merchant at Herat (April 2017).
3 Author's interview with an owner of manufacturing business in Herat (April 2017).
4 Asli Demirgu-Kunt & Vojislav Maksimovic, The World Bank Development Research Group, Firms as Financial Intermediaries: Evidence from Trade Credit Data 1 (Policy Research Working Paper 2696, 2001), https://openknowledge.worldbank.org/bitstream/handle/10986/19511/multi0page.pdf?sequence=1&isAllowed=y [hereinafter Demirgu-Kunt & Maksimovic, Firms as Financial Intermediaries: Evidence from Trade Credit Data (2001)]; Simon Johnson et al., *Courts and Relational Contracts*, 18(1) J. Law Econ. Organ. 221, 223 (2000) [hereinafter Simon Johnson et al., *Courts and Relational Contracts* (2000)]; Pınar Özlü & Cihan Yalcin, *The Trade Credit Channel of Monetary Policy Transmission: Evidence from Nonfinancial Manufacturing Firms in Turkey*, 48(4) Emerging Markets Finance and Trade 106 (2012) [hereinafter Özlü & Yalcin, *The Trade Credit Channel of Monetary Policy Transmission* (2012)]; F. Daniela Fabbri & Leora Klapper, The World Bank Development Research Group, Finance and Private Sector Team, Market Power and the Matching of Trade Credit Terms 4 (Policy Research Working Paper 4754, 2008) https://openknowledge.worldbank.org/bitstream/handle/10986/6913/WPS4754.pdf?sequence=1&isAllowed=y [hereinafter Fabbri & Klapper, Market Power and the Matching of Trade Credit Terms (2008)]; Neeltje Van Horen, Trade Credit as a Competitiveness Tool: Evidence from Developing Countries, 4 (Munich Personal RePEc Archive, 2004), https://mpra.ub.uni-muenchen.de/2792/1/MPRA_paper_2792.pdf [hereinafter Horen, Trade Credit as a Competitiveness Tool (2004)]; Go Yano & Maho Shiraishi, *Factors in the Development of Trade Credit: Case Study of Provinces in China*, 50(2) Emerging Markets Finance and Trade 131 (2014) [hereinafter Yano & Shiraishi, *Factors in the Development of Trade Credit* (2014)].

5 Author's interview with a merchant in Nangarhar (May 2017).
6 Raymond Fisman & Inessa Love, *Trade Credit, Financial Intermediary Development, and Industry Growth*, 58(1) J. Finance 353 (2003) [hereinafter Fisman & Love, *Financial Intermediary Development, and Industry Growth* (2003)].
7 Ying Ge & Jiaping Qiu, *Financial Development, Bank Discrimination and Trade Credit*, 31(2) J. Bank. Finance 514 (2007).
8 *Id.*
9 Leora Klapper et al., *Trade Credit Contracts*, 25(3) Rev. Financial Stud. 838, 840 (2012).
10 Anna Maria C. Menichini, *Inter-Firm Trade Finance at Times of Crisis*, 34(10) The World Economy 1788, 1803 (2011).
11 *Id.*
12 This finding is based on author's interviews with Afghan merchants in five major provinces of Afghanistan (Kabul, Herat, Nangarhar, Balkh, and Kandahar) between March and August 2017.
13 *See e.g.* Karen Clay, *Trade Without Law: Private-Order Institutions in Mexican California*, 13(1) J. L. Econ. Org. 202, 224 (1997) [hereinafter Clay, *Trade Without Law* (1997)]; Clay (1997b), Karen Clay, *Trade, Institutions, and Credit: Contract Enforcement on The California Coast 1830–1846*, 34 Explorations in Economic History 495, 506 (1997) [hereinafter Clay, *Trade, Institutions, and Credit* (1997b)].
14 *See* 3.2.10.
15 Author's interview with the owner of a manufacturing business at Herat (April 2017).
16 *Id.*
17 The description of weekly payment system of *ugraee* in Afghanistan presented here is based on typical facts reported by the interviewees in the author's interviews with Afghan merchants in five major provinces of Afghanistan (Kabul, Herat, Nangarhar, Balkh, and Kandahar) between March and August 2017.
18 The consequences of prevailing supply chain structure for innovation is discussed in Section 3.1.6.
19 Author's interviews with merchants in Nangarhar (May 2017).
20 Author's interviews with merchants in Herat (April 2017) and author's interviews with merchants in Kabul (June 2017).
21 Author's interviews with merchants in Nangarhar (May 2017).
22 Author's interview with the president of Herat *Sarrafi* Market (April 2017).
23 This finding is based on author's interviews with Afghan merchants in five major provinces of Afghanistan (Kabul, Herat, Nangarhar, Balkh, and Kandahar) between March and August 2017.
24 *See* discussion of court enforcement of written and verbal contracts in Chapter 2.
25 Author's interviews with merchants in Kabul (June 2017).
26 Author's interview with the owner of a construction company in Kabul (June 2017).
27 *Id.*
28 This finding is based on author's interviews with Afghan merchants in five major provinces of Afghanistan (Kabul, Herat, Nangarhar, Balkh, and Kandahar) between March and August 2017, as well as author's personal observations over several years of his work as accountant in Afghanistan's private sector between 2008 and 2013.
29 *Id.*
30 *Id.*
31 The description of process of credit transaction in Afghanistan presented here is based on typical facts reported by the interviewees in the author's interviews with Afghan merchants in five major provinces of Afghanistan (Kabul, Herat, Nangarhar, Balkh, and Kandahar) between March and August 2017.
32 This finding is based on author's interviews with Afghan merchants in five major provinces of Afghanistan (Kabul, Herat, Nangarhar, Balkh, and Kandahar) between March and August 2017, as well as author's personal observations over several years of his work as accountant in Afghanistan's private sector between 2008 and 2013.

33 In an interview with the author, the owner of a construction company talked about an American contractor refusing to pay and leaving the country and his failed attempt to collect the debt. Author's interview with the owner of a construction company in Kabul (June 2017).
34 Author's interview with a Kandahari merchant (July 2017).
35 *Id.*
36 *See e.g.* Guoqiang Long, Center for Global Development, China's Policies on FDI: Review and Evaluation 316 (2005), www.cgdev.org/sites/default/files/9780881323818-Ch12.pdf.
37 This finding is based on author's personal observations over several years of his work as accountant in Afghanistan's private sector between 2008 and 2013.
38 This finding is based on author's interviews with Afghan merchants in five major provinces of Afghanistan (Kabul, Herat, Nangarhar, Balkh, and Kandahar) between March and August 2017, as well as author's personal observations over several years of his work as accountant in Afghanistan's private sector between 2008 and 2013.
39 *See* website of Business and Marketing Services Agency of Afghanistan (last visited June 1, 2018), www.bamsa.org/
40 *Id.*
41 *Id.*
42 This finding is based on author's interviews with Afghan merchants in five major provinces of Afghanistan (Kabul, Herat, Nangarhar, Balkh, and Kandahar) between March and August 2017.
43 *See* Principles of Commercial Law (1958); Civil Code (1977).
44 Author's interview with a hygiene product importer in Herat (April 2017).
45 Author's interviews with merchants in Kabul (June 2017), author's interviews with merchants in Herat (April 2017), and author's interviews with merchants in Balkh (May 2017).
46 Author's interviews with merchants in Nangarhar (May 2017), and author's interviews with merchants in Kandahar (July 2017).
47 Author's interviews with merchants in Nangarhar (May 2017).
48 Author's interview with a Nangarhari merchant (May 2017).
49 Author's interviews with merchants in Kandahar (July 2017).
50 The facts reported in this paragraph is based on author's interview with the owner of a construction company in Kabul (June 2017).
51 This finding is based on author's interviews with Afghan merchants in five major provinces of Afghanistan (Kabul, Herat, Nangarhar, Balkh, and Kandahar) between March and August 2017.
52 Yano & Shiraishi, *Factors in the Development of Trade Credit* (2014), at 131.
53 Fisman & Love, *Financial Intermediary Development, and Industry Growth* (2003), at 355.
54 Yano & Shiraishi, *Factors in the Development of Trade Credit* (2014), at 131.
55 Chapter 4 discusses bank loans.
56 *See* Yano & Shiraishi, *Factors in the Development of Trade Credit* (2014), at 131.
57 Robert Cull et al., The World Bank, Formal Finance and Trade Credit During China's Transition 21 (Policy Research Working Papers 4204, 2007), https://openknowledge.worldbank.org/bitstream/handle/10986/7022/wps4204.pdf?sequence=1&isAllowed=y.
58 *Id.*
59 *See* Demirgu-Kunt & Maksimovic, Firms as Financial Intermediaries: Evidence from Trade Credit Data (2001), at 1.
60 *Id.*
61 Afghanistan's banking system is discussed in Chapter 4.
62 This finding is based on author's interviews with Afghan merchants in five major provinces of Afghanistan (Kabul, Herat, Nangarhar, Balkh, and Kandahar) between March and August 2017.

63 Emilia Garcia-Appendini & Judit Montoriol-Garriga, *Firms as Liquidity Providers: Evidence from the 2007–2008 Financial Crisis*, 109(1) J. Financial. Econ. 272, 290 (2013).

64 Jaleel Ahmad et al., *Investigation of Causal Relationship Between Trade Credit and Bank Loan During 2008 Financial Crisis*, 5(5) J. Asian Business Strategy 90, 97 (2015).

65 This finding is based on author's interviews with Afghan merchants in five major provinces of Afghanistan (Kabul, Herat, Nangarhar, Balkh, and Kandahar) between March and August 2017.

66 *Id.*

67 *See* Claudio Raddatz, *Credit Chains, and Sectoral Comovement, Does the Use of Trade Credit Amplify Sectoral Shock?* 92(4) Rev. Econ. Stat. 985, 986 (2010).

68 This finding is based on author's interviews with Afghan merchants in five major provinces of Afghanistan (Kabul, Herat, Nangarhar, Balkh, and Kandahar) between March and August 2017.

69 Bank loans are discussed further in Chapter 4.

70 *See* Law on Use of Movable Properties as Collateral in Banking Transactions (2009).

71 This finding is based on author's interviews with Afghan merchants in five major provinces of Afghanistan (Kabul, Herat, Nangarhar, Balkh, and Kandahar) between March and August 2017, as well as author's personal observations over several years of his work as accountant in Afghanistan's private sector between 2008 and 2013.

72 Da Afghanistan Bank's Public Credit Registry Department has set up a website where institutional and non-institutional users could check the existing security rights. However, until the date of writing this dissertation (May 2018), the website was not working. *See* Da Afghanistan Bank's Public Credit Registry, https://pcr.gov.af/.

73 Author's interview with a cell phone merchant in Kabul (June 2017).

74 *See* Chapter 2 for a more detailed discussion of Afghanistan Property Rights System.

75 Bank loans further in Chapter 4.

76 It is further discussed later in this chapter.

77 This finding is based on author's interviews with Afghan merchants in five major provinces of Afghanistan (Kabul, Herat, Nangarhar, Balkh, and Kandahar) between March and August 2017.

78 This finding is based on author's interviews with Afghan merchants in five major provinces of Afghanistan (Kabul, Herat, Nangarhar, Balkh, and Kandahar) between March and August 2017, as well as author's personal observations over several years of his work as accountant in Afghanistan's private sector between 2008 and 2013.

79 Author's interview with a Kabuli merchant (June 2017).

80 *See e.g.* Joshua Charap & Jelena Pavlovic, IMF Middle East and Central Asia Department, Development of the Commercial Banking System in Afghanistan: Risks and Rewards 18 (IMF Working Paper WP/09/150, 2009), www.imf.org/external/pubs/ft/wp/2009/wp09150.pdf; *see also* Da Afghanistan Bank, Strategic Plan (2017).

81 *Id.*

82 *See generally* Joseph A. Schumpeter, Capitalism, Socialism, and Democracy (1943); Acemoğlu and Robinson have also credited the rise of the West to the change in political institutions that allowed creative destruction to happen. *See* Daron Acemoğlu et al., *Institutions as A Fundamental Cause of Long-Run Growth, in* 1A Handbook of Economic Growth 385, 390 (Philippe Aghion and Steven N. Durlauf eds., Elsevier B.V. 2005).

83 This finding is based on author's interviews with Afghan merchants in five major provinces of Afghanistan (Kabul, Herat, Nangarhar, Balkh, and Kandahar) between March and August 2017, as well as author's personal observations over several years of his work as accountant in Afghanistan's private sector between 2008 and 2013.

84 *Id.*

85 *Id.*
86 *Id.*
87 *See* Appendix I.
88 This finding is based on author's interviews with Afghan merchants in five major provinces of Afghanistan (Kabul, Herat, Nangarhar, Balkh, and Kandahar) between March and August 2017.
89 *Id.*
90 Bank loans are discussed further in Chapter 4.
91 *See* Chapter 2.
92 *See* Section 3.2.7.
93 *See e.g.* Michael C. Jensen & William H. Meckling, *Theory of the Firm: Managerial Behavior, Agency Costs and Ownership Structure*, 3(4) J. Financial Econ 305 (1976).
94 *See* Ronald H. Coase, *The Problem of Social Cost*, 3 J. L. Econ. 1, 43 (1960); Ronald H. Coase, *The Nature of The Firm: Origin, Meaning, Influence*, 4 J. L. Econ. Org. 3, 4 (1988); *see also* Oliver E. Williamson, The Economic Institutions of Capitalism 20–21 (1985) [hereinafter Williamson, The Economic Institutions of Capitalism (1985)].
95 This finding is based on author's interviews with Afghan merchants in five major provinces of Afghanistan (Kabul, Herat, Nangarhar, Balkh, and Kandahar) between March and August 2017, as well as author's personal observations over several years of his work as accountant in Afghanistan's private sector between 2008 and 2013.
96 This finding is based on author's interviews with Afghan merchants in five major provinces of Afghanistan (Kabul, Herat, Nangarhar, Balkh, and Kandahar) between March and August 2017.
97 Kellee S. Tsai, *Back-Alley Banking: Private Entrepreneurs in China* 36 (Cornell University Press 2002).
98 *See* Civil Code (1977), arts. 1993–2102; *See also* Khan, The Islamic Law of Inheritance (2008).
99 This finding is based on author's interviews with Afghan merchants in five major provinces of Afghanistan (Kabul, Herat, Nangarhar, Balkh, and Kandahar) between March and August 2017.
100 This finding is based on author's interviews with Afghan merchants in five major provinces of Afghanistan (Kabul, Herat, Nangarhar, Balkh, and Kandahar) between March and August 2017, as well as author's personal observations over several years of his work as accountant in Afghanistan's private sector between 2008 and 2013.
101 *Id.*
102 *Id.*
103 Author's interview with a medicine merchant in Kabul (June 2017).
104 *See* Introduction and Chapter 2.
105 *See* Afghanistan Constitution (2014), art. 10 states, "The state shall encourage, protect as well as ensure the safety of capital investment and private enterprises in accordance with the provisions of the law and *market economy*" (emphasis added).
106 Ibraheem Bahiss, Taliban's ideological and policy positions on social justice (2021) http://library.fes.de/pdf-files/bueros/kabul/18739.pdf
107 *See* Chapter 4.
108 *Id.*
109 *See* The World Bank, Afghanistan—State Building, Sustaining, Growth, and Reducing Poverty 6 (World Bank 2005) [hereinafter The World Bank, State Building, Sustaining, Growth, and Reducing Poverty (2005)]; *see also* Integrity Watch Afghanistan, Curbing Illicit Financial Flows in Afghanistan: Money Laundering, Terrorist Financing, and *hawala* 28 (2015), https://iwaweb.org/wp-content/uploads/2016/04/IFF-report-English-2-for-screen.pdf [hereinafter Integrity Watch Afghanistan, Curbing Illicit Financial Flows in Afghanistan (2015)].

110 This finding is based on author's interviews with Afghan merchants in five major provinces of Afghanistan (Kabul, Herat, Nangarhar, Balkh, and Kandahar) between March and August 2017, as well as author's personal observations over several years of his work as accountant in Afghanistan's private sector between 2008 and 2013.
111 *Id.*
112 *Id.*
113 *See* Chapter 2.
114 Afghanistan's banking system as discussed in Chapter 4.
115 *See* Afghanistan Financial Services, Afghanistan Capital Markets Assessment: A Survey and Analysis of Current Capital Market Activities, the Demand for Capital, and the Basic Structure and Government Debt Markets (2010), www.ahg.af/data/AFS-Afghanistan-Capital-MarketsAssessment.pdf [hereinafter Afghanistan Financial Services, Afghanistan Capital Markets Assessment (2010)].
116 This finding is based on author's interviews with Afghan merchants in five major provinces of Afghanistan (Kabul, Herat, Nangarhar, Balkh, and Kandahar) between March and August 2017.
117 *Id.*
118 This finding is based on author's interviews with *Sarrafs* in five major provinces of Afghanistan (Kabul, Herat, Nangarhar, Balkh, and Kandahar) between March and August 2017.
119 *See* Chapter 4.
120 Author's interview with a Kabuli merchant (June 2017).
121 The problem of illegal funds in *Sarrafi* markets and its policy implications are discussed in Chapter 4 and Chapter 5.
122 This finding is based on author's interviews with *Sarrafs* in five major provinces of Afghanistan (Kabul, Herat, Nangarhar, Balkh, and Kandahar) between March and August 2017.
123 *See* Special Inspector General for Afghanistan Reconstruction, Quarterly Report to the United States Congress 165 (April 30, 2015), www.sigar.mil/pdf/quarterly reports/2015-04-30qr-section3-economic.pdf [hereinafter Special Inspector General, Quarterly Report to the United States Congress (2015)].
124 *See* Chapter 4 in context of Da Afghanistan Bank effort to outlaw the use of personal bank accounts by *Sarrafs*; *see also* Special Inspector General, Quarterly Report to the United States Congress (2015), at 165.
125 *See* Special Inspector General, Quarterly Report to the United States Congress (2015), at 165.
126 This finding is based on author's interviews with *Sarrafs* in five major provinces of Afghanistan (Kabul, Herat, Nangarhar, Balkh, and Kandahar) between March and August 2017.
127 *Id.*
128 *See* Office of the Economic Advisor, Mobile Banking in Afghanistan (PowerPoint Presentation, April 2017), http://afghaneconomics.com/research/Mobile_banking_scenario.pdf [hereinafter Office of the Economic Advisor, Mobile Banking in Afghanistan (2017)].
129 *See* Holzmann, Managed Labor Migration in Afghanistan (2018), at 12.
130 *See* Edwina A. Thompson, Trust Is the Coin of the Realm: Lessons from the Money Men in Afghanistan 221 (2011) [hereinafter Thompson, Trust Is the Coin of the Realm (2011)].
131 *See infra* Chapter 4.
132 This finding is based on author's interviews with *Sarrafs* in five major provinces of Afghanistan (Kabul, Herat, Nangarhar, Balkh, and Kandahar) between March and August 2017.
133 *Id.*
134 This finding is based on author's interviews with Afghan merchants in five major provinces of Afghanistan (Kabul, Herat, Nangarhar, Balkh, and Kandahar) between

March and August 2017, as well as author's personal observations over several years of his work as accountant in Afghanistan's private sector between 2008 and 2013.

135 I personally received my salary in the US dollar while working for the United States Institute for Peace in Afghanistan.

136 This finding is based on author's interviews with *Sarrafs* in five major provinces of Afghanistan (Kabul, Herat, Nangarhar, Balkh, and Kandahar) between March and August 2017.

137 *Id.*

138 *See* Chapter 2.

139 Author's interview with a *Sarraf* in Herat (April 2017).

140 Author's interview with the president of Herat *Sarrafi* Union (April 2017).

141 *Id.*

142 *Id.*

143 *Id.*

144 This finding is based on author's interviews with Afghan merchants in five major provinces of Afghanistan (Kabul, Herat, Nangarhar, Balkh, and Kandahar) between March and August 2017.

145 Author's interview with the president of Herat *Sarrafi* Union (April 2017).

146 *See* Qanun Asnad Qabel Mu'amela [Law of Negotiable Documents] (No. 971, 1387 [2009]), arts. 3(3).

147 *Id.*

148 *Id.*

149 *Id.*

150 The facts reported in this paragraph are based on author's interview with the president of Herat *Sarrafi* Union (April 2017).

151 *See* Section 3.1.2.

152 Author's interview with a Kabuli merchant (June 2017).

153 This finding is based on author's interviews with Afghan merchants in five major provinces of Afghanistan (Kabul, Herat, Nangarhar, Balkh, and Kandahar) between March and August 2017.

154 This finding is based on author's interviews with Herati merchants (April 2017).

155 This finding is based on author's interviews with Afghan merchants in five major provinces of Afghanistan (Kabul, Herat, Nangarhar, Balkh, and Kandahar) between March and August 2017.

156 Author's interview with a merchant in Herat (April 2017).

157 *See* Section 3.2.10.

158 Author's interview with a Herati *Sarraf* (April 2017).

159 *See* Chapter 4.

160 Afghanistan Financial Services, Afghanistan Capital Markets Assessment (2010).

161 *Id.*

162 Author's interview with a Herati *Sarraf* (April 2017).

163 This finding is based on author's interviews with Afghan merchants in five major provinces of Afghanistan (Kabul, Herat, Nangarhar, Balkh, and Kandahar) between March and August 2017.

164 *Id.*

165 *See* Section 3.2.10.

166 This finding is based on author's interviews with Afghan merchants in five major provinces of Afghanistan (Kabul, Herat, Nangarhar, Balkh, and Kandahar) between March and August 2017, as well as author's personal observations over several years of his work as accountant in Afghanistan's private sector between 2008 and 2013.

167 This finding is based on author's interviews with Afghan merchants in five major provinces of Afghanistan (Kabul, Herat, Nangarhar, Balkh, and Kandahar) between March and August 2017.

168 Measured by the combination of decline in the quality of business climate and business climate stability. *See* Chapter 2.

169 Author's interview with a Balkhi *Sarraf* (May 2017).

170 This finding is based on author's interviews with Afghan merchants in five major provinces of Afghanistan (Kabul, Herat, Nangarhar, Balkh, and Kandahar) between March and August 2017.

171 *Id.*

172 *Id.*

173 *See* Chapter 2.

174 *Id.*

175 *Id.*

176 Turkmenistan, Tajikistan, and Uzbekistan.

177 *See* Chapter 2.

178 *See e.g.* Clay, *Trade Without Law* (1997), at 224; Clay, *Trade, Institutions, and Credit* (1997b), at 34.

179 This finding is based on author's interviews with Afghan merchants in five major provinces of Afghanistan (Kabul, Herat, Nangarhar, Balkh, and Kandahar) between March and August 2017.

180 *Id.*

181 *Id.*

182 *See* Da Afghanistan Bank, Strategic Plan 2 (2017), at 46; Afghanistan Ministry of Commerce and Industries, Strategic Plan (2016), at 47. Da Afghanistan Bank has recently issued a license for Afghanistan's first Islamic Bank, "Islamic Bank of Afghanistan." *See Central Bank Grants IBA An Islamic Banking System License*, TOLONews (April 23, 2018), www.tolonews.com/business/central-bank-grants-iba-islamic-banking-system-license.

183 The low rate of bank use, discussed in Chapter 4, occurs despite the availability of Shari'ah-compliant financing in Afghanistan.

184 This finding is based on author's interviews with Afghan merchants in five major provinces of Afghanistan (Kabul, Herat, Nangarhar, Balkh, and Kandahar) between March and August 2017.

185 This finding is based on author's interviews with merchants in Kabul (June 2017).

186 *Id.*

187 *Id.*

188 This finding is based on author's interviews with Afghan merchants in five major provinces of Afghanistan (Kabul, Herat, Nangarhar, Balkh, and Kandahar) between March and August 2017.

189 This finding is based on author's interviews with merchants in Kandahar (July 2017).

190 This finding is based on author's interviews with merchants in Kabul (June 2017).

191 Thompson, Trust Is the Coin of the Realm (2011), at 248.

192 *Id.*

193 The description of *Gerawee* in Afghanistan presented here is based on typical facts reported by the interviewees in the author's interviews with Afghan merchants in five major provinces of Afghanistan (Kabul, Herat, Nangarhar, Balkh, and Kandahar) between March and August 2017, author's personal observations over several years of his work as accountant in Afghanistan's private sector between 2008 and 2013, and interview data collected for the author's previously published article, Haroun Rahimi, *The Customary Practice of Gerawee in Afghanistan: A Case for Transitioning to Real Equity-Based Finance*, 4 Indon. J. Int'l & Comp. L. 743 (2015) [hereinafter Rahimi, *The Customary Practice of Gerawee in Afghanistan* (2015)].

194 The total value of *Gerawee* in a province is estimated according to the following formula: the total number of active real estate agents × the median number of *Gerawee* brokered by a real estate agent per year × median value of a *Gerawee*. These are rough conservative estimates because not all *Gerawee*s are conducted via real estate agencies. If *Gerawor* and *Gerawee*-ee know each other, they may decide to bypass going to a real estate agency to avoid paying commission. The number of active real

estate agents, the median number of *Gerawees* brokered by a real estate agent per year, and the median value of a *Gerawee* is based on the estimates provided by an experienced real estate agent and Huquq Department in Herat, the president of Union of Real Estate Agents in Kandahar, an experienced real estate agent in Kabul, and an experienced real estate agent and Huquq Department in Balkh.

195 *See infra* Chapter 4.

196 As explained in Chapter 2, these four provinces represent less than half of Afghanistan's economy and less than one-third of Afghanistan's population; therefore, one could safely assume they only represent half of total value of *Gerawee*. Thus, extrapolating from that, the estimated total value of *Gerawee* would reach 900 million USD, which is almost 25% higher than total amount of outstanding bank loans.

197 This is based on the estimates provided by Huquq Department and an experienced real estate agent using the following formula: the total number of active real estate agents × the median number of *Gerawee* brokered by a real estate agent per year × median value of a *Gerawee*.

198 According to the data provided by the head of Da Afghanistan Bank regional office in Herat, the total amount of outstanding bank loans issued by provincial branches of banks in Herat for the year 2017 was 43.3 million USD. The actual bank loans held by Herati merchants may be higher because most banks in Afghanistan issue loans through their Kabul office. Therefore, the data on regional distribution of bank loans are not representative of actual bank loan distribution. It was not possible to obtain the data on outstanding loans for other provinces.

199 This finding is based on author's interviews with Afghan merchants in five major provinces of Afghanistan (Kabul, Herat, Nangarhar, Balkh, and Kandahar) between March and August 2017, author's personal observations over several years of his work as accountant in Afghanistan's private sector between 2008 and 2013, and interview data collected for the author's previously published article, Rahimi, *The Customary Practice of Gerawee in Afghanistan* (2015).

200 Author's interview with the president of Nangarhar Real Estate Agents' Union (May 2017).

201 Author's interview with an experienced real estate agent in Balkh (May 2017).

202 *See* Chapter 2.

203 The contrast between refusal of civil courts to enforce the terms of a *Gerawee*, on the one hand, and commercial courts' enforcement of interest-bearing bank loans and recognition of informally developed practice of *Sar qufli*, on the other, suggests attitude toward interest-bearing transactions and recognition of informal practices differ from commercial to noncommercial contexts. The prevailing attitudes in commercial courts is more business friendly than the prevailing attitude in noncommercial courts.

204 *See* Principles of Commercial Procedure (1965) and Civil Code (1977).

205 This will be discussed later in this chapter.

206 *See* Chapter 2.

207 This finding is based on author's interviews with Afghan merchants in five major provinces of Afghanistan (Kabul, Herat, Nangarhar, Balkh, and Kandahar) between March and August 2017, Author's personal observations over several years of his work as accountant in Afghanistan's private sector between 2008 and 2013, and interview data collected for the author's previously published article, Rahimi, *The Customary Practice of Gerawee in Afghanistan* (2015).

208 Thompson et al., An Introduction to the Property Law of Afghanistan (2015), at 59.

209 The Shari'ah-standing of *Gerawee*, an explanation of the term *mufti*, and the opinions of Islamic jurists regarding the practice is discussed later in this chapter.

210 This finding is based on author's interviews with Afghan merchants in five major provinces of Afghanistan (Kabul, Herat, Nangarhar, Balkh, and Kandahar) between March and August 2017, author's personal observations over several years of his work as accountant in Afghanistan's private sector between 2008 and 2013, and

interview data collected for the author's previously published article, Rahimi, *The Customary Practice of Gerawee in Afghanistan* (2015).

211 Nicholas Foster, *The Islamic Law of Real Security,* 15 Arab L.Q. 145 (2000) [hereinafter Foster, *The Islamic Law of Real Security* (2000)].

212 *Al-Majalla Al Ahkam Al Adaliyyah* [The Ottoman Courts Manual] (Hanafi) (last visisted February 19, 2015, 05:32 p.m.), http://legal.pipa.ps/files/server/ENG%20 Ottoman%20Majalle%20(Civil%20Law).pdf [hereinafter The Ottoman Courts Manual] (Majalla is a manual of Hanafi jurisprudence that was developed by Ottoman to be used by judges in Ottoman courts. The Majalla is considered to be an authoritative collection of the rulings of Hanafis on most issues.)

213 *Id.* art. 701.

214 Like selling the property without the consent of seller/debtor A.

215 Foster, *The Islamic Law of Real Security* (2000), at 159.

216 *See* The Ottoman Courts Manual.

217 Foster, *The Islamic Law of Real Security* (2000), at 145.

218 *See* The Ottoman Courts Manual.

219 Foster, *The Islamic Law of Real Security* (2000), at 147.

220 *Fiqh* refers to the human interpretation of Shari'ah. Shari'ah, that is, Islamic law, is only accessible through application of human reasons to the scripture. However, since the human reason is inevitably fallible, Muslim jurists distinguish between Shari'ah, which is Islamic law as understood by Allah, and the *Fiqh*, which is human understanding of Shari'ah and, therefore, inescapably subject to debate, evolution, and disagreement. For an explanation of meanings *Fiqh* and Shari'ah and their differences, *see* Clark B. Lombardi, State Law as Islamic law in Modern Egypt Ch. One (2006). In this dissertation, however, I often use Islamic law, Shari'ah, and *Fiqh* interchangeably.

221 *See* Wael Hallaq, *What is Sharia? in* 12 Yearbook of Islamic And Middle Eastern Law: 2005–2006 151 (2007); Rudolph Peters, *From Jurists Law to Statute Law or What Happens When the Shari'a Is Codified*, 7 Mediterranean Politics 82 (2002).

222 *Id.*

223 The *fatwas* discussed in this section are generally retrieved from these online sources of *fatwas*: www.islampp.com/ (Web: Sunni Tradition Fatwa [Juristic Legal Ruling] Collection); www.eslahonline.net (Web: Afghanistan Rectification Society). The discussion is also informed by the authors' many discussions with local muftis in Afghanistan.

224 Civil Code (1977).

225 *Id.*

226 *Id.*

227 *Id.*

228 *Id.*

229 Al-Qanun Al-Madani [Civil Code] (Lebanon) [hereinafter Lebanon Civil Code].

230 *Id.* arts. 473–486.

231 Code Civil [Civil Code] arts. 1659–1673 (Fr.) (vente à réméré) [hereinafter France Civil code].

232 Lebanon Civil Code, arts. 473–486.

233 Al-Qanun Al-Madani [Civil Code] (Egypt) [hereinafter Egypt Civil Code].

234 *See Id.*; Al-Qanun Al-Madani [Civil Code] (Syria) [hereinafter Syria Civil Code]; Al-Qanun Al-Madani [Civil Code] (Libya) [hereinafter Libya Civil Code].

235 *See* Al-Qanun Al-Madani [Civil Code] (Jordan) [hereinafter Jordan Civil Code].

236 Al-Qanun Al-Madani [Civil Code] (Iraq) [hereinafter Iraq Civil Code].

237 *Id.*

238 Lebanon Civil Code, arts. 473–486.

239 *Id.*

240 *See Id.*; France Civil Code, arts. 1659–1673.

241 *Id.*
242 Afghanistan Constitution (2014).
243 Civil Code (1977).
244 The description of *Sar qufli* in Afghanistan presented here is based on typical facts reported by the interviewees in the author's interviews with Afghan merchants in five major provinces of Afghanistan (Kabul, Herat, Nangarhar, Balkh, and Kandahar) between March and August 2017, as well as author's personal observations over several years of his work as accountant in Afghanistan's private sector between 2008 and 2013.
245 *See* Williamson, The Economic Institutions of Capitalism (1985), at Ch. 1, 2 and 3.
246 *Id.*
247 The comparable rent (in Arabic *ijarat al-meth'l*) refers to the amount of rent for a comparable property. For example, the comparable rent of a store would be the amount of rent for which a comparable store may be leased.
248 *See* Chapter 1.
249 Author's written communication via Facebook with the head of Huquq General Department at the Ministry of Justice (September 2017).
250 *See* Chapter 1.
251 *See* Law of Civil Procedure (1990).
252 Author's interview with Judge Sediqi, chief judge of Kabul's Primary Commercial Court (June 2017).
253 *Id.*
254 *See* Chapter 2.
255 Author's interview with Judge Sediqi, chief judge of Kabul's Primary Commercial Court (June 2017).
256 *Id.*; *see also* Afghanistan Supreme Court, Judicial Seminar (2017).
257 *See* Afghanistan Supreme Court, Judicial Seminar (2017), at 73.
258 *Id.*
259 Under Qanun Assasi Afghanistan [Afghanistan Constitution] 1343 [1964], art. 69 [hereinafter Afghanistan Constitution (1964)], which was in force at the time, in the absence of legislation, courts were required to use Hanafi jurisprudence to resolve disputes. Article 130 of Afghanistan Constitution (2014) contains a similar provision.
260 *See* Afghanistan Constitution (1964), art. 69.
261 *See* Afghanistan Constitution (2014), art. 130.
262 Afghanistan Supreme Court, Judicial Seminar 73–74 (1381 [2002]).
263 *Id.*
264 *Id.* at 74.
265 *Id.* at 74–82.
266 *Id.*
267 *Id.* at 74.
268 *Id.* at 75.
269 *Id.*
270 *Id.*
271 *Id.*
272 *Id.* at 77.
273 *Id.* at 78.
274 *Id.* at 80.
275 *Id.*
276 *Id.* at 81.
277 *Id.*
278 *Id.* at 82.
279 *Id.*
280 *Id.*
281 Afghanistan Supreme Court, Judicial Seminar (2017), at 172.

282 *Id.* at 336.
283 *Id.*
284 *Id.* at 336–337.
285 *Id.* at 337.
286 *Id.* at 184.
287 *Id.* at 185.
288 *Id.*
289 *Id.*
290 *Id.*
291 Author's interview with Judge Sediqi, chief judge of Kabul's Primary Commercial Court (June 2017).
292 *Id.*
293 Afghanistan Supreme Court, Judicial Seminar (2017), at 341.
294 *See* earlier discussions in this chapter.
295 *See* Chapter 1.
296 This observation is based on the author's knowledge of Afghanistan's judicial system as he has witnessed such assignment and reassignment.
297 *See* North, Change and Economic Performance 5 (1990), at 33; Hernando De Soto, The Mystery of Capital: Why Capitalism Triumphs in the West and Fails Everywhere Else 227 (2000).
298 *Id.*
299 *Id.*
300 Amin Tarzi, *Islam, Shari'a, and State Building under 'Abd al-Rahman Khan*, *in* Afghanistan's Islam: From Conversion to the Taliban 139 (Nile Green ed., University of Calafornia Press 2017) [hereinafter Tarzi, *Islam, Shari'a, and State Building under 'Abd al-Rahman Khan* (2017)]; Afghanistan Supreme Court, Tariskh Qaza [History of Judiciary], 95–97 [hereinafter Afghanistan Supreme Court, History of Judiciary]; Mohammad Hashim Kamali, Law in Afghanistan: A Study of the Constitution, Matrimonial Law, and Judiciary 37 (1985) [hereinafter Kamali, Law in Afghanistan (1985)].
301 *Id.*
302 *See* Tarzi, *Islam, Shari'a, and State Building under 'Abd al-Rahman Khan* (2017), at 139.
303 *Id.*
304 Haroun Rahimi, *What Can History Teach Us About Legal Reform in Afghanistan? A Historical Study of Codification of Substantive Private Law in Afghanistan* (Forthcoming).
305 *See* Tres Thompson et al., *Stanford Law School, Afghanistan Legal Education Project, An Introduction to the Commercial Law of Afghanistan* 36 (2nd ed. 2015), https://www-cdn.law.stanford.edu/wp-content/uploads/2015/12/Intro-to-Commercial-Law-of-Afg-2d-Ed.pdf.
306 *See* Tarzi, *Islam, Shari'a, and State Building under 'Abd al-Rahman Khan* (2017), at 139; Afghanistan Supreme Court, History of Judiciary, 95–97; Kamali, Law in Afghanistan (1985), at 37.
307 Haroun Rahimi, *What Can History Teach Us About Legal Reform in Afghanistan? A Historical Study of Codification of Substantive Private Law in Afghanistan* (Forthcoming).
308 *See* Ruchi Kumar, *The Decline of Afghanistan's Hindu and Sikh Communities*, Al Jazeera (January 1, 2017), www.aljazeera.com/indepth/features/2016/12/decline-afghanistan-hindu-sikh-communities-161225082540860.html [hereinafter Kumar, *The Decline of Afghanistan's Hindu And Sikh Communities* (2017)]; *see also* Sara Koplik, A Political and Economic History of the Jews of Afghanistan 38 (2015) [hereinafter Koplik, History of the Jews of Afghanistan (2015)].
309 *See* Thompson, Trust Is the Coin of the Realm (2011), at 117.

310 Kumar, *The Decline of Afghanistan's Hindu and Sikh Communities* (2017).
311 *See* Koplik, History of the Jews of Afghanistan (2015), at 38.
312 *See* Thompson, Trust Is the Coin of the Realm (2011), at 117.
313 *Id.*
314 Nadir Khan attempted to end the reign of non-Muslims (and non-Afghans for that matter) in the area of financial law. To do that, he summoned the assistance of a prominent Afghan businessman, Abdul Majid Zabuli, who founded Afghanistan's first joint stock company with a monopoly on export and currency exchange. He later founded Afghanistan's first bank as well. However, Zabuli's efforts were not successful at ending Hindus' control of Afghanistan's financial market. Although he was able to get around the prohibition of interest by charging a repayment fee instead of interest, his company did not run a sufficiently diverse portfolio and did not enjoy the same vast ethnic/religious network as Hindus. *See* Thompson et al., An Introduction to the Property Law of Afghanistan (2015), at 36.
315 The fact that they were not from any of the Afghan ethnic groups also helped Hindus to protect themselves against political turmoil and ethnic rivalry in the country. *See* Thompson, Trust Is the Coin of the Realm (2011), at 117.
316 *See* Tarzi, *Islam, Shari'a, and State Building under 'Abd al-Rahman Khan* (2017), at 139.
317 *Id.*
318 Afghanistan Supreme Court, Judicial Seminar (2017), at 190.
319 *Id.*
320 *Id.*
321 *Id.*
322 *Id.*
323 For an analysis of composition of Afghanistan's legislature, *see* Mohammad Bashir Mobasher, *Understanding Ethnic-Electoral Dynamics: How Ethnic Politics Affect Electoral Laws and Election Outcomes in Afghanistan*, 51 Gonz. L. Rev. 355 (2015–2016).
324 *See* Chapter 2.
325 "The *Afghan mindset is more arbitration oriented*, but people in Kabul clearly want to explore more formalized mediation. *The interest for formal mediation in the province* [Balkh] *the consultant visited was not as high*" (emphasis added). Pete Swanson, United States Agency for International Development, Report on Assessment of Potential for Commercial Mediation 6 (March 17, 2010).
326 *See* Chapter 1.
327 *Id.*
328 *See id.* and discussion of *Sar qufli* earlier in this chapter.
329 The description of informal dispute resolution in Afghanistan presented here is based on typical facts reported by the interviewees in the author's interviews with Afghan merchants in five major provinces of Afghanistan (Kabul, Herat, Nangarhar, Balkh, and Kandahar) between March and August 2017.
330 Author's interview with a hygienic products manufacturer in Herat (April 2017).
331 *Id.*
332 *Id.*
333 This finding is based on author's interviews with Afghan merchants in five major provinces of Afghanistan (Kabul, Herat, Nangarhar, Balkh, and Kandahar) between March and August 2017.
334 *See* e.g. Marcel Fafchamps, Market Institutions In Sub-Saharan Africa 10 (2004).
335 This finding is based on author's interviews with Afghan merchants in five major provinces of Afghanistan (Kabul, Herat, Nangarhar, Balkh, and Kandahar) between March and August 2017.
336 Author's interview with the vice president of Kandahar Chamber of Commerce and Industries (July 2017).

337 This finding is based on author's interviews with Afghan merchants in five major provinces of Afghanistan (Kabul, Herat, Nangarhar, Balkh, and Kandahar) between March and August 2017.
338 Author's interview with a Kabuli merchant (June 2017).
339 The description of informal dispute resolution in Afghanistan presented here is based on typical facts reported by the interviewees in the author's interviews with Afghan merchants in five major provinces of Afghanistan (Kabul, Herat, Nangarhar, Balkh, and Kandahar) between March and August 2017.
340 Author's interview with the vice president of Kandahar Chamber of Commerce and Industries (July 2017).
341 This finding is based on author's interviews with Afghan merchants in five major provinces of Afghanistan (Kabul, Herat, Nangarhar, Balkh, and Kandahar) between March and August 2017.
342 Author's interview with the vice president of Kandahar Chamber of Commerce and Industries (July 2017).
343 This observation is based on author's interviews with Afghan merchants in five major provinces of Afghanistan (Kabul, Herat, Nangarhar, Balkh, and Kandahar) between March and August 2017, as well as author's personal observations over several years of his work as accountant in Afghanistan's private sector between 2008 and 2013.
344 In 2017, 62% of the people pooled in 3,773 across 34 provinces of Afghanistan said that magistrate and judges are either all or most of them corrupt. This is the highest percentage of five institutions pooled. National government officers, members of parliament, local government officers, and the police were perceived as less corrupt. World Justice Program, The Rule of Law in Afghanistan 10 (2017), https://worldjusticeproject.org/sites/default/files/documents/WJP_Afghanistan_Report_2017_Final_Online-Edition-Reduced.pdf.
345 *See* discussion of *Sarrafi* markets earlier in this chapter.
346 Author's interview with a Kandahari merchant (July 2017).
347 *See infra* Chapter 2.
348 This finding is based on author's interviews with Afghan merchants in five major provinces of Afghanistan (Kabul, Herat, Nangarhar, Balkh, and Kandahar) between March and August 2017.
349 *Id.*
350 *See* discussion of *Sarrafi* markets earlier in this chapter.
351 The description of variation of informal dispute resolution practices in Afghanistan presented here is based on typical facts reported by the interviewees in the author's interviews with Afghan merchants in five major provinces of Afghanistan (Kabul, Herat, Nangarhar, Balkh, and Kandahar) between March and August 2017.
352 Author's interview with two dried fruits merchants in Kandahar (July 2017).
353 *Id.*
354 *Id.*
355 This finding is based on author's interviews with Afghan merchants in five major provinces of Afghanistan (Kabul, Herat, Nangarhar, Balkh, and Kandahar) between March and August 2017.
356 *See* Chapter 2.
357 For a historical discussion of *jirga* in the Pashtun context, *see* Barfield, Afghan Customary Law and Its Relationship to Formal Judicial Institutions (2003).
358 *See* Newell, The Politics of Afghanistan (1972), at 34.
359 *Id.* at 78.1
360 Identifying the consequences prevalence of *jirga* and avoidance of use of signed written documents in the business dealings on economic performance of predominately Pashtun provinces compared to more ethnically heterogeneous provinces will require additional research.

361 This finding is based on author's interviews with Afghan merchants in five major provinces of Afghanistan (Kabul, Herat, Nangarhar, Balkh, and Kandahar) between March and August 2017, as well as author's personal observations over several years of his work as accountant in Afghanistan's private sector between 2008 and 2013.
362 Author's interview with a merchant in Nangarhar (May 2017).
363 Author's interviews with merchants in Kabul (June 2017).
364 *Id.*
365 This assertion is based on author's interview with the owner of a construction company in Kabul (May 2017).
366 Author's interviews with merchants in Kandahar (July 2017).
367 *Id.*
368 *See* Afghanistan Demographic Estimates for the Years of 2002/03 until 2017/18.

References

Afghanistan Demographic Estimates for the Years of 2002/03 until 2017/18, http://cso.gov.af/fa/page/demography-and-socile-statistics/demograph-statistics/3897111

Afghanistan Financial Services, Afghanistan Capital Markets Assessment: A Survey and Analysis of Current Capital Market Activities, the Demand for Capital, and the Basic Structure and Government Debt Markets (2010), www.ahg.af/data/AFS-Afghanistan-Capital-MarketsAssessment.pdf

Afghanistan Ministry of Commerce and Industries, Ministry of Commerce and Industries Strategic Plan 2016–2020 (2016), http://moci.gov.af/Content/files/stratigic%20plan%20 2017.pdf

Afghanistan Rectification Society, www.eslahonline.net

Afghanistan Supreme Court, Judicial Seminar 190 (1395 [2017])

Afghanistan Supreme Court, Judicial Seminar 73–74 (1381 [2002])

Afghanistan Supreme Court, Tariskh Qaza [History of Judiciary]

AL-MAJALLA AL AHKAM AL ADALIYYAH [The Ottoman Courts Manual] (Hanafi), (February 19, 2015, 05:32 PM), http://legal.pipa.ps/files/server/ENG%20Ottoman%20 Majalle%20(Civil%20Law).pdf

Al-Qanun Al-Madani [Civil Code] (Egypt)

Al-Qanun Al-Madani [Civil Code] (Iraq)

Al-Qanun Al-Madani [Civil Code] (Jordan)

Al-Qanun Al-Madani [Civil Code] (Lebanon)

Al-Qanun Al-Madani [Civil Code] (Libya)

Al-Qanun Al-Madani [Civil Code] (Syria)

Amin Tarzi, *Islam, Shari'a, and State Building under 'Abd al-Rahman Khan, in* Afghanistan's Islam: From Conversion to the Taliban (Nile Green ed., University of California Press 2017)

Anna Maria C. Menichini, *Inter-Firm Tade Finance at Times of Crisis*, 34(10) The World Economy (American Economic Association 2011)

Asli Demirgu-Kunt & Vojislav Maksimovic, *The World Bank Development Research Group, Firms as Financial Intermediaries: Evidence from Trade Credit Data* (Policy Research Working Paper 2696, 2001), https://openknowledge.worldbank.org/bitstream/handle/10986/19511/multi0page.pdf?sequence=1&isAllowed=y

Asulnama Tijarat [Principles of Commercial Law] 1336 [1958]

Central Bank Grants IBA An Islamic Banking System License, TOLONews (April 23, 2018), www.tolonews.com/business/central-bank-grants-iba-islamic-banking-system-license.

Clark B. Lombardi, *State Law as Islamic law in Modern Egypt* (Brill Academic Publishers 2006)
Claudio Raddatz, *Credit Chains, and Sectoral Comovement, Does the Use of Trade Credit Amplify Sectoral Shock?* 92(4) Rev. Econ. Stat. (2010)
Code Civil [Civil Code] arts. 1659–1673 (Fr.) (vente à réméré)
Da Afghanistan Bank, Strategic Plan 2017–2021 (2017), http://dab.gov.af/fa/page/media/publications/strategic-plan
Da Afghanistan Bank's Public Credit Registry, https://pcr.gov.af/
Daron Acemoğlu et al., *Institutions as A Fundamental Cause of Long-Run Growth, in* 1A Handbook of Economic Growth (Philippe Aghion & Steven N. Durlauf eds., Elsevier B.V. 2005)
Douglas C. North, *Institutions, Institutional Change and Economic Performance* (Cambridge University Press 1990)
Edwina A. Thompson, *Trust Is the Coin of The Realm: Lessons from The Money Men in Afghanistan* (OUP Pakistan 2011)
Emilia Garcia-Appendini & Judit Montoriol-Garriga, *Firms as Liquidity Providers: Evidence from the 2007–2008 Financial Crisis*, 109(1) J. Financial. Econ (2013)
F. Daniela Fabbri & Leora Klapper, *The World Bank Development Research Group, Finance and Private Sector Team, Market Power and the Matching of Trade Credit Terms* (Policy Research Working Paper 4754, 2008), https://openknowledge.worldbank.org/bitstream/handle/10986/6913/WPS4754.pdf?sequence=1&isAllowed=y
Go Yano & Maho Shiraishi, *Factors in the Development of Trade Credit: Case Study of Provinces in China*, 50(2) Emerging Markets Finance and Trade (Taylor&Francis, Ltd 2014)
Guoqiang Long, Center for Global Development, China's Policies on FDI: Review and Evaluation (2005), www.cgdev.org/sites/default/files/9780881323818-Ch12.pdf
Hamid Khan, *The Islamic Law of Inheritance* (Oxford University Press 2008).
Haroun Rahimi, *The Customary Practice of Gerawee in Afghanistan: A Case for Transitioning to Real Equity-Based Finance*, 4 Indon. J. Int'l & Comp. L. (2015)
Haroun Rahimi, *What Can History Teach Us About Legal Reform in Afghanistan? A Historical Study of Codification of Substantive Private Law in Afghanistan* (Forthcoming).
Hernando De Soto, *The Mystery of Capital: Why Capitalism Triumphs in the West and Fails Everywhere Else* (Basic Books 2000)
Ibraheem Bahiss, *Taliban's Ideological and Policy Positions on Social Justice* (Freidrich-Ebert Stiftung 2021) http://library.fes.de/pdf-files/bueros/kabul/18739.pdf
Integrity Watch Afghanistan, Curbing Illicit Financial Flows in Afghanistan: Money Laundering, Terrorist Financing, and *hawala* (2015), https://iwaweb.org/wp-content/uploads/2016/04/IFF-report-English-2-for-screen.pdf
Jaleel Ahmad et al., *Investigation of Causal Relationship Between Trade Credit and Bank Loan During 2008 Financial Crisis*, 5(5) J. Asian Business Strategy (2015)
Joseph A. Schumpeter, *Capitalism, Socialism, and Democracy* (George Allen & Unwin Ltd 1943)
Karen Clay, *Trade, Institutions, and Credit: Contract Enforcement on The California Coast 1830–1846*, 34 Explorations in Economic History (Elsevier Academic Press 1997)
Karen Clay, *Trade Without Law: Private-Order Institutions in Mexican California*, 13(1) J. L. Econ. Org (Oxford University Press 1997)
Kellee S. Tsai, *Back-Alley Banking: Private Entrepreneurs in China* (Cornell University Press 2002).
Leora Klapper et al., *Trade Credit Contracts*, 25(3) Rev. Financial Stud. (Oxford University Press 2012)

Marcel Fafchamps, *Market Institutions in Sub-Saharan Africa* (MIT Press 2004)
Michael C. Jensen & William H. Meckling, *Theory of the Firm: Managerial Behavior, Agency Costs and Ownership Structure*, 3(4) J. Financial Econ (Springer 1976)
Mohammad Bashir Mobasher, *Understanding Ethnic-Electoral Dynamics: How Ethnic Politics Affect Electoral Laws and Election Outcomes in Afghanistan*, 51 Gonz. L. Rev. (2015–2016)
Mohammad Hashim Kamali, *Law in Afghanistan: A Study of the Constitution, Matrimonial Law, and Judiciary* (BRILL 1985)
Neeltje Van Horen, *Trade Credit as a Competitiveness Tool: Evidence from Developing Countries*, 4 (Munich Personal RePEc Archive, 2004), https://mpra.ub.uni-muenchen.de/2792/1/MPRA_paper_2792.pdf
Nicholas Foster, *The Islamic Law of Real Security*, 15 Arab L.Q. (BRILL 2000)
Office of the Economic Advisor, *Mobile Banking in Afghanistan* (PowerPoint Presentation, April 2017), http://afghaneconomics.com/research/Mobile_banking_scenario.pdf
Oliver E. Williamson, *The Economic Institutions of Capitalism* (Free Press 1985)
Joshua Charap & Jelena Pavlovic, IMF Middle East and Central Asia Department, Development of the Commercial Banking System in Afghanistan: Risks and Rewards 18 (IMF Working Paper WP/09/150, 2009), www.imf.org/external/pubs/ft/wp/2009/wp09150.pdf
Pete Swanson, United States Agency for International Development, Report on Assessment of Potential for Commercial Mediation (Mar. 17, 2010)
Pınar Özlü & Cihan Yalcin, *The Trade Credit Channel of Monetary Policy Transmission: Evidence from Nonfinancial Manufacturing Firms in Turkey*, 48(4) Emerging Markets Finance and Trade (2012)
Qanun Asnad Qabel Mu'amela [Law of Negotiable Documents] (No. 971, 1387 [2009]).
Qanun Assasi Afghanistan [Afghanistan Constitution] 1343 [1964]
Qanun Assasi Afghanistan [Afghanistan Constitution] 1382 [2014]
Qanun Rahn Amwal Manqul dar Mua'amalat Banki [Law on Use of movable Properties as Collateral in Banking Transactions] (No. 990, 1387 [2009])
Qanun Usul Muhakimat Madani [Law of Civil Procedure] (No. 722, 1369 [1990]).
Qanuni Madani [Civil Code] 1355 [1977]
Raymond Fisman & Inessa Love, *Trade Credit, Financial Intermediary Development, and Industry Growth*, 58(1) J. Finance. 353 (2003)
Richard S. Newell, *The Politics of Afghanistan* (Cornell University Press 1972)
Robert Cull et al., The World Bank, Formal Finance and Trade Credit During China's Transition (Policy Research Working Papers 4204, 2007), https://openknowledge.worldbank.org/bitstream/handle/10986/7022/wps4204.pdf?sequence=1&isAllowed=y
Robert Holzmann, World Bank, Managed Labor Migration in Afghanistan: Exploring Employment and Growth Opportunities for Afghanistan (2018), http://documents.worldbank.org/curated/en/746891516915310370/pdf/122987-WP-P158055-PUBLIC-SummaryReportFINALonline.pdf.
Ronald H. Coase, *The Nature of The Firm: Origin, Meaning, Influence*, 4 J. L. Econ. Org. 3, (1988)
Ronald H. Coase, *The Problem of Social Cost*, 3 J. L. Econ. (The University of Chicago 1960)
Ruchi Kumar, *The Decline of Afghanistan's Hindu and Sikh Communities*, Al Jazeera (January 1, 2017), www.aljazeera.com/indepth/features/2016/12/decline-afghanistan-hindu-sikh-communities-161225082540860.html
Rudolph Peters, *From Jurists Law to Statute Law or What Happens When the Shari'a is Codified*, 7 Mediterranean Politics (2002).

Sara Koplik, *A Political and Economic History of the Jews of Afghanistan* (BRILL 2015)
Simon Johnson et al., *Courts and Relational Contracts*, 18(1) J. Law Econ. Organ (Oxford University Press 2000)
Special Inspector General for Afghanistan Reconstruction, Quarterly Report to the United States Congress (April 30, 2015), www.sigar.mil/pdf/quarterlyreports/2015-04-30qr-section3-economic.pdf
Sunni Tradition Fatwa [Juristic Legal Ruling] Collection, www.islampp.com/
Thomas J. Barfield, United States Institute for Peace, Afghan Customary Law and Its Relationship to Formal Judicial Institutions (2003), www.usip.org/sites/default/files/file/barfield2.pdf.
Tres Thompson et al., Stanford Law School, Afghanistan Legal Education Project, An Introduction to the Property Law of Afghanistan (2015), https://www-cdn.law.stanford.edu/wp-content/uploads/2016/05/ALEP-Property-Law-1st-Ed_English.pdf.
Wael Hallaq, *What is Sharia? in* 12 Yearbook of Islamic and Middle Eastern Law: 2005–2006 (Cambridge University Press 2007)
Website of Business and Marketing Services Agency of Afghanistan (June 1, 2018), www.bamsa.org/
The World Bank, *Afghanistan—State Building, Sustaining, Growth, and Reducing Poverty* (World Bank 2005)
World Justice Program, The Rule of Law in Afghanistan (2017), https://worldjusticeproject.org/sites/default/files/documents/WJP_Afghanistan_Report_2017_Final_Online-Edition-Reduced.pdf.
Ying Ge & Jiaping Qiu, *Financial Development, Bank Discrimination and Trade Credit*, 31(2) J. Bank. Finance 514 (2007)

3 Afghanistan's Formal Financial Institutions

Afghanistan's formal financial institutions have not been able to provide credits in a way that can be used by Afghan merchants. That is why banks in Afghanistan have held as high as 3 billion USD in excessive reserves,[1] while Afghan merchants have increasingly faced financing problems.[2] The approach reflected in the Government's Strategic Policies of the (now toppled) Islamic Republic of Afghanistan on institutional reforms aimed to improve access to credit—which, if judged by their content, strongly reflect the policy prescriptions of the State-Centered Theory—was ineffective. The approach failed because it completely disregards the existing informal institutions, seeking to displace them with formal institutions modeled on international best practices. This approach has led Da Afghanistan Bank to unsuccessfully attempt to outlaw deposit-keeping and loan distributions by the *Sarrafs*.

The first part of this chapter describes the state of formal financial institutions in Afghanistan before the Taliban takeover triggered the current banking crisis. To do so, it starts by discussing the boundaries of formal financial institutions in Afghanistan. Specifically, it discusses the attempts by Da Afghanistan Bank to deny *Sarrafs* a formal role as a financial intermediary. This case illustrates the Afghan former government's problematic approach to institutional reform. The impetus behind Da Afghanistan Bank's anti-*Sarraf* attempt, which can be gleaned from the discourse around the policy, was to incentivize the use of banks in Afghanistan. However, this study shows that this policy was based on false assumptions and could not be implemented. After determining the boundaries of formal financial institutions, the chapter describes the state of the banking system in Afghanistan before the Taliban takeover, showing why and how banks' role as credit providers not only failed to improve but also was on a decline.

The second part of this chapter describes the content of former Afghan Government Strategic Policies aimed at improving access to credit for Afghan merchants. The content of these policies is used to illustrate how the former Afghan government's approach to institutional reform followed the policy prescriptions of State-Centered Theory in that these policies completely disregard the institutional landscape of Afghanistan's credit economy and the opportunities and challenges it presents for creating formal institutions that offer credit in a way that meets the needs of Afghan merchants.

DOI: 10.4324/9781003245476-4

Formal Financial Intermediaries in Afghanistan: Are *Sarrafs* Included?

The financial intermediaries of Afghanistan's formal financial system are difficult to identify. There are four main candidates for inclusion as financial intermediaries in the formal financial system of Afghanistan: (1) banks; (2) microfinance institutions, which are mostly run as charitable organizations; and (3) insurance companies, which play a minor role in the financial system due to underdevelopment of insurance industry in Afghanistan; and (4) non-bank actors (*Sarrafs*). The first three candidates can be easily included within the formal financial system because, according to formal rules, they can, *inter alia*, perform the function of pooling savings for investment purposes. In other words, they move funds from the parties with excessive capital to parties needing capital. Of these three categories of financial intermediaries, this chapter focuses on banks and the formal rules that govern the operation of *Sarrafs*.

There are nine microfinance institutions in Afghanistan[3] whose estimated collective loan portfolio in 2018 exceeded 131 million USD issued to more than 148,000 small borrowers.[4] However, this study does not focus on microfinance institutions because they are most often run as charitable organizations with an endowment and do not primarily hold deposits from savers (e.g. FMFB-A).[5] This study also declines to focus on insurance companies because the insurance industry is in its nascent stage of development in Afghanistan and, therefore, does not play a significant role in the financial system.[6]

The fourth category of financial intermediaries is less straightforward. There are two types of non-bank actors in Afghanistan's financial system. The first are *Sarrafi* (FX),[7] which literally means money exchanger. According to formal rules, they can only engage in the exchange of different currencies.[8] The second are Money Service Providers,[9] which according to formal rules, in addition to currency exchange, can also engage in domestic and international money transfers, popularly known as *hawala*.[10] Money Service Providers can also buy, sell, and discount checks.[11] This study has called FXs and Money Service Providers collectively by their popular name in Afghanistan, *Sarraf* (singular), *Sarrafs* (plural), and *Sarrafi* (adjective). *Sarrafs*, according to formal rules, are barred from keeping deposits and issuing loans.[12] They, as explained in Chapter 3, nonetheless, de facto perform these functions and other functions formally reserved for banks. Therefore, I have divided the discussion of formal rules concerning the operations of *Sarrafs*: this chapter analyzes the formal rules governing the operation of *Sarrafs*, while Chapter 3 discussed the de facto functions of *Sarrafs* using interview data.

Formal Regulations of Sarrafs

The difference between FX and Money Service Providers is that the latter can legally exchange currencies and execute *hawala*, while the former can only exchange currencies.[13] However, both FX and Money Service Providers, in practice, do much more than execute *hawala* or exchange currency, as described in the previous chapter. The formal requirements for acquiring a Money Service Provider license are stricter compared to obtaining an FX license.[14] The distinction between FXs and Money Service Providers is much blurrier in practice. They both perform *hawala* and execute currency exchanges and perform several other functions.[15]

In addition to the many licensed *Sarrafs* that operate from a permanent place of business (such as a store or an office), there are many more mobile *Sarrafs* that hold neither a license nor operate from a permanent place of business. They have significantly less capital (not more than a few thousand dollars) compared to established *Sarrafs* (whose capital can be as high as millions of dollars). Mobile *Sarrafs* stand on the street near the *Sarrafi* market, or inside the *Sarrafi* market, or on other streets, holding their money at hand. They do not execute *hawala*—because they do not have a permanent address, no one would trust them with a *hawala*—but only buy and sell different currencies. They often have an account with an established *Sarraf*. The Da Afghanistan Bank in 2016 made efforts to issue licenses to mobile *Sarrafs*. However, this has not happened; therefore, they are not, generally, reflected in Da Afghanistan Bank reports.[16]

Between 2013 and 2019, according to Da Afghanistan Bank data, the number of licenses issued for FXs and Money Service Providers has increased from 1,900 to 3,200, which shows a 68% increase.[17] In the second quarter of 2019, the latest time the data was made available, the proportion of FX and Money Service Providers is roughly 48% FXs and 52% Money Service Providers, while the number of FX has increased at a faster rate between 2013 and 2019.[18] According to the latest Da Afghanistan Bank report, there are currently 3,200 FX and Money Service Provider license holders in Afghanistan.[19] This number does not reflect the actual number of *Sarrafs* in Afghanistan. According to informal estimates, in Kabul only 80% of *Sarrafs* hold licenses; the figures for provinces is expectedly much lower.[20]

Prior to 2016, *Sarrafs* were licensed from Da Afghanistan Bank, but otherwise, there were very few substantive regulations concerning the operation of *Sarrafi* markets. In 2016, Da Afghanistan Bank enacted a regulation concerning *Sarrafs*, Regulation of Organizing the Activities of *Sarrafs* and Money Service Providers ("Regulation").[21] The Regulation has been very controversial. Da Afghanistan Bank promulgated the Regulation with the aim of preventing money laundering and terrorism financing (I.2 Regulation).[22]

One year after promulgation of the Regulation, when the Da Afghanistan Bank attempted to call an election to elect a new president of the *Sarrafi* union, under a provision of the Regulation, *Sarrafs* staged a nationwide strike to protest the Regulation.[23] The Regulation fundamentally disrupted the operation of *Sarrafs*. The National Council of *Sarrafs*, which is comprised of *Sarrafs*' provincial unions, was established in February 2016 to organize *Sarrafs* effort on the national level with the aim of resisting the Da Afghanistan Bank regulations.[24] In their public statements in relation to the strike, they demanded the changes in 22 provisions of the Regulation.[25]

The strike lasted four days (February 6–10, 2018) and disrupted the business and personal lives of Afghans.[26] According to the International Monetary Fund data, 90% of financial transactions in Afghanistan are conducted through *Sarrafs*.[27] Only 10% of the Afghanistan population uses banks.[28] Another World Bank report discussed earlier suggested that 16% of Afghan families rely on the money sent by a family member working abroad, which is almost exclusively transferred via *Sarrafs*.[29] This means a *Sarrafs*' strike has great consequences for the livelihood of Afghans.

The National Council of *Sarrafs*, in a statement issued to declare the conclusion of the strike, stated that they reached an agreement with Da Afghanistan Bank to revise 22 provisions of the Regulation after Chief Executive of Afghanistan's Government Abdullah and Second Vice President Danish got involved.[30] Da Afghanistan Bank spokesman, in a statement issued concerning the possible revision of the Regulation, said some provisions are based on Afghanistan banking laws and would not be changed.[31] The provisions barring *Sarrafs* from deposit-keeping and lending is one of those provisions. The Islamic Republic fell without clarifying the status of the Regulation.

The Regulation sets forth conditions for obtaining an FX or Money Service Provider license, restricts the type of financial services *Sarrafs* can legally engage in, and grants FinTRACA (Financial Transaction and Reports Analysis Center for Afghanistan)[32] broad monitoring and disciplinary authority over *Sarrafs*.[33] Although it was not required by the Regulation, in early 2018 Da Afghanistan Bank recently decided to suspend the issuance of Money Service Provider and FX licenses in urban centers altogether in order to "contain the expansion of *traditional markets* and better control of the existing markets" (emphasis added).[34] The call for reelection of the head of *Sarrafs*' union, who did not hold either a Money Service Provider or FX license as the Regulation required, was the straw that broke the camel's back.[35]

To illustrate the ways the Regulation aimed to regulate the *Sarrafi* markets in Afghanistan, I review the main points of contentions between *Sarrafs* and the Da Afghanistan Bank in the context of the 2018 strike. These contentions illustrate the fundamentals of the regulatory scheme that Da Afghanistan Bank is seeking to impose on *Sarrafs*.

A main point of contention in the recent strike was Da Afghanistan Bank's decision to halt the issuance of *Sarraf*'s license in the major urban centers. Da Afghanistan Bank instituted a stay on issuing licenses for urban centers of five major provinces studied here (Kabul, Herat, Nangarhar, Balkh, and Kandahar), as well as Kunduz.[36] Da Afghanistan Bank wanted to limit the number of active *Sarrafs* to incentivize Afghans to use the formal banking system. A main demand of the National Council of *Sarrafs* was to lift this stay.[37]

The authority of the FinTRACA to suspend and revoke *Sarrafs*' licenses was another contentious issue in the recent strike.[38] The National Council of *Sarrafs* demands that FinTRACA should not be able to suspect or revoke a license without the agreement of the National Council of *Sarrafs*.[39] *Sarrafs* also objected to provisions of the Regulation which imposed strict reporting obligations.[40]

To prevent tax evasion, the Regulation bars *Sarrafs* from using personal bank accounts for their business deposits (Regulation 3.3.a).[41] The National Council of *Sarrafs* claims this rule jeopardizes the personal security of *Sarrafs* by making the information of their capital easily available.[42]

A main driver of *Sarraf*'s 2018 strike was to protest against Da Afghanistan Bank's attempt to reject *Sarrafs*' status as financial intermediaries in Afghanistan. The Regulation prohibits *Sarrafs* from accepting deposits unless the deposit is held for *hawala* purposes (3.2.1.b Regulation and 3.2.1.c).[43] The National Council of *Sarrafs* demanded this prohibition be lifted.[44] According to the spokesman for the National Council of *Sarrafs*, the Da Afghanistan Bank agreed to a compromise on this provision as a part of the deal to end the strike as well.[45] However, Da Afghanistan Bank's spokesman said that allowing *Sarrafs* to accept deposits and issue loans would violate Afghanistan banking law which restricts those functions to banks; therefore, a compromise is not possible.[46] This contention has not been resolved yet.

To prevent money laundering and transfer of funds for illegal activities, the Regulation requires *Sarrafs* to demand, record, and keep information (the identity of the parties involved, source of the money, and the purpose of transaction) on all their regular and non-regular clients, especially high-risk clients (e.g. political figures) (4.2 Regulation).[47] The National Council of *Sarrafs* believes the current requirements are very demanding, and it advocates for more relaxed client information recording requirements.[48] According to FinTRACA 2017 report, *Sarrafs* did not report a single suspicious financial transaction since the Regulation came into force, suggesting a low level of cooperation.[49]

What Is Wrong with the Sarrafi *Regulation?*

The Regulation, along with several other pieces of legislation, are enacted to ensure the integrity of Afghanistan financial market; to ensure the continued inclusion of Afghanistan in international financial systems; to curb the source of revenues for the insurgent groups (at the time, chief among them was Taliban); and to increase the cost of illegal economic activities. For example, during 2016, under the Regulation, FinTRACA froze the bank accounts of 12 *Sarrafs* suspected of money laundering and drug trafficking.[50]

However, the Regulation is based on false assumptions about the informal institution of *Sarrafi* markets, which is reflective of the influence of State-Centered Theory. For example, another purpose for the Regulation offered by the Da Afghanistan Bank's spokesman "is to contain the *traditional market*"[51] (emphasis added). In effect, Da Afghanistan Bank, by barring *Sarrafs* from accepting deposits and issuing loans, is trying to strengthen the position of banks as the main financial intermediaries in Afghanistan. The rationale for restricting the scope of legal activities for *Sarrafs* is that it will shift the supply of funds (deposits), and demand for funds (loans), to banks. As a result, the Regulation is meant to improve access to credit through banks by displacing the informal institutions of *Sarrafi* markets.

There are three main problems with the approach espoused by the Regulation. First, depositing funds with *Sarraf*s does not generally remove funds from the banking system. *Sarraf*s hold most of their funds in banks.[52] Therefore, outlawing deposit-keeping by *Sarraf*s will not increase the bank deposits significantly. Second, Afghan banks, at least until the Taliban takeover, have held excessive reserves, which they have been unable to distribute in loans.[53] Therefore, banning *Sarraf*s from issuing loans will hinder access to credit by restricting Afghan merchants' access to short-term working capital loans. Short-term working capital loans are a vital source of financing for Afghanistan's supply chain. Finally, given the low penetration rate of Afghanistan's banking system,[54] the Afghan government's low regulatory capacity, and limited control in large parts of the country, unreasonable restriction of *Sarraf*s will only ensure illegal continuation of their functions, which will further reduce the impact of the formal rules over the de facto operation of the financial system.[55]

By conflating measures designed to combat illegal transfer of funds with measures to outlaw Afghanistan's "traditional market," State-Centered-Theory-based Regulation not only will hinder access to credit for Afghan merchants, especially small- and medium-sized businesses, but also hurts the chance of anti-money laundering efforts. The approach I advocate for, Grounded Institutional Reform, proposes that instead of outlawing the effective working financial system in Afghanistan, Da Afghanistan Bank should use the offer of inclusion in the legal financial system as a legal financial intermediary to incentivize *Sarraf*s to comply with anti-money laundering efforts. This way Da Afghanistan Bank can introduce self-interest compatible incentives to encourage cooperation with anti-money laundering efforts despite the low regulatory capacity of the Afghanistan government. This approach will also improve access to credit for Afghan merchants by ensuring the continued supply of short-term working capital loans and competition and cooperation between banks and *Sarraf*s—instead of a blind attempt to displace the informal institutions. This approach to institutional reform and its challenges is further discussed in Chapter 5.

Taliban took over Da Afghanistan Bank in August of 2021 and put their head of financial operation during their period of insurgency in charge of Afghanistan's banking sector. While the Taliban don't share the terrorism financing and money laundering concerns of the Islamic Republic, and generally have favorable attitudes toward the Afghan informal economy, they nonetheless have had frictions with the *Sarrafi* markets as they tried to curb the devaluation of the national currency and curb the outflow of foreign currency from Afghanistan. Taliban reported arresting many *Sarraf*s in connection with smuggling of USD out of the country. Taliban have also banned the *Booli* practice where *Sarraf*s hold an open auction to set the market rate for AFN/USD exchange, fearing that market speculation will further devaluate the AFN. In short, the tension between the Central Bank and the *Sarrafi* markets are likely to continue under Taliban rule as well even though the points of tensions may shift.

Banks in Afghanistan

Afghans have a very low rate of bank use. Afghans are one of the least banked populations in the world. According to the Global Findex database for 2017, Afghanistan has the lowest share of bank accounts per adult population after the Central African Republic.[56] According to the International Monetary Fund data for 2019, there were only 183 depositors with commercial banks per 1,000 adult Afghans with a minuscule increase of a little more than 1% increase since 2015.[57] That being said, the number of depositors increased by fivefold between 2008 and 2015 (from 36.4 to 181.09 per 1,000 adults), mostly due to the government policy to distribute government employees' salaries through bank accounts.[58]

Banks have not penetrated a large portion of Afghanistan's population and territory. In 2004, the number of commercial bank branches per 100,000 adults was 0.37, and then it peaked in 2010 going as high as 2.39 per 100,000 adults.[59] But then the number started declining and dropped to 1.87 in 2019. The number of ATMs per 100,000 adults, on the other hand, has steadily increased from near zero in 2004 to 1.64 per 100,000 adults in 2019.[60]

According to the Da Afghanistan Bank data, as of the third quarter of 2019, there are a total of 13 active banks in Afghanistan: three state-owned banks, eight private commercial banks, and two branches of foreign banks.[61] Over the last decade, the number of banks has been generally stable, but a private commercial bank and a branch of a foreign bank were closed between 2018 and 2019.

The use of bank loans by Afghan merchants is very low. According to World Bank data for 2014, only 2% of Afghan firms used bank loans for investment,[62] while 3.9% of firms used bank credit to finance working capital.[63] This percentage must have decreased because since 2014 the supply of bank loans in Afghanistan has experienced a consistent decline, suggesting a corresponding decrease in the percentage of firms using bank loans.[64] Throughout this period (2013–2019), however, banks have maintained an average excessive reserves of more than 3 billion USD, measured by averaging the difference between the total value of deposits and the total value of gross loans published by Da Afghanistan Bank.[65] As late as the third quarter of 2019, despite a period of decline in the total value of deposits, the banks in Afghanistan still held roughly 2.7 billion USD more in deposits than they distributed in loans.

Trust in Banks

Even before the Taliban takeover triggered a run on banks, most Afghans did not use banks for savings because (1) they tend to not trust banks;[66] (2) they have limited access to banks; and (3) when they have accounts with banks, it has been costly to access their savings. The government needs to encourage savings in banks because they are the only institutions that can effectively pool savings for investment in Afghanistan. Informal substitutes like *Sarraf*'s loans and *Gerawee* have either limited or no long-term financing potential. Afghanistan needs to improve the regulatory framework to regain people's trust in banks and pursue policies to improve access to and performance of banks.[67] However, as things stand, it is unlikely to happen in the short or medium term.

Afghans' distrust of banks predated the Taliban takeover. Afghans, generally, distrust banks,[68] arguably, because the highly unstable history of Afghanistan has undermined Afghans' trust in the durability of formal institutions—a belief that has been again reconfirmed by the havoc unleashed on the banking sector following Taliban takeover of the country. Furthermore, banks cannot be Afghans' main option for saving because banks have limited reach in Afghanistan.[69] Furthermore, Afghans also do not save in banks because it has been expensive to access their money when they need it even before the current liquidity crunch. For example, I used to receive my university salary in Herat, Afghanistan, in form of a wire deposit in a Kabul Bank account, but I would withdraw a large sum of my salary at once as soon as I could. I did so because I knew that it would take me a long time to withdraw the money should I need it, so I preferred to keep the cash. When I was in Herat for this field research in 2017, two available Kabul Bank's ATMs, in Afghanistan's second-largest urban center, were not working. When they did work, there was often a line.[70] There were some banks who fared better, for example, Afghanistan International Bank, before the Taliban takeover.

The most serious blow to the credibility of the financial sector before the Taliban takeover was the Kabul Bank scandal. Kabul Bank, established in 2004, was the largest private commercial bank in Afghanistan. However, in 2010, Kabul Bank was taken over by the Da Afghanistan Bank due to fear that it might collapse after a 1 billion USD fraud in Kabul Bank surfaced.[71] The 1 billion USD fraud consisted of fraud, embezzlement, and forgery involving powerful political and economic figures in Afghanistan.[72] Almost half of the loss is due to improper loans to the owners; many of whom are also powerful political figures in Afghanistan.[73] Kabul Bank is still under receivership of the Da Afghanistan Bank, as the few attempts at auctioning Kabul Bank to the private sector have proven unsuccessful.[74] The Kabul Bank scandal has had a disastrous impact on the Afghanistan bank industry. However, it is almost impossible to isolate the precise effect of the Kabul Bank scandal on the industry because there are numerous confounding factors and also because Da Afghanistan Bank only recently started to release periodic reports on the status of banking industry starting in 2012.

The low trust in banks does not mean that Afghans trust *Sarrafs* more—albeit it is unclear if the near-collapse of the financial sector following Taliban takeover has changed that or not. On the contrary, during my field work in 2017, most interviewees expressed that they trusted banks more than *Sarrafs*. This is expected because *Sarrafs* go bankrupt more often than banks, and when do, they have limited assets for debt recovery. No major bank has gone bankrupt in Afghanistan, at least post-2001. In short, although Afghans did not generally save in banks, partly out of fear of losing their savings, *Sarrafs* are not a more credible saving option. As a result, saving in financial intermediaries remains low. Instead, Afghans usually use a portfolio of liquid and illiquid commodities to hold their limited savings.[75]

The higher rate of *Sarrafs* use by Afghan merchants, combined with a relatively higher level of trust in banks (at least at the time of my field research), indicate that it is the ability of *Sarrafs* to meet Afghan merchants' needs that explains their popularity compared to banks, not a sentimental preference for the use of traditional institutions. The flip side of this argument also holds true: low demand for bank loans is not a function of low trust in banks but a result of formal lending requirements that Afghan merchants cannot satisfy for reasons described previously.

Banks' Total Assets

According to Da Afghanistan Bank data, between 2013 and 2019, the total asset of banks measured in US dollars (based on prevailing USD/AFN exchange rate at each reporting interval) has decreased by almost 17%. Part of this decrease is explained by the devaluation of Afghan currency in relation to USD during the same period. The analysis that follows uses US dollars because, given Afghanistan's dependence on external resources and pervasiveness of foreign currencies,[76] it is a better indicator of the macroeconomic trends.

In the first quarter of 2013, banks in Afghanistan held total assets of 4.6 billion USD. By the third quarter of 2017, banks' total assets in Afghanistan decreased to 3.82 billion USD. Of the total assets of banks, between 2013 and 2017 (the period for which the breakdown data is available), roughly 10% was held by branches of the foreign banks, and their share has been shrinking; state-owned banks owned roughly a quarter of the assets, and their share has been shrinking as well; private commercial banks have held more than half of the assets, and their share has been expanding between 2013 and 2017.

According to the Da Afghanistan Bank data, at least between 2013 and 2017, almost half of the banks' assets were cash in the vault and claims on Da Afghanistan Bank. The second category of the banks' assets is interbank claims that make up almost a quarter of the banks' total assets. The third category is loans that make up roughly 15% of the banks' total assets. Banks' fixed assets have stayed roughly the same (3% of total assets). Investment makes up roughly 7% of the banks' total assets.

Between 2013 and 2017, the share of cash in total assets of banks has increased by 7%, the share of interbank claims has decreased by 3%, the share of investment has increased by 4%, and the share of loans has decreased by almost 5%.

Banks' Total Deposits

Between 2013 and 2019, the total amount of deposits in banks, measured in USD based on the contemporary prevailing exchange rate, decreased by 17%, if measured in US dollars. Again, a portion of this change is explained by the devaluation of the Afghan currency. Between 2013 and 2019, the value of Afghan currency in relation to USD depreciated by almost 60%.[77]

At the end of 2013, measured in the contemporary USD rate, the total amount of deposits held by banks was 4.9 billion USD. At the end of the third quarter of 2019, deposits held by banks fell to 3.8 billion USD.

Demand deposits make up roughly three quarters of total bank deposits, and their share has been marginally increasing between 2013 and 2017. Savings deposits make up almost one-fifth of total deposits, but its share has marginally decreased in the same period. Time deposits have been increasing. They made up 4.48% of total deposits in 2013. In 2017, the share of time deposits rose to 5.38%. The smaller and decreasing share of saving deposits highlight the limited capacity of banks in Afghanistan to pool savings.

The share of state-owned banks, commercial private banks, and branches of foreign banks in deposits is roughly the same as their share in total assets: 10%, 65%, and 26%, respectively. The only difference is that state-owned banks have been able to increase their share of deposits from 11% in 2013 to 26% in 2014. From 2014 forward (at least until 2017), the share of state-owned banks in deposits has stabilized.

Banks' Loans

Bank loans do not play a large role in financing businesses in Afghanistan. A Survey of Afghanistan Capital Market Assessment ("Capital Assessment") in 2010 found that only 5% of their sample relied on banks for capital (14.81 million USD).[78] Capital Assessment only included large businesses. Capital Assessment defined a large business as a business with more than 30 employees or an initial capital investment of 250,000 USD or more.[79] (However, the 2009 Business Survey estimated that only 10% of the business establishments in Afghanistan had more than five employees.)[80]

Two World Bank Enterprise Surveys in 2008 and 2014 found that only, respectively, 1.4% and 2% of firms used banks to finance investment.[81] The same two surveys found that only 2.5% (2008) and 3.9% (2014) of firms used banks to finance working capital.[82]

Since the last survey in 2014, the use of bank loans as a source of capital is on the decline. According to Da Afghanistan Bank data, between 2013 and 2019, the total of banks' gross loans, measured in US dollars using contemporary USD/AFN exchange rate, has decreased by almost 343 million USD, which represents a 39% decline.[83] Again if one measures the total gross loans in Afghani, the decline is lower given that Afghani significantly depreciated during this time interval.

Banks in Afghanistan, as reported between 2013 and 2019, have had on average more than 3 billion USD excessive reserves measured by the average of differences between total deposits and total gross loans in USD based on the contemporary exchange rate, that they have not been able to distribute in loans.[84] Even toward the end of 2019, banks in Afghanistan were very liquid, holding 2.7 billion USD more in deposits than the gross value of their combined loan portfolio. Banks' ability to pool savings to finance investment has declined as evidenced by decrease in deposits and deposit-loan ratios.

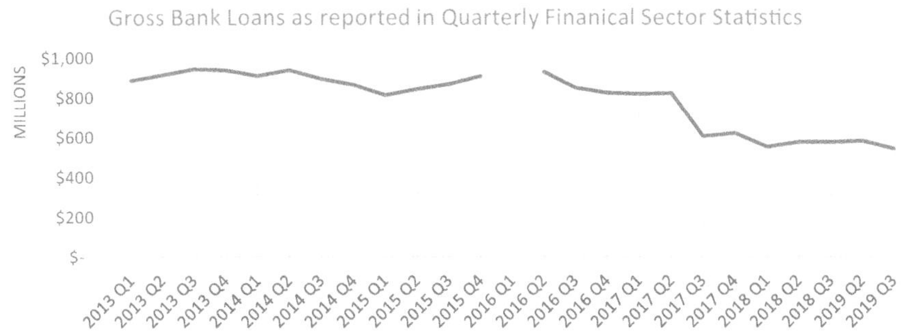

Figure 3.1 Total Gross Loans Distributed in Afghanistan (2013–III 2019)

The decline in the bank loans issued is not due to decrease in demand. According to Business Climate Reports, the percentage of businesses reporting a problem with access to finance increased between 2014 and 2016.[85] In 2014, according to the 2014 Business Climate Report, 36% of businesses surveyed reported that they had a problem accessing finance. In 2015, this percentage rose to 43.5%. By the end of 2016, the percentage of businesses reporting a problem accessing finance rose to 47%.

According to the 2016 Business Climate Report, Afghan businesses cite the following reasons as to why they do not use banks' loans: very high-interest rate (52%),[86] excessive collateral requirements (26%), need for political connections (12%), and too difficult business or project plan (11%).[87] According to the 2016 Business Climate Report, this is a pattern that has been consistently observed since 2014.[88]

These surveys, supported by interview data, reveal three main challenges to bank-based financing in Afghanistan: (1) a highly uncertain environment has caused interest rates to increase, making it difficult for merchants to use bank loans for investment; (2) an inefficient formal property rights system, making it difficult to collateralize bank loans; and (3) low economic literacy among Afghan businesses, making it difficult for businesses to comply with the banks' requirements and for the banks to assess loans' applicants effectively.

Interview data confirm the Business Climate Report findings. Interview data highlights two additional related challenges that prevent merchants from using bank loans for investment: (1) inflexible repayment terms make it difficult for Afghan businesses who operated in an unpredictable business climate to use loans from banks and (2) the short term of bank loans (bank loans repayment terms in Afghanistan does not exceed three years). Since merchants operate in a highly uncertain environment, it makes it difficult for them to use bank loans to finance long-term investments.[89]

The Business Climate Report data shows significant regional and sectoral variation in the percentage of businesses that reported having a problem with access to finance.[90] Access to finance, as used in the survey, is meant to represent access to investment financing, commonly bank loans. However, Business Climate Report data reflect the attitude toward bank loans, not the actual access/usage. This is because the overwhelming majority of surveyed businesses did not have a bank loan, nor had they necessarily applied for bank loans. Therefore, the survey reflects the business attitudes toward bank loans rather than the actual experience of participants.

According to Business Climate Report data, the five major provinces ranked according to the percentage of businesses that reported having a problem with access to finance, from high to low, are Kandahar, Nangarhar, Kabul, Herat, and Balkh.[91] Balkh has both the lowest business registry of the five major provinces and a low proportion of smaller businesses, which may explain why Balkhis are less likely to say they have a problem with access to finance.[92] Stated differently, low market competition in Balkh may reduce the need for financing.

The Business Climate Report data suggest that there is no significant difference in the percentage of businesses that report problems with access to finance based on business size.[93] Similarly, the Business Climate Reports does not show any particular temporal pattern in the sectorial variation of the percentage of businesses that report a problem with access to finance.[94] The scattered temporal distribution of sectoral ease of access to financing illustrates the highly volatile business climate in Afghanistan. According to the Business Climate Report data, business sectors that reported having a problem with access to credit from worst to best: agriculture, manufacturing, construction, trade, and service, based on the percentage of access of businesses to finance.[95]

The Da Afghanistan Bank data for the same period show that the distribution of loans by sector has drastically changed between 2013 and 2017. In 2013, the sectors that received the most bank loans were ranked in the following order: trade, commercial real estate and construction, service, consumer loans, manufacturing, power and energy, and residential mortgage loans to individuals.[96] The ranking in 2017 was as follows: service, manufacturing, commercial real estate and construction, communication, trade, power and energy, mines and dams and infrastructure, agricultural loans, residential mortgages to individuals, and consumer loans.[97] A small part of this transformation in the distribution of bank loans between 2013 and 2017 is a change in the categorization of loans as is evident by the decrease in the share of the category of "other loans."[98] However, as it can be seen from the figure in the next section, this can only explain a small part of the change in the distribution of loans. The Da Afghanistan Bank data clearly show that the share of service and manufacturing has significantly expanded, while the share of trade and commercial real estate and construction has significantly contracted.[99]

Commercial banks are the main issuers of bank loans in Afghanistan. Private commercial banks issue more than 90% of the total bank loans in the country.[100] Although state-owned banks hold a quarter of the banks' total assets and deposits, they only issue 7% of loans. Branches of foreign banks hold 10% of banks' total assets and deposits but issued only a little more than 1% of total loans in 2016. Between 2013 and 2017, private commercial banks expanded their share

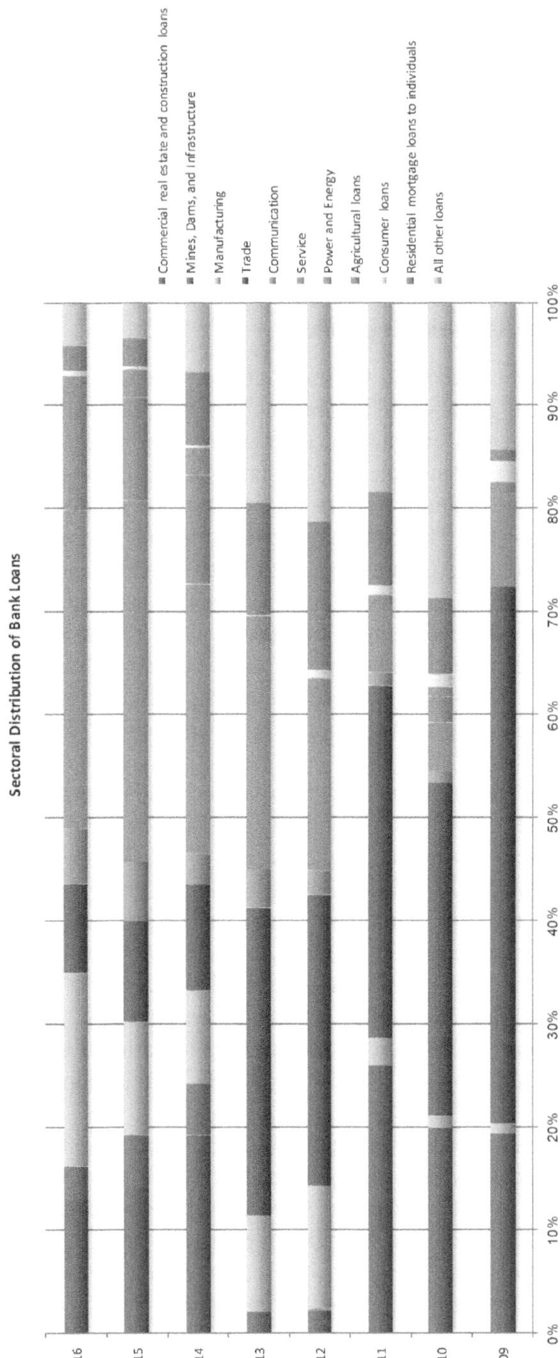

Figure 3.2 Sectoral Distribution of Bank Loans in Afghanistan (2009–2016)

of total loans by 3%, while branches of foreign banks reduced their share by 4%. State-owned banks' share of total bank loans overall had marginally increased by roughly 1%.

The percentage of nonperforming loans has steadily increased in Afghanistan. In 2012, according to Da Afghanistan Bank data, only 5.31% of loans were nonperforming in Afghanistan. This rate has steadily increased from 2012 to 2016. In 2016, according to Da Afghanistan Bank, 12.67% of loans were nonperforming. The increase in the rate of nonperforming loans is expected as the economic conditions in this period deteriorated.

Government Strategic Policies Aimed to Improve Access to Credit during the Islamic Republic

The Afghan government adopted several strategic policies to improve access to credit for Afghans in general and Afghan merchants in particular. The Afghanistan National Peace and Development Framework ("the National Framework") (2017–2021) and its predecessor, Afghanistan National Development Strategy (2008–2013), were the previous Afghan government's national strategic plans for achieving self-reliance.[101] The National Framework and National Development Strategy both formulated Afghanistan's high-level developmental priorities and guidelines.[102] Like the National Development Strategy, the National Framework, Afghanistan's national development framework until the Republic collapsed, underscores key reforms and priority investments needed to achieve its developmental goals.[103] The National Framework highlights institutional reforms needed to improve access to credit for Afghan merchants and achieve financial inclusion for Afghans.[104]

Different units of the previous Afghan government also formulated strategic plans to achieve Afghanistan's developmental goals in their respective jurisdictions. Afghanistan's Ministry of Commerce and Industries, Afghanistan's Ministry of Economics, and Afghanistan's Central Bank (Da Afghanistan Bank) developed strategic plans which set forth reform and investment priorities needed to improve access to credit for Afghan merchants and improve Afghanistan's financial system. These strategies are the Ministry of Commerce's Strategic Plan 2016–2020 ("Commerce Strategy"),[105] Ministry of Economics' Afghan Government Economic Plan ("National Economic Plan") 2013,[106] and Da Afghanistan Bank's Strategic Plan ("Banking Strategy") 2017–2021.[107]

These strategic plans, which made up the Afghan government's latest strategic plans in their respective sector (in some cases they are the first or only strategic plan formulated for their respective sector) until the collapse of the Republic in August of 2021, illustrate the Afghan government's approach to institutional reform during the Republic. It can be surmised from their content that they were informed by State-Centered Theory as they primarily focus on reforms that feature using formal institutions that have proven successful in other contexts (e.g. Credit Bureau and export bank).

In line with the State-Centered Theory's model for institutional reform, the former Afghan Government's Strategic Policies disregard the entrepreneurially developed informal institutions that are currently the source of credit for most Afghan merchants, in effect, seeking to displace them with formal institutions modeled on international best practices. Formal institutions have made up a very small source of finance for Afghan merchants. Only 1% to 3% of Afghan merchants use bank credit.[108] Reflecting State-Centered Theory's limiting approach, the former Government Strategic Policies aimed to create new formal institutions and/or reform the existing formal institutions, as if formal institutions are the only institutional recourse that Afghans have. However, none of the Government's Strategic Policies appear to recognize the need to understand the existing institutions used by Afghan merchants nor prescribes the formulation of institutional reforms as a correction or supplement to the informal institutions. Government Strategic Policies seem to assume that outside of formal institutions, Afghanistan is an institutional vacuum. Thus, they forgo the institutional knowledge and potential held by informal institutions in Afghanistan and overlook the interaction between formal and informal institutions.

Concerning the access to credit, in particular, the former Government's Strategic Policies' view of the credit institutions is limited to formal institutions, particularly bank loans. This explains why they correctly identify most of the problems of access to bank loans and some of the changes that must be made to improve access to bank loans. They generally failed, however, to improve access to credit for Afghan merchants. This failure is rooted in a narrow understanding of Afghanistan's existing credit institutions and unwillingness to leverage existing informal credit institutions.

This section initially reviews the provisions of four Government Strategic Policies (the National Framework, Commerce Strategy, National Economic Plan, and Banking Strategy) aimed at institutional reforms to improve access to credit as well as Afghanistan's Ministry of Justice's Strategic Plan ("Justice Strategic Plan") (2014–2018).[109] These documents collectively represent the approach to institutional reform under the period of the foreign-backed Republic in Afghanistan. Chapter 5 will focus on a critical assessment of the theoretical approach informing Government Strategic Policies, offering an alternative approach for institutional reform for countries like Afghanistan.

Afghanistan National Peace and Development Framework (2017–2021)

The National Framework (2017–2021) set forth the now toppled Islamic Republic of Afghanistan's national development strategy aimed to achieve self-reliance and increase welfare for Afghans.[110] It envisioned transforming Afghanistan's economy from "one of import and distribution to one where a thriving private-sector—from small farmers and urban businesses and to large manufacturers—can successfully export Afghan products regional and global markets."[111]

The National Framework underscored the need to clarify property titles, provide reliable supply of electricity, provide access to transport, and ensure the personal safety of Afghan merchants.[112] It also recognized the need to promote exports by improving access to credit.[113] Concerning the housing market, the National Framework highlighted the importance of regulatory reform to unleash the value trapped in the urban housing market. It states,

> Regulatory reform can . . . unleash investment by the poor. We are offering incentives to the urban poor to invest in their houses and small businesses through a national program for *land certification* that provides *tenure security* in all large and medium-sized cities[114] (emphasis added).

The strategy acknowledged land tenure insecurity is a factor contributing to the creation of a poverty trap in Afghanistan's urban centers.[115]

Mobile banking and e-payment were being hailed as effective ways to reach a large section of the population. Recognizing this opportunity, the National Framework stresses the potentials of mobile banking and e-payment to reduce interest rates and transaction costs.[116]

The National Framework's section on financial sector reforms focused on two main strategies: (1) creating a robust financial regulatory system and (2) incentivizing loan distribution by banks and savings in banks.[117] It proposed a list of reforms aimed at creating a robust system of financial oversight such as establishing a unit within Da Afghanistan Bank to monitor financial system risk. While recognizing its importance, the National Framework did not offer a strategy to incentivize banks to lend to private enterprises. To incentivize savings in banks, the strategy proposed the creation of a national financial inclusion strategy to allow citizens better access to banking services by December 2017.[118] The strategy, National Financial Inclusion Strategy (2020–2024), was later adopted with technical support from the World Bank.[119] Da Afghanistan Bank also has a financial inclusion department tasked with the implementation of financial inclusion strategy in Afghanistan.[120]

Ministry of Economics Afghan Government Economic Plan (National Economic Plan) (2013)

In 2013 the Ministry of Economics developed and adopted its National Economic Plan as a strategic instrument to unify the Afghan government's institutional reform efforts to induce economic growth and trade.[121] The National Economic Plan aimed to unify government institutional reform by setting unified developmental priorities.[122]

As a priority for the agricultural sector, the National Economic Plan prescribed the creation of an agricultural bank to improve access to credit for Afghan farmers.[123] As a priority for the industrial sector, the National Economic Plan prescribed the creation of mechanisms offering long-term loans for investment in large developmental projects.[124] To stimulate urban development, the National Economic Plan proposed a supply of long-term loans to facilitate homeownership.[125]

The National Economic Plan does not offer an analysis of the viability of any of these propositions, nor does it contains specific mechanisms for operationalizing these propositions.

Ministry of Commerce and Industries Strategic Plan (Commerce Strategy) (2016–2020)

The Commerce Strategy contains strategies, plans, and projects in the area of commerce and industry based on the Afghanistan government's strategic priorities set forth in the National Framework. Of all the Government Strategic Policies, the views reflected in the Commerce Strategy are most closely aligned with the views of Afghan merchants. It is likely because the Ministry of Commerce and Industries, compared to other ministries, has built better partnerships with business associations. The Commerce Strategy analysis of challenges to commerce and building of industries in Afghanistan underscores these root causes: (1) limited access to bank loans with favorable terms, (2) poor infrastructure, (3) instability, (4) weak rule of law, (5) weak property rights, and (6) limited access to financial services.[126]

The Commerce Strategy identifies ineffective formal dispute resolution and weak property rights as main challenges to commerce in Afghanistan. About formal resolution of commercial disputes, it states, "Resolving disputes at commercial courts is inefficient and time-consuming. The average length of a commercial dispute is 1258 days and commercial courts have no regard for the needs [of] businesses."[127] The Commerce Strategy also identifies weak property rights as a challenge impeding productive activities in Afghanistan. Acknowledging that "roughly 80% of land ownership is held or transferred informally without formal deed,"[128] the Commerce Strategy recognizes the negative effects of the absence of a comprehensive and reliable titling system on development of commerce and industries in Afghanistan.[129] To remedy the problems caused by weak property rights, the Commerce Strategy advocates for a fundamental transformation of the property rights system in Afghanistan.[130]

The Commerce Strategy recognizes that the industrial sector is dominated by small- and medium-sized and family enterprises engaging in trade and production of low value-added products[131] and identifies the problem of high transaction costs in Afghanistan. It states, "Transaction cost in Afghanistan is still high because administrative procedures are complex, the registration procedures are complicated and cumbersome, there are excessive regulations, loan distribution frameworks are weak, laws and regulations are inefficient."[132] The Commerce Strategy argues that Afghanistan's low technology level and low trade volume contribute to high transaction costs.[133] According to the Commerce Strategy, most Afghan businesses do not have access to foreign markets.[134]

When analyzing the problems of Afghanistan's financial sector, the Commerce Strategy highlights high-interest rates, lack of access to long-term loans, and willingness of banks tendencies to only lend to highly qualified merchants through their Kabul office as main problems of access to start-up and investment financing in Afghanistan.[135] Among its findings, the Commerce Strategy underscores the lack of credit information and scarcity of formal titles as main causes of problems of access to investment financing in Afghanistan.[136] The Commerce Strategy also asserts that loan enforcement by the Afghan judiciary is unreliable, which disincentivizes banks from issuing loans. On the demand side, the Commerce Strategy maintains that Afghan merchants believe the cost of borrowing is too high, and they cannot satisfy the collateral of bank loans.[137] Citing a recent survey conducted by the Ministry of Commerce and Industries, the Commerce Strategy recognizes religious objection to interest as a main obstacle against bank loan distribution.[138]

According to the Commerce Strategy's assessment, limited access to formal credit has required Afghans to continue relying on informal sources of credit, like personal savings and family loans, and to rely on the *hawala* system for transfer of funds.[139] To address these problems, the Commerce Strategy's strategic plans to strengthen the private sector in Afghanistan focus on thirteen objectives, including (1) improvement of legal framework, (2) improvement of access to loans, and (3) increased inclusion of informal economic activities in the formal economy.[140] As such, the Commerce Strategy proposes adoption of a credit guaranty scheme that partially guarantees private-bank-issued loans as a way of lowering the cost of borrowing and improving access to loans in Afghanistan.[141] In addition, as a way of alleviating the religious objections to bank loans, the Commerce Strategy underscores the need for enactment of laws and regulations, with the collaboration of Da Afghanistan Bank, to support the Islamic banking industry in Afghanistan.[142] Those regulations were later enacted by Da Afghanistan Bank. Further, the Commerce Strategy advocates for conducting a viability study and enacting laws and regulations, with the aim of creating different programs to improve access to commercial loans, especially export credit devices.[143]

The Commerce Strategy also proposes creating a Credit Bureau that would collect and process credit data and produce credit reports to help banks assess credit risk. It also advocates for conducting a viability study to assess creating a security and capital market in Afghanistan to increase liquidity of Afghanistan's capital market.[144]

Concerning inclusion of informal economic activities in the formal economy, the Commerce Strategy claims, "features of informal economy are limited access to credit, low-quality products, and jobs, weak labor rights protection, unfair competition with businesses in the formal economy, tax evasion, lower contribution to job creation and government revenue."[145] The Commerce Strategy maintains that the Afghan government should incentivize informal businesses to join the formal economy by proposing a two-prong strategy: (1) reducing the barriers for inclusion by simplifying registration processes, removing excessive tax burden, and improving property rights protection; and (2) offering incentives to joining the formal economy by offering better access to loans and support for business expansion.[146]

Afghanistan Central Bank Strategic Plan (Banking Strategy) (2017–2021)

The Banking Strategy sets forth a number of strategic objectives, which include (1) increasing the effectiveness of monetary policy to support economic growth and economic stability, (2) creating a better legal framework to ensure the integrity of the financial system and increase people's trust in the banking system, (3) expanding financial services, (4) increasing the security and effectiveness of payment systems and reducing risk in the payment system and creating a centralized system for a securities market.[147]

In order to achieve its second strategic objective, the Banking Strategy proposes enactment and revisions of several laws and regulations, including Da Afghanistan Bank law, negotiable document law, Islamic banking regulation, and anti-money laundering laws and regulations.[148] Concerning securitization of bank loans, the Banking Strategy proposes the revision of banks' immovable mortgage law, creation of a collateral registration system, creating an electronic system of credit information reports, and a public awareness campaign to promote the use of a collateral registration system.[149] The Banking Strategy also proposes the creation of an especial Islamic banking fund to promote Islamic finance in Afghanistan.[150] In order to achieve its third objective, the Banking Strategy proposes a study of obstacles and challenges of expansion of financial services in Afghanistan.[151] Before the collapse of the Republic, Da Afghanistan Bank did enact a series of rules and regulations in order to facilitate the growth of the Islamic finance sector in Afghanistan.

Ministry of Justice Strategic Plan (Justice Strategic Plan) (2014–2018)

The Department of Huquq, which is a department of the Ministry of Justice, is the primary enforcement authority when it comes to enforcing court decisions in noncriminal cases. However, improving the enforcement of court judgments is not included in the Ministry of Justice Strategic priorities. The Justice Strategic Plan not only fails to recognize the effects of ineffective and uncertain judgment enforcement on the popularity of formal dispute resolution and hence stabilization of rule of law but also neglects to prioritize improving enforcement of court judgments.

The Justice Strategic Plan focused on seven strategic objectives: (1) law reform and increasing the effectiveness of legislation, (2) public access to justice, (3) transparency and accountability, (4) capacity building, (5) infrastructure, (6) coordination and cooperation with domestic and international organizations, and (7) security.[152] The Justice Strategic Plan proposes personnel capacity building, infrastructure projects, and promotion of cooperation and coordination mechanisms as ways to achieve its strategic objectives.[153] However, the Justice Strategic Plan omits the issue of court judgment enforcement and thereby fails to address this problem. As this study shows, the uncertainty of court judgements' enforcement was a main impediment against the use of formal dispute resolution by Afghan merchants and thus was an important challenge to overcome to create an economy that operates according to formal rules.

Analysis of Afghan Government Strategic Policies

Government Strategic Policies of the now toppled Islamic Republic have a narrow view of Afghanistan's institutional landscape, which this study argues is reflective of the influence of State-Centered Theory. These strategies propose solutions which disregard the value of working informal institutions. While these strategies most often correctly diagnose the problems of credit transacting in Afghanistan, their solutions do not get traction in Afghanistan. The Government Strategic Policies' proposed solutions, if effectively implemented, may solve the problem of credit transacting in Afghanistan; however, they are attempting to replace working institutions rather than using them as building blocks to create better institutions. Therefore, their implementation requires much more regulatory and administrative capacity than the Afghan government ever held. By ignoring the wealth of existing institutional knowledge and networks, Government Strategic Policies overstretched the limited regulatory and administrative power of the Afghan government in trying to overcome the resistance from the current users of working institutions to impose these new institutions.

The governance expectations reflected in Afghanistan's Government Strategic Policies, as Thomas in his aptly named book *Govern Like Us* argues, was based on what governments in developed countries are capable of doing.[154] He argues, it is impossible to require Afghanistan to build effective and universal-access institutions across the arrays of domains, as formulated in various plans and strategy documents.[155] This study concurs with Thomas that while most of Government Strategic Policies' proposed formal institutions are good institutional outcomes—given the limited capacity of informal institutions to provide long-term financing—they are more likely to be created and penetrate Afghanistan's financial system if they are built incrementally using existing formal institutions as building blocks—based on Grounded Institutional Reform.

Afghanistan's Government Strategic Policies underscore the need for property rights reform and a titling system to unleash the value currently trapped in the housing market in Afghanistan cities. However, they do not mention *Gerawee*, which is helping Afghans raise some capital against the value of their houses in absence of secure tenure and land certification. Instead of building on and correcting the working institutions, once again the Government Strategic Policies advocate for creation of new formal institutions.

In addition, the Government Strategic Policies underscore the need to improve access to credit information for banks to assess borrowers. However, they completely disregard the wealth of credit information that *Sarrafs* possess. *Sarrafs* conduct 90% of financial transactions in Afghanistan[156] and have ongoing financial interactions with Afghan merchants. Providing banks access to this wealth of information can greatly improve banks' ability to assess risks and will reduce their reliance on scarce formal deeds. For example, the Government Strategic Policies could propose use of *Sarrafs* as guarantors for bank loans, which would encourage banks to outsource creditworthiness assessment and monitoring to *Sarrafs*.

Government Strategic Policies, on the other hand, propose creation of new formal institutions like a Credit Bureau.

Concerning the promotion of exports, the Government Strategic Policies acknowledge the importance of encouraging exports by providing better access to commercial and export financing. However, they disregard the potential of short-term working capital loans, which have been financing import and supply chains. Instead, they propose creation of a new formal institution, namely, an export bank. About the capital market, they stress the need to improve liquidity in Afghanistan's capital market. However, they do not mention *Sar qufli* as a way of commodifying future revenue tied to a place of business. Instead, they focus on the creation of new formal institutions like securities markets.

State-Centered-Theory-based Government Strategic Policies do not recognize the existing informal institutions in Afghanistan's institutional landscape as possible building blocks of solutions to the problem of access to credit for Afghan merchants.

The only Government Strategic Policies that mentioned the informal economy and informal institutions is the Commerce Strategy. This is most likely due to collaboration between the Ministry of Commerce and Industries and business associations in Afghanistan. However, the Commerce Strategy only refers to the informal economy and informal institutions in the context of incentivizing inclusion of informal businesses in the formal economy. While the Ministry of Commerce correctly underscores the need to design incentive-based mechanisms of promoting inclusion in the formal economy, it only discusses the need to reduce the barriers to and increase the benefit of inclusion in formal economy. The Commerce Strategy does not mention the need to build on and correct informal institutions to increase the reach and acceptance of the formal economy and formal institutions. The Commerce Strategy does not mention the need to draw on the existing institutions. Thus, while the Commerce Strategy highlights an important and often missing component of institutional reform in Afghanistan, it does not go far enough to advocate for the use of informal institutions as building blocks for devising institutional solutions to the problem of credit transacting in Afghanistan, as Grounded Institutional Reform does.

The prevailing institutional reform approach in Afghanistan is discussed in more detail in Chapter 5, where this book proposes an alternative approach to institutional reform for countries like Afghanistan that have poor infrastructure, limited market expansion opportunities, and a reformist but weak government.

Formal institutions in Afghanistan have generally failed to provide credit to Afghan merchants in a way that works for the Afghan context; therefore, Afghan merchants generally do not use bank loans. The now toppled Islamic Republic's approach to institutional reform appears to strongly reflect the influence of State-Centered Theory and was responsible for the inability of the Afghan government to improve access to credit for Afghan merchants. Drawing upon a critical review of informal institutions and their effects on access to credit in the Afghan context (presented in Chapter 3), this book, in the next chapter, proposes a new approach to institutional reform which empowers the Afghan government to use the working informal institutions to create formal institutions that work for the Afghan context.

Notes

1 Calculated by the author as the difference between total of gross bank deposits and total of gross bank loans based on Da Afghanistan Bank, Quarterly Statistics of I-2013 until II-2017.
2 Calculated by the author based on Afghanistan Chamber of Commerce Industries, Business Tendency Survey Reports.
3 Da Afghanistan Bank, Strategic Plan (2017), at 11.
4 *See* Mix Market, www.themix.org/mixmarket/countries-regions/afghanistan (last visited February 18, 2018). See also Afghanistan MicroFinance Association, Annual Report (2019), http://ama.org.af/wp-content/uploads/2020/10/01Annual-Report-2019.pdf.
5 *See* the First MicroFinance Bank of Afghanistan, http://fmfb.com.af/.
6 According to Da Afghanistan Bank, there are four insurance companies active in Afghanistan (one public and three private). *See* Da Afghanistan Bank, Strategic Plan (2017), at 11. The contribution of insurance industry to GDP in 2016–2017, according to Afghanistan Statistics Department, measured in gross underwritten premium was 2.45 million USD, Afghanistan Central Statistics Organization, Sectoral Contribution to the GDP.
7 Da Afghanistan Bank, Muqarrara Tanzim Fa'aliat hai Sarrafan va Fraham Konandagan Khadamat Puli [Regulation of Sarrafs and Money Service Providers' Activities] 1395 [2016], arts. 6(1)(g) and 6(1)(h) [hereinafter Regulation of Sarrafs and Money Service Providers' Activities (2016)].
8 *Id.* art. 3(2)(2).
9 *Id.* art. 6(1)(e).
10 *Id.* art. 3(2)(1).
11 *Id.* art. 3(2)(1).
12 *Id.* 3.2.1.c.
13 *Id.* arts. 3(2)(1) and 3(2)(2).
14 *Id.* arts. 2(4)-2(7).
15 *See* Chapter 3 for a discussion of the de facto functions of *Sarrafs*.
16 Regulation of Sarrafs and Money Service Providers' Activities (2016), art. 2(1)(d).
17 Calculated by the author based on Da Afghanistan Bank, Quarterly Statistics of I-2013 until II-2017.
18 *Id.*
19 *Id.*
20 Integrity Watch Afghanistan, Curbing Illicit Financial Flows in Afghanistan (2015), at 34.
21 In 2014, the international Financial Action Task Force (FATF), an independent intergovernmental body tasked with combating money laundering and financial crimes, had threatened to categorize Afghanistan as a "high-risk and non-cooperative jurisdiction," which would have effectively blacklisted Afghanistan's financial system, if Afghanistan failed to follow FATF's recommendation and enact effective anti-money laundering laws. Being blacklisted from the international financial system would have effectively shut Afghanistan out of the international financial system, which would have had consequences for the Afghan economy, effectively shutting Afghanistan out of international financial system. To avoid this, the Afghanistan government has passed a series of legislations and took several measures to create a robust system of financial oversight. As a result of these efforts, in June 2017 FATF certified that Afghanistan met its commitment to implement FATF's recommendations and removed Afghanistan

from the FATF's monitoring process for the first time after five years, effectively removing Afghanistan from the gray list. The Regulation was part of Afghanistan's reforms to meet FATF recommendations. *See* FATF, Improving Global AML/CFT Compliance: On-going Process—23 June 2017, www.fatf-gafi.org/countries/a-c/afghanistan/documents/fatf-compliance-june-2017.html (last visited April 10, 2018).

22 Regulation of *Sarrafs* and Money Service Providers' Activities (2016).

23 Khairullah Rasooli, *Afghan Sarrafs Have Closed Saraya Shahzadaha [Kabul's Sarrafi Market] in Protest*, VOADari (February 2, 2018), www.darivoa.com/a/money-changers-closed-saraye-shazada-money-changing-market/4242561.html [hereinafter Rasooli, *Afghan Sarrafs Have Closed Saraya Shahzadaha* (2018)].

24 *National Council of Sarrafs is Established*, The Daily Afghanistan (September 29, 2017), www.dailyafghanistan.com/national_detail.php?post_id=141831.

25 Rasooli, *Afghan Sarrafs Have Closed Saraya Shahzadaha* (2018).

26 *Kabul's Sarrafs Have Ended Their Strike*, BBC Persian (February 21, 2018), www.bbc.com/persian/business-43022961 [hereinafter *Kabul's Sarrafs Have Ended Their Strike* (2018)].

27 *See* Integrity Watch Afghanistan, Curbing Illicit Financial Flows in Afghanistan (2015), at 28; *see also* The World Bank, State Building, Sustaining, Growth, and Reducing Poverty (2005), at 6.

28 Special Inspector General, Quarterly Report to the United States Congress (2015), at 165.

29 Holzmann, Managed Labor Migration in Afghanistan (2018), at 12.

30 *Kabul's Sarrafs Have Ended Their Strike* (2018).

31 *Id.*

32 FinTRACA is part of Da Afghanistan Bank's Financial Intelligence Unit.

33 Regulation of *Sarrafs* and Money Service Providers' Activities (2016). According to the FinTRACA annual report for 2017, within one-year life of the Regulation FinTRACA revoked and suspended 33 MSPs' licenses and imposed 3.8 million AFN (approx. 56,000 USD) fines on MSPs. FinTRACA has imposed almost the same amounts of fine (3.55 million AFN) against banks in the same period. *See* Da Afghanistan Bank, Financial Intelligence Unit, Annual Report 2017: Financial Transactions and Reports Analysis Center of Afghanistan (FinTRACA), www.fintraca.gov.af/Report.html [hereinafter Da Afghanistan Bank, FinTRACA Report 2017].

34 Rasooli, *Afghan Sarrafs Have Closed Saraya Shahzadaha* (2018).

35 *Id.* (Quoting Da Afghanistan Bank's Spokesman).

36 *Id.*

37 Haji Qzi Mir Afghan Safi, The President of Kabul's Sarrafs' Union, Facebook (February 7, 2018), www.facebook.com/qazishirinaqa/posts/350963322045553. According to the spokesman of the National Council of *Sarrafs*, Da Afghanistan Bank has agreed to lift the stay as part of a deal to end the strike. Interview Clip, Facebook, *End of Sarraf's Strike* (VOA Dari, February 2018), www.facebook.com/voadari/videos/1718723204840376/ [hereinafter Safi, *End of Sarraf's Strike* (2018)].

38 The Regulation provides FinTRACA with enforcement authority—13.4 Regulation authorizes FinTRACA to impose pecuniary fine (between 50,000 AFN-500,000 AFN), suspend and revoke FX and MSP licenses. Regulation of *Sarrafs* and Money Service Providers' Activities (2016). FinTRACA, using this authority, has revoked and suspended 33 MSPs' licenses in 2017. *See* Da Afghanistan Bank, FinTRACA Report 2017.

39 The National Council of *Sarrafs* also demands that the revoked licenses be reinstated. *See* Safi, *End of Sarraf's Strike* (2018).

40 The Regulation requires *Sarrafs* to report every currency exchange transaction in excess of 500,000 AFN to FinTRACA. Furthermore, the Regulation requires *Sarrafs* to report a *hawala* (and other financial transactions) in excess of 500,000 AFN (approx. 7,250 USD). *See* Regulation of *Sarrafs* and Money Service Providers' Activities (2016) (6.4.a Regulation). The National Council of *Sarrafs* claims these requirements

are impractical and demand that it be removed. It demands the Da Afghanistan Bank increases the transaction threshold to 1mAFN (approx. 14,500 USD). *See* Safi, *End of Sarraf's Strike* (2018). According to FinTRACA 2017 annual report, FXs and MSPs reported 71,012 large cash transactions. *See* Da Afghanistan Bank, FinTRACA Report 2017.

41 Regulation of *Sarrafs* and Money Service Providers' Activities (2016).

42 Currently, *Sarrafs* use multiple personal bank accounts to hold deposits at a number of banks. *Sarraf* owners objected to the requirement to combine these accounts into a centralized account because the consolidation would make them security targets if insurgents or criminals could easily determine their assets. *See* interview with the spokesman of National Union of *Sarrafs*; Safi, *End of Sarraf's Strike* (2018).

43 Regulation of *Sarrafs* and Money Service Providers' Activities (2016).

44 Safi, *End of Sarraf's Strike* (2018).

45 Interview with the spokesman of National Union of Sarrafs, Safi, *End of Sarraf's Strike* (2018).

46 *Kabul's Sarrafs Have Ended Their Strike*, BBC Persian (February 21, 2018), www.bbc.com/persian/business-43022961.

47 Regulation of *Sarrafs* and Money Service Providers' Activities (2016).

48 *See* Safi, *End of Sarraf's Strike* (2018). For example, the Regulation prohibits *Sarrafs* from conducting a transaction without recording a copy of the national ID or passport of the parties involved. Regulation of *Sarrafs* and Money Service Providers' Activities (2016) (4.2 Regulation). The National Council of *Sarrafs* argues that a large number of Afghans, who make up a large percentage of their customers, do not have either of these documents. *See* interview with the spokesman of National Union of Sarrafs, Safi, *End of Sarraf's Strike* (2018).

49 Da Afghanistan Bank, FinTRACA Report 2017.

50 *Id.*

51 Rasooli, *Afghan Sarrafs Have Closed Saraya Shahzadaha* (2018) (quoting Da Afghanistan Bank's spokesman).

52 Special Inspector General for Afghanistan Reconstruction, Quarterly Report to the United States Congress 165 (April 30, 2015), www.sigar.mil/pdf/quarterlyreports/2015-04-30qr-section3-economic.pdf.

53 *See* Chapter 1.

54 According to International Monetary Fund data, in 2015 there were 189 bank accounts per 1,000 adults in Afghanistan, and there were only 2.5 bank branches for every 100,000 Afghans. International Monetary Fund, Bank Accounts Per 1,000 Adults, Bank Accounts Per 1,000 Adults in Afghanistan for the Years of 2008 until 2015, www.theglobaleconomy.com/Afghanistan/bank_accounts/; International Monetary Fund, Bank Branches Per 100,000 people, Bank Branches Per 100,000 people in Afghanistan for the Years of 2004 until 2015, www.theglobaleconomy.com/Afghanistan/bank_branches/ [hereinafter International Monetary Fund, Bank Branches Per 100,000 people in Afghanistan].

55 *See infra* Chapter 4.

56 https://globalfindex.worldbank.org/#GF-ReportChapters.

57 https://data.worldbank.org/indicator/FB.CBK.DPTR.P3?locations=AF.

58 https://data.worldbank.org/indicator/FB.CBK.DPTR.P3?locations=AF.

59 https://data.worldbank.org/indicator/FB.CBK.BRCH.P5?locations=AF.

60 https://data.worldbank.org/indicator/FB.ATM.TOTL.P5?locations=AF.

61 The data in this paragraph is calculated by the author based on Afghanistan Supreme Court, Judicial Activities Reports for the Years of 2012 until 2017.

62 The World Bank, World Bank Development Indicators, Percentage of Firms Using Banks to Finance Investment, Percentage of Firms Using Banks to Finance Investment in Afghanistan for the Year 2014, https://data.worldbank.org/indicator/IC.FRM.

BNKS.ZS?locations=AF [hereinafter The World Bank, Percentage of Firms Using Banks to Finance Investment in Afghanistan for the Year 2014].

63 The World Bank, World Bank Development Indicators, Percentage of Firms Using Banks to Finance Working Capital, Percentage of Firms Using Banks to Finance Working Capital in Afghanistan for the Year 2014, https://data.worldbank.org/indicator/IC.FRM.BKWC.ZS?locations=AF [hereinafter The World Bank, Percentage of Firms Using Banks to Finance Working Capital in Afghanistan for the Year 2014].

64 Calculated by the author based on Afghanistan Supreme Court, Judicial Activities Reports for the Years of 2012 until 2017.

65 *Id.*

66 In 2012, according to GALLUP® survey, when asked do you have confidence in the financial institutions or banks, 56% of Afghans answered NO while only 29% said YES (15% said don't know or refused). *See* Steve Crabtree, *European Countries Lead World in Distrust of Banks* (May 20, 2013), http://news.gallup.com/poll/162602/european-countries-lead-world-distrust-banks.aspx [hereinafter Crabtree, *European Countries Lead World in Distrust of Banks* (2013)].

67 *See* Chapter 3 for a comparison of the functionality of *Sarrafs* versus bank lending.

68 *See* Crabtree, *European Countries Lead World in Distrust of Banks* (2013).

69 There are 2.47 branch per 100,000 persons. *See* International Monetary Fund, Bank Branches per 100,000 people in Afghanistan.

70 The Afghan government is working to improve access to banking services through mobile banking with some success. According to the International Telecommunication Union, in 2016, the number of mobile cellular subscription per 100 people in Afghanistan was 66, The International Telecommunication Union, Afghanistan: Mobile Phone Subscribers per 100 people, www.theglobaleconomy.com/Afghanistan/Mobile_phone_subscribers_per_100_people/. That is a very high user rate compared to bank users. As of 2017, there are 357,000 mobile banking services provided by three main telecommunication companies in Afghanistan (Roshan's M-Pisa, Etisalat's M-*hawala*, and AWCC's My money). There are 10 mobile banking users per 1,000 adults in Afghanistan, according to a 2017 report. Mobile banking services include person-to-person money transfer, salary disbursement, bill payments, and top-up, and merchant payment. These services vary by provider. While mobile banking is still in its early stages of development in Afghanistan, it shows great potential for increasing financial inclusion. *See* Office of the Economic Advisor, Mobile Banking in Afghanistan (2017).

71 *See* Independent Joint Anti-Corruption Monitoring and Evaluation Committee, MEC Update on Kabul Bank Scandal (Press Release, October 2, 2016), www.mec.af/index.php/news-events/press-releases; *Kabul Bank Fraud: Ghani Reopens Afghan Corruption Case*, BBC News (October 1, 2014), www.bbc.com/news/world-asia-29450821.

72 *Id.*

73 *Id.*

74 *Id.*

75 *See* Landell Mills Development Consultant, UKAid, Overcoming the Access to Finance Paradox in Afghanistan: Experience from the Afghanistan Business Innovation Fund 2 (2016), https://static1.squarespace.com/static/553f9958e4b06d466cd3ce1e/t/599ea0eaf9a61e5bdb7a9087/1503568115954/APA-ABIF-financing-KP-010916.pdf [hereinafter Mills, Overcoming the Access to Finance Paradox in Afghanistan (2016)].

76 *See* Chapters 1 and 2.

77 Calculated by the author Based on Da Afghanistan Bank, Monthly Average USD For the Years of 1385 Hijri Until 1396 Hijri.

78 The Assessment also found that only 1% of their sample of large businesses used *Sarraf* for investment (1.19 million USD). The Assessment survey only asked about one-year or longer-term financing. *Sarrafs*, as I discussed in Chapter 3, do not often provide long-term financing to large businesses. *See* Afghanistan Financial Services, Afghanistan Capital Markets Assessment (2010).

79 *Id.*

80 Business Establishment Survey (2010).

81 The World Bank, Percentage of Firms Using Banks to Finance Investment in Afghanistan for the Year 2014.

82 The World Bank, Percentage of Firms Using Banks to Finance Working Capital in Afghanistan for the Year 2014.

83 Calculated by the author based on Da Afghanistan Bank, Quarterly Statistics of I-2013 until II-2017.

84 Calculated by the author based on Da Afghanistan Bank, Quarterly Statistics of I-2013 until II-2017.

85 The Business Climate Report data in this section is calculated by the author based on Afghanistan Chamber of Commerce Industries, Business Tendency Survey Reports.

86 According to the IMF data, real interest rate, defined as bank lending interest rate minus inflation in Afghanistan between 2008 and 2016 was on average 10.91%. *See* International Monetary Fund, Afghanistan: Real Interest Rate (Bank Lending Rate Minus Inflation) for the Years of 2008 until 2016, www.theglobaleconomy.com/Afghanistan/Real_interest_rate/.

87 Calculated by the author based on Afghanistan Chamber of Commerce Industries, Business Tendency Survey Reports.

88 *Id.*

89 *Id.*

90 Calculated by the author based on Afghanistan Chamber of Commerce Industries, Business Tendency Survey Reports.

91 *Id.*

92 *See* Chapter 2.

93 Calculated by the author based on Afghanistan Chamber of Commerce Industries, Business Tendency Survey Reports.

94 *Id.*

95 *Id.*

96 Calculated by the author based on Da Afghanistan Bank, Annual Economic and Statistical Reports for the Years of 1384 Hijri until 1395 Hijri, http://dab.gov.af/en/page/media/publications/annual-economic-and-statistical-bulletin [hereinafter Da Afghanistan Bank, Economic and Statistical Reports for the Years of 1384 until 1395 Hijri].

97 Calculated by the author based on Da Afghanistan Bank, Economic and Statistical Reports for the Years of 1384 until 1395 Hijri

98 *Id.*

99 *Id.*

100 The data in the two following paragraphs is calculated by the author based on Da Afghanistan Bank, Economic and Statistical Reports for the Years of 1384 until 1395 Hijri.

101 *See* Islamic Republic of Afghanistan, National Peace and Development Framework (2016); Islamic Republic of Afghanistan, National Peace and Development Framework (2008).

102 *Id.*

103 *Id.*

104 *See* Islamic Republic of Afghanistan, National Peace and Development Framework (2016).

105 Afghanistan Ministry of Commerce and Industries, Strategic Plan (2016).

106 Afghanistan Ministry of Economics, Economic Policy (2013).
107 Da Afghanistan Bank, Strategic Plan (2017).
108 *See* the discussion of bank loans earlier in this chapter.
109 Afghanistan Ministry of Justice, Five Strategic PLANS (2013). I was unable to find the Afghanistan Supreme Court's strategic plan.
110 Islamic Republic of Afghanistan, National Peace and Development Framework (2016), at 1.
111 *Id.*
112 *Id.* at 19.
113 *Id.*
114 *Id.*
115 *Id.* at 26.
116 *Id.* 19.
117 *Id.* at 22.
118 *Id.*
119 www.dab.gov.af/sites/default/files/2020-06/National%20Financial%20Inclusion%20Strategy%20for%20Afghanistanfinal.pdf.
120 Da Afghanistan Bank Financial Inclusion Department, http://dab.gov.af/en/page/about-the-bank/departments/mortgage (last visited April 10, 2018).
121 Afghanistan Ministry of Economics, Economic Policy (2013).
122 *Id.*
123 *Id.* at 8.
124 *Id.* at 9.
125 *Id.* at 14.
126 Afghanistan Ministry of Commerce and Industries, Strategic Plan (2016), at 13.
127 *Id.* at 12.
128 *Id.* at 13.
129 *Id.*
130 *Id.*
131 *Id.* at 14.
132 *Id.*
133 *Id.* at 14–15.
134 *Id.*
135 *Id.*
136 *Id.*
137 *Id.* at 46.
138 *Id.*
139 *Id.* at 15.
140 *Id.* at 25–26.
141 *Id.* at 47.
142 *Id.*
143 *Id.* at 49.
144 *Id.*
145 *Id.* at 55.
146 Commerce Strategy refers to a Business Formalization Strategy that has already been adopted by the Ministry of Commerce. However, I was not able to access the Stagey. *Id.*
147 Da Afghanistan Bank, Strategic Plan (2017).
148 *Id.* at 35.
149 *Id.* at 38.
150 *Id.* at 46.
151 *Id.* at 51.
152 Afghanistan Ministry of Justice, Five Strategic Plan (2013), at 11–14.

153 *Id.* at 15–20.
154 M. A. Thomas, Govern Like Us: U.S. Expectations of Poor Countries 21 (2015) [hereinafter Thomas, Govern Like Us (2015)].
155 *Id.* at 202.
156 *See* Integrity Watch Afghanistan, Curbing Illicit Financial Flows in Afghanistan (2015), at 28; *see also* The World Bank, State Building, Sustaining, Growth, and Reducing Poverty (2005), at 6.

References

Afghanistan Central Statistics Organization, Business Establishment Survey 2009 (2010), http://cso.gov.af/en/page/1500/1494/6

Afghanistan Central Statistics Organization, Sectoral Contribution to the GDP for the Years of 2002/03 until 2016/17, http://cso.gov.af/fa/page/ict/11328/11332

Afghanistan Chamber of Commerce Industries, Business Tendency Survey Reports of II-2014, IV-2014, I-2015, II-2015, III-2015, IV-2015, I-2016, II-2016, III-2016, IV-2016, I-2017, II-2017, and III-2017, www.acci.org.af/surveys-and-studies.html

Afghanistan Financial Services, Afghanistan Capital Markets Assessment: A Survey and Analysis of Current Capital Market Activities, the Demand for Capital, and the Basic Structure and Government Debt Markets (2010), www.ahg.af/data/AFS-Afghanistan-Capital-MarketsAssessment.pdf

Afghanistan MicroFinance Association, Annual Report (2019), http://ama.org.af/wp-content/uploads/2020/10/01Annual-Report-2019.pdf

Afghanistan Ministry of Economics, Economic Policy of Government of Afghanistan (2013), http://moec.gov.af/Content/files/Policy_National_Economic.pdf

Afghanistan Ministry of Justice, Five Strategic Plan: Law and Justice 2014–2018 (2013), http://moj.gov.af/Content/files/Estrategi.pdf

Afghanistan Supreme Court, Quarterly Judicial Activities Reports for the Years of 2012 until 2017, http://supremecourt.gov.af/fa/page/court-reporting

Da Afghanistan Bank, Annual Economic and Statistical Reports for the Years of 1384 Hijri until 1395 Hijri, http://dab.gov.af/en/page/media/publications/annual-economic-and-statistical-bulletin

Da Afghanistan Bank, Currency Hijri Monthly Average USD For the Years of 1385 Hijri Until 1396 Hijri, http://dab.gov.af/en/page/monetary-policy/rates-statistics/currency-hijri-average

Da Afghanistan Bank Financial Inclusion Department, http://dab.gov.af/en/page/about-the-bank/departments/mortgage (last visited April 10, 2018)

Da Afghanistan Bank, Financial Intelligence Unit, Annual Report 2017: Financial Transactions and Reports Analysis Center of Afghanistan (FinTRACA), www.fintraca.gov.af/Report.html

Da Afghanistan Bank, Muqarrara Tanzim Fa'aliat hai Sarrafan va Fraham Konandagan Khadamat Puli [Regulation of Sarrafs and Money Service Providers' Activities]

Da Afghanistan Bank, Quarterly Financial Sector Financial Statistics for the Period of I-2013 until II-2017, http://dab.gov.af/en/page/financial-supervision/financial-statistics/banks

Da Afghanistan Bank, Strategic Plan 2017–2021 (2017), http://dab.gov.af/fa/page/media/publications/strategic-plan

FATF, Improving Global AML/CFT Compliance: On-going Process—23 June 2017, www.fatf-gafi.org/countries/a-c/afghanistan/documents/fatf-compliance-june-2017.html (last visited April 10, 2018)

Haji Qzi Mir Afghan Safi, The President of Kabul's Sarrafs' Union, Facebook (February 7, 2018), www.facebook.com/qazishirinaqa/posts/350963322045553

Independent Joint Anti-Corruption Monitoring & Evaluation Committee, MEC Update on Kabul Bank Scandal (Press Release, October 2, 2016), www.mec.af/index.php/news-events/press-releases

Integrity Watch Afghanistan, Curbing Illicit Financial Flows in Afghanistan: Money Laundering, Terrorist Financing, and *hawala* 28 (2015), https://iwaweb.org/wp-content/uploads/2016/04/IFF-report-English-2-for-screen.pdf

International Monetary Fund, Afghanistan: Real Interest Rate (Bank Lending Rate Minus Inflation) for the Years of 2008 until 2016, www.theglobaleconomy.com/Afghanistan/Real_interest_rate/

International Monetary Fund, Bank Accounts Per 1000 Adults, Bank Accounts Per 1000 Adults in Afghanistan for the Years of 2008 until 2015, www.theglobaleconomy.com/Afghanistan/bank_accounts/

International Monetary Fund, Bank Branches Per 100,000 people, Bank Branches Per 100,000 people in Afghanistan for the Years of 2004 until 2015, www.theglobaleconomy.com/Afghanistan/bank_branches/

The International Telecommunication Union, Afghanistan: Mobile Phone Subscribers per 100 people, www.theglobaleconomy.com/Afghanistan/Mobile_phone_subscribers_per_100_people/

Interview Clip, Facebook, *End of Sarraf's Strike* (VOA Dari, February 2018), www.facebook.com/voadari/videos/1718723204840376/

Interview with the Spokesman of National Union of Sarrafs, Safi, *End of Sarraf's Strike* (2018)

Islamic Republic of Afghanistan, Afghanistan National Development Strategy 2008–2013 (2008), http://mfa.gov.af/en/page/6547/afghanistan-national-development-strategy/afghanistan-national-development-strategy-ands

Islamic Republic of Afghanistan, Afghanistan National Peace and Development Framework 2017–2021 (2016), http://policymof.gov.af/afghanistan-national-peace-and-development-framework-anpdf/

Kabul Bank Fraud: Ghani Reopens Afghan Corruption Case, BBC News (October 1, 2014), www.bbc.com/news/world-asia-29450821

Kabul's Sarrafs Have Ended Their Strike, BBC Persian (February 21, 2018), www.bbc.com/persian/business-43022961

Khairullah Rasooli, *Afghan Sarrafs Have Closed Saraya Shahzadaha [Kabul's Sarrafi Market] in Protest*, VOA Dari (February 2, 2018), www.darivoa.com/a/money-changers-closed-saraye-shazada-money-changing-market/4242561.html

Landell Mills Development Consultant, UKAid, Overcoming the Access to Finance Paradox in Afghanistan: Experience from the Afghanistan Business Innovation Fund 2 (2016) https://static1.squarespace.com/static/553f9958e4b06d466cd3ce1e/t/599ea0eaf9a61e5bdb7a9087/1503568115954/APA-ABIF-financing-KP-010916.pdf

M. A. Thomas, *Govern Like Us: U.S. Expectations of Poor Countries* (Columbia University Press 2015)

Mix Market, www.themix.org/mixmarket/countries-regions/afghanistan, (last visited February 18, 2018)

National Council of Sarrafs is Established, The Daily Afghanistan (September 29, 2017), www.dailyafghanistan.com/national_detail.php?post_id=141831

Office of the Economic Advisor, Mobile Banking in Afghanistan (PowerPoint Presentation, April 2017), http://afghaneconomics.com/research/Mobile_banking_scenario.pdf

Robert Holzmann, World Bank, Managed Labor Migration in Afghanistan: Exploring Employment and Growth Opportunities for Afghanistan 12 (2018), http://documents.worldbank.org/curated/en/746891516915310370/pdf/122987-WP-P158055-PUBLIC-SummaryReportFINALonline.pdf

Special Inspector General for Afghanistan Reconstruction, Quarterly Report to the United States Congress (April 30, 2015), www.sigar.mil/pdf/quarterlyreports/2015-04-30qr-section3-economic.pdf

Steve Crabtree, *European Countries Lead World in Distrust of Banks* (May 20, 2013) http://news.gallup.com/poll/162602/european-countries-lead-world-distrust-banks.aspx

The World Bank, *Afghanistan—State Building, Sustaining, Growth, and Reducing Poverty* (World Bank 2005)

The World Bank, World Bank Development Indicators, Percentage of Firms Using Banks to Finance Investment, Percentage of Firms Using Banks to Finance Investment in Afghanistan for the Year 2014, https://data.worldbank.org/indicator/IC.FRM.BNKS.ZS?locations=AF

The World Bank, World Bank Development Indicators, Percentage of Firms Using Banks to Finance Working Capital, Percentage of Firms Using Banks to Finance Working Capital in Afghanistan for the Year 2014, https://data.worldbank.org/indicator/IC.FRM.BKWC.ZS?locations=AF

4 A Critique of the Approach to Institutional Reform in Afghanistan and a Proposal for a New Approach

Grounded Institutional Reform

Formal institutions in Afghanistan have not been able to improve access to credit for Afghan merchants because they have generally failed to overcome the fundamental problems with and barriers to credit transactions in Afghanistan (highly volatile business climate, uncertain contract enforcement, and inefficient property rights system).[1] In spite of deficient formal institutions, in Afghanistan, a number of informal institutions have emerged that alleviate some of the credit constraints on Afghan merchants. These informal institutions include risk-sharing trade credit operations, short-term working capital loans, *Gerawee*, and *Sar qufli*.[2] Informal institutions such as these have been able to significantly improve access to working capital financing while marginally improving access to investment financing and liquidity in capital markets. The success of these informal institutions is due, primarily, to their ability to adapt to the context of Afghanistan, overcoming the fundamental problems of credit transacting in Afghanistan. However, the existing informal institutions have not been able to significantly improve access to investment financing due to their limited capacity to pool savings for investment purposes, and their extralegal practices may have negative consequences on long-term economic growth and attraction of foreign investment. To improve access to investment financing, Afghanistan needs to undertake a series of institutional reforms to create formal institutions that work for the Afghan context using the working informal institutions as building blocks.

The existing theories of institutional development are not helpful in the case of Afghanistan. Accordingly, the models of institutional reforms developed based on the existing theories do not respond to the financial reality of the Afghan context. The literature provides two distinct theories of institutional development and, correspondingly, two different models for institutional reform. One theory focuses on the role of the state as suppliers of formal institutions and creators of preconditions for economic growth. As such, this theory's model for institutional reform posits that less-developed countries can achieve economic growth by creating good formal institutions based on institutional best practices (e.g. strong property rights, good contract enforcement institutions). The other theory focuses on private entrepreneurs as suppliers of informal institutions and drivers of economic growth. This theory's model for institutional reform posits that the informal institutions developed by the economic entrepreneurs to support and expand their

DOI: 10.4324/9781003245476-5

economic ventures stimulate economic growth and supply of formal institutions. However, neither theory is helpful in the case of Afghanistan where the government has failed to supply workable formal institutions, and the development of entrepreneur-supplied informal institutions are bounded by poor infrastructure and limited market expansion opportunities. As such, these models of institutional reforms do not work in the Afghan context. This book proposes a synthetic approach to institutional reform in countries like Afghanistan, countries that have poor infrastructure, limited market expansion opportunities, and a reformist but weak government: this approach is Grounded Institutional Reform.

Designed to improve access to finance in countries like Afghanistan, Grounded Institutional Reform posits that the best way to create workable formal institutions is to leverage the working informal institutions. In this chapter, the Grounded Institutional Reform approach is applied to features found in Afghanistan to illustrate how it works in context. This book argues that to ensure Afghanistan's economy can move toward reliance on formal institutions and thereby remedy the shortcomings of the informal institutions, the Afghan government needs to use working, informal institutions as building blocks for creating formal institutions that work for the Afghan context—i.e. Grounded Institutional Reform. By leveraging working informal institutions, the Afghan government can utilize the wealth of existing institutional knowledge and networks and incentivize inclusion in the formal institutions.

The Afghan government's institutional reforms, so far, have generally been unsuccessful. This book argues that institutional reforms in Afghanistan have failed because they have only focused on formal institutions. Reformers have not been willing to use working informal institutions as building blocks to create formal institutions that work in the Afghan context. Institutional reforms in Afghanistan have failed to create formal institutions that gain tractions either because the formal institutions fail to solve the problems of credit transacting, and/or the Afghan government does not have sufficient capacity to overcome the resistance from the existing financial intermediaries of working informal institutions (but not the users of the informal institutions who are responsive to the workability of institutions). Therefore, creation and expansion of formal institutions, which has often meant outlawing informal institutions, has resulted in increased decoupling. Nevertheless, outlawing the informal institutions has not resulted in increased prevalence of formal institutions; instead, it has ensured the continued operation of informal institutions illegally—decoupling the formal rules and rules-in-use.

Grounded Institutional Reform creates conditions under which invested users of informal institutions (i.e. financial intermediaries) can increase some of their gains while accepting some losses (mostly during the initial period of transition), by voluntary inclusion in the newly created formal institutions. Thus, by rendering inclusion self-interest-compatible, Grounded Institutional Reform incentivizes voluntary compliance and reduces the need for overstretched and limited coercive power and administrative capacity of the state. For example, as explained in Chapter 4, Grounded Institutional Reform–based regulation of *Sarraf*s would offer formal recognition of deposit-keeping and loan distribution to incentivize *Sarrafs* to comply with the reporting and transparency regulations.

Grounded Institutional Reform represents two fundamental differences from the tried Afghan government strategy aimed to include informal businesses into the formal economy (which is mostly found in the Commerce Strategy).[3] First, the tried strategy uses two basic tools to incentivize inclusion in the formal economy: (1) ad hoc incentive packages (e.g. tax breaks or pardon of fines for unpaid taxes), which increase the benefit of inclusion; and (2) reduction of barriers to entry into the formal economy by simplifying registration and compliance requirements, which decrease the cost of inclusion.[4] While these are both important components of an inclusion strategy, they fall short. Grounded Institutional Reform posits that in order to incentivize the users of informal institutions to use formal institutions, formal institutions must incorporate the working informal institutions. Stated differently, in order to formalize Afghanistan's economy, formal institutions must absorb the working informal institutions.

Second, the current inclusion strategy only focuses on the users of informal institutions, that is, users of financial services. Grounded Institutional Reform, however, posits that given the limited coercive power of the Afghan state and the significant influence of informal financial intermediaries, in order to successfully formalize Afghanistan's financial sector (and Afghanistan's economy in general), the resistance from existing financial intermediaries of informal institutions must be curtailed. Grounded Institutional Reform overcomes this resistance by ensuring the existing financial intermediaries continue to have a role (although an altered role) in the formal institution and, therefore, have an incentive to comply with the formal rules and cooperate with the reform process.

The tenets of Grounded Institutional Reform stem from three main observations borne out of field research in Afghanistan. The relationships between these tenets and this research is described in the following three points:

(1) A main impediment against acceptance of formal institutions is that they have failed to overcome the problems of credit transacting in Afghanistan. Existing informal institutions, on the other hand, have been able to overcome the problems of credit transacting (albeit mostly for working capital financing); therefore, they can serve as good models for workable institutions in the context of Afghanistan. Grounded Institutional Reform posits that by using exiting informal institutions as building blocks for formal institutions, the Afghan government can tailor the formal institutions for the Afghan context.

(2) Informal institutions are used to conducting the overwhelming majority of business dealings in Afghanistan (90% of financial transactions are conducted through *Sarrafs*). A move toward formal institutions requires an incredible amount of institutional learning. The use of working informal institutions as building blocks for workable formal institutions will capitalize on existing institutional knowledge and, therefore, reduce the cost of transitioning to the use of these formal institutions.

(3) Existing informal institutions have created a powerful group of financial intermediaries who are heavily invested in the continued existence of these institutions. Any attempt to replace the existing informal institutions will have to overcome the resistance from this powerful group of financial intermediaries (as the failed attempt to regulate the *Sarrafi* market illustrates). Grounded Institutional Reform will reduce this resistance by ensuring a role (albeit an altered role) for existing financial intermediaries in the formal institutions. Thus, it incentivizes compliance and reduces decoupling by creating conditions under which inclusion in the formal institutions is self-interest-compatible for existing financial intermediaries.[5]

Grounded Institutional Reform finds support in Dani Rodrik's writing. Drawing on the experiences of successful reforms in China, South Korea, and Taiwan, Rodrik argues against adoption of institutional best practices. Instead, he argues that reformists are best served by operationalizing sound economic principles (such as appropriate incentives, property rights, sound money, and fiscal solvency) through policy experimentation.[6] He argues that these sound economic principles come "institution-free" and should be implemented through policies that are designed best on the existing institutional landscape.[7] In line with the premise of Grounded Institutional Reform, Rodrik argues, "[t]he pre-existing institutional landscape will typically *offer both constraints and opportunities*, requiring creative shortcuts or bold experiments. From this perspective, the 'art' of reform consists of *selecting appropriately from a potentially infinite menu of institutional designs*" (emphasis added).[8]

Grounded Institutional Reform finds support in the legal reform literature as well. Dixit, summarizing the lessons for developing countries, argues that "it is not always necessary to create replicas of western-style state legal institutions from scratch; *it may be possible to work with such alternative institutions as are available and build on them*"[9] (emphasis added). Similarly, Berkowitz, Pistor, and Richard found that countries that developed their legal systems internally adapted the imported legal codes to the local conditions or had knowledge of foreign legal codes achieved superior legal institutions compared to the countries that simply transplanted foreign legal orders.[10]

Grounded Institutional Reform has close affinity with the approach proposed by Andrews, Pritchett, and Woolcock in their book *Building State Capability: Evidence, Analysis, Action.*[11] Drawing on their research and experience in education, health, public financial management, and governance, in line with the arguments presented here, they criticize the orthodoxy in the international development organizations like World Bank[12] for failing to consider the implementation capacity of the states, "pushing states to do too much too fast," and distorting the process of problem-driven institutional development in the developing countries by advocating for adoption of international "best practices," effectively pursuing a policy of "institutional isomorphism."[13] In close affinity with the basic insight of Grounded Institutional Reform, they underscore the destructive hegemony of institutional transplantation over existing working institutions, stating,

> When certain forms are perceived as "best practices," their unwitting transplantation prevent *new forms from emerging, and displaces existing models*—or, as is often the case, is justified by simply *pretending they are not there at all*, succumbing to the "*illusion of the blank slate*" (emphasis added).[14]

Andrews, Pritchett, and Woolcock argue that the institutional ecology created by the international organizations and local agencies alike, they argue, enables inefficient and effective institutions to persist through "isomorphic mimicry," causing developing countries to get stuck.[15] Isomorphic mimicry allows an inefficient and effective institution to continue to receive resources and resist reform by looking like a legitimate institution conflating "looks like" with "does" and "form" with "function."[16] Drawing on their research and experience, they propose a new approach for institutional development, *Problem-Driven Iterative Adaptation.* It begins "with generating locally nominated and prioritized problems, and . . . works iteratively to identify customized *'best fit' responses* (sometimes by exploiting the existing variation in implementation outcomes)"[17] (emphasis added).

Much like the arguments presented here, Problem-Driven Iterative Adaptation posits that institutional design must take account of the implementational capacity of the state or it will result in decoupling. Divergence of the notional practice (de jure) and actual practice (de facto) does not only render the particular policy ineffective, but it also has lasting effects as it can result in a loss of what they call "normative traction."[18] The continued enactment of best practices in low capability environments, they argue, can sever the connection between notional policy and the ground, exponentially reducing the ability of notional policy to enact change on the ground—loss of normative traction.[19]

While Grounded Institutional Reform has close kinship with Problem-Driven Iterative Adaptation, it differs from it in several key aspects: first, the latter is generally proposed as a better approach to reforming government institutions such as education systems, while Grounded Institutional Reform is mostly concerned with economic institutions. Furthermore, Problem-Driven Iterative Adaptation focuses on creating an institutional environment where different institutions are judged by their ability to produce desirable outcomes by improving on their targeted problem areas rather than matching an acceptable institutional form. Grounded Institutional Reform, on the other hand, while recognizing institutional isomorphism and isomorphic mimicry as part of its diagnosis of the tried approach in Afghanistan, proposes an alternative approach to institutional reform which uses the existing informal institutions as building blocks for creating workable formal institutions. In other words, Problem-Driven Iterative Adaptation is an approach on how we should (or rather, should not) evaluate the effectiveness and fitness of different institutions. Grounded Institutional Reform builds on this evaluative approach by going one step further and positing how we should design formal economic institutions that can effectively ameliorate their targeted problems.

This chapter develops the argument for Grounded Institutional Reform then applies it to the context of Afghanistan. This chapter describes the existing models of institutional development, showing how they fail to explain the case of countries like Afghanistan. Next, it examines the rationale for the Afghan government's aversion to informal institutions, reflecting both the practical problems of formalizing (even revised) informal institutions and the problematic formulation of institutional reform based on the existing institutional development model. The chapter concludes by describing a number of ways Afghanistan can build on existing informal institutions to incentivize compliance and improve the workability of formal institutions in Afghan context, that is, apply Grounded Institutional Reform. While here Grounded Institutional Approach is only applied to credit and dispute resolution institutions in the context of commerce in Afghanistan, this approach has broad application not only in other domains within Afghanistan, such as access to justice and state-building, but also in other countries where the triangle of poor infrastructures, limited market development opportunities, and a willing but weak government is present.

Grounded Institutional Reform: *A Revised Approach for the Countries with Poor Infrastructure, Limited Market Expansion Opportunities, and a Willing Government*

Neither Entrepreneurial Institutional Theory nor State-Centered Theory can fully explain the institutional development in the case of Afghanistan. My research has identified entrepreneur-driven institutional development in the context of Afghanistan. Like Chinese entrepreneurs, Afghan merchants have also developed informal credit institutions to ameliorate the constraining effects of deficient formal institutions.[20] However, at the same time, my research highlights the shortcomings of entrepreneurial institutional development in countries with poor infrastructure and limited market expansion opportunities. Afghan merchants have not been able to expand their economic activities because of poor infrastructure that fragments the domestic markets and limits production and export. As a result, they have not developed working informal institutions that can sustain and facilitate an expanding and diversifying business climate. Neither have they generated sufficient demand for formalization of existing informal institutions except in limited cases (e.g. *Sar qufli*).

I propose a new approach to designing economic reform. Grounded Institutional Reform responds to the problems of developing workable formal institutions in Afghanistan in ways that Entrepreneurial Institutional Theory and State-Centered Theory cannot. The limitation of State-Centered Theory is that when applied to a context like Afghanistan, the formal institutions imported from outside based on best practices fail to take hold because they are not suited to solve the specific problems of transacting that local merchants face and instead aim to coercively replace the entrenched working informal institutions. Also, Entrepreneurial Institutional Theory does not fully suit the case of Afghanistan because entrepreneurs in Afghan-like contexts cannot expand their businesses due to poor infrastructure and limited market access. In the absence of innovation incentives generated by the possibility of market expansion, entrepreneurs have few incentives to continually improve the efficiency of informal institutions. Stated differently, Entrepreneurial Institutional Theory breaks down when applied in the context of countries like Afghanistan because private entrepreneurs are trapped in a vicious cycle and cannot, without external support, supply and sustain institutions necessary to stimulate economic growth.

Finally, the state, in the context of countries like Afghanistan, differs from the state envisioned by State-Centered Theory or Entrepreneurial Institutional Theory. It differs from the state envisioned by State-Centered Theory because it does not possess sufficient coercive power and administrative capacity to overcome resistance from the invested users of informal institutions. It differs from the state envisioned by Entrepreneurial Institutional Theory because it is willing to attempt to create strong formal institutions, either under pressure from the international community on which it depends for resources—a strong incentive for the now toppled Islamic Republic—or under domestic pressures generated by a desire to achieve performance legitimacy—a strong incentive for the caretaker government installed by the Taliban. Thus, unlike Entrepreneurial Institutional Theory-envisioned states, the Afghan state is willing, but unlike State-Centered-Theory-envisioned states, it has limited capacity to impose better formal institutions.

Grounded Institutional Reform corrects the problematic assumptions of Entrepreneurial Institutional Theory and State-Centered Theory about the role of states in institutional development in the context of less-developed countries. In a break with Entrepreneurial Institutional Theory, Grounded Institutional Reform overcomes the low entrepreneurial capacities of less-developed economies by allowing the state to play a proactive supporting role by incorporating working informal institutions. Grounded Institutional Reform incorporates the need for a proactive role for the state in less-developed countries with limited entrepreneurial capacities, advocated for by State-Centered Theory, but ensures context-sensitivity and user-readiness by absorbing working informal institutions within formal institutions. Grounded Institutional Reform overcomes the limited coercive power and administrative capacity of the states in less-developed countries by leveraging the existing informal institutions by incorporating the existing institutional knowledge, networks, and beneficiaries.

Rationales for Anti-Informal Institutions Positions: The Problems of Formalizing Informal Institutions in Afghanistan

Institutional reforms in Afghanistan have generally been informed by State-Centered Theory.[21] However, there are several specific theoretical and practical reasons why Afghan governments—at least during the Islamic Republic—have shown an aversion to the absorption of informal institutions. While these reasons are borne out by research on Afghanistan's case, this book argues, they also represent a general trend in less-developed countries which have poor infrastructure, limited market expansion opportunities, and a reformist but weak state.

There are several reasons why the Afghan government did not choose to absorb working informal institutions. These reasons are both theoretical and practical. The first practical reason is that informal institutions in Afghanistan are entangled with illegal economic activities. Secondly, informal institutions are hard to manipulate because they do not function according to transparent rules. Additionally, the users of informal institutions resist formalization to (a) safeguard themselves against predatory behavior of regulators, (b) evade taxes, and (c) ensure the continued use of informal institutions to support illegal economic activities. This book argues that given the limited coercive power and administrative capacity of the Afghan state, absorption of informal institutions is the most effective way to remedy the practical problems of informal institutions in Afghanistan and can help fully eliminate these problems in the long run.

In addition to these practical reasons, there are two main theoretical reasons, which are squarely rooted in State-Centered Theory, that further explain why the Afghan government did choose to use working informal institutions to create formal institutions that work for the Afghan context. The first theoretical reason is concerned with the formal institutions and why they have not worked in Afghanistan. There is a belief that formal institutions have failed to gain traction in Afghanistan because of the stickiness of informal institutions, and the absence of effective formal institutions. The former is generally evidenced by the pervasive use of informal institutions. Concerning the latter, in accordance with State-Centered Theory, good institutions are understood to use best institutional practices. Therefore, formal institutions that have worked well in other countries have been adopted as good formal institutions.

As to the second theoretical reason that the Afghan government did not choose to use working informal institutions, there is a belief that informal institutions have no place in a modern economy. Informal institutions are deemed to represent backwardness: to modernize the country and the economy, informal institutions must be uprooted.[22] This book argues that these theoretical justifications are not valid: formal institutions have failed to gain traction because they cannot overcome the problems of credit transacting in Afghanistan, and informal institutions contain a wealth of useful institutional knowledge and networks that can contribute to the creation of workable formal institutions in Afghanistan and ensure a smooth transition to a more formalized economy.

Theoretical Underpinning of Anti-Informal Institutions in Afghanistan

The tried Afghan government's theoretical approach to institutional reform generally reflects a preference for State-Centered Theory.[23] Its approach to institutional reform is rooted in the idea that the stickiness of informal institutions is the reason formal institutions do not stick. From this point of view, curbing informal institutions and adopting better formal institutions based on institutional best practices will ensure that informal institutions gain traction in Afghanistan. The tried government approach was also rooted in the idea that informal institutions are backward and must be uprooted. Replacing formal institutions, and/or outlawing formal institutions, will ensure Afghanistan transitions from a backward economy into a modern economy, the thinking goes. These two theoretical propositions can be surmised from the content of the now toppled Islamic Republic's Government's Strategic Policies for institutional reforms (Government's Strategic Policies) and the discourse around the *Sarrafi* regulation.[24] They are also firmly rooted in State-Centered Theory.

The problem with these theoretical propositions is that they break down when applied to the Afghan context. They are imported insights from State-Centered Theory, and they are either generally held positions within the field of institutional reforms, informed by neo-liberal economic theories and writings of State-Centered Theory institutionalists, or they are normative propositions about what a developed economy (and country) should look like. Insofar as these theoretical propositions have empirical support, that support has been generated in entirely different contexts that do not share sufficient features or characteristics with Afghanistan. In short, these theoretical propositions either do not fit Afghanistan's context, or when they do, they overreach.

Concerning the first theoretical proposition, that is, stickiness of informal institutions, my research shows that stickiness of informal institutions is not likely an explanation for the continued use of informal institutions. Afghan merchants do not use bank loans not because they are used to the old way of doing business and are more comfortable with existing informal institutions but because the current model of bank loans does not work for the context of Afghanistan. Relatedly, this research shows that the theoretical proposition that adoption of institutional best practices (e.g. Credit Bureau) will ensure the success of formal institutions is not well-founded. Afghan governments should instead adopt institutions that overcome the problems of credit transacting with full consideration of the Afghan context. Therefore, due consideration should be given to the problems of credit transacting in Afghanistan and the solutions that have emerged to overcome those problems, instead of seeking to adopt institutional solutions whose workability has not been tested in the context of Afghanistan.

Concerning the second theoretical proposition, the backwardness of informal institutions, this normative statement is also not supported by the findings of my research in Afghanistan. While the prevailing informal institutions having limited capacity to finance long-term investment and attract foreign investors, they have significantly improved access to working capital financing in Afghanistan, reducing the capital constraints on Afghan merchants and ensured competitiveness of Afghan markets and thus lower prices.[25] Assuming *a priori* that informal institutions are inefficient closes the door on leveraging the institutional knowledge and networks that have emerged to solve the problems of credit transacting in a way that works for the context of Afghanistan. It closes the door on learning about the institutional solutions that have emerged and developed incrementally in a bottom-up way to inform the design of formal institutions that will be effective for the Afghan context.

While anti-informal-institutions critics often justify their positions by citing North's theory, this author believes that Grounded Institutional Reform finds equal or greater support in North's writings. North contends that an economy which functions according to formal rules is more efficient than an economy that is governed by informal institutions.[26] However, North also argues that formal institutions only enhance efficiency if they are appropriate for the context in which they are used (hence, North's aversion to institutional engineering).[27] This book takes the position that the appropriateness of formal institutions for the context of their use can be greatly improved if effective informal institutions are used as building blocks for formal institutions that work for that context, that is, Grounded Institutional Reform. If formalization is conducted by building on and correcting the existing working informal institutions, the formal institutions will work for the context, and formalization will be met with less resistance.

Ironically, stickiness of theoretical propositions which are not supported by empirical in-context studies are the reason why institutional reforms most often disregard the value of existing institutions that have developed in context. The attempt to achieve institutional isomorphism based on unifying theory of institutional reforms, coupled with limited in-context studies, has biased reformists against using the effective elements of working informal institutions.

Practical Problems of Absorbing Informal Institutions in Afghanistan

In addition to theoretical impediments to adopting Grounded Institutional Reform in Afghanistan, which are mostly problematic, this section explores the practical problems impeding the absorption of informal institutions in Afghanistan.

Informal Institutions Are Entangled with Illegal Economic Activities

According to the Ministry of Finance under the now toppled Islamic Republic, 65% of all financial flows in the country are illicitly earned, transferred, or used.[28] *Sarrafs* are the financial service providers of choice of Afghans, especially those who are involved in the illegal economy. *Sarrafs* handle 90% of financial transactions in Afghanistan.[29] Therefore, *Sarrafs* are closely entangled with illegal economic activities. According to Thompson's estimate for the years 2004–2005, almost 30% of *hawala* volume (approx. 2 billion USD) came from opium trade alone.[30] The production of opium has been consistently increasing since 2005; therefore, it is safe to assume that contribution of opium to *hawala* has correspondingly increased.[31] There are early indications that with Taliban in power and the deepening of economic crisis, the drug economy (not only opium but also the nascent meth industry) is expanding.

The prevalence of the opium industry, then Taliban insurgency, and the prevalent corruption during the Islamic Republic together have created a large illegal economy in Afghanistan. The main components of that economy included poppy cultivation, opium trade and production, and corruption. According to conservative estimates, the value of Afghanistan's illegal economy, measured by corruption and opium alone, would amount to roughly one-third of the country's GDP before Taliban's takeover.[32] While Taliban takeover may improve corruption figures, it is also likely to increase the share of the drug economy. The illegal economy is likely to continue.

United Nations Office on Drugs and Crime's estimated data for the period between 2008 and 2015 suggest that the production and trade value of opium received by Afghan farmers and traffickers was roughly the same as the contribution of legal agriculture to the GDP.[33] According to Integrity Watch Afghanistan biannual reports, in 2016, almost 3.5 million Afghans reported that they had paid 2.89 billion USD in bribes over the last year.[34]

The estimated total value of the illegal economy, taking into account only opium production and sales and bribes, could be calculated for 2010, 2012, and 2014. In 2012, the estimated value of bribes paid and money from the opium industry received by Afghans was 4.71 billion USD, which is equal to 30% of the legal economy GDP (15.74 billion USD calculated at the current price).[35] In 2014, the estimated total value of the illegal economy was 5.56 billion USD, which is 27% of the legal economy measured by GDP at current price (20.25 billion USD).[36] In 2014, the total estimated value of Afghanistan's illegal economy was 7.06 billion USD, which compared to 34% of the GDP calculated at the current price for that year (20.48 billion USD).[37]

Interviews conducted for this study show that the illegal economy interacts in several complicated ways with Afghanistan's financial system.[38] Money from opium exports are used to finance imports. According to several interviewees, some merchants, who are also engaged in the opium trade, import products (most often cars) in exchange for opium exports. Thus, they are able to sell the products (e.g. cars) for a lower price than legal importers in the Afghanistan market, make a good profit, and launder opium money at the same time. This puts the businesses which are not involved in the export of opium at a serious disadvantage.

Sarrafs are the main financial service providers that facilitate the financing of legal imports by opium export and also transfer and launder bribes and revenue from opium trade. Therefore, a significant portion of funds that *Sarrafs* hold for their clients come from the illegal economy. *Sarrafs* use these funds, along with the funds generated from legal business activities, to finance short-term working capital loans, medium-term loans, and equity investment. *Sarrafs* extensively use banks to hold and transfer funds, a significant portion of which comes from illegal economy; hence, illicit funds are not contained in the *Sarrafi* markets.

In short, given the pervasiveness of Afghanistan's illegal economy, illicit funds routinely mesh into legal economic activities (e.g. finance import of legal products, supply of working capital loans to legal businesses, and legal business ventures), mixed with the legal funds and travel through both the *Sarrafi* and formal banking system. As a result, finding and fighting illegal funds in Afghanistan is incredibly difficult even before considering the uber-complicated question of US and UN sanctions on Taliban.

The governments under now toppled Islamic Republic, under pressure from the international community, enacted numerous pieces of legislation and created a number of oversight bodies to curb the illegal funds in Afghanistan's financial system. The Regulation of the *Sarrafi*, discussed in Chapter 4, was one of these efforts. Under the Regulation, a number of reporting and vetting processes were instituted to improve the transparency and accountability in the operation of *Sarrafi* markets. However, the Regulation was met with fierce resistance from *Sarraf* Unions and was finally suspended.[39] Until the end of the Republic, the fate of the Regulation is unclear.

Fighting the illicit funds is of utmost importance not only because it jeopardizes the inclusion of Afghanistan's financial system in the global financial system but also because the illegal economy disadvantages the legal economy in Afghanistan. However, the Regulation did not represent the right approach to achieve the desired result of curbing illegal funds in Afghanistan; hence, it failed. This book argues that a regulation designed based on Grounded Institutional Reform could practically contain illegal funds and ensure continued access to working capital finance in Afghanistan (see Section 4.1.2.)

The current Regulation, in addition to institution of transparency and accountability-enhancing measures, outlaws deposit-keeping and loan distributions by *Sarrafs*. *Sarrafs* rely on deposit-keeping and loan distribution to ensure the continued demand for their currency exchange and *hawala* services. By outlawing deposit-keeping and loan distributions, the Regulation, in effect, removed any incentive for *Sarrafs* to comply with the Regulation.

Unlike the transparency and accountability measures of the Regulation, which are based on a practical need to fight illegal funds in the financial system, banning *Sarrafs* from keeping deposits and issuing loans is based on problematic theoretical propositions. The first theoretical justification is that banks in Afghanistan have failed to gain tractions because merchants are used to using *Sarrafs* (i.e. stickiness of informal institutions). Therefore, Da Afghanistan Bank's Regulation was aimed at increasing the use of banks by outlawing *Sarrafs*' financing services. The second theoretical justification was that *Sarrafs* represent and sustain Afghanistan's traditional economy, which must be curtailed. This is a normative stance which is not rooted in a thorough understanding of Afghanistan's institutional landscape.

The banning of deposit-keeping and loan distribution by *Sarrafs* is not based on a practical analysis of the need of Afghanistan's economy; rather it is based on a problematic theoretical position informed by State-Centered Theory. As this study has shown, the failure of formal institutions to gain tractions in Afghanistan is due to their inability to overcome the problems of credit transacting—that is why the low rate of use *Sarraf*'s financing in Balkh is not correlated with increased use of banks' financing. On the other hand, *Sarraf*'s short-term working capital loans are a very significant source of working capital financing in Afghanistan, which ensures Afghan merchants can issue trade loans despite Afghanistan's highly volatile business climate, thus ensuring market competition and lower prices.

A regulation designed based on Grounded Institutional Reform can remedy the problems of the *Sarrafi* market while ensuring the continued supply of working capital finance for Afghan merchants. With the Grounded Institutional Reform regulation, the *Sarrafs* would be allowed to engage in financing (deposit-keeping and loan distribution). This would ensure that *Sarrafs*' *hawala* and currency exchange services are continued to be demanded. Thus, *Sarrafs* would have incentives to comply with the Regulation. The Grounded Institutional Reform regulation would enhance some of the benefits of formalization for *Sarrafs*, based on empirical research that shows *Sarrafs* finance supply chains in Afghanistan, while imposing transparency and accountability-enhancing measures to curb the negative influence of illegal funds on Afghanistan's economy and stability.

Unlike the current Regulation, Grounded Institutional Reform regulation is likely to be successful because it reduces the resistance of the powerful group of financial intermediaries by offering them targeted finance-enhancing concessions while imposing much needed transparency and accountability-enhancing measures. The Regulation of *Sarrafs* failed, in part, because it did not offer an incentive for *Sarrafs* to comply; therefore, they organized to resist the Regulation at all costs, which resulted in failure of the Regulation. The Regulation of *Sarrafs* failed because it attempted to bundle much-needed transparency and accountability-enchaining measures with anti-informal institutions measures ("containing the traditional market") and offered the *Sarrafs* no incentive to comply with either.[40]

Regulations based on Grounded Institutional Reform will likely face resistance. However, by absorbing the working informal institutions, resistance will be reduced because it will ensure a role for *Sarrafs* in the formal financial system. Furthermore, Grounded Institutional Reform's approach to regulating *Sarrafs* has a better chance of success because the numbers of *Sarrafs* who knowingly engage in supporting Afghanistan's illegal economy is limited. Stated differently, a small number of *Sarrafs* handle the majority of funds from the illegal economy in Afghanistan.[41] Therefore, the current Regulation, by targeting the entirety of the *Sarrafi* market, based on theoretical justifications that have limited grounding in the context of Afghanistan, alienated the entire *Sarrafi* markets, which ensured its failure. Grounded Institutional Reform regulation, on the other hand, through targeted absorption of informal institutions of *Sarrafi* markets, increases its likelihood of success by targeting the practical problems of informal institutions.

Taliban relation to the illegal economy is complicated. On the one hand, during their insurgency, they have acted as both a regulator and beneficiary of the illegal markets, and now that they are in government but still a sanctioned group, they maintain close contact with the illegal economy as a survival strategy. On the other hand, now that they are in power, they have expressed a strong desire to be accepted in the international community and signaled their willingness to take actions to facilitate inclusion by holding international law, including taking actions against the illegal economy. Moreover, now that Taliban are the de facto government, they have different interests when it comes to regulating the illegal markets and taxation, which may bring their views closer to other governments when it comes to the illegal economy. In any case, while the sanctions stand and the humanitarian crisis goes unabated, it is hard to assess what Taliban may do if they can achieve the status of the legal government of Afghanistan and what kind of regulatory approach they are to take to the illegal and informal markets of Afghanistan. One thing is for sure: they are more sympathetic to the informal institutions and much more skeptical of the imported institution solutions. This combination, while destructive in other areas, could be positive in reforming trade and credit institutions.

Informal Institutions Are Hard to Manipulate

While the rules that make up the informal institutions are understood by those who use them, even though they may not be able to articulate them, they are not transparent to outsiders. Therefore, Grounded Institutional Reform, which aims to use informal institutions as building blocks for workable formal institutions, faces the problem of identifying how informal institutions operate. Stated differently, information about the mechanics of informal institutions is generally hard to obtain by those who design institutional reforms; therefore, it will be more difficult to design institutional reforms that take into account the mechanics and working dynamics of informal institutions.

Due to the hegemony of State-Centered Theory institutional reform discourse, reformists within the government and international organizations tend to focus on formal institutions because formal institutions are more transparent; they are easier to identify. The training of most reformists does not prepare them to look for or study informal institutions. Alternatively, the reformists' training most often biases them in favor of formal institutions and against informal institutions. In short, institutional reformists tend to have an information deficiency, both in access to information and processing the information, when it comes to informal institutions.

This informational deficiency surrounding informal institutions makes it difficult to design institutional intervention to manipulate working informal institutions, making it more likely that reformists only focus on formal institutions inside the country and look to formal institutions in other countries for designing institutional reforms. Thus, reformists are likely to forgo the wealth of institutional knowledge and networks held within working informal institutions and inevitably resort to coercion to impose imported institutional solutions. As a result, institutional reforms run a high risk of failure especially in the countries like Afghanistan, where, due to historical underdevelopment of formal institutions, informal institutions are more pervasive.

This study posits that informal deficiency surrounding informal institutions can be remedied. If institutional reformists change their attitudes toward informal institutions from one of contempt to one of learning and commit to an in-depth study of working informal institutions, reformists can overcome their informational deficiency. Thus, they can design and implement institutional reforms that use working informal institutions as building blocks for creating formal institutions that work for the context of Afghanistan and will ensure that the formal institutions will gain traction and not be met with unsurmountable resistance.

The informational deficiency of reformists concerning informal institutions is a reason why, in the context of Afghanistan, courts have been the first to implement Grounded Institutional Reform through selective formalization of informal institutions. Courts have continuous interaction with the user of informal institutions who resort to courts to compensate for the deficiency of informal enforcement mechanisms. This provides courts with information that can be used to devise targeted intervention to selectively formalize informal institutions. This explains why courts have been able to effectively formalize informal institutions like *Sar qufli* with positive consequences for capital liquidity and access to credit.[42]

The judiciary has an informational advantage over other rule-making bodies due to its repeated interactions with the users of informal credit institutions. Court disputes are the main locus of interaction between formal and informal institutions in Afghanistan. The judiciary can draw on its informational advantage and rule-making power to lend support of formal institutions to the informal institutions in cases where this support can help increase the utility of informal institutions. The case of *Sar qufli* shows that the Afghan judiciary has the capacity to improve the utility of informal credit transaction through incremental, bottom-up, and demand-led interventions.

The Users of Informal Institutions Resist Formalization

Any institutional arrangement produces winners and losers by creating a certain distribution of resources.[43] An institutional reform, to be successful, must either forcefully overcome the resistance from the invested users of existing institutions or ensure that transition to a new institutional arrangement is beneficial enough to a large enough group of users that a transition becomes possible without considerable coercive power.[44]

Formalization of informal institutions in Afghanistan poses the same problem. Existing informal institutions have invested users who will resist formalization. This renders any attempt to change informal institutions (whether it be formalizing them or replacing them) difficult.[45] One important group of invested users identified here are financial intermediaries that have developed under informal institutions (most notably *Sarrafs*). The user of financial services of these financial intermediaries, on the other hand, are responsive to the workability and cost of alternative institutional solutions as they are not inextricably linked to the prevailing informal institutions.

The tried inclusion strategies tend to focus only on users of informal institutions but not on those who function as maintainers of those institutions (i.e. invested users).[46] Existing informal institutions have created a powerful group of financial intermediaries (e.g. *Sarrafs* and real estate agents) who are invested in the continued existence of current institutional arrangements. What adds to this difficulty, in the context of Afghanistan and other underdeveloped countries, is the limited coercive power and administrative capacity of the Afghan government, coupled with the pervasiveness and entrenchment of informal institutions. According to the World Bank 2020 Governance Index, the Afghan government falls within the lowest percentile consistently ranking one of the worst countries across the recorded measurements which are important for formulation and implementation of policies and regulation.[47] These reports collectively provide strong evidence that the Afghan state have limited coercive and administrative capacity—this includes the Afghan state under the Taliban rule as well.

As Thomas has argued, the implementation of the institutional reforms formulated in the range of Government Strategic Policies is out of reach for governments like those of Afghanistan.[48] Concurring with Thomas' argument, Grounded Institutional Reform will reduce the difficulty of formalizing informal institutions by providing incentives to users as well as invested users of existing informal institutions to formalize. Grounded Institutional Reform incorporates the existing informal institutions while altering them. Thus, it offers a mixed package of benefits and costs. It offers invested users of informal institutions the opportunity to increase some of the current benefits they receive by granting them formal legal recognition while imposing costs upon them to curb the negative aspects of the informal institutions. Therefore, depending on the informal institutions and their efficiency, Grounded Institutional Reform will either reduce or eliminate the resistance to the formalization of informal institutions. As a result, it draws on an incentive-based model, instead of a coercive model, to implement institutional reform by inducing compliance and reducing the need to use the state's limited coercive power.

Absorption of informal institutions, under Grounded Institutional Reform, must be coupled with efforts to improve the quality of formal institutions, especially curbing corruption. Invested users and not-invested users of existing informal institutions resist formalization not only to ensure they can continue to engage in illegal activities (e.g. handle illegal funds or evade taxes) but also to protect themselves against predatory behavior of regulators. Formalization makes the users of information institutions visible to the corrupt officials who may misuse their regulatory power to extract rent from informal financial intermediaries and users of informal institutions. Therefore, to incentivize those who are involved in informal institutions to join the formal economy and subject themselves to formal institutions, the Afghan government must ensure not only that invested users have an incentive to comply with the formal institutions but also that they are protected against predatory behavior of regulators. Thus, improvement of formal institutions goes hand in hand with Grounded Institutional Reform.

Grounded Institutional Reform focuses on formal institutional design and process of formalization to make them fit for the context of Afghanistan. However, *if the government does not seriously fight the corruption in formal institutions, regardless of their content and design, no model of formal institutions and formal institutional design can ensure that formal institutions will gain traction in Afghanistan.*

What Would Reforms Based on Grounded Institutional Reform Look Like in Afghanistan?

This section provides a number of possible institutional reforms as illustrative applications of Grounded Institutional Reform in the context of Afghanistan. These examples are drawn from research findings conducted for this study and will show how Grounded Institutional Reform-based solutions differ from the tried Afghan Government's Strategic Policies which reflect the State-Centered-Theory-based solutions.[49]

Government Strategic Policies have a narrow view of Afghanistan's institutional landscape; therefore, they propose solutions that disregard the wealth of working informal institutions. While they most often correctly diagnose the problems of credit transacting in Afghanistan, their solutions do not get traction in Afghanistan. While most of the Government Strategic Policies' proposed formal institutions may be necessary institutional outcomes, they are more likely to get traction and work for the Afghan context if they are built incrementally using existing formal institutions as building blocks, that is, if they are revised using Grounded Institutional Reform.

Government Strategic Policies do not recognize Afghanistan's existing informal institutions, such as *Gerawee*, *Sar qufli*, or short-term working capital loans, as possible building blocks for solutions to the problem of access to credit for Afghan merchants. The only Government Strategic Policies that mention the informal economy and informal institutions is the Commerce Strategy.[50] This is most likely due to the collaboration between the Ministry of Commerce and business associations in Afghanistan, which has partially remedied the informational deficiency of institutional reform concerning the informal economy. However, the Commerce Strategy only refers to the informal economy and informal institutions in the context of incentivizing inclusion of informal businesses in the formal economy. While the Commerce Strategy correctly underscores the need to design incentive-based mechanisms to promote inclusion in the formal economy, it only discusses the need to reduce the barriers to and increase the benefit of inclusion in the formal economy. The Commerce Strategy does not mention the need for building on and correcting informal institutions as a way of increasing the workability and acceptance of the formal economy and formal institutions. The Commerce Strategy does not mention the need to draw on the existing institutions. Thus, while the Commerce Strategy highlights an important and often missing component of institutional reform in Afghanistan, it does not go far enough to advocate for the use of informal institutions as building blocks for devising institutional solutions to the problem of credit transacting in Afghanistan.

Government Strategic Policies underscore the need for property right reforms and creation of an effective titling system to unleash the value trapped in the housing market in Afghanistan cities. However, they do not mention *Gerawee*, which currently is helping Afghans raise capital against the value of their houses in the absence of secure tenure and land certification. Instead of building on and correcting these working institutions, Government Strategic Policies again advocate for creation of new formal institutions.

Facilitating the absorption of *Gerawee* by formal institutions, which could be aided by placing *Gerawee* transactions under the jurisdiction of commercial courts, can improve access to long-term financing while the Afghan government reforms formal property rights in the country. Likewise, Government Strategic Policies disregard the potential of the network of local real estate agents in implementing and maintaining an updated and comprehensive system of property titling. However, local real estate agents, who are acting as institutional entrepreneurs to facilitate *Gerawee* and *Sar qufli* transactions despite the current informality of property rights, can be used to partially privatize the creation and maintenance of a comprehensive system of property titling. Local real estate agents have an incentive to obtain information about the legal status of the properties in their locality. They also have an informational advantage due to their continuous interaction with the property users and property owners in their locality as well as their intimate knowledge of property transactions that are occurring. Afghan laws already require the registration of property transactions (e.g. lease and sale) with a registered real estate agent to improve tax collection. The Afghan government can leverage real estate agents' networks and information to create and maintain an updated and comprehensive property tilting system. Real estate agents offer a possible way to privatize creation or maintenance of property registration system, at least in major urban centers.

To solve the information problem that banks face in Afghanistan, Government Strategic Policies acknowledge the need to improve access to credit information to enable banks to assess borrowers. However, this idea completely disregards the wealth of credit information *Sarrafs* possess. *Sarrafs* conduct 90% of financial transactions in Afghanistan[51] and have ongoing financial interactions with Afghan merchants. Providing banks access to this wealth of information can greatly improve banks' ability to assess risks and will reduce their reliance on scarce formal deeds. For example, the Government Strategic Policies could propose the use of *Sarrafs* as guarantors for banks loans. This would encourage banks to outsource creditworthiness assessment and monitoring to *Sarrafs*. Government Strategic Policies, on the other hand, propose creation of new formal institutions like a Credit Bureau. A Credit Bureau would not work for the context of Afghanistan because it relies on information about formal credit practices, which, due to the low rate of formal credit use, are scarce in Afghanistan.

To expand Afghanistan's limited export, Government Strategic Policies underline the importance of inducing exports through providing better access to commercial and export financing. However, this disregards the potentials of short-term working capital loans, which are already financing import and supply chains. Instead, they propose creation of a new formal institution, namely, an export bank. Such a bank may help, but it requires resources that the Afghan government does not have and institutional knowledge that Afghan merchants do not possess.

Concerning the capital market, Government Strategic Policies stress the need to improve liquidity in Afghanistan's capital market. However, they do not mention

Sar qufli as a way of commodifying future revenue tied to a place of business. Instead, they focus on creation of new formal institutions like security markets. While a capital market, if successfully created, may improve capital market liquidity in Afghanistan, *Sar qufli* is currently delivering the same result although in significantly limited contexts. Leveraging *Sar qufli*, by supporting its use in other transactions where the value created by the use of a property is not easily movable, could have an immediate and positive consequences for liquidity in Afghanistan's capital market.

Notes

1 *See* Chapters 1 and 3.
2 *See* Chapter 1.
3 *See* Section 4.3. and Afghanistan Ministry of Commerce and Industries, Strategic Plan (2016), at 55.
4 *Id.*
5 Lau, Qian, and Roland argue that China was able to liberalize agricultural sector because it managed to implement reform without creating losers. China employed a two-track system that allowed for the liberalization *on the margin* while keeping the plan system intact. The two-track system was critical, they argue, to achieving political support for the reform, maintaining its momentum, and minimizing its adverse social implications. Dani Rodrik, discussing Lau, Qian, and Roland's research, observed that the two-track system was successful because it "*preserved the income streams of initial claimants*" (emphasis added). Lawrence J. Lau et al., *Reform without Losers: An Interpretation of China's Dual-Track Approach to Transition*, 108(1) The Journal of Political Economy 120, 136 (2000) and Dani Rodrik, *Growth Strategies* 980 (Elsevier B.V. 2004) [hereinafter Rodrik, *Growth Strategies* (2004)].
6 Rodrik, *Growth Strategies* (2004), at 985.
7 *Id.*
8 *Id.*
9 Avinash Dixit, Lawlessness and Economics 4 (2004).
10 *See* Jean-Francois Richard et al., *Economic Development, Legality, and the Transplant Effect*, 47(1) European Economic Review 165, 197 (2003). *See also* Pistor, who argues that legal transplantation can backfire; Katharina Pistor, the Standardization of Law and its Effect on Developing Economies 17 (G-24 Discussion Paper No. 4, July 2000), http://unctad.org/en/docs/pogdsmdpbg24d4.en.pdf.
11 Matt Andrews et al., Building State Capability: Evidence, Analysis, Action 44–45 (2017) [hereinafter Andrews et al., Building State Capability (2017)].
12 It is worth nothing that all three authors have worked with different international organizations, like World Bank, extensively.
13 Andrews et al., Building State Capability (2017).
14 *Id.* at 46. Willful ignorance of potentials of *Sarrafs*, *Sar qufli*, and *Gerawee* to relax the credit constrains of Afghan merchants is a great example of justifying institutional displacement using "illusion of the blank slate."
15 *Id.*
16 An example of isomorphic mimicry from Afghanistan would be ineffective lending model enduring because it looks likes the lending model that has been successful in other countries.
17 Andrews et al., Building State Capability (2017), at 5.
18 *Id.* at 58.

19 *Id.* at 59. An example of loss of normative traction in Afghanistan would be the Da Afghanistan Bank's attempt to outlaw deposit-keeping and loan distribution by *Sarrafs*. This policy, if reinstated, would surely fail to stop *Sarrafs* from keeping deposits and issuing loans, ensuring that those practices continue despite being against the formal rules. Such outcome would undermine the Da Afghanistan Bank's ability to regulate *Sarrafi* markets in the future as it severs any real connection between formal policies and laws and the operation of *Sarrafs*. In effect, by doing too much too soon, Da Afghanistan Bank would ensure it could not do much in the future.

20 *See* Chapter 1.

21 *See* Chapter 4.

22 *See* Chapter 2, the discourse around regulation of *Sarrafi* markets.

23 *See* Chapter 2.

24 *Id.*

25 *See* Chapter 1.

26 Douglas C. North, Institutions, Institutional Change and Economic Performance 46–47 (Cambridge University Press 1990).

27 *Id.*

28 Integrity Watch Afghanistan, Curbing Illicit Financial Flows in Afghanistan (2015), at 34.

29 *See Id.*; *see also* The World Bank, State Building, Sustaining, Growth, and Reducing Poverty (2005), at 6.

30 Thompson, Trust Is the Coin of the Realm (2011), at 248.

31 Annual poppy cultivation measured in hectare has increased from 8,000 hectares in 2001 to 74,000 hectares in 2002, and 183,000 hectares in 2015. Annual opium production in the same period has also risen. In 2001, Afghanistan only produced an estimated of 185 tons of opium. This number increased to 3,400 tons in 2002 and 3,300 tons in 2015. *See* United Nations Office on Drugs and Crime, Afghanistan Opium Survey, at 12 and 33.

32 Calculated by the author based on United Nations Office on Drugs and Crime, Afghanistan Opium Survey, Integrity Watch Afghanistan, National Corruption Survey (2016) and Afghanistan Central Statistics Organization, GDP by Sector for the Years 2002/03 until 2016/17.

33 *Id.*

34 *See* Integrity Watch Afghanistan, National Corruption Survey (2016).

35 Calculated by the author based on United Nations Office on Drugs and Crime, Afghanistan Opium Survey, Integrity Watch Afghanistan, National Corruption Survey (2016), and Afghanistan Central Statistics Organization, GDP by Sector for the Years 2002/03 until 2016/17.

36 *Id.*

37 *Id.*

38 The description of interactions between Afghanistan's financial market and illegal economy is based on author's interviews with Afghan merchants in five major provinces of Afghanistan (Kabul, Herat, Nangarhar, Balkh, and Kandahar) between March and August 2017.

39 *See* Chapter 3.

40 *See* Chapter 3.

41 This observation based on author's interviews with *Sarrafs* in five major provinces of Afghanistan (Kabul, Herat, Nangarhar, Balkh, and Kandahar) between March and August 2017.

42 *See* Chapter 2.

43 *See* Jack Knight, Institutions and Social Conflict 14 (1992).

44 *Id.*

45 *See* Chapter 3.

46 *See* e.g. Afghanistan Ministry of Commerce and Industries, Strategic Plan (2016), at 55.

47 World Bank, Worldwide Governance Indicators: Afghanistan for the Years 1996 to 2020, http://info.worldbank.org/governance/wgi/index.aspx#reports.
48 *See* Section 4.3.6. and Thomas, Govern Like Us (2015), at 202.
49 *See* Section 5.2 for a discussion on how a Grounded Institutional Reform–informed regulation of the *Sarrafi* market would be different than the current failed regulation.
50 *See* Chapter 3.
51 *See* Integrity Watch Afghanistan, Curbing Illicit Financial Flows in Afghanistan (2015), at 28; *See* also The World Bank, State Building, Sustaining, Growth, and Reducing Poverty (2005), at 6.

References

Afghanistan Current GDP by Sector for the Years 2002/03 until 2016/17, http://cso.gov.af/fa/page/ict/11328/888

Afghanistan Ministry of Commerce and Industries, Ministry of Commerce and Industries Strategic Plan 2016–2020 (2016), http://moci.gov.af/Content/files/stratigic%20plan%20 2017.pdf

Avinash Dixit, *Lawlessness and Economics* (Princeton University Press 2004)

Dani Rodrik, *Growth Strategies* (Elsevier B.V. 2004)

Edwina A. Thompson, *Trust Is the Coin of The Realm: Lessons from The Money Men in Afghanistan* (OUP Pakistan 2011)

Integrity Watch Afghanistan, Curbing Illicit Financial Flows in Afghanistan: Money Laundering, Terrorist Financing, and *hawala* (2015), https://iwaweb.org/wp-content/uploads/2016/04/IFF-report-English-2-for-screen.pdf

Integrity Watch Afghanistan, National Corruption Survey 2016: Afghan Perceptions and Experiences of Corruption (2016), https://iwaweb.org/national-corruption-corruption-survey-2016/

Jack Knight, Institutions and Social Conflict 14 (1992)

Jean-Francois Richard et al., *Economic Development, Legality, and the Transplant Effect*, 47(1) European Economic Review (2003)

Katharina Pistor, the Standardization of Law and its Effect on Developing Economies (G-24 Discussion Paper No. 4, July 2000), http://unctad.org/en/docs/pogdsmdpbg24d4.en.pdf

Lawrence J. Lau et al., *Reform without Losers: An Interpretation of China's Dual-Track Approach to Transition*, 108(1) The Journal of Political Economy (2000)

M. A. Thomas, Govern Like Us: U.S. Expectations of Poor Countries (2015)

Matt Andrews et al., *Building State Capability: Evidence, Analysis, Action* (Oxford University Press 2017)

United Nations Office on Drugs and Crime, Afghanistan Opium Survey 2015: Cultivation and Production, www.unodc.org/documents/crop-monitoring/Afghanistan/_Afghan_opium_survey_2015_web.pdf

The World Bank, *Afghanistan—State Building, Sustaining, Growth, and Reducing Poverty* (World Bank 2005)

Conclusions and Recommendations

Credit transactions raise a number of fundamental problems in the context of Afghanistan. The highly uncertain business climate of Afghanistan increases the borrowing costs and renders adherence to fixed repayment terms challenging. Formal property rights cannot be used to secure credit transactions because formal deeds are scarce, the titling system is a failure, and the formal property rights system does not reflect the practical needs of the property rights owners in Afghanistan. Formal contract enforcement institutions have not been able to reliably enforce credit transactions because underdevelopment of formal property rights and the instability of Afghanistan's business climate have made it difficult to hold the debtors accountable.

Formal institutions have not been able to overcome the fundamental problems of credit transacting in the Afghan context. As such, bank loans were seldom used to finance investment even before Taliban takeover triggered a financial crisis. For example, although banks in Afghanistan held sufficient reserves, Afghan merchants increasingly found it difficult to obtain bank loans. The stickiness of informal credit institutions cannot explain the low demand for bank loans because, as the case of Balkh shows, the use of formal credit institutions is not inversely correlated with the use of informal credit. The low demand for bank loans is likewise not entirely attributable to Shari'ah-based opposition to interest: interest-friendly (or at least natural) attitudes do not positively correlate with the increased use of bank loans, and there is pervasive use of informal credit institutions that incorporate the time value of money. Similarly, low trust in banks cannot explain the low demand for bank loans because Afghan merchants—before the Taliban return to power caused a run on the banking system—generally expressed more confidence in banks compared to *Sarraf*s. Thus, the inability of formal institutions to provide credit in a way that works for the Afghan context is the primary explanation for the low demand for bank loans and, consequently, the inability of formal institutions to improve access to credit for Afghan merchants.

Afghans have instead developed a number of informal institutions to facilitate credit transactions. In Afghanistan, market competition animates the supply of trade credit by sellers/creditors who are most often importers. *Sarraf*'s short-term working capital loans help sellers/creditors meet their financial obligations to their foreign suppliers despite unpredictable cash flow from their domestic

DOI: 10.4324/9781003245476-6

buyers/debtors. There exists a feedback loop: low barriers to entry increases market competition and animates the supply of trade credit and *Sarraf*'s short-term working capital loans, while the access to trade credit and *Sarraf*'s short-term working capital loans reduces the barriers to entry and ensure the competitiveness of markets. On the demand side, the risk-sharing-enabling feature of trade credit is the primary cause of demand for trade credit. Trade credit arrangements allow buyers/debtors to pass the market risk to sellers/creditors; sellers/creditors are able to engage in these risk-sharing arrangements because they have been able to minimize moral hazard and reduce principal-agent problems through a weekly payment system that consists of regular monitoring and short-term cash extractions. My research shows that the informality of credit institutions has limited exclusionary effects for Afghans. Afghan merchants can rely on a range of social and institutional networks to form credit transactions with other merchants within Afghanistan. However, informal credit institutions put outsiders at a disadvantage, hindering the attraction of foreign investment to Afghanistan.

Sarrafs provide short-term working capital loans to sellers/creditors to entice customers to utilize their *hawala* and currency exchange business. These short-term loans are often executed in the form of a credit *hawala*, whereby a *Sarraf* executes a *hawala* paying a merchant-client's foreign suppliers when the client does not have sufficient funds with the *Sarraf* with the expectation that the merchant-client will reimburse the *Sarrafs* in a short time by collecting on receivable from his domestic debtors. Thus, *Sarraf*'s short-term working capital loans help sellers/creditors, who are often importers, bridge the gap between Afghanistan's uncertain business climate that operate under risk-sharing arrangements and foreign markets that require adherence to fixed-term payments.

In addition to supply chain financing, informal institutions have been able to provide partial access to investment financing as well. Despite underdeveloped formal private property rights, Afghan merchants are able to raise long-term capital against the value of their real estate using *Gerawee*. Estimated figures suggest that *Gerawee* is an important source of investment financing for Afghan merchants. However, the unwillingness of courts to recognize the lender's security right in the property and the bilateral nature of the transaction have limited the financing capacity of *Gerawee*.

To improve liquidity in the capital market, Afghan merchants have adopted *Sar qufli* to commodify future business reputation in cases where reputation is closely tied to a place of business. *Sar qufli* has evolved organically in Afghanistan and other places to curtail the opportunistic behaviors that arise from the problem of assets specified in commercial lease of immovable property. Afghan courts have recognized the legal validity and Shari'ah-compliance of *Sar qufli*, increasing its popularity. *Sar qufli* and the judicial jurisprudence that has developed in connection to it have the capacity to improve liquidity in the capital markets in cases where the use of a property creates additional value that cannot be easily separated from the property.

Another way to raise capital in Afghanistan is equity financing, which is facilitated by family businesses. Family businesses are not only very common in

Afghanistan but also positively correlate with the success of the business enterprise because they help Afghans pool capital, prevent dilution of capital across generations, and ensure that the business has continued access to a pool of agents whose interests are aligned with the interest of the business.

These informal institutions are good but not great. They have significantly improved access to working capital financing for Afghan merchants while bringing about some improvements in access to investment financing and liquidity of the capital market. However, the emergent informal institutions only have limited capacity for pooling savings for investment purposes because they are not capable of scaling up or drawing in funds from savers. Thus, they are not a substitute for effective formal institutions. The Afghan government needs to create better formal institutions.

The Afghan government's approach during the period of the Republic aimed at improving access to credit through reforming formal institutions generally failed. This book argues that this failure was rooted in an unwillingness to use the existing informal institutions as building blocks for creating workable formal institutions. Using the content of the Government's Strategic Polices as evidence, the former Afghan government's approach reflects the policy prescriptions of State-Centered Theory. Thus, the Afghan government strategy has aimed to displace the functioning but inadequate informal institutions with imported, untried (in the Afghan context) formal institutions, rather than incorporating successful informal institutions into new formal institutions that can meet Afghan merchants in the Afghan context. This book makes the case that neither imported formal credit institutions nor entrepreneur-supplied informal institutions have been able to provide adequate access to investment financing in Afghanistan. The former has failed because formal institutions have not been able to provide credit in a way that works for the Afghan context or because the Afghan government does not have sufficient coercive power and administrative capacity to overcome resistance from the invested users of the existing informal institutions. The latter has failed because poor infrastructure and limited market expansion opportunities limit the incentive for the supply of informal institutions and improvement of existing informal institutions to sustain credit transactions in a more complex and inclusive way.

Showing that institutions created by both State-Centered Theory and Entrepreneurial Institutional Theory have failed to provide adequate investment financing for Afghan merchants, this dissertation proposes a new approach. It proposes Grounded Institutional Reform as an approach that would enable the Afghan government to create workable formal institutions in Afghanistan by absorbing the working informal institutions. By building on and reshaping the working informal institutions, the Afghan government can harness the problem-solving abilities of Afghan entrepreneurs to create formal institutions that work for the Afghan context and ensure user-readiness of the formal institutions. By ensuring a continued role, albeit an altered one, for the invested actors in the existing informal institutions, Grounded Institutional Reform will also help the Afghan government induce compliance with the formal rules, reducing the need to rely on the limited coercive power of the state.

This book proposes Grounded Institutional Reform based on a critical assessment of Afghanistan's informal institutions. It finds that Afghanistan's informal institutions are popular because they are able to provide credits on terms acceptable to Afghan merchants. Thus, it is the ability of informal institutions to overcome the credit transacting problems that explain their popularity, not the fact that they are informal or traditional institutions. This, this book has argued, creates an invaluable opportunity for the Afghan government to harness the potentials of existing informal institutions to create formal institutions that can meet the needs of Afghan merchants in their context while enabling formalization of Afghanistan's economy. This is the opportunity that Grounded Institutional Reform is trying to seize.

While this book has only applied Grounded Institutional Reform to credit institutions, this approach is scalable and can be applied to institutional reform in other areas both within and outside Afghanistan. Within Afghanistan, for example, Grounded Institutional Reform can be used to design reform to improve access to justice for Afghans by building upon informal institutions such as *shuras* and *jirgas*. Application of this approach in the area of access to justice would require in-depth studies of the problems of access to justice and informal institutions to identify what is working with the informal institutions and why. Grounded Institutional Reform can also be applied to reforms in other less-developed countries. This book provides three suitability criteria for the application of this approach to economic institutions of other less-developed countries: poor infrastructure, limited market expansion opportunities, and weak but reformist government.

In addition to an assessment of credit institutions, this book also produces interesting findings about dispute resolution institutions in Afghanistan. This research finds that Afghan merchants avoid the use of courts not because they are invariably against the use of formal, adversarial dispute resolution institutions but because formal dispute resolutions are most often ineffective. The high rate of court use for commercial cases where court judgments are both necessary and effective disproves the commonly held hypothesis that Afghan merchants are invariably opposed to the use of formal, adversarial dispute resolution. Informal dispute resolution effectively resolves most common disputes among Afghan merchants. However, they often disregard the formal rules of property rights, the principle of limited liability, and hinder depersonalization of business dealings in Afghanistan.

The available statistics on the use of courts during the period of the Republic suggest that merchants in predominately Pashtun provinces use courts significantly less often than the merchants in ethnically diverse provinces or predominantly non-Pashtun provinces. This observation is robust even if one controls for the business size. Cultural aversion to the use of signed written documents in the course of business dealings, combined with the cultural salience of *jirga*, which provides a focal point for dispute resolution, and ethnic homogeneity are responsible for the reduced rate of court use in predominately Pashtun provinces.

The research presented here suggests that jurisdictional rules have important consequences for the formalization of informal credit institutions in Afghanistan. Commercial courts, compared to civil courts, at least during the Republic, are more likely to recognize informally developed financial institutions that are incongruent with the normative stance in the broader society. This divergence of judicial attitude is due to the history of commercial law in Afghanistan, the type of actors involved in commercial transactions, and the specialized nature of commercial transactions.

Drawing on the research presented here, this book makes the following specific recommendations for Afghanistan to reform credit and dispute resolution institutions:

> Afghanistan needs to reform formal property rights to create clear rules of determining legal ownership and to create an integrated system of legal, reliable, and up-to-date titling to reduce the cost of transactions in property, the ability to effectively use the property for collateralization. The current unsupportive property rights system is a fundamental problem of credit transacting in Afghanistan. Creating an effective system of formal property rights will have an enormously positive effect on access to credit and formalization of Afghanistan's economy.

The volatility of Afghanistan's business climate increases the borrowing costs, preventing productive investments with considerable positive externalities from taking place. Afghanistan needs to reduce the borrowing costs to stimulate more investments and job creation. One way the government can accomplish this goal is by introducing targeted and performance-linked credit guarantee schemes to lower the cost of capital. The high volatility of the business climate increases the cost of borrowing in Afghanistan; the government can reduce this cost through partial guarantee of the repayment of business loans. This will incentivize the distribution of loans by banks and increase investment. There has already been a pilot project to test this model in Northern Afghanistan with positive results.[1]

If the Afghan banking sector survives sanction-induced crisis, the Afghan government should improve the loan distribution to stimulate economic growth. Afghan merchants do not use bank loans because they cannot satisfy the collateral requirement of banks. Banks require collateral to ensure the creditworthiness of the borrower. One mechanism by which banks can reduce their reliance on collateral is to use an alternative measure of creditworthiness. However, the scarcity of credit data hinders the use of alternative measures of creditworthiness in Afghanistan. *Sarrafs* hold rich data on the financial flow and creditworthiness of their clients. *Sarrafs* currently use this information to issue short-term working capital loans to their clients without even the use of a written contract. Afghanistan should incentivize *Sarrafs* to share information with banks and the proposed Credit Bureau, if established. If *Sarrafs* are properly incentivized to share credit information with banks, it will greatly improve the ability of banks to assess risk and creditworthiness, facilitating loan distributions.

In addition to high borrowing costs and demanding collateral requirements, low financial literacy on the side of Afghan merchants and low professional capacity on the side of banks are also hindering the distribution of business loans. The Afghan government can increase distribution of bank loans by improving the financial literacy of Afghan merchants and improving the professional capacity of banks' loan officers. Thus, the Afghan government should support and implement financial literacy programs for Afghan businesses, as well as training programs for bank staff.

Banks in Afghanistan face problems when it comes to attracting savers as well. After the Kabul Bank corruption scandal, people's trust in banks has suffered. Then Taliban takeover triggered a bank run that destroyed any remaining trust in the banking system. The Afghan government needs to improve banking regulations to restore people's trust in banks and incentivize savings in banks. Afghans generally do not trust the durability of formal institutions for good reasons; therefore, banks have a higher burden convincing people to deposit their savings. The Kabul Bank scandal has seriously undermined the trust of Afghans in the banks and Taliban takeover, and the subsequent liquidity crisis destroyed whatever was left of that trust. However, banks are the most important institution for pooling of savings for investment purposes. As such, the Afghan government must undertake measures to safeguard the integrity of financial institutions and restore the public trust in banks.

In conjunction with reforming the banking system, Afghanistan also needs to improve the non-banking sources of credit. *Sar qufli* has been able to improve liquidity in the capital market by making it easier for developers to recover their capital costs. *Sar qufli* has also helped solve the asset specificity problem by encouraging investment in immovable properties by the renter-businesses. To improve certainty and predictability in the *Sar qufli* market, the Afghan government should enact legislation based on the judicial jurisprudence developed in connection with *Sar qufli. Sar qufli* has the capacity to expand to other settings where the use of a property creates additional value that cannot be easily separated from the property. The Afghan government needs to enact legislation to unleash the broader potential application of *Sar qufli.*

Like *Sar qufli, Gerawee* too has been effective in alleviating the capital constraints of Afghan merchants. However, unlike *Sar qufli*, the development of *Gerawee* is hindered by the unwillingness of courts to recognize and protect creditor rights in the *Gerawee* transactions. To unleash the value trapped in the housing market, the Afghan government needs to improve the formal protection of financiers in the *Gerawee*. This book argues the government can achieve this goal by assigning *Gerawee* creditors. This book proposes transferring the jurisdiction over *Gerawee* cases to commercial courts in cases where the borrower is a merchant. Commercial courts during the Republic were more likely to lend formal support to the *Gerawee* transaction, thereby improving the rights of creditors and unleashing the potential trapped in the housing market to finance productive activities. We do not know much about the attitude of the Taliban judiciary, but there are reasons to be hopeful for some continuity.

Sarrafs play an important role in financing supply chains in Afghanistan. The Afghan government should promulgate regulations, using the Grounded Institutional Reform approach, to facilitate the financing role of *Sarrafs*, especially for exporters. If the Taliban wish to end the isolation of the Afghan financial sector, they need to consider anti-money laundering and counter terrorism-financing measures seriously. To curb the amount of illegal funds in the *Sarrafi* markets, instead of outlawing deposit-keeping and loan distribution by *Sarrafs*, the Afghan government should enact regulations that facilitate the financing role of *Sarrafs* in exchange for compliance with transparency and reporting requirements. Such regulations not only will have a greater chance of success, thereby curbing illegal funds, but also will improve access to working capital financing by ensuring that *Sarrafs* will continue to provide credit-*hawala* to merchants.

To ensure effective performance of policies and improve contract enforcement, Afghanistan needs to reform commercial procedures and improve court judgment enforcement. Enforcement costs are an important factor in the use of credit transactions. Afghan merchants will not enter into a credit transaction if they are not reasonably sure, *ex ante*, that the transaction will be enforced. Currently, the majority of non-bank credit transactions are enforced by informal institutions. While these informal institutions are effective in most cases, they put outsiders at a disadvantage and do not uphold the principles of limited liability or separation of private property. Therefore, the Afghan government needs to encourage the use of formal dispute resolution institutions by removing barriers to the use of courts and improving court judgment enforcement. Currently, the two formal institutions in charge of formal dispute resolutions, the Judiciary and the Ministry of Justice, either do not have a strategic policy or do not prioritize judgment enforcement and commercial court procedures reform in their strategic policies. The Afghan government needs to undertake reforms of commercial court procedures and judgment enforcement to improve the comparative competitiveness of formal dispute resolution in relation to informal dispute resolution.

Creating good formal institutions in less-developed countries is an immensely difficult task. Grounded Institutional Reform posits that an effective way to approach this task is to set reasonable expectations and utilize the potential of organically developed institutions. Instead of starting by looking outside to find solutions, Grounded Institutional Reform suggests that the governments of less-developed countries should seriously consider the potential of informally developed institutions because they capture the collective efforts of indigenous economic entrepreneurs over a long period to solve their institutional problems.

Note

1 *See* Mills, Overcoming the Access to Finance Paradox in Afghanistan (2016); *see also* Organisation For Economic Co-Operation And Development, Private Sector Development Policy Handbook, Improving Access to Finance for SMEs in Central Asia through Credit Guarantee Schemes (2013), www.oecd.org/global-relations/AccesstoFinanceforSMEs.pdf.

References

Landell Mills Development Consultant, UKAid, Overcoming the Access to Finance Paradox in Afghanistan: Experience from the Afghanistan Business Innovation Fund (2016), https://static1.squarespace.com/static/553f9958e4b06d466cd3ce1e/t/599ea0eaf9a61e5bdb7a9087/1503568115954/APA-ABIF-financing-KP-010916.pdf

Organisation for Economic Co-Operation and Development, Private Sector Development Policy Handbook, Improving Access to Finance for SMEs in Central Asia through Credit Guarantee Schemes (2013), www.oecd.org/global-relations/AccesstoFinanceforSMEs.pdf.

Bibliography

Constitutions/Quran

The Holy Quran (Abdullah Yusuf Ali, trans, Wordsworth Classics of World Literature 2001)

Qanun Assasi Afghanistan [Afghanistan Constitution] 1343 [1964]

Qanun Assasi Afghanistan [Afghanistan Constitution] 1366 [1987]

Qanun Assasi Afghanistan [Afghanistan Constitution] 1382 [2014]

Foreign Law

Al-Qanun Al-Madani [Civil Code] (Egypt)

Al-Qanun Al-Madani [Civil Code] (Iraq)

Al-Qanun Al-Madani [Civil Code] (Jordan)

Al-Qanun Al-Madani [Civil Code] (Lebanon)

Al-Qanun Al-Madani [Civil Code] (Libya)

Al-Qanun Al-Madani [Civil Code] (Syria)

Code Civil [Civil Code] (Fr.)

AL-MAJALLA AL AHKAM AL ADALIYYAH [The Ottoman Courts Manual] (Hanafi), (last visited February 19, 2015, 05:32 PM), http://legal.pipa.ps/files/server/ENG%20Ottoman%20Majalle%20(Civil%20Law).pdf.

Statutes

Asulnama Tijarat [Principles of Commercial Law] 1336 [1958]

Qanun Asnad Qabel Mu'amela [Law of Negotiable Documents] (No. 971, 1387 [2009])

Qanun Estimlak Zamin [Law of Land Expropriation] (No. 794, 1380 [2000])

Qanun Rahn Amwal Manqul dar Mua'amalat Banki [Law on Use of Movable Properties as Collateral in Banking Transactions] (No. 990, 1387 [2009])

Qanun Rahn Amwal Qair-Manqul dar Mua'amalat Banki [Law on Use of Immovable Properties as Collateral in Banking Transactions] (No. 990, 1387 [2009])

Qanun Sherkathai Sahami va Mahdud Al-Masuliat Afghanistan [Corporation and Limited Liabilities Law of Afghanistan] (Law No. 913, 1385 [2006])

Qanun Survey Arazi va Sabt Survey Sakenin [The Law Concerning Land Survey and Registration of Settlement Survey] 1355 [1976]

Qanun Survey va Ehsaya Arazi [Land Survey and Statistics Law] 1344 [1965]

Qanun Tanzim Umur Malikiat [Law of Managing Ownership Affairs] 1387 [2008]
Qanun Tanzim Umur Zamindari Emirat Islami Afghanistan [Islamic Emirate of Afghanistan's Land Management Law] (No. 795, 1381 [2001])
Qanun Tarz Tahsil Huquq [Law of Enforcement of Rights] (No. 786, 1377 [1999]).
Qanun Tashkil va Salahiat Quva Qazaiee [Laws on Organization and Jurisdiction of Judiciary] (No. 851, 1384 [2005])
Qanun Usul Muhakimat Madani [Law of Civil Procedure] (No. 722, 1369 [1990])
Qanun Zamin [Law on Land] (No. 783, 1376 [1997])
Qanuni Madani [Civil Code] 1355 [1977]
Usul Muhakimat Tijrati [Principles of Commercial Procedure] (No. 1–4, 1343 [1965])

Regulations

Da Afghanistan Bank, Muqarrara Tanzim Fa'aliat hai Sarrafan va Fraham Konandagan Khadamat Puli [Regulation of *Sarrafs* and Money Service Providers' Activities] 1395 [2016]

Presidential Decrees

Farman Eslah Arazi [Land Reform Decree] (No. 8, 1359 [1980])
Farman Rayees Jumhur Afghanistan dar bara Isterdad Amval That Malikiat Duwlat [The Decree of the President of Republic of Afghanistan with regard to Return of the Properties under the Control of the Government to their Owners] (Law No. 715, 1369 [1991])

Judicial Decisions

Afghanistan Supreme Court, Judicial Seminar (1381 [2002])
Afghanistan Supreme Court, Judicial Seminar 190 (1395 [2017])
Afghanistan Supreme Court, Mutahadulmal [Decision] (No. 307–369, 1385 [2007])

Government Policies

Afghanistan Ministry of Commerce and Industries, Ministry of Commerce and Industries Strategic Plan 2016–2020 (2016), http://moci.gov.af/Content/files/stratigic%20plan%20 2017.pdf
Afghanistan Ministry of Economics, Economic Policy of Government of Afghanistan (2013), http://moec.gov.af/Content/files/Policy_National_Economic.pdf
Afghanistan Ministry of Justice, Five Strategic Plans: Law and Justice 2014–2018 (2013), http://moj.gov.af/Content/files/Estrategi.pdf
Da Afghanistan Bank, Strategic Plan 2017–2021 (2017), http://dab.gov.af/fa/page/media/publications/strategic-plan
Islamic Republic of Afghanistan, Afghanistan National Development Strategy 2008–2013 (2008), http://mfa.gov.af/en/page/6547/afghanistan-national-development-strategy/afghanistan-national-development-strategy-ands
Islamic Republic of Afghanistan, Afghanistan National Peace and Development Framework 2017–2021 (2016), http://policymof.gov.af/afghanistan-national-peace-and-development-framework-anpdf/

Economic Reports

Economic Reports by the Afghan Government

Afghanistan Central Statistics Organization, Afghanistan Current GDP by Sector for the Years 2002/03 until 2016/17, http://cso.gov.af/fa/page/ict/11328/888.

Afghanistan Central Statistics Organization, Afghanistan Demographic Estimates for the Years of 2002/03 until 2017/18, http://cso.gov.af/fa/page/demography-and-socile-statistics/demograph-statistics/3897111.

Afghanistan Central Statistics Organization, Afghanistan GDP in Constant Prince by the Sector for the Years of 2002/03 until 2016/17, http://cso.gov.af/fa/page/ict/11328/11330.

Afghanistan Central Statistics Organization, Afghanistan Import and Export Annual Data for the Years of 2008/09 until 2016/17, http://cso.gov.af/fa/page/economy-statistics/6323/annual-trade.

Afghanistan Central Statistics Organization, Agricultural Survey Data for the Years of 2008 until 2017.

Afghanistan Central Statistics Organization, Business Establishment Survey 2009 (2010), http://cso.gov.af/en/page/1500/1494/6

Afghanistan Central Statistics Organization, Business Establishment Survey 2015 (2016), http://cso.gov.af/en/page/1500/1494/6.

Afghanistan Central Statistics Organization, Sectoral Contribution to the GDP for the Years of 2002/03 until 2016/17, http://cso.gov.af/fa/page/ict/11328/11332.

Afghanistan Central Statistics Organization, The National Risk and Vulnerability Assessment: Afghanistan Living Conditions Survey 2005, http://cso.gov.af/en/page/1500/1494/nrav-report.

Afghanistan Central Statistics Organization, The National Risk and Vulnerability Assessment: Afghanistan Living Conditions Survey 2007–2008, http://cso.gov.af/en/page/1500/1494/nrav-report.

Afghanistan Central Statistics Organization, The National Risk and Vulnerability Assessment: Afghanistan Living Conditions Survey 2011–2012, http://cso.gov.af/en/page/1500/1494/nrav-report.

Afghanistan Central Statistics Organization, The National Risk and Vulnerability Assessment: Afghanistan Living Conditions Survey 2013–2014, http://cso.gov.af/en/page/1500/1494/nrav-report.

Afghanistan Central Statistics Organization, The National Risk and Vulnerability Assessment: Afghanistan Living Conditions Survey 2016–2017, http://cso.gov.af/en/page/1500/1494/nrav-report.

Afghanistan Chamber of Commerce Industries, Business Tendency Survey Reports of II-2014, IV-2014, I-2015, II-2015, III-2015, IV-2015, I-2016, II-2016, III-2016, IV-2016, I-2017, II-2017, and III-2017, www.acci.org.af/surveys-and-studies.html.

Business Registry Data for the Years of 2014/15 until 2016/17 For Kabul, Herat, Kandahar, Balkh, and Nangarhar, Received by the author from Afghanistan Central Business Registry's Directory Through Head of Office of Business Registry at Afghanistan Ministry of Commerce (September 23, 2017).

Da Afghanistan Bank, Annual Economic and Statistical Reports for the Years of 1384 Hijri until 1395 Hijri, http://dab.gov.af/en/page/media/publications/annual-economic-and-statistical-bulletin.

Da Afghanistan Bank, Currency Hijri Monthly Average USD For the Years of 1385 Hijri Until 1396 Hijri, http://dab.gov.af/en/page/monetary-policy/rates-statistics/currency-hijri-average.

Da Afghanistan Bank, Financial Intelligence Unit, Annual Report 2017: Financial Transactions and Reports Analysis Center of Afghanistan (FinTRACA), www.fintraca.gov.af/Report.html.

Independent Joint Anti-Corruption Monitoring & Evaluation Committee, MEC Update on Kabul Bank Scandal (Press Release, October 2, 2016), www.mec.af/index.php/news-events/press-releases

Economic Reports by NGOs and other Organizations

Afghanistan Financial Services, Afghanistan Capital Markets Assessment: A Survey and Analysis of Current Capital Market Activities, the Demand for Capital, and the Basic Structure and Government Debt Markets (2010), www.ahg.af/data/AFS-Afghanistan-Capital-MarketsAssessment.pdf

Building Markets, Afghan Women's Economic Participation Survey Report (2013) http://buildingmarkets.org/products-services-/afghan-women-economic-participation.

Central Intelligence Agency World Factbook: Afghanistan, www.cia.gov/Library/publications/the-world-factbook/geos/af.html.

Equality for Peace and Development, Afghanistan Gender Equality Report Card: Evaluating The Government of Afghanistan's Commitments to Women and Gender Equality 67 (2015)

Integrity Watch Afghanistan, Curbing Illicit Financial Flows in Afghanistan: Money Laundering, Terrorist Financing, and *hawala* (2015), https://iwaweb.org/wp-content/uploads/2016/04/IFF-report-English-2-for-screen.pdf

Integrity Watch Afghanistan, National Corruption Survey 2016: Afghan Perceptions and Experiences of Corruption (2016), https://iwaweb.org/national-corruption-corruption-survey-2016/

International Monetary Fund, Islamic Republic of Afghanistan: Detailed Assessment Report on Anti-Money Laundering and Combating the Financing of Terrorism 24 (IMF Country Report No.11/317 2011), www.imf.org/external/pubs/ft/scr/2011/cr11317.pdf

International Monetary Fund, Islamic Republic of Afghanistan: Detailed Assessment Report on Anti-Money Laundering and Combating the Financing of Terrorism (IMF Country Report No.11/317 2011), www.imf.org/external/pubs/ft/scr/2011/cr11317.pdf

Richard Ghiasy et al., International Council of Swedish Industry, Afghanistan's Private Sector: Status and Ways Forward 5 (SIPRI and NIR 2015), www.sipri.org/publications/2015/afghanistans-private-sector-status-and-way-forward.

Special Inspector General for Afghanistan Reconstruction, Quarterly Report to the United States Congress (October 30, 2017), www.sigar.mil/pdf/quarterlyreports/2017-04-30qr.pdf

Special Inspector General for Afghanistan Reconstruction, Quarterly Report to the United States Congress (April 30, 2015), www.sigar.mil/pdf/quarterlyreports/2015-04-30qr-section3-economic.pdf

The International Telecommunication Union, Afghanistan: Mobile Phone Subscribers per 100 people, www.theglobaleconomy.com/Afghanistan/Mobile_phone_subscribers_per_100_people/.

The World Bank, Afghanistan National Reconstruction and Poverty Reduction—the Role of Women in Afghanistan's Future (2005), http://siteresources.worldbank.org/AFGHANISTANEXTN/Resources/AfghanistanGenderReport.pdf.

The World Bank, *Afghanistan—State Building, Sustaining, Growth, and Reducing Poverty* (World Bank 2005).

UNHCR, Iran Fact Sheet (February 2016), www.unhcr.org/en-us/protection/operations/50002081d/iran-fact-sheet.html

UNHCR, Pakistan Fact Sheet (December 2015), www.unhcr.org/en-us/protection/operations/5000210e9/pakistan-fact-sheet.html.

United Nations Assistance Mission in Afghanistan, Protection of Civilian in Armed Conflict 2017 Annual Report (2017), https://unama.unmissions.org/sites/default/files/afghanistan_protection_of_civilians_annual_report_2017_final_6_march.pdf.

United Nations Office on Drugs and Crime, Afghanistan Opium Survey 2015: Cultivation and Production, www.unodc.org/documents/crop-monitoring/Afghanistan/_Afghan_opium_survey_2015_web.pdf

UNICEF, UNICEF Global Database on adjusted Net Attendance Rates (April 2021), https://data.unicef.org/wp-content/uploads/2021/04/Adjusted-net-attendance-rate_2021-1.xlsx

Judicial Reports

Afghanistan Supreme Court, Quarterly Judicial Activities Reports for the Years of 2012 until 2017, http://supremecourt.gov.af/fa/page/court-reporting

IMF Data

International Monetary Fund, Afghanistan: Real Interest Rate (Bank Lending Rate Minus Inflation) for the Years of 2008 until 2016, www.theglobaleconomy.com/Afghanistan/Real_interest_rate/

International Monetary Fund, ATM machines Per 100,000 people, ATM machines Per 100,000 people in Afghanistan for the Years of 2004 until 2015, www.theglobaleconomy.com/Afghanistan/bank_branches/

International Monetary Fund, Bank Accounts Per 1000 Adults, Bank Accounts Per 1000 Adults in Afghanistan for the Years of 2008 until 2015, www.theglobaleconomy.com/Afghanistan/bank_accounts/

International Monetary Fund, Bank Branches Per 100,000 people, Bank Branches Per 100,000 people in Afghanistan for the Years of 2004 until 2015, www.theglobaleconomy.com/Afghanistan/bank_branches/

World Bank Data

The World Bank, World Bank Development Indicators, Foreign Direct Investment Net Inflows in current USD, Afghanistan's Direct Investment Net Inflows in current USD for the Years of 2001 until 2015, https://data.worldbank.org/indicator/BX.KLT.DINV.CD.WD?end=2016&locations=AF&start=2001

The World Bank, World Bank Development Indicators, Foreign Direct Investment Net Outflows in current USD, Afghanistan's Direct Investment Net Outflows in current USD for the Years of 2001 until 2016, https://data.worldbank.org/indicator/BM.KLT.DINV.CD.WD?end=2016&locations=AF&start=2003

The World Bank, World Bank Development Indicators, GDP at Constant Price from 2015 in USD, Afghanistan's GDP at Constant Price from 2015 in USD for the Years of 2001 until 2020, (Last Updated at January 29, 2022), https://data.worldbank.org/indicator/NY.GDP.MKTP.KD?end=2020&locations=AF&start=2001

The World Bank, World Bank Development Indicators, GDP at Current USD, Afghanistan's GDP (Last Updated at January 01, 2018) https://data.worldbank.org/indicator/NY.GDP.MKTP.CD?locations=AF

The World Bank, World Bank Development Indicators, GDP Growth by Annual Percent, Afghanistan's GDP Growth by Annual Percent 2003–2016, https://data.worldbank.org/indicator/NY.GDP.MKTP.KD.ZG?locations=AF.

The World Bank, World Bank Development Indicators, GDP Growth by Annual Percent, Afghanistan's GDP Growth by Annual Percent 2006–2016, https://data.worldbank.org/indicator/NY.GDP.MKTP.KD.ZG?locations=AF

The World Bank, World Bank Development Indicators, Life expectancy at birth up to total years, Afghanistan's Life expectancy at birth up to total years for the Years of 2000 until 2019, https://data.worldbank.org/indicator/SP.DYN.LE00.IN?end=2019&locations=AF&start=2001

The World Bank, World Bank Development Indicators, Maternal mortality ratio for modeled estimate, per 100,000 live births, Afghanistan's Maternal mortality ratio for modeled estimate, per 100,000 live births for the Years of 2000 until 2017, https://data.worldbank.org/indicator/SH.STA.MMRT?end=2017&locations=AF&start=2000

The World Bank, World Bank Development Indicators, Mortality Rates for Infants per 1,000 Live Births, Afghanistan's Mortality Rates for Infants per 1,000 Live Births for the Years of 2001 until 2019, https://data.worldbank.org/indicator/SP.DYN.IMRT.IN?end=2019&locations=AF&start=2001

The World Bank, World Bank Development Indicators, Net official development assistance received in current USD, Afghanistan's Net official development assistance received in current USD for the Years of 1960 until 2015, https://data.worldbank.org/indicator/DT.ODA.ODAT.CD?locations=AF

The World Bank, World Bank Development Indicators, Net Portfolio Investment in current USD, Afghanistan's Net Portfolio Investment in current USD for the Years of 2008 until 2016, https://data.worldbank.org/indicator/BN.KLT.PTXL.CD?end=2016&locations=AF&start=2008

The World Bank, World Bank Development Indicators, New Business Registered, Afghanistan's New Business Registered 2006–2016, https://data.worldbank.org/indicator/IC.BUS.NREG?locations=AF

The World Bank, World Bank Development Indicators, Percentage of Firms Using Banks to Finance Investment, Percentage of Firms Using Banks to Finance Investment in Afghanistan for the Year 2014, https://data.worldbank.org/indicator/IC.FRM.BNKS.ZS?locations=AF

The World Bank, World Bank Development Indicators, Percentage of Firms Using Banks to Finance Working Capital, Percentage of Firms Using Banks to Finance Working Capital in Afghanistan for the Year 2014, https://data.worldbank.org/indicator/IC.FRM.BKWC.ZS?locations=AF

The World Bank, World Bank Development Indicators, Personal remittances received in current USD, Afghanistan's Personal remittances received in current USD for the Years of 2008 until 2016, https://data.worldbank.org/indicator/BX.TRF.PWKR.CD.DT?end=2016&locations=AF&start=2008

The World Bank, World Bank Development Indicators, Political Stability Index, Afghanistan's Political Stability Score for the Years of 1996 until 2016, www.theglobaleconomy.com/Afghanistan/wb_political_stability/

The World Bank, World Bank Development Indicators, Poverty headcount ratio at national poverty lines For the Percentage of population, Afghanistan's Poverty headcount ratio at national poverty lines For the Percentage of population for the Years of 2007 until 2016, *https://data.worldbank.org/indicator/SI.POV.NAHC?locations=AF*

The World Bank, World Bank Development Indicators, School Enrollment by primary Gross Percentage, Afghanistan's School Enrollment by primary Gross Percentage for the Years of 2001 until 2019, https://data.worldbank.org/indicator/SE.PRM.ENRR?end=2019&locations=AF&start=2001

The World Bank, World Bank Development Indicators, Unemployment Rate, Afghanistan's Unemployment Rate Between 1991–2017, www.theglobaleconomy.com/Afghanistan/Unemployment_rate/

The World Bank, World Bank Development Indicators, Youth Unemployment, Afghanistan's Youth Unemployment Rate Between 1991–2017, www.theglobaleconomy.com/Afghanistan/Youth_unemployment/

The World Bank, Worldwide Governance Indicators: Afghanistan for the Years 1996 to 2016, http://info.worldbank.org/governance/wgi/index.aspx#reports

Scholarly Books

1 Friedrich A. Hayek, Law, Legislation and Liberty, Vol 1: Rules and Order (1973)

Afghanistan Supreme Court, Tariskh Qaza [History of Judiciary] (No Date Posted), http://supremecourt.gov.af/Content/files/Tarikh_Qaza_dar_afg.doc.

Amin Saikal, *Modern Afghanistan: A History of Struggle and Survival* (2004)

Anselm L. Strauss & Juliet Corbin, *Basics of Qualitative Research: Grounded Theory Procedures and Techniques* (4th ed., SAGE Publications, Inc 2015).

Anselm L. Strauss & Barney Glaser, *The Discovery of Grounded Theory: Strategies for Qualitative Research* (1967)

Anver Greif, *Institutions and the Path to Modern Economy* (Cambridge University Press 2006)

Avinash Dixit, *Lawlessness and Economics* (Princeton University Press 2004)

Chrysostomos Mantzavinos, *Individuals, Institutions, and Markets* (Cambridge University Press 2001)

Clark B. Lombardi, *State Law as Islamic law in Modern Egypt* (BRILL Academic Publishers 2006)

Coimbatore K. Prahalad, *The Fortune at the Bottom of the Pyramid: Eradicating Poverty Through Profits* (Pearson Prentice Hall 2004).

Dani Rodrik, *Growth Strategies* (Elsevier B.V. 2004)

Dani Rodrik, *One Economics, Many Recipes: Globalization, Institutions and Economic Growth* (Princeton University Press 2007)

Daren Acemoğlu, *Introduction to Modern Economic Growth* (Princeton University Press 2009)

Douglas C. North, *Institutions, Institutional Change and Economic Performance* (Cambridge University Press 1990)

Douglass C. North, *The Process of Economic Change* (Princeton University Press 2005)

Douglas C. North et al., *Violence and Social Order: A Conceptual Framework for Interpreting Recorded Human History* (Cambridge University Press 2009)

Douglas C. North & Robert Paul Thomas, *The Rise of the Western World: A New Economic History* (Cambridge University Press 1973)

Edwina A. Thompson, *Trust Is the Coin of The Realm: Lessons from The Money Men in Afghanistan* (OUP Pakistan 2011)

Eirik G. Furubotn & Rudolph Richter, *Institutions and Economic Theory: The Contribution of the New Institutional Economics* (University of Michigan Press 2000)
Gilles Dorronsoro, *Revolution Unending: Afghanistan, 1979 to the Present* (John King trans.) (Columbia University Press 2005).
Hamid Khan, *The Islamic Law of Inheritance* (Oxford University Press 2008)
Hernando De Soto, *The Mystery of Capitalism: Why Capitalism Triumphs in the West and Fails Everywhere Else* (Basic Books 2000)
Jack Knight, *Institutions and Social Conflict* (Cambridge University Press 1992)
Jean-Philipe Platteau, *Institutions, Social Norms, and Economic Development* (Cambridge University Press 2000)
Joseph A. Schumpeter, *Capitalism, Socialism, and Democracy* (George Allen & Unwin Ltd 1943)
Kellee S. Tsai, *Back-Alley Banking: Private Entrepreneurs in China* (Cornell University Press 2002)
M. A. Thomas, *Govern Like Us: U.S. Expectations of Poor Countries* (Columbia University Press 2015)
Marcel Fafchamps, *Market Institutions in Sub-Saharan Africa* (The MIT Press 2004)
Matt Andrews et al., *Building State Capability: Evidence, Analysis, Action* (Oxford University Press 2017)
Maxwell J. Fry, *The Afghan Economy* (Cambridge University Press 1974)
Melanie Birks & Jane Mills, *Grounded Theory: A Practical Guide* (2nd ed., SAGE Publications Ltd 2015)
Mohammad Hashim Kamali, *Law in Afghanistan: A Study of the Constitution, Matrimonial Law, and Judiciary* (BRILL 1985).
Oliver E. Williamson, *The Economic Institutions of Capitalism* (Free Press 1985)
Oliver E. Williamson, *The Mechanisms of Governance* (Oxford University Press 1996)
Richard S. Newell, *The Politics of Afghanistan* (Cornell University Press 1972)
Sara Koplik, *A Political and Economic History of the Jews of Afghanistan* (BRILL 2015)
Sonja Opper & Víctor Nee, *Capitalism from Below: Markets and Institutional Change in China* (Harvard University Press 2012)
Timur Kuran, *The Long Divergence: How Islamic Law Held Back the Middle East* (Princeton University Press 2010)
Tres Thompson et al., *Stanford Law School, Afghanistan Legal Education Project, An Introduction to the Commercial Law of Afghanistan* (2nd ed., University of California Press 2015), https://www-cdn.law.stanford.edu/wp-content/uploads/2015/12/Intro-to-Commercial-Law-of-Afg-2d-Ed.pdf.
Yoram Barzel, *Economic Analysis of Property Rights* (Cambridge University Press 1989)

Scholarly Articles

Alejandro Ramirez et al., *Economic Growth and Human Development* (Economic Growth Center Discussion Paper No. 787, 1997), www.econ.yale.edu/growth_pdf/cdp787.pdf
Amin Tarzi, *Islam, Shari'a, and State Building under 'Abd al-Rahman Khan, in* Afghanistan's Islam: From Conversion to the Taliban 129 (Nile Green ed., University of California Press 2017)
Anna Maria C. Menichini, *Inter-Firm Trade Finance at Times of Crisis*, 34(10) The World Economy 1788 (2011)

Anver Greif & David D. Latin, *A Theory of Endogenous Institutional Change*, 98(4) Am. Pol. Sc. Rev. 633 (2004)

Armen A. Alchian, *Some Economics of Property Rights*, 30(4) II Politico 816 (1965)

Asli Demirgu-Kunt & Vojislav Maksimovic, *The World Bank Development Research Group, Firms as Financial Intermediaries: Evidence from Trade Credit Data* (Policy Research Working Paper 2696, 2001), https://openknowledge.worldbank.org/bitstream/handle/10986/19511/multi0page.pdf?

Avner Greif, *Cultural Beliefs and the Organization of Society: A Historical and Theoretical Reflection on Collectivist and Individualist Societies*, 102(5) J. Political. Econ. 912 (1994)

Claudio Raddatz, *Credit Chains, and Sectoral Comovement, Does the Use of Trade Credit Amplify Sectoral Shock?* 92(4) Rev. Econ. Stat. 985 (2010)

Coimbatore K. Prahalad & Stuart L. Hart, *The Fortune at the Bottom of the Pyramid*, Strategy+Business (First Quarter of 2002), https://people.eecs.berkeley.edu/~brewer/ict4b/Fortune-BoP.pdf

Conor Foley, *Norwegian Refugee Council, a Guide to Property Law in Afghanistan* (2nd ed. 2011), www.nrc.no/globalassets/pdf/reports/a-guide-to-property-law-in-afghanistan.pdf

Dani Rodrik, *The New Development Economics: We Shall Experiment, But How Shall We Learn?* Harvard Kennedy School Faculty Research Working Paper Series (No. 100, 2008), https://research.hks.harvard.edu/publications/getFile.aspx?Id=317

Daniel H. Cole & Peter Z. Grossman, *The Meaning of Property Rights: Law versus Economics?* 78(2) Land Economics 317 (2002)

Daron Acemoğlu et al., *Institutions as A Fundamental Cause of Long-Run Growth*, *in* 1A Handbook of Economic Growth 385 (Philippe Aghion & Steven N. Durlauf eds., Elsevier B.V. 2005)

Douglas W. Allen, *Transaction Costs*, *in* Encyclopedia of Law & Economics 893 (Bouckaert et al. ed. 1999), www.sfu.ca/~allen/allentransactioncost.pdf.

Edward L. Glaeser & et al., *Do Institutions Cause Growth?* 9(3) J. Econ. Growth 271 (2004)

Eirik G. Furubotn & Rudolph Richter, *The New Institutional Economics: An Assessment*, *in* the New Institutional Economics: A Collection of Articles from the Journal of Institutional and Theoretical Economics 15 (Eirik Furubotn & Rudolph Richter eds., Texas A & M Press 1991)

Emilia Garcia-Appendini & Judit Montoriol-Garriga, *Firms as Liquidity Providers: Evidence from the 2007–2008 Financial Crisis*, 109(1) J. Financial. Econ. 272 (2013)

Fali Huang, *The Transition from Relational to Legal Contract Enforcement*, SMU Economics & Statistics Working Paper Series (Paper No. 23, 2006)

Floortje Kljin, Afghanistan Research & Evaluation Unit, *Finding the Money: Informal Credit Practices in Rural Afghanistan* (A Synthesis Paper 2007)

Gary D. Libecap, *Property Rights in Economic History*, 23 Explorations in Economic History 227 (1986)

Go Yano & Maho Shiraishi, *Factors in the Development of Trade Credit: Case Study of Provinces in China*, 50(2) Emerging Markets Finance and Trade 114 (2014)

Gretchen Helmke & Steven Levitsky, *Informal Institutions and Comparative Politics: A Research Agenda*, 2(4) Perspectives on Politics 725 (2004)

Harold Demsetz, *The Cost of Transacting*, 82 Q. J. Econ. 33 (1968)

Haroun Rahimi, *The Customary Practice of Gerawee in Afghanistan: A Case for Transitioning to Real Equity-Based Finance*, 4 Indon. J. Int'l & Comp. L. 743 (2015).

Jaleel Ahmad et al., *Investigation of Causal Relationship Between Trade Credit and Bank Loan During 2008 Financial Crisis*, 5(5) J. Asian Business Strategy 90 (2015)

Jean-Francois Richard et al., *Economic Development, Legality, and the Transplant Effect*, 47(1) European Economic Review 165 (2003)

John Shuhe Li, *Relation-based Versus Rule-based Governance: An Explanation of the East Asian Miracle and Asian Crisis*, 11(4) Rev. Int. Econ. 651 (2003)

Julio Faundez, *Douglas North's Theory of Institutions: Lessons for Law and Development*, 8 Hague J. R. L. 373 (2016).

Karen Clay, *Trade Without Law: Private-Order Institutions in Mexican California*, 13(1) J. L. Econ. Org. 202 (1997)

Karen Clay, *Trade, Institutions, and Credit: Contract Enforcement on The California Coast 1830–1846*, 34 Explorations in Economic History 495 (1997).

Katharina Pistor, The Standardization of Law and its Effect on Developing Economies, (G-24 Discussion Paper No. 4, July 2000), http://unctad.org/en/docs/pogdsmdpbg24d4.en.pdf.

Kenneth J. Arrow, *The Organization of Economic Activity: Issues Pertinent to the Choice of Market versus Non-Market Allocation, in* 1 The Joint Economic Committee of Congress, the Analysis and Evaluation of Public Expenditures: The PBB-System 47 (Joint Committee of Congress 1969)

Kevin E. Davis & Michael J. Trebilcock, *The Relationship between Law and Development: Optimists versus Skeptics*, 56(4) Am. J. Comp. Law 895 (2008), www.fgv.br/processoseletivo/md/Ingresso2017/The-Relationship-between-Law.pdf

Lawrence J. Lau et al., *Reform without Losers: An Interpretation of China's Dual-Track Approach to Transition*, 108(1) The Journal of Political Economy 120 (2000)

Leora Klapper et al., *Trade Credit Contracts*, 25(3) Rev. Financial Stud. 838 (2012)

Luis Angeles, *Institutions, Property Rights, and Economic Development in Historical Perspective*, 64(2) Kyklos Int. Rev. Social Sciences 157 (2011).

Maliti Musole, *Property Rights, Transaction Costs and Institutional Change: Conceptual Framework and Literature Review*, 7 Progress in Planning 43 (2009)

Marcel Fafchamps, *Trade Credit in Zimbabwean Manufacturing*, 25(5) World Development 795 (1997)

Martin Ravallion & Shaohua Chen, *World Bank, What Can New Survey Data Tell Us about Recent Changes in Distribution and Poverty*, 11(2) The World Bank Economic Review 357 (1997)

Michael C. Jensen & William H. Meckling, *Theory of the Firm: Managerial Behavior, Agency Costs and Ownership Structure*, 3(4) J. Financial Econ 305 (1976)

Michael T. Hannan & John Freeman, *Structural Inertia and Organizational Change*, 49(2) Amer. Sociological Rev. 149 (1984)

Mohammad Bashir Mobasher, *Understanding Ethnic-Electoral Dynamics: How Ethnic Politics Affect Electoral Laws and Election Outcomes in Afghanistan*, 51 Gonz. L. Rev. 355 (2015–2016)

Neeltje Van Horen, *Trade Credit as a Competitiveness Tool: Evidence from Developing Countries* (Munich Personal RePEc Archive 2004), https://mpra.ub.uni-muenchen.de/2792/1/MPRA_paper_2792.pdf.

Nicholas Foster, *The Islamic Law of Real Security*, 15 Arab L.Q. 145 (2000).

Paul Pierson, *Increasing Returns, Path Dependence, and the Study of Politics*, 94(2) Am. Political Sci. Rev. 251 (2000)

Philip Keefer & Stephen Knack, *Why Don't Poor Countries Catch-up? A Cross-National Test of an Institutional Explanation*, 34 Econ. Inquiry 590 (1997)

Pınar Özlü & Cihan Yalcin, *The Trade Credit Channel of Monetary Policy Transmission: Evidence from Nonfinancial Manufacturing Firms in Turkey*, 48(4) Emerging Markets Finance and Trade 102 (2012)
Raghuram G. Rajan & Luigi Zingales, *Financial Dependence and* Growth, 88 Am. Econ. Rev. 559 (1998)
Raymond Fisman & Inessa Love, *Trade Credit, Financial Intermediary Development, and Industry Growth*, 58(1) J. Finance. 353 (2003)
Richard A. Posner, *Creating a Legal Framework for Economic Development*, 13(1) The World Bank Research Observer 2 (1998)
Robert G. King & Ross Levine, *Finance and Growth: Schumpeter Might Be Right*, 108 Q. J. Econ 717 (1993)
Robert G. King & Ross Levine, *Finance, Entrepreneurship, and Growth: Theory and Evidence*, 32 Journal of Monetary Economics 513 (1993)
Ronald H. Coase, *Blackmail*, 74 Va. L. Rev. 655
Ross Levine, *Financial Development and Economic Growth: Views and Agenda*, 35 J. Econ. Lit 688 (1997)
Ross Levine, *The Legal Environment, and Long Run Economic Growth*, 30 J. Money, Credit, & Banking 596 (1998)
Ross Levine, *Finance and Growth: Theory and Evidence*, *in* Handbook of Economic Growth 865 (Philippe Aghion & Steven Durlauf eds., Elsevier B.V. 2005)
Ross Levine *et al.*, *Financial Intermediation and Growth: Causality and Causes*, 46 Journal of Monetary Economics 31 (2000)
Rudolph Peters, *From Jurists Law to Statute Law or What Happens When the Shari'a is Codified*, 7 Mediterranean Politics 82 (2002)
Shahid Yusuf & Joseph E. Stiglitz, *Development Issues: Settled and Open*, *in* Frontiers of Development Economics: The Future in Perspective 227 (Gerald M. Meier & Joseph E. Stiglitz eds., World Bank and Oxford University Press 2000)
Shamshad Pasarlay, *Islam and the Sharia in the 1993 Mujahideen—Draft Constitution of the Islamic State of Afghanistan: A Comparative Perspective*, 3 Indon. J. Int'l & Comp. L. 183 (2016)
Simon Johnson et al., *Courts and Relational Contracts*, 18(1) J. Law Econ. Organ. 221 (2000)
Timothy Besley & Maitreesh Ghatak, *Property Rights and Economic Development*, *in* 5 Handbook of Development Economics 4528 (Dani Rodrik & Mark Rosenzweig eds., Elsevier B.V. 2010)
Wael Hallaq, *What is Sharia? in* 12 Yearbook of Islamic and Middle Eastern Law: 2005–2006 151 (2007)
The World Bank, *The Problem of Social Cost*, 3 J. L. Econ. 1 (1960)
The World Bank, *Toward A Theory of Property Rights*, 57(2) Am. Econ. Rev. 347 (1967)
The World Bank, *The Nature of The Firm: Origin, Meaning, Influence*, 4 J. L. Econ. Org. 3 (1988)
The World Bank, *The Institutional Structure of Production*, 82(4) Am. Econ. Rev. 719 (1992)
The World Bank, *What Can History Teach Us About Legal Reform in Afghanistan? A Historical Study of Codification of Substantive Private Law in Afghanistan* (Forthcoming)
Wenfeng Wu et al., *Trust and The Provision of Trade Credit*, 39(C) J. Bank. Finance 146 (2014)
Ying Ge & Jiaping Qiu, *Financial Development, Bank Discrimination and Trade Credit*, 31(2) J. Bank. Finance 513 (2007)

Articles by NGO and other Organizations

Ales Bulir & A. Javir Hamann, International Monetary Fund, Volatility of Development Aid: An Update (IMF Staff Papers 54, 2007)

Daniela Fabbri & Leora Klapper, The World Bank Development Research Group, Finance and Private Sector Team, Market Power and the Matching of Trade Credit Terms (Policy Research Working Paper 4754, 2008), https://openknowledge.worldbank.org/bitstream/handle/10986/6913/WPS4754.pdf?sequence=1&isAllowed=y.

David Stanfield, Jonathan Reed, and M. Yasin Safar, Emerging Markets Group, Description of Procedures for Producing Legal Deeds to Record Property Transactions in Afghanistan 12 (2005), www.terrainstitute.org/pdf/Description%20of%20Procedures.pdf

David Stanfield et al., Terra Institute, Description of Procedures for Producing Legal Deeds to Record Property Transactions in Afghanistan (2005), www.terrainstitute.org/pdf/Description%20of%20Procedures.pdf

Guoqiang Long, Center for Global Development, China's Policies on FDI: Review and Evaluation 315 (2005), www.cgdev.org/sites/default/files/9780881323818-Ch12.pdf.

International Fund for Agricultural Development, Sending Money Home: Worldwide Remittance Flows to Developing Countries (2007), https://publications.iadb.org/handle/11319/1072.

Joshua Charap & Jelena Pavlovic, IMF Middle East and Central Asia Department, Development of the Commercial Banking System in Afghanistan: Risks and Rewards (IMF Working Paper WP/09/150, 2009), www.imf.org/external/pubs/ft/wp/2009/wp09150.pdf

Kate Meagher, Women in Informal Employment: Globalizing and Organizing, Unlocking the Informal Economy: A Literature Review on Linkages Between Formal and Informal Economies in Developing Countries (WIEGO Working Paper No. 27, 2013) www.vumelana.org.za/wp-content/uploads/2014/03/Document-49-Meagher_WIEGO_WP27.pdf.

Landell Mills Development Consultant, UKAid, Overcoming the Access to Finance Paradox in Afghanistan: Experience from the Afghanistan Business Innovation Fund (2016), https://static1.squarespace.com/static/553f9958e4b06d466cd3ce1e/t/599ea0eaf9a61e5bdb7a9087/1503568115954/APA-ABIF-financing-KP-010916.pdf

Liz Alden Wiley, Afghan Research and Evaluation Unit, Land Rights in Crisis: Restoring Land Tenure to Afghanistan (2003), https://reliefweb.int/report/afghanistan/land-rights-crisis-restoring-tenure-security-afghanistan

Liz Alden Wily, Afghanistan Research & Evaluation Unit, Looking for Peace on the Pastures: Rural Land Relations in Afghanistan (2004), https://areu.org.af/wp-content/uploads/2015/12/437E-Looking-for-Peace-on-the-Pastures-Rural-Land-Relations-in-Afghanistan-SP-web.pdf.

Liz Alden Wiley, Afghan Research and Evaluation Unit Putting Rural Land Registration in Perspective: The Afghanistan Case (2004), http://citeseerx.ist.psu.edu/viewdoc/download?doi=10.1.1.521.8602&rep=rep1&type=pdf

Liz Alden Wily, Afghanistan Research and Evaluation Unit, Land, People and The State of Afghanistan: 2002–2012 (2013), www.areu.org.af/Uploads/EditionPdfs/

Martha Alter Chen, Women in Informal Employment: Globalizing and Organizing, The Informal Economy: Definitions, Theories and Policies (WIEGO Working Paper No. 1, 2012), www.wiego.org/sites/default/files/publications/files/Chen_WIEGO_WP1.pdf.

Organisation For Economic Co-Operation and Development, Private Sector Development Policy Handbook, Improving Access to Finance for SMEs in Central Asia through

Credit Guarantee Schemes (2013), www.oecd.org/global-relations/AccesstoFinancefor-SMEs.pdf

Patrick M. Jost & Harjit Singh Sandhu, Interpol General Secretariat, The Hawala Alternative Remittance System and Its Role in Money Laundering (2000), www.nmta.us/assets/docs/hawala.pdf.

Pete Swanson, United States Agency for International Development, Report on Assessment of Potential for Commercial Mediation (March 17, 2010)

Richard H. Adams, Jr., The World Bank, Economic Growth, Inequality, and Poverty: Findings from a New Data Set (Policy Research Working Paper 2972, 2003) http://siteresources.worldbank.org/INTPGI/Resources/14021_WPS_2972_adams.pdf.

Robert Cull et al., The World Bank, Formal Finance and Trade Credit During China's Transition (Policy Research Working Papers 4204, 2007), https://openknowledge.worldbank.org/bitstream/handle/10986/7022/wps4204.pdf?sequence=1&isAllowed=y.

Robert Holzmann, World Bank, Managed Labor Migration in Afghanistan: Exploring Employment and Growth Opportunities for Afghanistan (2018), http://documents.worldbank.org/curated/en/746891516915310370/pdf/122987-WP-P158055-PUBLIC-SummaryReportFINALonline.pdf.

Sahay et al., IMF Staff Discussion Note, Rethinking Financial Deepening: Stability and Growth in Emerging Markets (SDN, August 15, 2015)

Stephen Haber *et al.*, *Political Institutions and Financial Development*, *in* Political Institutions and Financial Development 1 (Stephen Haber et al., eds. Stanford University Press 2008)

Thomas A. Timberg, Nathan Association Inc., *Informal Remittance Systems and Afghanistan* (2003), www.researchgate.net/profile/Thomas_Timberg/publication/241852212_Informal_Remittance_Systems_and_Afghanistan/links/55e09b6d08ae2fac471c2c6f/Informal-Remittance-Systems-and-Afghanistan.pdf?origin=publication_detail

Thomas J. Barfield, United States Institute for Peace, Afghan Customary Law and Its Relationship to Formal Judicial Institutions (2003), www.usip.org/sites/default/files/file/barfield2.pdf.

World Justice Program, *The Rule of Law in Afghanistan* (World Justice Project 2017)

News Articles

Afghanistan Chamber of Commerce and Industries, *Start of Export via Kabul-Almaty, Kazakhstan by Kam Air Airline* (February 21, 2018), ACCI.org, www.acci.org.af/da/component/content/article/38-news/1313-n.html.

Ahmad Hanayesh, *Yaqubi: Taliban Collect Taxes from People in The Districts of Kapisa Where They Have Control, Radio Azadi*, https://da.azadiradio.com/a/28560065.html

Anjana Pasricha, *India and Afghanistan Open Air Freight Corridor to Bypass Pakistan*, VOANews (June 21, 2017), www.voanews.com/a/india-afghanistan-air-freight-corridor-opens/3909537.html

BAZAR: Afghanistan-Turkey Air Corridor Discussed, TOLONews (May 13, 2018), www.tolonews.com/business/bazar-afghanistan-turkey-air-corridor-discussed

BBC Afghanistan Division, *Freedom House: More than One Million and Two Hundred Thousands Jaribs Are Grabbed in Afghanistan*, BBC Persian (February 21, 2016), www.bbc.com/persian/afghanistan/2016/02/160221_k05_landgrab_house_of_freedom_report

BBC Afghanistan Division, *Land Management Development Program Has Begun in Afghanistan*, BBC Persian (February 15, 2018), www.bbc.com/persian/afghanistan-43073751

Central Bank Grants IBA An Islamic Banking System License, TOLONews (April 23, 2018), www.tolonews.com/business/central-bank-grants-iba-islamic-banking-system-license

Douglass C. North—Prize Lecture: Economic Performance through Time, December 9, 1993, Nobelprize.org, www.nobelprize.org/nobel_prizes/economic-sciences/laureates/1993/north-lecture.html (posted May 24, 2018) (North and Robert W. Fogel won the 1993 Sveriges Riksbank Prize in Economic Sciences in Memory of Alfred Nobel)

Haidarshah Omid, *Afghan Refugees Contribute 10% To Country's Gross Income*, TOLONews (February 07, 2018), www.tolonews.com/business/afghan-refugees-contribute-10-country%E2%80%99s-gross-income

Indonesia, Turkey, and Dubai, UAE, See Zarmina Mohammadi, *Afghanistan-Indonesia to Open Air Corridor*, TOLONews (February 6, 2018), www.tolonews.com/index.php/business/afghanistan-indonesia-open-air-corridor

Kabul Bank Fraud: Ghani Reopens Afghan Corruption Case, BBC News (October 1, 2014), www.bbc.com/news/world-asia-29450821

Kabul to Have Air Corridors with Ankara, Dubai, 1TVNews.af (April 28, 2018), www.1tvnews.af/en/news/afghanistan/34318-kabul-to-have-air-corridors-with-ankara-dubai

Kabul's Sarrafs Have Ended Their Strike, BBC Persian (February 21, 2018), www.bbc.com/persian/business-43022961

Karim Amini, *Ongoing ARG-Jamiat Rift Affects Investment in Balkh*, TOLO News (February 02, 2018), www.tolonews.com/afghanistan/ongoing-arg-jamiat-rift-affects-investment-balkh.

Khairullah Rasooli, Saraffan dar Sarasar Afghanistan emrooz a'etesab kari kardan [*Sarrafs* in Afghanistan Staged a Nationwide Strike Today], VOADari (December 29, 2017), www.darivoa.com/a/Afghan-money-changer-union-made-a-strike-across-Afghanistan/4182373.html

Khairullah Rasooli, *Afghan Sarrafs Have Closed Saraya Shahzadaha [Kabul's Sarrafi Market] in Protest*, VOADari (February 2, 2018), www.darivoa.com/a/money-changers-closed-saraye-shazada-money-changing-market/4242561.html

Matin Sahak, *Powerful Afghan Governor Defying President Ghani Agrees to Go*, Reuters (March 22, 2018), www.reuters.com/article/us-afghanistan-governor/powerful-afghan-governor-defying-president-ghani-agrees-to-go-idUSKBN1GY1PU

Matthew Rosenberg, *Audit Says Kabul Bank Began as 'Ponzi Scheme,'* N.Y. Times (November 26, 2012) www.nytimes.com/2012/11/27/world/asia/kabul-bank-audit-details-extent-of-fraud.html

Mujib Mashal & Salman Masood, *Cutting Off Pakistan, U.S. Takes Gamble in Complex Afghan War*, N. Y. Times (January 5, 2018), www.nytimes.com/2018/01/05/world/asia/pakistan-aid-afghan-war.html

National Council of Sarrafs is Established, The Daily Afghanistan (September 29, 2017), www.dailyafghanistan.com/national_detail.php?post_id=141831

New Findings Reveal Taliban Collect Tax in Ghazni, TOLO News (January 10, 2018), www.tolonews.com/afghanistan/new-findings-reveal-taliban-collecting-tax-ghazni

Nimrooz Authorities: Taliban Collect Taxes from Merchants on Khashrood—Delaram High Way, Radio Azadi (January 1, 2018), https://da.azadiradio.com/a/28958957.html

Ra'is Amniat Melli Afghanistan: Iran va Russia ta hududi be Taliban kumak mikonan [The Head of Afghanistan's Intelligence Agency: Iran and Russia Help Taliban to Some Extent], BBC Persian (February 4, 2018), www.bbc.com/persian/afghanistan-42937425

Ruchi Kumar, *The Decline of Afghanistan's Hindu and Sikh Communities*, Al Jazeera (January 1, 2017), www.aljazeera.com/indepth/features/2016/12/decline-afghanistan-hindu-sikh-communities-161225082540860.html

Samira Zafari, *One Million and Six Hundred Thousand Jarib of Public Land Has been Usurped in Afghanistan*, ArianaNews.AF (December 21, 2017), https://ariananews.af/%DB%8C%DA%A9-%D9%85%DB%8C%D9%84%DB%8C%D9%88%D9%86-%D9%88-%D8%B4%D8%B4-%D8%B5%D8%AF-%D9%87%D8%B2%D8%A7%D8%B1-%D8%AC%D8%B1%DB%8C%D8%A8-%D8%B2%D9%85%DB%8C%D9%86-%D8%AF%D9%88%D9%84%D8%AA%DB%8C-%D8%AF/?lang=fa

Staff Report, *Pakistan Reopens Key Afghan Trade Route for Trial Run*, Daily Times (March 10, 2018), https://dailytimes.com.pk/212864/pakistan-reopens-key-afghan-trade-route-for-trial-run/

Steve Crabtree, *European Countries Lead World in Distrust of Banks* (May 20, 2013), http://news.gallup.com/poll/162602/european-countries-lead-world-distrust-banks.aspx

Taliban Collect Taxes in Farah, 8am.af (September 13, 2017), http://8am.af/1396/10/10/ghazni-has-become-the-talibans-tax-area/; http://8am.af/1396/07/22/the-taliban-collect-taxes-in-farah/

Multimedia

Da Afghanistan Bank has agreed to lift the stay as part of a deal to end the strike, Interview Clip, Facebook, *End of Sarraf's Strike* (VOA Dari, February 2018), www.facebook.com/voadari/videos/1718723204840376/

Haji Qzi Mir Afghan Safi, *The President of Kabul's Sarrafs' Union*, Facebook (February 7, 2018), www.facebook.com/qazishirinaqa/posts/350963322045553

Lant Pritchet on Poverty, Growth, and Experiments, EconTalk (May 22, 2017) www.econtalk.org/archives/2017/05/lant_pritchett_1.html

Ministry of Foreign Affairs of Afghanistan, *Counting down the hours now to RECCA VII (Ashgabat, November 14–15, 2017)!* Video Clip Posted on Facebook (Jan. 2018), www.facebook.com/mfa.afghanistan/videos/1551999691524672/

Office of the Economic Advisor, Mobile Banking in Afghanistan (PowerPoint Presentation, Apr. 2017), http://afghaneconomics.com/research/Mobile_banking_scenario.pdf

Websites

Afghanistan Analyst Network, www.afghanistan-analysts.org/miscellaneous/aan-resources/the-government-of-national-unity-deal-full-text/.

Afghanistan Chamber of Commerce and Industries, www.acci.org.af/

Appendix I

List of Interviewees

Province	*Name of Company or Individual*	*Companies' Activities*	*Sector(s)*	*# of Employees*	*Annual Dealings*
Balkh	Abdul Qayoom & Sons	*Sarrafi* and *Hawala*, Chair of Balkh's *Sarrafi* Union	*Sarrafi*		
Balkh	Al-Mubashir Group	Produces cakes, chocolates, and gum	Manufacturing/Trade	100	
Balkh	Bashir Naweed Group	Imports rods, construction materials, and food items, and produces bricks and washing products	Manufacturing/ Processing/Trade		
Balkh	Fahim Farzam Group	Imports and produces cooking oil	Manufacturing/Trade	70	
Balkh	Hamid Sadat Co.	Imports and sells raw materials, produces bottled water	Processing/Trade	52	
Balkh	Jamshid Rahim Co.	Buys fruits from farmers, processes and exports dried fruit	Processing/Trade	13 permanent, up to 200/day	
Balkh	Judge Abdullah Muhammadi	Chief Judge of Primary Commercial Court in Balkh	Commercial Court		
Balkh	Kabul Cam Co.	Produces Chocolate	Manufacturing	20	
Balkh	Khaled Tayba Co.	Imports and exports food and wood	Trade	12	
Balkh	Mazar Money Services	*Sarrafi* and *Hawala*	*Sarrafi*		
Balkh	Nasir Ahmad Qasemi	General Manager of Balkh's Chamber of Commerce and Industry	Chamber of Commerce		
Balkh	Navid Munib Tomato Paste Production Co.	Produces tomato paste, distributes food	Processing/Trade		
Balkh	Roof Bitumen Production Co. of the North East	Imports, sells, and installs roof bitumen, also a board member on Balkh's Union of Manufacturers	Services/Trade	40	

Balkh	Roshan Zada Group	Produces PVC, imports construction Materials, grains, and exports sesame and Zira; the president of Balkh's Union of Manufacturers and president of Balkh's Oil and Gas Union	Manufacturing/Trade	40	
Balkh	Sadat Cola Production Co.	Produces nonalcoholic beverages	Manufacturing	200	
Balkh	Sarrafi Sayed Hishmat	*Sarrafi* and *Hawala*, and sells phone top-ups	*Sarrafi*/Trade		
Balkh	Sayed Jamal Co.	Imports tractors, wheat, and flavorings; produces plastic bags, pipes, and flavorings; exports animal skins	Manufacturing/Trade	40 (prior 200, downsized)	
Herat	Bahar Ahmad Marble Factory	Processes marble	Manufacturing/Processing	17	
Herat	Biranj Co.	Assembles motorcycles and tricycles	Assembly/Manufacturing	200	
Herat	Fawad Sediqi Group	Imports oil and gas from Central Asia and sells across Afghanistan	Trade		$20 Mil.
Herat	Haji Abdul Wudud Faizzada	President of the Herat Union of Manufacturers	Union		
Herat	Haji Sa'ad Khatibi	President of Herat Chamber of Commerce and Industry	Chamber of Commerce		
Herat	Herat Marble Processing Co.	Processes Marble	Processing/Trade		
Herat	Ibrahim Yahya Co.	Manufactures, imports furniture	Manufacturing/Trade	15	
Herat	Judge Ali Ahmad Ahmadi	Appellate Judge at the Commercial Dewan of the Herat Court of Appeals	Commercial Dewan		
Herat	Judgement Enforcement		Huquq Dept.		

(*Continued*)

(Continued)

Province	*Name of Company or Individual*	*Companies' Activities*	*Sector(s)*	*# of Employees*	*Annual Dealings*
Herat	Mubarak Group	Imports and exports rugs and carpets, produces hygiene products, and owns and operates a printing company	Manufacturing/Services/ Trade	200	
Herat	Nadem Group	Imports construction materials from Iran and Uzbekistan	Trade	12	$20 Mil.
Herat	Najm Co.	Imports and distributes tea	Trade		
Herat	Noorzai Group	Produces UPVC, profiles, and electric cable; imports raw materials and sells to other factories; and owns a *Sarrafi*	Manufacturing/*Sarrafi*/ Trade		
Herat	Pamir Group	Assembles motorcycles, produces bottled water and party energy drink	Assembly/Manufacturing	360	
Herat	Rahimi Sarrafi	*Sarrafi* and *Hawala*, Chair of Herat's Sarrafi Union	*Sarrafi*		
Herat	Sarrafi Arman Masooud	*Sarrafi* and *Hawala*	*Sarrafi*		
Herat	Taha Co. and Shahid Cookie & Cake Factory	Produces cookies and cakes	Manufacturing/Trade		
Herat	Talash Asia Production Co.	Produces wheel caps of different sizes and models for cars, trucks, motorcycles, and tricycles	Manufacturing	40	
Herat	Talaya Co.	Produces tissues, shampoo, and cleaning products	Manufacturing	40	
Herat	Turkani & Sediqi Sarrafi	*Sarrafi* and *Hawala*	*Sarrafi*		

Herat	Yusufi Group	Imports machinery, e.g. generators and construction machines, exports valuable minerals	Trade	210
Kabul	Abdul Hakeem Sanaee Co.	Provides transportation and custom clearance services	Services	
Kabul	Adeel Co.	Processes marble and natural stones	Processing/Trade	
Kabul	Afghan Polyethylene Co.	Produces 3D panels used in construction	Manufacturing/Services	
Kabul	Amirian Group	Imports and distributes cell phones and accessories, produces stoves	Manufacturing/Trade	
Kabul	Aziz Faizy	Head of Afghanistan Center of Commercial Dispute Resolution	ACCDR	
Kabul	Hekmat Afghan Construction	Construction and logistics company, imports electronics and seed for chicken	Services/Trade	
Kabul	Judge Sediqi	Chief judge of Kabul primary commercial court	Primary Commercial Court	
Kabul	Khedmat Group	Imports machinery, processes marble and other minerals	Processing/Trade	
Kabul	Parwiz Wahid Co.	Imports drugs and pharmaceutical products	Trade	
Kabul	Salim Karwan Group	Imports construction materials, owns and operates an oil refinery, owns a construction company	Manufacturing/Processing/Services/Trade	
Kabul	Sarrafi Khosti	*Sarrafi* and *Hawala*; former president of Kabul *Sarrafi* Union	*Sarrafi*	
Kandahar	Amin Karimi Box Production	Produces boxes and owns and operates a printing company	Manufacturing/Services	
Kandahar	Brothers Co.	*Sarrafi* and *Hawala*	*Sarrafi*	
Kandahar	Eng. Ab. Baqi Banaee	VP of Kandahar Chamber of Commerce and Industry	Chamber of Commerce	

(*Continued*)

(Continued)

Province	*Name of Company or Individual*	*Companies' Activities*	*Sector(s)*	*# of Employees*	*Annual Dealings*
Kandahar	Erfan Ahmad Co.	Buys fruit from farmers, processes, and exports dried fruit	Manufacturing/ Processing/Trade		
Kandahar	Haji Ghulam Rasul Sarraf	*Sarrafi* and *Hawala*	*Sarrafi*		
Kandahar	Judge Rahim	Chief judge of Kandahar primary commercial court	Primary Commercial Court		
Kandahar	Miami Co.	Distributes cleaning products	Trade		
Kandahar	Milko Co.	Produces dairy products, e.g. yogurt and ice cream	Manufacturing/Processing	250	
Kandahar	Nazir Ahmad Forwarding	Forwarding and transportation services	Services		
Kandahar	Negah Afghan Co.	Produces bottled water	Manufacturing/Processing	23	
Kandahar	Noori Afghan Co.	Imports and distributes home appliances	Trade		
Kandahar	Noorzai Group (Kandahar)	Produces UPVC, profiles, and electric cable, imports and sells raw materials, owns and operates a *Sarrafi*	Manufacturing/ Trade/*Sarrafi*		
Kandahar	Sadiq Co.	Produces juice, bottled water, and ice; president of Kandahar's Union of Manufacturing	Manufacturing/Processing		
Kandahar	Sardar Rush Iodine Salt	Produces iodized salt	Manufacturing/Processing		
Kandahar	Wali Hootak Co.	Owns and operates a large supermarket, furniture store, and home appliance store	Trade		
Kandahar	Zmaray Ae'temad Co.	Distributes imported blankets	Trade		
Nangarhar	Admin Officer of Primary Commercial Court	Admin officer of the primary commercial court in Nangarhar	Primary Commercial Court		

Nangarhar	Al-Madina Manufacturing Co.	Produces aluminum plates	Manufacturing		$20,000 Initial Capital
Nangarhar	Bashir Faheem Co.	Imports food	Trade		
Nangarhar	Faqir Wahab Co.	Imports household goods, e.g. dishwashing liquids	Trade	40	
Nangarhar	Getz Pharma -Afghanistan Representative	Imports drugs and pharmaceutical products for Pakistan	Trade		$2.5 Mil.
Nangarhar	Haji Taj Muhammad	A major importer and distributor of fabrics	Trade		
Nangarhar	Javid Afghan Co.	Imports and produces iron rods	Manufacturing/Trade	225	
Nangarhar	Judge Munir	Appeal judge at the commercial dewan of Nangarhar's court of appeals	Commercial Dewan		
Nangarhar	Manager at Nangarhar Chamber of Commerce		Chamber of Commerce		
Nangarhar	Muhammad Asif Sarrafi	*Sarrafi* and *Hawala*	*Sarrafi*		
Nangarhar	Muhammad Kamal Sarrafi	*Sarrafi* and *Hawala*	*Sarrafi*		
Nangarhar	Nawi Sediqzai Co.	Imports household necessities, e.g. cooking oil and washing powder	Trade	18	
Nangarhar	Omid Sajid Basit Co.	Imports and distributes drugs from Pakistan	Trade		
Nangarhar	Qasim Ma'raj and Ma'raj Shirak Co.	Imports rugs and carpets from Pakistan	Trade	3	
Nangarhar	Samiullah Fahim Co.	Imports iron rods	Trade		

Appendix II

Pool of Interview Questions

Name of interviewee:
Name of interviewee's business:
Number of employees:
A rough estimate of annual dealings:
Ethnicity:
A short description of business:

A) Starting a Business (8 questions)

1 When did you first start your business?
2 Where did you get the money to start your business?
3 Did you have family members, relatives, or close friends who were involved in the same or similar business when you started your business?
4 How did you first establish business relations (e.g. drawing on personal, family relations, or drawing on ethnic or religious connections)?
5 Did you have to conduct your business (buy and sell) in cash when you first started your business?
6 Did you have a relation with a *Sarraf* through family, relatives, or friends when you first started your business?
7 Do you have a relation with a *Sarraf*(s) now? How old is your relation?
8 If you answered question number 6 negatively and question number 7 in positively, how did you establish a relation with a *Sarraf*?

B) Business Structure (6 questions)

1 Is your business registered? If yes, with what governmental entity?
2 What is the legal form of your business?
3 How many equity partners do you have?
4 What kind of relations did you and your equity partners have before you became partners?
5 Are you a member of a business association? Name them.
6 Did you and your employees know each other before your hired them?

C) Preventive Institutions (26 questions)

1 Who are the people you do business with (e.g. suppliers, customers, *Sarraf*, government, etc.)?
2 Can you estimate how much your business is done on credit?
3 How do you decide to give someone credit?
4 Do you have to personally know the people you do business with?
5 If you answered question number 4 positively, from where do you know the people you do business with?
6 If you answered question number 4 negatively, do you need to trust the people you do business with?
7 If you answered question number 6 positively, what makes you trust a person if you don't know him/her personally?
8 If you answered question number 6 negatively, how do you make sure that your business partner does not cheat without trust?

***

9 Can you estimate, in the last year, how many of your dealings involved a late payment? What was the average length of delay?
10 Do you still do business with the people that delayed their payments? Why?
11 Did you change the conditions of your dealings after the delayed payment? How?
12 In the last year, how many of your dealings involved a late delivery of goods/services? What was the average length of delay?
13 Do you still do business with the people that delayed the delivery? Why?
14 Did you change the conditions of your dealings after the delayed delivery? How?
15 In the last year, how many of your dealings resulted in complete nonpayment or complete failure to deliver good/service?
16 Do you still do business with the people who did not pay or did not deliver the goods/service? Why?
17 Did you change the conditions of your dealings after nonpayment or failure to deliver good/service? How?
18 In the last year, how many of your dealings involved other disagreements as to what each party's obligation was?
19 Do you still do business with the people you had the disagreements with? Why?
20 Did you change the conditions of your dealings after the disagreement? How?

***

21 Do you collect evidence (receipt, written contract, etc.) when you enter into a business agreement so you can prove it? What do you collect?
22 Do you collect evidence on all your agreements? If the answer is no, for what kind of agreements do you collect evidence?
23 If you answered question number 21 positively, to whom do you think you need to prove the agreement?

24 Do you record the conditions of agreements too? How do you record the conditions of agreements?
25 Do you record the conditions of agreements for all your agreements? If the answer is no, for what kind of agreements do you record the conditions of the agreement?
26 If you do record the conditions of agreements, why do you do it? When do you think you will need the record? And for whom?

D) Dispute Resolution Institutions (48 questions)

1 Can you estimate, over the last year, how many disputes you had with the people you do business with?
2 With whom do you usually have disputes (e.g. suppliers, old customers, new customers, *Sarrafs*)?
3 What were the most common disputes?
4 What were the most common sources of disputes?
5 What do you do first when you have a dispute with someone?
6 Do you try to preserve the relationship with the other party?
7 How do you decide if you should try to preserve the relations despite the dispute or if you should stop doing business with the other party?
8 Do you compromise so you can still do business with the other party? How do you decide if you should compromise?

***

9 Are disputes and the need for compromise an important cost to your business?
10 Can you estimate, over the last year, how much money, roughly, you lost due to disputes and compromise (e.g. time, bribe, gifts, forgone profit, etc.)?
11 If there was a way so you did not have to compromise (e.g. someone made the other party honor the contract without you having to compromise), would that reduce the cost of your business significantly?
12 How would you change the kind of deals you make, the price you charge, or any other thing about your business if you did not have to consider the cost of disputes or compromise?

***

13 Do you resort to the superintendent of your market when you have a dispute?
14 Can you estimate, over the last year, how many times you resorted to the superintendent for a dispute?
15 How and when do you decide that you need to involve the superintendent of your market?
16 For what kind of disputes do you involve the superintendent more often? Why?
17 Does involving the superintendent increase the cost or length of the dispute? Why? What are the costs and sources of delays?

18 Does involving the superintendent help resolve the dispute? How?
19 Do you like to involve the superintendent? Why? Why not?

***

20 Can you estimate, over the last year, how many times you resorted to business associations for a dispute?
21 How and when do you decide to involve the business associations in your dispute?
22 For what kind of disputes do you involve associations more often? Why?
23 Does involving the business associations increase the cost or length of the dispute? Why? What are the cost and sources of delays?
24 Does involving associations help resolve the dispute?
25 Do you like to involve the associations? Why? Why not?

***

26 Over the last year, how many times did you go to Huquq for a dispute?
27 How and when do you decide to go to Huquq?
28 For what kind of dispute do you involve Huquq more often? Why?
29 Does involving Huquq help resolve the dispute?
30 Does involving the Huquq increase the cost or length of the dispute? What are the costs or source of delay?
31 Do you like involving Huquq in a dispute? Why? Why not?

***

32 Over the last year, how many times have you resorted to the courts to resolve a dispute?
33 How and when do you decide to go to court?
34 For what kind of dispute do you involve the courts more often? Why?
35 Does involving the courts help resolve the dispute?
36 Does involving the courts increase the cost or length of the dispute? What are the costs or source of delay?
37 Do you like involving the courts in a dispute? Why? Why not?

***

38 Have you known any businessmen who have resorted to threats to persuade other parties to resolve a dispute?
39 When and how do you think businessmen decide that they need to threaten the other party?
40 For what kind of disputes and against what kind of people do you think businessmen are more likely to resort to threat?
41 Has threatening the other party been an effective way to resolve a dispute when it is used by other businessmen? Why? Why not?

***

42 Can you estimate, over the last year, how many times you resorted to the police station for a commercial dispute?

43 Can you estimate, over the last year, how many disputes you know of that at one point involved police?
44 Why did you or the disputants that you know resort to the police?
45 What is usually the result when you or the people you know go to the police?

***

46 What are other ways you use to resolve a dispute? Describe.
47 How and when do you decide to resort to these methods?
48 Are they effective?

E) Access to Credit (40 questions)

1 Can you estimate, what percentage of your supply do you acquire on credit?
2 Can you estimate, how many suppliers do you have business with?
3 Do you have a credit line with all of them? If no, what determines whether you have cash or credit relations with a supplier?
4 Do you acquire your cash and credit supply from the same supplier? Why? Why not?
5 Do you have relations with several suppliers to procure the same product?
6 If the answer to question number 5 is yes, why do you maintain relations with several suppliers for procuring the same product?
7 Why do you think suppliers give you credit?
8 Do you have personal relations with all your suppliers?
9 What is your payment schedule to your suppliers? Do you pay them regularly or do you use a different schedule for each contract?
10 How much can you increase your credit supply and how fast?
11 What does it take to increase your credit supply? Explain.
12 If someone offered a lower price for your supply, what would you do? Do you switch suppliers? Why? Why not?

***

13 Do you have a bank loan(s)? If the answer is yes, answer the following questions:
14 From how many banks? What is the rough estimate of the total amount?
15 What form are the loan(s) in (loan, *murabaha*, *ijara*, etc.)?
16 For what use did you take the loan(s)?
17 What kind of collateral do borrowers generally provide for the loan(s)?
18 Did you know anyone from the bank personally before you applied for the loan?
19 What were the factors that you considered when you decided to apply for a loan (e.g. interest rate, religious doctrines, etc.)?
20 Do you owe *Sarraf*(s) money? If the answer is yes, answer the following questions:

21 To how many *Sarraf*(s) do you owe money? What is the rough total of the debt?
22 What form are debt(s) in (loan, *murabaha*, *ijara*, etc.)?
23 What are the sources of debt? For what use did you take the money from *Sarraf*(s)?
24 What kind of collateral is generally required for the debt, if any?
25 If you did not provide collateral, how do you think *Sarraf*(s) know they can trust that you will repay the debts?
26 Did you know the *Sarraf*s personally before you acquired the debt?
27 Can you estimate, how long did you have a relation with the *Sarraf* before you acquired the debt? How long personally? How long professionally?
28 What are the conditions of a debt?

a Do you pay interest? How much?
b What are your repayment schedules? Are they regular or debt-specific?

29 What were the factors that you considered when you decided to acquire a debt from a *Sarraf* (e.g. interest rate, religious doctrines, etc.)?
30 Do you prefer *Sarrafs* to banks? Why?
31 Is there a source of credit that you prefer to *Sarraf*s (e.g. family and/or friends, suppliers, banks, etc.)? Rank them.
32 Over the past year, have you wanted to expand your business (e.g. open a new store, enter a new line of business, expand your inventory, produce new products)? If the answer is yes, answer the following questions:
33 Have you been able to expand your business partially or completely as you wanted?
34 What were the main obstacles to expansions?
35 Was access to credit one of the main obstacles?
36 Which one of the following sources of credit have you tried for expansion, and what was the result?

a Family, relatives, and friends:
b *Sarraf*s and money dealers:
c Banks and moneylenders:
d Suppliers and business partners:
e Starting a partnership with someone:

37 What were the factors that you used to decide for and against any of the above options?

***

38 Over the last year, have you faced a cash shortage?
39 Which one of the following sources of credit did you use to solve your liquidity problem, and what was the result?

a Family, relatives, and friends:
b *Sarraf*s and money dealers:

c Banks and moneylenders:
d Suppliers and business partners:
e Starting a partnership with someone:

40 What were the factors that you used to decide for and against any of the above options?

F) Networks (3 questions)

1 List five suppliers that you do the most business with. Describe your relationships with them and how you first got to know them.

***

2 List five customers that you do the most business with. Describe your relationships with them and how you first got to know them.

***

3 List your five sources of credit. Describe your relationships with them and how you first got to know them.

Index